Grade Aid

for

Lilienfeld, Lynn, Namy, and Woolf

Psychology
From Inquiry to Understanding

prepared by

Managing Editor: Amy Hackney-Hansen
Georgia Southern University

MyPsychLab Editor: Kimberley Duff
Cerritos College

Patricia Kowalski
University of San Diego

Annette Kujawski Taylor
University of San Diego

PEARSON

Boston   New York   San Francisco
Mexico City   Montreal   Toronto   London   Madrid   Munich   Paris
Hong Kong   Singapore   Tokyo   Cape Town   Sydney

ISBN-13: 978-0-205-60754-9
ISBN-10:   0-205-60754-3

Printed in the United States of America

10 9 8 7 6 5 4 3 2 1   11 10 09 08 07

TABLE OF CONTENTS

NUMBERED TEXT LEARNING OBJECTIVES

Even though the chapter learning objectives are not numbered in the text, we have provided a numbered list to make referencing them throughout this workbook much more convenient.

CHAPTER 1

1.1 Distinguish common from uncommon sense
1.2 Describe naive realism and its perils
1.3 Differentiate popular psychology information from misinformation
1.4 Describe the importance of science as a set of safeguards against biases
1.5 Identify the key features of scientific skepticism and distinguish it from pathological skepticism
1.6 Identify and explain six key principles of critical thinking that will be used throughout the text
1.7 Describe pseudoscience and its differences from science and metaphysics
1.8 Describe the prevalence of pseudoscientific beliefs
1.9 Identify seven key warning signs of pseudoscience
1.10 Describe the motivational factors that predispose us to pseudoscientific beliefs
1.11 Describe the role that scientific illiteracy may play in the public's acceptance of pseudoscience
1.12 Explain the importance of cognitive factors as contributors to pseudoscientific thinking
1.13 Identify key logical fallacies in psychological thinking that can predispose us to pseudoscientific beliefs
1.14 Describe the dangers of pseudoscience

CHAPTER 2

2.1 Explain what research designs accomplish that we can't discover by intuition alone
2.2 Identify heuristics and biases that prevent us from thinking clearly about psychology
2.3 Distinguish the types of designs and the conclusions that we can draw from each
2.4 Identify the potential pitfalls of each design that can lead to faulty conclusions
2.5 Explain the ethical obligations of researchers toward their research participants
2.6 Describe both sides of the debate on the use of animals as research subjects
2.7 Explain how to calculate measures of central tendency
2.8 Identify uses of various measures of central tendency and dispersion
2.9 Show how statistics can be misused for purposes of persuasion
2.10 Identify flaws in research designs
2.11 Identify skills for evaluating psychological claims in the popular media

CHAPTER 3

3.1 Identify the parts of the nervous system that play a role in sensation and perception
3.2 Track the parts of the nervous system that play a role in motor functions
3.3 Clarify the relationship between the nervous system and the body
3.4 Identify the parts of the brain that play a role in emotion
3.5 Clarify how the autonomic nervous system works in emergency and everyday situations
3.6 Describe what hormones are and how they affect behavior
3.7 Distinguish the parts of neurons and what they do

CHAPTER 12

12.1   Explain how stress is defined and approached in different ways
12.2   Identify different approaches to measuring stress
12.3   Describe Selye's general adaptation syndrome
12.4   Explain the tend and befriend response to stress
12.5   Describe the diversity of stress responses, including PTSD, anxiety, and depression
12.6   Describe how the immune system functions
12.7   Describe the field of psychoneuroimmunology
12.8   Explain the contributions of the biopsychosocial model to understanding psychophysiological disorders
12.9   Describe the role of personality in everyday experience, and socioeconomic factors in coronary heart disease, and stress in asthma and ulcers
12.10 Describe the role of social support and different types of control in coping with stress
12.11 Explain how spirituality, hardiness, selfenhancement, and rumination may influence responses to stress
12.12 Identify the goals and practices of behavioral medicine and health psychology
12.13 Distinguish alternative from complementary medicine
12.14 Describe different alternative medical approaches and compare their effectiveness with placebos

CHAPTER 13

13.1   Identify the ways in which social situations influence the behavior of individuals
13.2   Explain how and why our attributions about the causes of others' behavior are accurate in some cases but biased in others
13.3   Explain the power of our observations of others to influence our thoughts, beliefs, and decisions
13.4   Determine the factors that influence when we conform to the behaviors and beliefs of others
13.5   Recognize the dangers of group decision making and identify ways to avoid mistakes common in group decisions
13.6   Identify the contexts that maximize or minimize obedience to authority
13.7   Recognize why individuals may not help others in distress in group contexts
13.8   Distinguish those aspects of a situation that increase or decrease the likelihood of helping
13.9   Describe the social and individual difference variables that contribute to human aggression
13.10 Describe how attitudes relate to behavior
13.11 Evaluate theoretical accounts of how and when we alter our attitudes
13.12 Identify common and effective persuasion techniques and how they're exploited by pseudoscientists
13.13 Distinguish prejudice and stereotypes as beliefs from discrimination as a behavior
13.14   Identify theoretical explanations of the causes of prejudice
13.15 Identify ways to combat prejudice

CHAPTER 14

14.1   Distinguish between the two major approaches to studying personality
14.2   Describe how twin and adoption studies shed light on genetic and environmental influences on personality
14.3   Describe the core assumptions of psychoanalytic theory
14.4   Distinguish among the three Freudian agencies of the psyche and explain their interactions
14.5   Identify the five psychosexual stages of psychoanalytic theory
14.6   Describe key criticisms of psychoanalytic theory
14.7   Identify the central features of neo-Freudian theories
14.8   Identify the core assumptions of behavioral views of personality
14.9   Identify the core assumptions of social learning theories of personality and their differences from traditional behavioral views
14.10   Describe key criticisms of behavioral and social learning approaches
14.11   Explain the concept of self-actualization and its role in humanistic models
14.12   Identify Maslow's characteristics of self-actualized individuals
14.13   Describe key criticisms of humanistic approaches
14.14   Describe key challenges to trait models of personality
14.15   Explain what personality traits can and can't predict
14.16   Identify models of personality structure and their implications and limitations
14.17   Identify cultural influences on personality
14.18   Identify key criticisms of trait models
14.19   Describe structured personality tests, particularly the MMP1-2, and their methods of construction
14.20   Describe projective tests, particularly the Rorschach, and their strengths and weaknesses
14.21   Identify common pitfalls in personality assessment

CHAPTER 15

15.1   Identify criteria for defining mental disorders
15.2   Describe conceptions of diagnoses across history and cultures
15.3   Identify common misconceptions about psychiatric diagnoses, and the strengths and limitations of the current diagnostic system
15.4   Identify popular misconceptions about the law and mental illness
15.5   Describe the many ways people experience anxiety
15.6   Identify explanations of anxiety disorders that center on the environment, catastrophic thinking, and biological causes
15.7   Identify the characteristics of different mood disorders
15.8   Identify risk factors for suicide
15.9   Describe the interplay of life events and interpersonal behavioral, cognitive, and biological factors in producing the symptoms of depression
15.10   Describe depersonalization, dissociative amnesia, and fugue
15.11   Explain the controversies surrounding dissociative disorders, especially dissociative identity disorder
15.12   Recognize the characteristic symptoms of schizophrenia

SUCCESS IN INTRODUCTORY PSYCHOLOGY (AND BEYOND): HOW TO AVOID SOME COMMON MISCONCEPTIONS

As you begin this course, you probably believe you already know a lot about psychology. You might also believe you know how to study in order to do well in this course. As a check of your knowledge, answer the following questions True or False:

T or F Psychology is primarily interested in abnormal behavior and its treatment.
T or F If you want to learn in college you should focus on your grades.
T or F If you want to remember something you should repeat it over and over.

How well do you think you did? If you are like most students, you answered "True" to each of these questions. Actually, the correct answer to each of the questions is "False." Don't feel bad if you answered these questions incorrectly. They were designed to challenge common misconceptions you might have about both psychology and the tools needed to achieve academic success.

Misconceptions exist in most subjects (e.g., ostriches don't really stick their heads in the ground), but especially in psychology. Throughout the text and this Grade Aid you will learn about many misconceptions people hold. For example, the answer to the question "Psychology is primarily about abnormal behavior," is false. Many people think of psychology as the study of abnormal behavior. It is true that some psychologists study behavior that deviates from what is typical and other psychologists study and apply psychological knowledge to aid individuals demonstrating problematic behavior. However, psychology is much broader than the study of abnormal behavior. Most of psychology deals with the normal processes involved in thinking and behaving and many of the applications of psychology are of value to the ordinary individual. For example, among the many things psychologists study is how we learn—something that should be of particular practical interest to you as a college student. Your psychology course, therefore, will help you learn to differentiate claims that are unlikely to make accurate predictions, show you how common beliefs are not really supported by objective evidence, and teach you how to learn in college. Although you will learn more about what cognitive psychologists say about learning in the next section of this Grade Aid , here are a few study tips related to common misconceptions.

MISCONCEPTION: MEMORIZING INFORMATION IS THE BEST WAY TO LEARN

Many introductory psychology students are just beginning their college careers. They often believe that the same study strategies that worked for them in high school will be good enough for college. Many of these techniques involve attempts to memorize information through rehearsal. Although such strategies may have helped students get by in high school, they are neither effective nor efficient methods of study at college. Students often spend much more time and effort studying than they need to and are surprised when their efforts don't pay off. Why don't their efforts pay off? Their efforts don't pay off because their study strategies do not involve an effort to *understand* the material.

I'm going to try to demonstrate this point with an exercise. DO NOT READ AHEAD!
Take 20 seconds to memorize the words below. Ready, Go.

I spoon eating a got bowl haven't of I'm oatmeal a but

WITHOUT LOOKING BACK, close your eyes and repeat the words. How did you do?
Now try this second example, the same way:

I'm eating a bowl of oatmeal but I haven't got a spoon.

Now repeat the words. How did you do?

These two examples contained EXACTLY the same words. Why was the second sample easier to remember? Because it was meaningful. The words made sense. Even if it is silly, they at least made a sentence. There is overwhelming evidence (as you will see in Chapter 7 on Memory and in the next section of this Grade Aid) that it's easier and more efficient when we try to remember something that's meaningful, compared to trying to memorize something that's meaningless. Therefore, the prerequisite for studying for a test is to first understand the material. Before you try to commit material to memory in a way that will enable you to perform well on an exam, you must first complete the process of understanding. This process does not occur during the last minutes before an exam. Rather it's an ongoing process requiring your actively thinking about the material throughout the semester. This Grade Aid includes the kinds of activities that will help you learn how to think about the material at a meaningful level. By reading the text, completing the Grade Aid activities, and reviewing your class notes regularly, you will be developing your understanding of the material.

MISCONCEPTION: YOU WILL LEARN BEST IF YOU FOCUS ON GRADES

Not only do students believe that rehearsal is an effective learning strategy, students also believe that they will learn in college by focusing on grades. Grades *are* valuable as reflections of what you have learned and may be used by potential graduate programs and employers as indicators of your knowledge. Thinking about being evaluated can help you focus, prioritize, and avoid distractions when necessary. However, a focus on grades as a reason for studying is not enough to motivate you to *learn* the material. Research shows that when students are focused on a goal that is extrinsic to the task of learning (grades, awards, money), they tend to use superficial strategies and shortcuts to reach their goal—the grade (Nolen, 1996). They are also more likely to be negatively affected by anxiety and more likely to give up when confronted with obstacles. In contrast, when students focus on the task of learning itself, they use strategies that engage them in the process of learning, seek challenges, and show better retention (Dweck & Leggett, 1988: Elliot & McGregor, 1999). By being motivated to learn the material, students are more likely to engage in strategies that result in meaningful, enduring forms of learning and students are more likely to enjoy the process of learning.

Wanting to learn will make little difference if you cannot motivate yourself to exert the effort necessary to engage in effective learning strategies. Most of the students we have met in our 50 (combined) years of teaching say they want to learn and many do know some of the more effective strategies for learning. The majority, however, meet their doom in their lack of self-regulation. Self-regulation involves something called "metacognition" or what you know about what you know, and the motivational and problem-solving skills you put to work in monitoring and improving you knowledge. Self-regulation requires identifying goals and engaging in behaviors that lead to accomplishing your goals (Schunk & Zimmerman, 2001). For example, should your goal be to understand the material in class, self-regulation would involve your monitoring your understanding, figuring out what you need to do if you do not understand, and motivating yourself to actually do what it is you need to do. That is, it involves thought, motivation, and behavior. Monitoring your understanding of the material, therefore, is critical. Self-regulation involves stopping to think about whether you really understand the material and if not, doing something about it.

This Grade Aid provides opportunities for you to monitor your learning. Before the practice tests we have included opportunities for you to stop and reflect on how well you know the material before you attempt the test. After taking and scoring the test, you can use your actual score as feedback on both whether you understand the material and whether you are accurately judging your understanding of the material.

Finding out that you do not really know the material as well as you think should indicate the need to do something to improve your understanding.

Another critical component of self-regulation is actually motivating yourself to engage in the behaviors that are necessary to improve your learning. Not only should you check your understanding by reviewing your notes regularly, but you must review them far enough before an exam that if they do not make sense, you can get clarification before you start to study. Figuring out what kind of help you need and how to get it will take some thinking. Perhaps you will need to review the material, ask the teacher, or do some additional research. The important thing is to know when you need help understanding the material and to get help when you need it. You cannot and will not do well in college unless you take some responsibility for motivating yourself to do the things you need to do in order to learn. Learning and the good grades that reflect that you've learned involve some effort, some engagement, and some self-regulation.

SOME FINAL MISCONCEPTIONS ON TEST-TAKING AND ESSAY-WRITING

Students hold many misconceptions about test-taking. For example, students believe that cramming the night before the test keeps the information fresh, you shouldn't change your answer, and you should study differently for different types of tests. All of these beliefs have been challenged when looked at objectively. Cramming is ineffective (the next section will elaborate), when you study for any type of test as if it were an essay test you are more likely to study for understanding, and reflection can contribute to your changing a wrong answer to a right answer. In fact, taking your time to think about questions is a critical test taking strategy. In contrast, students tend to rush through tests, possibly to just get them over with. When taking multiple choice tests, they either pick the first answer that sounds good or think of the multiple choice questions as something they either know the answer to or they don't—and they don't take time to stop and think about it.

Advice on taking multiple choice tests:
1) Take your time and THINK.
2) Read each question and each option fully and carefully.
3) BEFORE reading the options, think of a reasonable response on your own.
4) Go through each option as if it were a TRUE/FALSE question.
5) Exclude those that are clearly false.
6) Ask your professor questions, if you find a term ambiguous.
7) Think carefully about your remaining options.

What about essays:
The biggest problem students have with essay tests (and this is true about all students—freshman as well as seniors) is that they don't make their point clearly enough and don't provide clear evidence to support the point. I think students assume professors know the answer so why should you have to explain what you're talking about. Students who do poorly on essay exams either float around describing examples of something without ever clearly stating what point they're trying to make with the examples. OR make some general statement and assume the professor accepts the statement without ever providing examples that demonstrate or clarify the statement. If your answer seems brief, it is probably incomplete!

One method for writing essays is called the X123 method (Kerrigan, 1987). The first thing you write is your X statement: A clear statement of your point. The answer to the essay question. It's what you want to say. The 123 then are each statements that support, demonstrate, and clarify your point. Take this example:

Essay question: What is one major reason students perform less well than they expect on an exam?
X Students are inefficient at studying.

1. Students often wait until right before the exam to do the reading.
2. Students often wait right before the exam to review their notes.
3. Students often try to study what they don't first understand. Then fill out the essay, providing evidence and giving examples to support your 123 statements.

As a final point, the purpose of this Grade Aid is to actively engage you in the process of learning about psychology. We hope that as you use this study tool you will develop your ability to think critically, you will become actively engaged in thinking your course material, and you will learn that learning about psychology is both a valuable *and* an enjoyable experience.

References

Dweck, C. S., & Leggett, E. (1988). A social-cognitive approach to motivation and personality, *Psychological Review, 95*, 256–273.

Elliot, A. J., & McGregor, H. A. (1999). Text anxiety and the hierarchical model of approach and avoidance achievement motivation. *Journal of Personality and Social Psychology, 76*, 628–644.

Kerrigan, W. (1987). *Writing to the Point*. New York: Harcourt Brace Jovanovich.

Kuhn, D. (1999). A developmental model of critical thinking. *Educational Researcher, 28*, 16–25, 46.

Nolen, S. B. (1996). Why study? Reasons for learning influence strategy selection *Educational Psychology Review, 8*(4), 335–355.

Schunk, D. H., & Zimmerman, B. J. (2001). *Self-Regulated Learning and Academic Achievement: Theoretical Perspectives*. Mahwah, NJ: Lawrence Erlbaum Associates Publisher.

Cognitive psychology is the scientific study of those behaviors related to thinking. What can cognitive psychology teach you about how to learn? Fortunately, MUCH! A wealth of good evidence shows what works best when it comes to things such as remembering—probably the heart and soul of student life— cramming all that information into your head for longer than just a few days, or even for just a few weeks.

As you will learn in Chapter 7 on Memory, remembering something involves three steps: encoding, storage, and retrieval. First you have to *encode* the information, or you have to get it in. Second, you have to *store* it someplace. Let's not worry about where for now, but how. If you don't store it in such a way that you can find it, well, later, when you need the information, encoding it will have been a wasted effort. Finally, you have to be able to *retrieve* the information, whenever you want to. The information must be available: you got it in and you got it stored somewhere, AND it must be accessible: you can put your (mental) finger right on it.

Because cognitive psychology can teach you so much, picking a starting point could be difficult. Except that it's not: you can begin your studying where cognitive psychologists begin to look at how best to remember, and that is with . . .

ORGANIZATION

LESSON #1: ORGANIZE INFORMATION BEFORE YOU SIT DOWN TO STUDY IT.

How Do We Know?
In a landmark study, Bower, Clark, Lesgold, and Winzenz (1969) gave people four lists of 28 words each, either organized hierarchically or arranged randomly. What did they find? People who studied the organized lists for only 2 minutes per list remembered nearly 100% of the words after only one study session! People who had the randomly organized list remembered less than 80% after four study sessions.

How to Do It:

1. Use the chapter outlines and sections of the textbook to organize material in a hierarchical format.

2. Create concept maps. Concept mapping imposes order on what might seem like TOO MUCH information.

3. Use CHUNKING. To make a "chunk," group together larger units of information into smaller units. For instance, rather than remembering FBICIAKGB as a long string of letters, you could chunk it into FBI, CIA, and KGB.

LESSON #2: CREATE SCHEMAS TO GUIDE YOUR CURRENT LEARNING AND INTEGRATE THE OLD AND THE NEW LEARNING.

How Do We Know?
A "schema" is an organized framework of past experiences. For example, you have a classroom schema. The first time you walked into a college classroom you knew pretty much what to do and what to expect: you dressed a certain way, you came in and took a seat, you might have introduced yourself to people sitting around you, you took out a pen and paper, etc. Schemas provide "cognitive economy," which

means you don't have to relearn everything from scratch each time you need to know about something. Instead, you can call to mind your previous experiences and use them to guide your learning.

How to Do It:

1. Think of similar material you have learned in the past and bring it up from memory. Examine it for relatedness. If you find a match, niche your new information into your existing framework.

2. If you are sure the information is completely new to you, start a new schematic framework, but you will need to access it more often during early learning!

3. Incidentally, the lesson on chunking applies here as well: you can use your schemata (plural of *schema*) to help you integrate new information with old.

LESSON #3: IF YOU CAN'T REMEMBER SOMETHING, SWITCH PERSPECTIVES: CALL UP A DIFFERENT SCHEMA

How Do We Know?
In a clever study, Anderson and Pichert (1978) asked people to remember stories of two boys playing hooky from school. Some people were asked to remember the story from the perspective of a burglar; others were asked to remember the story from the perspective of a potential home buyer. The story involved various details, such as how big the rooms were (homebuyer interest) and different electronic devices (burglar interest) the boys used, such as a television set and small appliances in the kitchen. When Anderson and Pichert asked their participants to recall the stories, they did pretty well, but they performed even better when each group was divided in half. One subgroup recalled the story again, keeping the same perspective. The other subgroup was told to switch perspectives: the potential homebuyers were asked to think of themselves as burglars, and the potential burglars now were asked to think of themselves as homebuyers. What did they find? The people who kept the same perspective recalled just a little less the second time. Those who switched recalled substantially more. Their interpretation: switching perspectives provided a new plan for searching memory.

How to Do It:

If you are stuck in this way, just close your eyes for a minute and deactivate your current path for searching memory; deactivate you schema. Start over again and ask yourself what a related path might be, and go there. For example, maybe you encoded the biological bases of memory with your brain schema, rather than your memory schema. If searching one path doesn't work, try another reasonable path.

IMAGERY

LESSON #1: MAKE PICTORIAL REPRESENTATIONS OF VERBAL KNOWLEDGE WHENEVER POSSIBLE.

How Do We Know?
In another "landmark" study, Shepard (1967) showed subjects hundreds of pictures and 2 hours later gave a recognition task where each "old" picture was paired with a novel picture. Well, here is another no-brainer: Performance was nearly perfect. One week later recognition was still correct at 87%. When the same task was done with words, immediate recognition was only 88%. Yes, we now have evidence we can point to that pictures are better than words for remembering things.

How to Do It:
Create concept maps. It is much easier to bring to mind a picture and remember most of its details, than it is to remember words. Make concept maps for every chapter. This Grade Aid will give you some examples, but they are more limited to subsections of chapters, and really, it's best if you make your own.

LESSON #2: TAKE ABSTRACT CONCEPTS AND MAKE THEM AS CONCRETE AND IMAGEABLE AS POSSIBLE.

How Do We Know?
In the 1960s, Alan Paivio conducted a series of studies that showed that memory is stronger for things that are "imageable," such as concrete nouns, than for abstract concepts. In one study Paivio asked people to memorize pairs of words. Among the word pairs were four types: (1) concrete words paired with concrete words, (2) concrete words paired with abstract words, (3) abstract words paired with concrete words, and (4) abstract words paired with abstract words. He found that memory was best, in order, through conditions 1, 2, 3 and 4.

How to Do It:

Remember what we have learned so far: Memory is best if you connect concepts together. It is best to match concrete concepts together. However, much information in psychology is abstract, so you need to go to Paivio's condition 2: match concrete and abstract concepts together. During encoding you need to find related concepts: one concrete and one concrete or abstract. Make a mental image of the first concept: It should be unambiguous. Next, make an image of the abstract concept, even if it is ambiguous. Let's say you want to remember that short-term memory lasts about 30 seconds. "Memory" is a difficult concept for which to form an unambiguous mental image but a stopwatch stopped at 30 seconds can be easy to image. So a stop watch that has a computer memory chip background could work in this case. According to Paivio's dual code theory you will be storing two memories: the verbal one and the visual one. Then, during retrieval, if one path fails, you have a second path to search, and violà—twice the probability of retrieving the information.

MNEMONICS

Mnemonics are well-documented to have positive effects especially at **encoding,** but also at **storage and retrieval.** Many mnemonic devices—techniques to help you remember—are available. Some of these are called technical mnemonics and require you to learn specific techniques and memorize specific information first. Other are called naïve mnemonics because you can make them up as you go along. Whatever works!

LESSON #1: USE INTERACTIVE IMAGERY WHENEVER POSSIBLE.

How Do We Know?
Most of the technical mnemonics make use of imagery, particularly interactive imagery. You've already seen that memory for pictures is superior to that for words, and that dual-coding information for both verbal and imagery cues is superior to a single code. Now you will see evidence that making your images interactive works best. In a creative study examining the use of logos to accompany a company's name, Lutz and Lutz (1977) showed that people better remembered a company when the image of what the company does is integrated with the name of the company.

How to Do It:

Be creative! One common mnemonic is the "peg" system in which first a rhyme is memorized, such as "One is a bun, two is a shoe, three is a tree, four is a door, etc." Then, to-be-remembered ideas are reduced to an image, and these images are "hung" on the "pegs." The simplest example is of a list of errands you need to run. Let's say you needed to go to the grocery store, get gas, pick up the dry cleaning, and stop by the library. You could makes images of a large hamburger bun with groceries sticking out of the middle as the meat, a shoe-shaped car getting gas, with laces going between the gas tank and the pump, a tree with clothes on hangers blowing around in the wind, and a book-shaped door that opens up into shelves of books. This system works very well for memorizing lists or anything in sequence, such as events in history that need to be remembered in the order in which they occurred.

LESSON #2: USE VERBALLY BASED TECHNIQUES WHENEVER POSSIBLE.

How Do We Know?
The research literature is fairly consistent in showing that imagery works best; but some things just cannot be imaged in an unambiguous way. Here is where verbal mnemonics come into play. Reducing the cognitive load makes remembering easier. Psychologists have known this since George Miller first published his classic paper on the capacity of short-term memory in 1956. In addition, a review paper (see Bellezza, 1981; Cook, 1989) on the efficacy of verbally based techniques show that when imagery is not possible, verbal techniques work very well, and certainly MUCH better than just using simple rehearsal. Finally, independent studies of acronym use among introductory psychology students by Stalder (2005) showed that not only were the acronyms effective, but the task of coming up with acronyms, in particular, motivated students to study harder by looking for places where using an acronym would be appropriate, and then implementing their usage.

How to Do It:

Sometimes the material you need to learn is not amenable to images. For these situations, verbally based mnemonics come in handy. They include:
   A. Acrostics – In this type of "first letter mnemonic," you take the first letter of a list of things you need to memorize, such as the musical notes that are written on the "lines." Many a child has learned the sentence—Every Good Boy Does Fine—which stands for the notes E, G, B, D, F written in order from the bottom-most to the top-most line of the music staff.
   B. Acronyms – This "first letter mnemonic" takes the first letter of each word in a list and makes the letters into a word. For instance, "Roy G Biv" stands for the colors in a spectrum: Red, Orange, Yellow, Green, Blue, Indigo, and Violet.
   C. Narrative Methods – In this method you take the terms you need to remember and weave them into a story or a rhyme. For example: to spell correctly most children learn: "I before E, except after C…")
   D. Anything that works for you!

Again, you need some creativity and may need to rearrange concepts, but here is one you can use for the chapter on memory to help you remember the difference between proactive and retroactive interference— most beginning psychology students end up guessing because they just can't remember it: PORN, which is an acronym for Proactive interference Old material dominates Retroactive interference New material dominates. Or you can remember the difference between proactive and retroactive interference this way: *Pr*oactive interference occurs because of the *Pr*imacy effect and *Re*troactive interference occurs because of the *Re*cency effect.

DEPTH OF PROCESSING

This approach has its roots in **encoding**, to enhance **retrieval**. Craik and Lockhart (1972) published the seminal paper on depth, or levels of processing. Their basic premise is simple: The type of processing performed on material during encoding predicts later probability of remembering the material. Deep processing—processing for meaning, which focuses on (1) elaboration and (2) making individual bits of material distinct—is far superior to shallow processing, where the material is processed for its physical elements, as occurs during mindless rote repetition.

In describing shallow versus deep processing, Craik and Lockhart suggested two types of rehearsal: In rote rehearsal a person simply repeats to themselves over and over and over again the material, but at the same level of encoding (e.g., just memorizing the sounds of the words, without attaching any real meaning to what is being memorized). In elaborative rehearsal a person works on the material while repeating it, so that meaningfulness is considered—the material is connected to other things that are already known and interpreted in that light; the material is niched into an existing framework, or schema, and takes on a distinctive place in that framework.

LESSON #1: ATTACH MEANING TO NEW INFORMATION BY CONNECTING IT TO WHAT YOU ALREADY KNOW.

How Do We Know?
Here is an example of a study by Hyde and Jenkins (1973). They presented people with lengthy lists of words and asked them to perform one of several tasks. One type of task was a physical task: the person just had to note on paper whether the word was written in uppercase or lowercase letters. Another type of task was a semantic processing task: the person just had to note whether the meaning of the word indicated something pleasant. They were NEVER TOLD TO MEMORIZE the words. Well, in a surprise recall task, those who processed for meaning—that is, they used deep processing during encoding, recalled almost all of the words. Those people who processed only for physical characteristics—that is, they used shallow processing during encoding, recalled almost none of the words. So, without even trying, using deep processing provided strong memory for the material.

How to Do It:

When you study, don't just "memorize" terms. Each time you study a term make sure you are also telling yourself something about the meaning of that term. Later, your chances of remembering that information will be far greater than if you just sat and repeated the terms over and over again to yourself.

LESSON #2: MAKE NEW INFORMATION AS DISTINCT AS POSSIBLE.

How Do We Know?
One of the lessons from studying serial position effects, as well as the reasons for why depth of processing approaches might work other than the focus on meaning has to do with distinctiveness of material. Give a person a list of 20 unrelated words and ask him or her to recall it right away and you will find that they are more likely to remember the first few and the last few words; but are unlikely to remember the words in the middle, UNLESS there is something distinctive about those words in the middle. Then people show a spike in remembering.

How to Do It:

Simply take each concept you need to know and make it unique in some way. For example, you could think about not just the ways that things are alike, but also the ways in which they contrast. In fact, compare and contrast types of essay items are frequently used to assess higher-level thinking. The reasoning is that such items require students both elaborate (compare) the information and make it distinct (contrast).

LESSON #3: RELATE MATERIAL TO YOURSELF WHENEVER POSSIBLE.

How Do We Know?
Rogers, Kuiper, and Kirker (1977) presented a lengthy list of adjectives to people and then asked people to merely decide whether the words described the person. Of course, they had other comparison groups of people who performed other types of encoding tasks. But here is the important thing they found: Those people who performed the self-reference incidental task remember the most words during a surprise recall task.

How to Do It:

Now, you may not always be able to make these self-references, because not all material is going to relate to you. For example, it is hard to learn mathematical formulas in this way (although of course, processing them for meaning is possible, just probably not as a self-reference). However, whenever possible in a class such as psychology, when you learn a principle, think of examples in your own life that relate to the correct principle. THIS IS ESPECIALLY IMPORTANT WHEN YOU MUST OVERCOME INITIALLY INCORRECT PRECONCEPTIONS. Remember what we've told you before: most students come into an introductory psychology class thinking they already know a lot about human behavior—after all they have at least 18 years of human behavior in their own repertoire. But remember this: MUCH of the information reflects naïve science: knowledge based on an extremely limited sample (yourself and the people you know) and tends to be biased. Therefore, whenever you come up to information that seems to go against your existing knowledge, trying to find those examples which in the past you might have thought were exceptions, and dismissed as such, are now really important to focus on.

LESSON #4: IT IS BEST TO COME UP WITH YOUR OWN UNIQUE AND ORIGINAL EXAMPLES.

How Do We Know?
Slamecka and Graf (1978) showed that when people are asked to come up with examples of anything—whether it is generating mental images or schema-based frameworks to find a niche for new information—it always produces MUCH better memory for the information if a person comes up with his or her own image, framework, example, etc. Having the information provided for you is never as good as providing it for yourself.

How to Do It:

When you are studying, it is best to (1) put everything in your own words, (2) come up with your own original examples of the various principles you are reading about. Do not become overly focused on examples provided in your text—they are there as examples to illustrate the principles, but they are not the most important information in your studies. Being able to generate your own examples shows that you understand the principles you are working with—in this class and any other!

ENCODING SPECIFICITY

Tulving and Thomson (1973) stand out in the history of modern cognitive research for providing definitive evidence that **encoding** operations and **retrieval** operations are interwoven, and should not be considered as separate. They called their principles **encoding specificity** because it shows that the conditions and context that are specific to the encoding operations being performed need to be reinstated at retrieval for maximizing the retrieval process.

LESSON #1: MATCHING LEARNING AND RECALL CONTEXTS AND CONDITIONS AS MUCH AS POSSIBLE MAXIMIZES RECALL.

How Do We Know?

Tulving and Thomson asked people to study word pairs. Later, they presented people with two retrieval tasks: one was a recall task in which they presented one of the words originally studied in pairs, and the person had to remember the word that was paired with it. In a second task, recognition, Tulving and Thomson presented all of the to-be-remembered words, but without the paired words to act as cues. Instead, the target words were embedded with other words and only the targets needed to be picked out, i.e., recognized. Now, normally, most people would predict, as many studies do find, that recognition is MUCH easier than recall. However, in the situation that Tulving and Thomson created, of having words studied in pairs, they found that if they reinstated the encoding context by providing one of the words in each pair, people performed MUCH better on the recall task than on the recognition task.

How Do We Know MORE?

Well, in an interesting study Godden and Baddeley (1975) took this hypothesis a step further. They had two groups of participants who were all certified scuba divers. They asked one group of participants to learn a list of words while sitting on land. The other group learned the same list of words while under water. Each group was then split in half again. For the recall phase half of each group recalled the words under the same conditions, and half under the other conditions. So there were four groups: those who learned on land and recalled the words on land, those who learned on land but recalled the words under water, those who learned the words underwater and recalled them on land, and those who learned and recalled the words under water. What did they find? Those whose learning and recall contexts matched, recalled FAR MORE words, than those who changed context between learning and recall.

How to Do It:

Find a place to study that is most like the place in which you will be tested. For many students this might mean studying consistently in a classroom that is much like the classroom they usually have their own class in but that is consistently vacant at a time that the student has free for studying.

LESSON #2: IF YOU MUST CHANGE CONTEXTS BETWEEN LEARNING AND TESTING, IMAGINE YOURSELF IN THE LEARNING CONTEXT.

How Do We Know?

Sometimes, just imaging yourself in a specific location is all it takes. Smith (1979) replicated the classic test of having participants study and learn in the same or different context, but added an extra twist with an extra group of participants. The extra group changed rooms but each individual was asked to imagine him or herself in the learning room—to mentally reinstate the learning context. Smith found that those participants performed just as well as those who did not change rooms at all!

How to Do It:

Now we come to the conventional wisdom often mentioned in study skills Web sites: pick a place to study, study there consistently, and do nothing else in that place. Why? Because you will maximize your ability to remember what you studied if you can recreate your own learning context during a testing situation. Furthermore, if you can pick a seat in class and always sit in that seat, you can also help yourself to retrieve lecture information by literally being in the same context as you were during lecture.

Also, don't study with music on, unless you plan to be humming the same music to yourself throughout the test—likely to annoy your classmates should you hum out loud!

LESSON #3: MATCH YOUR INTERNAL STATES AND MOODS AT BOTH LEARNING AND TESTING TIMES.

How Do We Know?
A final tidbit related to all of the cue-dependent learning and forgetting: Ample evidence, as reviewed by Eich (1989), indicates for state-dependent learning is indeed effective. So, what is state-dependent learning? Well, just as context can serve as a retrieval cue, so too can your internal states (and moods for that matter!).

How to Do It:

Are you likely to take your test at about midnight when you are completely mentally drained? Not likely, because classes do not take place at such times. The lesson here is that you should not study in a state of mind that is unlike the state of mind you are likely to be in during the test.

A second lesson can come from this coordination of state and mood as well. Do you suffer from test anxiety? Simulate test anxiety during your study sessions: have a cup of coffee or two to increase arousal levels. But then, during the test, do NOT compound your test anxiety by having coffee on that day! Remember: increasing arousal during study has the purpose of matching encoding and retrieval operations. On the other hand: no test anxiety? Then just be sure to match your internal states as much as possible at encoding and retrieval.

MASSED VERSUS DISTRIBUTED PRACTICE

Studies on the spacing effect go back more than 100 years. The evidence over this time frame has been consistent: for **acquisition** of information, massed practice is good. But for long-term **retention** of material distributed practice is best. This recommendation is partly based on Ebbinghaus's classic forgetting curve, which Ebbinghaus described in the late 1800s, but still holds true today. Ebbinghaus found that most forgetting occurs shortly after initial learning—in fact most new information is rapidly forgotten. What remains tends to be long-lived, but it tends to not be much after a single learning session. Thus, the more learning sessions, the more that is remembered later on. Another reason for the superiority of distributed practice is what is called attenuation of attention. What does this fancy phrase mean? It means that the more you repeatedly study the same exact information, the less you are likely to attend to it—you experience a feeling of already knowing it. Another reason has to do with familiarity. As you repeatedly study the same information it feels familiar; your sense *at that moment* is that you "know" it. But what about the next day or the next week? "LATER" is a better test of what you actually know. Finally, it is difficult to maintain close attention for a long enough study session to master the large amounts of new information you are exposed to in your college classes. You need a break! Take it! Go back LATER.

LESSON #1: DISTRIBUTED PRACTICE IS CONSISTENTLY SUPERIOR TO MASSED PRACTICE (CRAMMING) FOR LONG-TERM RETENTION OF MATERIAL.

How Do We Know?
In one of a series of related studies, Landauer and Bjork (1978) asked students to memorize first and last name pairs. They had different groups of students study the names under different conditions. In one condition they simply used massed practice. In another condition they varied the length of the interval for distributed practice. In a final set of conditions they had what they called expanding and contracting

intervals. In the expanding intervals the spacing between learning sessions started out short and was lengthened (expanded) over time. In the contracting interval condition the sequencing was opposite: at first the intervals were long, and then were progressively shortened (contracted). If you had to guess which of these many conditions was best, which would you think? If you thought it was the expanding condition you would be correct: While you are still learning the material, shorter intervals are good. Remember that massed practice is best for acquisition. But then lengthening the interval progressively is best. It allows the most time for consolidation to take place.

How to Do It:

Don't Cram! PLAN AHEAD and set up times in which you will study; then start out each study session with a review of the previous study session(s). At first you might want to review from the just previous session, but over time, as you accumulate more information you can begin to expand your study sessions. So session 1 you first learn something. Session 2 you go over material from session 1 and then go into new material. Now, at session 3 you might go over session 2 material and learn new material. At session 4 you should probably review material back from study session 1 and then review what you just learned at study session 3 and move on to new material and so on…always review the new material from the previous study session but then go back and review some of the prior material as well before moving on to new material.

METACOGNITION

Metacognition is the big daddy of everything that cognitive psychology can tell us about learning. *Meta* comes from ancient Greek, meaning "behind," "beyond," or "after." Thus, metacognition is knowledge beyond what you know—it is what you know about your own knowledge—and what you don't know! How much control do you believe you exercise over your thinking, and how much of it do you just let "happen"? Remember: Some students who perform poorly study for many more hours than others who perform well. One of the reasons for this appears to be a difference in metacognition—good students spend more time on what they don't yet know well enough, and skimming what they already know. Unfortunately, students who perform poorly tend to not know what they know and don't know and so spend too much time on what they already know, and not enough time on what they don't yet know well.

Most educators discuss metacognition as involving a plan of action, following through with the plan by implementing and maintaining it, and finally, by evaluating the plan—is it producing the desired effect on learning? Good metacognitive awareness requires a LOT of effort, pure and simple, but it is the best guarantee you will ever have of maximizing your learning.

LESSON #1: CONTROLLING YOUR OWN LEARNING IS YOUR BEST CHANCE TO MAXIMIZE YOUR ABILITIES, BUT IT TAKES A LOT OF EFFORT.

How Do We Know?
Dunlosky and Lipko (2007) reviewed studies, as well as carrying out their own research. What they found was that students of all ages need to monitor their progress on an ongoing basis. Time and time again studies show that students overestimate their knowledge and need to remain constantly vigilant to what works and in which situations.

How to Do It:

BEGIN WITH THE PAST: What have you done in the past that has worked for you? Did you read? Memorize? Summarize? Stop and review in your own words? Which study habits have worked best? Worst?

DURING: Throughout the course, ask yourself: How am I doing? Am I on the right track? What information is important to remember? What do I need to do if I do not understand? Does my text have a study guide or a Web site where I can quiz myself?

AFTER: Evaluating your approach to studying answers these questions. How well did you do on assignments/tests? What could you have done differently? Do you need to go back through the task to fill in any "blanks" in your understanding?

BEWARE OF OVERCONFIDENCE: One element resulting in poor metacognition is overconfidence. Dunning, Heath, and Suls (2004) reviewed the literature for the past decades to conclusively show that flawed self-assessment is pervasive. In terms of students: the poorest performing students show the highest confidence in what they think they know.

LESSON #2: DO NOT STOP STUDYING UNTIL YOU HAVE OVERLEARNED THE MATERIAL.

How Do We Know?

In a sense this lesson harkens back to several previous ones, such as distributed practice. Rohrer and Pashler (2007) asked students to memorize word lists until they knew the lists completely. Some of the students continued to memorize them, and others stopped at that point. A week later, those who overlearned the lists remembered them much better. Nine weeks later, it makes no difference. However, in another study they had students either learn the material, and then learn it again after a time lapse. In this case, those students who overlearned by studying again after a time lapse remembered more at both the 1-week and 9-week test dates. Why might overlearning be helpful, especially in the short run? Shiffrin (1988) showed that if you practice a task more, your ability to use the information becomes more automatic, thereby freeing up resources—the task takes less effort. However, for a task to remain automatic it needs continued practice. Thus, distributing the learning sessions is most helpful. Finally, another reason students are often told to overlearn is that for most classroom material there really isn't a "criterion" of understanding that students can study to achieve. The best way to not fall prey to overconfidence that the "criterion" has been reached is to continue to study.

How to Do It:

Probably the easiest way to know what you do and don't know is to quiz yourself—but NOT right after studying. Of course, you know what you just finished studying. Quiz yourself a few days later. THEN go back over what you missed. Briefly gloss over what you think you knew well—you may have heard the saying, "You can never have too much of a good thing." Well, similarly, you can never study your lessons too many times.

References

Anderson, R. C., & Pichert, J. W. (1978). Recall of previously unrecallable information following a shift in perspective. *Journal of Verbal Learning and Verbal Behavior, 17*, 1–12.

Borkowski, J. G., Carr, M., Rellinger, E., & Pressley, M. (1990). Self-regulated cognition: Interdependence of metacognition, attributions, and self-esteem. In B. F. Jones & L. Idol (Eds.), *Dimensions of Thinking and Cognitive Instruction* (pp. 53–92). Mahwah: NJ.

Bower, G. H., Clark, M. C., Lesgold, A. M., & Winenz, D. (1969). Hierarchical retrieval schemes in recall of categorized word lists. *Journal of Verbal Learning and Verbal Behavior, 8*, 323–343.

Brewer, W. F., & Treyens, J. C. (1981). Role of schemata in memory for places. *Cognitive Psychology, 13*, 207–230.

Craik, F. I. M., & Lockhart, R. S. (1972). Levels of processing: A framework for memory research. *Journal of Verbal Learning and Verbal Behavior, 11*, 671–684.

Dunlosky, J., & Lipko, A. R. (2007). Metacomprehension: A brief history and how to improve its accuracy. *Current Directions in Psychological Science, 16*(4), 228–232.

Dunning, D., Heath, C., & Suls, J. M. (2004). Flawed self-assessment. *Psychological Science in the Public Interest, 5*(3), 69–106.

Eich, E. (1989). Theoretical issues in state dependent memory. In H. L. Roediger & F. I. M. Craik, *Varieties of Memory and Consciousness* (pp. 331–354), Hillsdale, NJ: Lawrence Erlbaum and Associates Publishers.

Godden, D. R., & Baddeley, A. D. (1975). Context-dependent memory in two natural environments: On land and underwater. *British Journal of Psychology, 66*, 325–331.

Hyde, T. S., & Jenkins, J. J. (1973). Recall for words as a function of semantic, graphic, and syntactic orienting tasks. *Journal of Verbal Learning and Verbal Behavior, 12*, 471–480.

Kruger, J., & Dunning, D. (1999). Unskilled and unaware of it: How difficulties in recognizing one's own incompetence lead to inflated self-assessments. *Journal of Personality and Social Psychology, 77*(6), 1121–1134.

Landauer, T. K., & Bjork, R. A. (1978). Optimum rehearsal patterns and name learning. In M. Gruneberg, H. Morris & R. Sykes (Eds.), *Practical Aspects of Memory* (pp. 625–632). London: Academic Press.

Lutz, K. A., & Lutz, R. J. (1977). Effects of interactive imagery on learning: Application to advertising. *Journal of Applied Psychology, 62*(4), 493–498.

Miller, G. A. (1956). The magical number seven, plus or minus two: Some limits on our capacity for processing information. *Psychological Review, 63*(2), 81–97.

Paivio, A., Walsh, M., & Bons, T. (1994). Concreteness effect on memory: When and why? *Journal of Experimental Psychology: Learning, Memory and Cognition, 20* (5), 1196–1204.

Payne, D. G., & Wenger, M. J. (1992). Improving memory through practice. In D. J. Herrmann, H. Weingartner & A. Searleman, (Eds.), *Memory Improvement* (pp. 187–209). New York: Springer-Verlag.

Rogers, T. B., Kuiper, N. A., & Kirker, W. S. (1977). Self-reference and the encoding of personal information. *Journal of Personality and Social Psychology, 35*(9), 677–688.

Rohrer, D., & Pashler, H. (2007). Increasing retention time without increasing study time. *Current Directions in Psychological Science, 16*, 183–186.

Shepard, R. N. (1967). Recognition memory for words, sentences, and pictures. *Journal of Verbal Learning and Verbal Behavior, 6*, 156–163.

Shiffrin, R. M. (1988). Attention. In R. C. Atkinson, R. J. Herrnstein, G. Lindzey, & R. Dun (Eds.), *Stevens' Handbook of Experimental Psychology* (pp. 739–811). John Wiley & Sons.

Slamecka, N. J., & Graf, P. (1978). The generation effect: Delineation of a phenomenon. *Journal of Experimental Psychology: Human Learning and Memory, 4*(6), 592–604.

Smith, M. S. (1979). Remembering in and out of context. *Journal of Experimental Psychology: Human Learning and Memory, 5*(5), 460–471.

Tulving, E., & Thomson, D. M. (1973). Encoding specificity and retrieval processes in episodic memory. *Psychological Review, 80*, 352–373.

Winn, W., & Snyder, D. (1996). Cognitive perspectives in psychology. In D. H. Jonassen (Ed.), *Handbook of Research for Educational Communications and Technology* (pp. 112–142). New York: Macmillan.

CONCEPT MAPPING

What are all of these "bubble maps"? And why do I need to deal with them?

If you are like our students, you are probably asking yourself these questions. The answer to the first question is that the "bubble" maps are actually concept maps. They represent material in a way that makes learning easier and more efficient, and they make it more likely that the information will stick in your memory. It is a way to organize the material for deeper learning.

The reason you may *want* to deal with the maps (rather than "need" to) is that doing so will maximize the chances that you will actually *learn* the material. That is, if you really want to learn the material (rather than just try to memorize it for a test and forget it) and you want to do so in an efficient way, concept maps can help you achieve your goals.

Why can't I just make an outline?

You could, and some students do, even after being introduced to concepts maps. Remember from the study skills section you just read, that actively engaging in thinking about the information, organizing the information, and relating it to other things you know, results in greater understanding and greater likelihood of retention. Concept mapping does everything outlines do and more. Concept maps organize information, but they also allow you to "visualize" concepts and their relationships in a layout format. This visualization can give you one more cue for retrieval. In addition, unlike an outline, which is organized from top to bottom, concepts maps can be read from top to bottom, but also from bottom to top, left to right and right to left!

How do I know it works? Isn't this just more "busywork?"

In Chapter 7, Memory, you will read about deep and shallow processing and you will see that the research evidence strongly supports deep processing—processing for meaning, based on elaborating the relationships between new and old knowledge. This is how it works—elaborating relationships on many levels. On the other hand, the research evidence is overwhelming that knowledge learned by rote tends to be quickly forgotten because it is not processed deeply. Thinking about how concepts are related to one another helps you encode the information so that it is easier to retrieve the information when you want it.

Another benefit of concept mapping is that a large amount of information can be efficiently summarized so that you can pull together information you already know and understand about a topic, and combine it with new information you are learning. In this way, it is not just more "busywork," which usually does NOT lead to deeper learning. Therefore, summarizing in this way is important because it aids memory, and it encourages high-level, critical thinking, which is so important in university work.

So, tell me again, why I want to do these exercises, and maybe apply this technique in other classes?

Concept mapping lets you organize information.
Concept mapping lets you see all your basic information on one page.
Concept mapping lets you see the relationships among key ideas more clearly.
Concept mapping lets you add new information as you learn it.
Concept mapping lets you integrate separate maps into larger, more complex structures.
Bottom line: Concept mapping results in better understanding of underlying ideas and, as a result, better retrieval of information.

How do you make a map?

Many concept maps use a hierarchical organization, although that format is not necessary. If hierarchical organization is desired, the most inclusive, most general concepts are placed at the top of the map, with the less general, more specific concepts arranged hierarchically below. Thus, the map will show the relationship of the subordinate (lower) concepts to each superordinate (higher) concept.

Each important term you learn is a node, or concept. A node is usually shown as a circle or bubble, with the term written within it. Lines connect the nodes, to show which concepts are related, and the nature of the relationship. These lines have a one-sided arrow if one concept flows from the other, or a two-sided arrow if there is a back-and-forth relationship between the two concepts, or no arrows at all. Each connecting line is labeled and tells how the concepts relate. A concept might link to another as "a part of," "for example," "located in," or "produces." Map guidelines are flexible—use what helps YOU understand. Here is a simple concept map—as you will see, they can be about any topic, not just psychology.

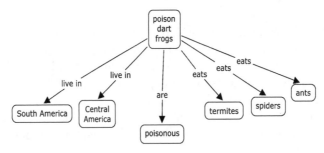

What do I do with the maps in the Grade Aid?

In this Grade Aid you will sometimes be given a partially completed concept map and your task will be to fill in the remaining circles with concepts, based on the relationships provided to you. Some concept maps will have an answer provided at the end of the chapter's activities. Your maps could differ based on your choice of concepts; it's not a matter of finding the completely "right" or "wrong" answers! Take advantage of the flexibility of concept maps to show multiple relationships.

Sometimes, the answers section will only provide a list of concepts that could be included by you. Other times we will provide you with a set of concepts and ask you to construct the map. The answers section may or may not include a completed map because the final mapping may be related to your prior knowledge, your understanding of the relationships between concepts, and how much information you have gleaned from the text. Most of the time the concept maps are not suggested to you. We encourage you to develop your own maps. You might want to map out entire chapters, linking together the individual maps we are providing you with.

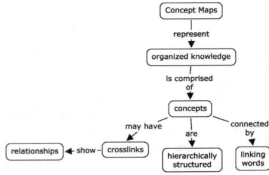

Can you give me an example?

EVALUATING WEB SITES

Throughout this Grade Aid, you will be asked to access the Internet—either to find information on your own, or to go to a site that we recommend for a particular activity. The Web is probably among the most wonderful inventions of our time—the information that is now instantly available to you is nothing short of amazing. But it is also the greatest source of misinformation, misconceptions, and just plain old gobbledy-gook imaginable. The following resources provide useful information on evaluating Web sites:

http://lib.nmsu.edu/instruction/evalcrit.html
http://kathyschrock.net/abceval/
http://www.library.cornell.edu/olinuris/ref/research/webeval.html
http://www.lib.msu.edu/link/critical.htm
http://www.lib.berkeley.edu/TeachingLib/Guides/Internet/Evaluate.html

As you read through a few of the these recommended Web sites you should keep in mind these basic criteria:

AUTHORITY—Who is the author? What are his or her qualifications or credentials? Who is the publisher? What bias would you expect of this publisher if any? What reputation do these sources have?

VERIFIABILITY—Are the claims made verifiable? Are there accurate, traceable sources?

CURRENCY OR TIMELINESS—Is the information given current? When was the last time the page was updated?

RELEVANCE—Is the material truly related to what you need to know?

BIAS VERSUS OBJECTIVITY—Is the language used loaded? Are points of view given that show a range of opinion? Are you being sold anything?

ORDERLINESS—Is the page arranged in an order that makes sense?

CLARITY—Is the information clearly stated? Does the author use obscure language?

ACCURACY—Is the information given out of context? Are the data used compatible?

NAVIGABILITY—Do all of the links work?

SCHOLASTIC REVIEWS—Has this site received any rewards?

HOUSING—What type of domain houses this Web page?

The bottom line in evaluating Web sites: Use every critical thinking skill you have ever been taught, either in this textbook or in any book you have read or course you have taken. The Web will provide you with quality information, but it will also provide you with the lowest-quality information. It will be up to you to determine the difference.

PROLOGUE:
HOW PSYCHOLOGY BECAME A SCIENCE

BEFORE YOU READ ... CHAPTER PREVIEW

The study of psychology is both a fascinating and a challenging journey. It is fascinating because as humans we have a natural interest in learning about ourselves; challenging because of characteristics of the subject of study. The 10 challenges in studying humans described in the prologue reflect the difficulties in studying abstract concepts that are multiply determined, where the mere act of observing can change behavior, and both the immediate and larger cultural environment can influence what is being observed.

Some claim that psychology is a young science, dating its birth from Wilhelm Wundt's establishment of the first psychological laboratory in 1879. Actually, psychology, like all of the sciences, has roots in early philosophy. Many of the questions studied by psychologists originated in the speculations of the philosophers. A new psychology was born as investigators developed ways of quantifying their observations. In addition, by developing a critical view of how human observation can be biased, the new psychology was also able to differentiate itself from spiritualism. Learning about these biases and how to avoid them will be a main theme of this textbook.

Five major theoretical orientations have played a role in shaping the field. Structuralism aimed to identify the basic elements of experience through the method of introspection. The school of functionalism hoped to understand the adaptive purposes of behavior. Behaviorism grew out of the belief that psychological science must be completely objective. The cognitivist view emphasized the importance of mental processes in understanding behavior. Psychoanalysis, focusing on unconscious processes and urges, has been criticized as retarding the progress of scientific psychology because of its lack of scientific rigor.

Today the field of psychology is diverse. A major controversy in the field involves whether clinical psychology should continue to reflect a scientific orientation or whether clinical practice should reflect clinical judgment and intuition. In addition to clinical practice, psychology has found its way into our everyday lives through other applications from advertising and testing to security and safety. There are many types of psychologists. Clinical and counseling psychologists conduct therapy. School psychologists develop intervention programs for children in school settings. Industrial organizational psychologists work in companies and business and are involved in maximizing performance. Forensic psychologists work in prisons or court settings. Many other psychologists conduct research. Developmental psychologists study systematic change over time. Experimental psychologists study learning and thinking and biopsychologists study biological basis of behavior.

Three great debates that have shaped the field of psychology reflect psychology's origins in philosophy. The nature–nurture debate asks, "Are our behaviors attributable to something we are born with or to our experiences in our environment?" The free will–determinism debate asks, "To what extent are behaviors freely selected?" The mind–body debate asks, "Are our behaviors entirely due to the action of our physical body or are they also influenced by a nonmaterial soul?"

1

BEFORE YOU READ ... TERM IDENTIFICATION

---

applied research (p. 14)
basic research (p. 14)
behaviorism (p. 11)
black box (p. 11)
cognition (p. 12)
compatibilism (p. 20)
critical multiplism (p. 13)
emic (p. 5)
etic (p. 6)
evolutionary psychology (p. 19)
functionalism (p. 11)
individual differences (p. 5)
introspection (p. 8)
jangle fallacy (p. 4)
just-so stories (p. 19)
levels of explanation (p. 2)

Meehl's maxim (p. 3)
mind–body dualists (p. 21)
mind–body monists (p. 21)
multicollinearity (p. 3)
multiply determined (p. 3)
mysterians (p. 3)
paranormal (p. 8)
psychoanalysis (p. 12)
psychology (p. 2)
reactivity (p. 5)
reciprocal determinism (p. 4)
reflexivity (p. 4)
scientist–practitioner gap (p. 9)
single-variable explanations (p. 3)
structuralism (p. 10)

AS YOU READ ... PRACTICE ACTIVITIES

WHAT IS PSYCHOLOGY? BASIC QUESTIONS AND KEY CHALLENGES

1. Although coming up with a definitive definition of psychology poses a challenge, coming up with questions that we might expect psychology to answer should be relatively easy. Write down 6 or more questions you would like to have answered throughout your journey into psychology. Come back and revisit these questions as the semester goes on. You may find, after reading chapters 1 and 2 that science cannot answer the questions as asked, and you may need to reframe them; or you may find excellent answers as the semester goes along.

2. In many "reality" television programs, the "contestants" know that their every behavior is being recorded. How do you think reactivity affects their behavior? Do you think their response changes over time? How and why?

3. Compare "emic" and "etic" approaches to studying the effects of culture on behavior. Note that throughout this Grade Aid you will be asked to "compare" two or more concepts rather frequently. When you do so, examine both how the concepts are alike and how they might differ from one another.

Prologue

PSYCHOLOGY IN HISTORICAL PERSPECTIVE: WHAT A LONG, STRANGE TRIP IT'S BEEN

1. True scientific psychology has always had to coexist with, and differentiate itself from, psychical and spiritualistic studies. Scientific psychologists have been debunking these latter beliefs for well over a century and still they persist. What are some modern day nonscientific disciplines that compete with psychological science? Why do you think that these types of beliefs are so persistent?

2. Match these major historical events in the history of psychology, to their dates.

    _____ Neisser launches field of cognitive psychology.

    _____ Wilhelm Wundt opens first laboratory devoted to scientific psychology and thereby psychology is born as a new discipline.

    _____ Milgram publishes classic studies on obedience.

    _____ Ivan Pavlov discovers classical conditioning.

    _____ Daniel Kahneman is first psychologist to win a Nobel Prize.

    _____ William James writes *Principles of Psychology.*

    _____ John Watson starts field of behaviorism

    1879; 1890; 1910; 1913; 1963; 1967; 2002

THE GREAT THEORETICAL FRAMEWORKS OF PSYCHOLOGY

1. Compare structuralism and functionalism's contributions to the early development of psychology as an independent discipline.

2. Match the following theoretical frameworks to their proponents and to their definitions.

Structuralism	Ulric Neisser	sought to identify basic purpose of thoughts, feelings, and behaviors
Functionalism	John B. Watson	sought to understand elements of psychology
Behaviorism	Edward Titchener	examined the effects of "thinking" in behavior
Cognitivism	William James	uncovered general laws of learning by examining external, objective behavior

THE MULTIFACETED WORLD OF MODERN PSYCHOLOGY

1. Imagine that you are committed to a future in some field of psychology. Which type of psychologist would you want to be, and why?

2. A public speaking phobia can be interpreted differently by the different types of psychologists. Pick three different types of psychologists and suggest the mechanisms they might use to interpret a public speaking phobia.

Prologue

3. This chapter only briefly mentions some types of psychologists, such as social, personality, cross-cultural, quantitative, and sports psychologists. Go to the Internet and find out a little bit more about each of these types of psychology and briefly describe each of them here.

THE GREAT DEBATES OF PSYCHOLOGY

1. After reading about the "Great Debates of Psychology" in the Prologue, skim through the rest of your text and find examples you believe illustrate each of these concepts. The Prologue provides you with many ideas of the chapters that cover the different areas of psychology where good examples can be found.

   a. nature

   b. nurture

   c. free will

   d. determinism

   e. actions of the body that affect behavior

   f. actions of the mind that affect behavior

THE PSYCHOLOGICAL JOURNEY

1. Psychology, as a complete journey has a vast interdisciplinary perspective, combining elements of philosophy, sociology, anthropology, biology, neuroscience, chemistry, physics, and mathematics. On the one hand these interrelationships are exactly what makes psychology a fascinating discipline to most people. On the other hand, they may sometimes seem a bit overwhelming! Which aspects excite you the most? Why? Which aspects worry you the most? Why? How can you plan ahead to take the worry out of those aspects of this journey?

AS YOU READ ... CONCEPT MAP ACTIVITIES

ACTIVITY 1: Provide your own original examples for these 10 things that make psychology challenging.

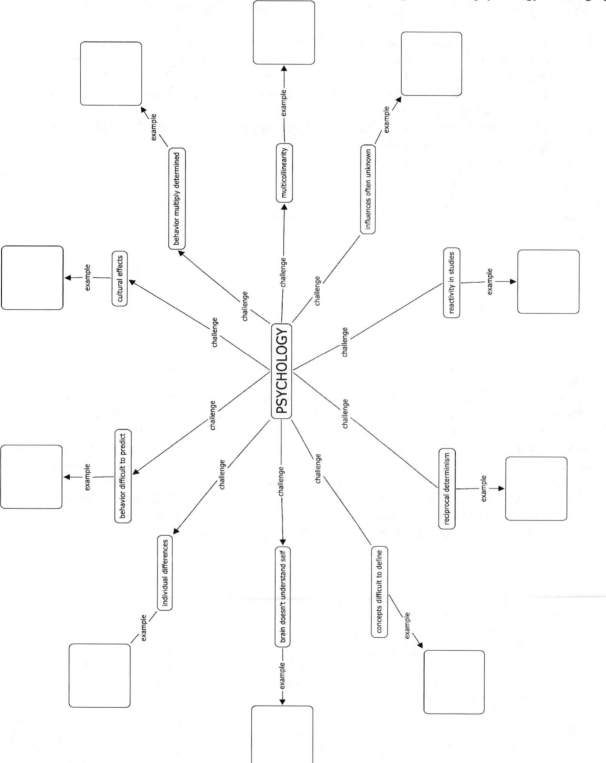

Author activity content supported by *IHMC Cmap Tools* Copyright ©1998-2007 Institute for Human & Machine Cognition

Prologue

AS YOU READ ... MYTH OR REALITY?

Myth: Parapsychology is the name for a subtype of psychology.
Reality: Parapsychology has little if any true psychological science to back it up.

1. Go to http://www.parapsychology.org and read about parapsychology.
   a. Evaluate the quality of this Web site using the guidelines in the Prologue to this Grade Aid.
   b. Evaluate parapsychology in terms of psychological science's "Great Theoretical Frameworks" as delineated in your text. Does parapsychology fit in with any of these frameworks? If not, why not? If so, which ones and how?
   c. Which of psychology's subtypes would parapsychology best fit with? Why? Is it easy to "niche" parapsychology into the standard subtypes of psychology? Why or why not?

2. If you accept a definition of psychology as a systematic, scientific consideration of human and animal behavior, then programs in parapsychology may fall short. To get an example of typical programs in parapsychology, see http://www.directoryofschools.com/American-Institute-of-Holistic-Theology/Programs.htm At this Web site you will find information about how you can receive a B.S., M.S., or Ph.D. in Parapsychic Science. Link to http://www.aiht.edu/catalog/parapsychic_courses.asp .
   a. How do the descriptions of these programs differ from a standard college program of study? Do they show the same breadth of instruction across disciplines? Compare the requirements to achieve your degree, to the program of study described at the second link. It is a 61-unit program with no general education courses included and culminates in a Bachelor of Science degree.
   b. Why do you think this program might be a detriment to a good education?

As You Read ... Put Your Critical Thinking Skills to the Test

1. You know you want to major in psychology (well, maybe you don't, but imagine that you do) but are not sure of exactly what you can do with a degree in psychology. After reading in your text about the types of psychologists, you can also go to http://www.apa.org/topics/psychologycareer.html or http://www.uni.edu/walsh/linda1.html to read more about the different careers within psychology. Develop two or three distinct career paths you might want to take, and what you will need to do to get from here (where you are now), to there (where you want to be eventually).

AS YOU READ ... MYPSYCHLAB CONNECTION

What Is Psychology? Basic Questions and Key Challenges
Psychology in Historical Perspective: What a Long, Strange Trip It's Been
Explore the *Psychology Timeline* to see the timeline of significant events in the field of psychology and biographies of contributors to the field.

The Great Theoretical Frameworks of Psychology
Take a **Quick Review** quiz on the *The Great Theoretical Frameworks of Psychology* to review the various theoretical perspectives.

The Multifaceted World of Modern Psychology
Explore the types of psychologists with *Psychologists at Work* to learn more about the work and various fields of psychologists.

The Great Debates of Psychology
Take a **Quick Review** quiz on the *The Great Debates of Psychology* and see if you understand the debates that have helped to shape the field of psychology

---

AFTER YOU READ ... PRACTICE TEST #1

Before beginning this practice test, estimate the percent you expect to get correct.
Anticipated percent correct: _____

1. Josiah believes that many of the questions that he has about human nature and behavior are too complex to really have definitive answers. Josiah's belief typifies the beliefs of
   a. alienists.
   b. empiricists.
   c. physicists.
   d. mysterians.

2. The finding that the causes for any specific behavior are not only multiply determined, but also overlap, is called
   a. reflexivity.
   b. multicollinearity.
   c. reciprocal determinism.
   d. a single-variable explanation.

3. Parents often use different disciplinary techniques even among their own children, each of whom might have a unique personality and temperament. This situation illustrates the principles of
   a. critical multiplism.
   b. introspection.
   c. reciprocal determinism.
   d. reflexivity.

4. The year 1879 is often considered the "birth year" of psychology as an independent laboratory science, because in 1879
   a. Ivan Pavlov discovered classical conditioning.
   b. Sigmund Freud wrote, *The Interpretation of Dreams*.
   c. Charles Darwin published, *The Origin of the Species*.
   d. Wilhelm Wundt developed and opened the first psychology laboratory.

5. Cyndi and her friends are sitting around a table at the campus coffee shop, systematically comparing their own inner thoughts on how they "know" that they have an ability called "memory." Cyndi and her friends are engaging in
   a. spiritualism.
   b. introspection.
   c. compatibilism.
   d. psychoanalysis.

6. Lenny has been using crystals with his clients during psychotherapy sessions because he has personally experienced their healing powers. Shirley, who uses cognitive behavioral therapy because she has studied the research behind it, seriously frowns on Lenny's use of crystals with his clients. Lenny and Shirley illustrate
   a. the scientist-practitioner gap.
   b. the advantages of critical multiplism.
   c. the distinction between basic and applied research.
   d. the distinction between an emic and an etic approach.

7. Carlos is a landscaper who picks plants for outdoor living spaces based on how well the scents and colors of the plants blend together. He tries to understand why some plants are more aesthetically pleasing to his clients. Carlos's approach to landscaping best reflects
   a. functionalism.
   b. structuralism.
   c. behaviorism.
   d. empiricism.

8. Which approach to psychology was advocated by Edward Titchener in the late 1800s?
    a. Humanistic psychology
    b. Psychoanalysis
    c. Functionalism
    d. Structuralism

9. Who is recognized as the founder of behaviorism?
    a. Carl Rogers
    b. John Watson
    c. Edward Titchener
    d. Hermann Ebbinghaus

10. The theoretical framework that focused on examining our external, objective behaviors is
    a. behaviorism.
    b. structuralism.
    c. functionalism.
    d. psychoanalysis.

11. The downfall for behaviorism may have been its overreliance
    a. exclusively on internal behaviors.
    b. exclusively on external behaviors.
    c. on partitioning the components of each behavior.
    d. on trying to figure out the workings of the black box.

12. The difference between a clinical psychologist and a psychiatrist is that
    a. a clinical psychologist can do group therapy and a psychiatrist cannot.
    b. a clinical psychologist uses Freudian methods and a psychiatrist does not.
    c. a clinical psychologist has a Ph.D. degree and a psychiatrist has an M.D. degree.
    d. a psychiatrist treats major disorders; a psychologist treats minor disorders.

13. The current view of psychoanalysis is that
    a. Freud himself seemed to suffer from psychological problems; his theories reflect his struggles.
    b. some of its claims can be empirically verified, but most cannot.
    c. since Freud's time, most elements have been verified with research studies.
    d. unconscious drives best explain why some people develop repressed memories.

14. Dr. Brown is researching the effects of loud noise on auditory development in monkeys. Dr. Grace is examining how loud noise in the classroom affects test taking. Dr. Brown is doing _____ research, whereas Dr. Grace is doing _____research.
    a. basic; applied
    b. invasive; theoretical
    c. structural; functional
    d. qualitative; quantitative

15. Carmen's career goal is to become a therapist. Her best plan may be to
    a. earn a Ph.D. in clinical psychology.
    b. earn a Psy.D. or a master's degree in social work.
    c. go to medical school and specialize in psychotherapy.
    d. avoid programs that require a research-based dissertation.

16. Professor Cunningham is a biological psychologist. She most likely studies which of these behaviors?
    a. What is the best temperature for assembly line work
    b. Which aspects of memory loss are normal as we get older
    c. How hormone levels change during stressful experiences
    d. How often a person buys a lotto ticket based on how often they win

17. These days the nature–nurture debate is more focused on
    a. why the debate has been dead since the genome project has now finished mapping out nature's contributions to behavior.
    b. how nature and nurture work together.
    c. determining exactly which genes are responsible for which of our behaviors.
    d. delineating the failures of genetics to predict behaviors, supporting the nurture account.

18. Evolutionary psychology
    a. provides readily testable hypotheses.
    b. depends on the overall strength of organisms relative to one another.
    c. applies the theory of natural selection to human and animal behavior.
    d. suggests hypotheses that provide deep explanations of human and animal behavior.

19. Some scientists argue that free will is an illusion. Support for this notion comes from
    a. the finding that so many of our behaviors only occur through great effort on our part.
    b. evidence of our direct access to the cause of our behaviors.
    c. B. F. Skinner's argument that we are not conscious of all of the stimuli in the environment that elicit a behavioral response from us.
    d. the effects of mental illness on our ability to act freely.

20. If you were a news reporter, which headline would best capture a story on the mind–body debate?
    a. Do we really "think" or do we just respond to stimuli?
    b. Are our actions attributable to our soul or to our mind?
    c. Does a soul underlie our behavior, or does the brain drive our behavior?
    d. Can we make our own choices for our behaviors or do environmental contingencies control us?

After completing the test, calculate your percent correct
(/ 20 =   ) x 100 = _____.

How accurate were your expectations? Does your performance suggest the need for additional study? For the items you missed, go back and identify why the "correct" answer is the best answer.

AFTER YOU READ ... PRACTICE TEST ANSWER KEYS

Practice Test 1.

1. d (p. 3)
2. b (p. 3)
3. c (p. 4)
4. d (p. 7)
5. b (p. 8)
6. a (p. 9)
7. a (p. 11)
8. d (p. 10)
9. b (p. 11)
10. a (p. 11)
11. b (p. 12)
12. c (p. 16)
13. b (p. 13)
14. a (p. 14)
15. b (p. 16)
16. c (p. 17)
17. b (p. 18)
18. c (p. 19)
19. c (p. 20)
20. c (pp. 20–21)

AFTER YOU READ ... CONCEPT MAPPING ACTIVITY ANSWERS

ACTIVITY 1: Provide your own original examples for these 10 things that make psychology challenging.

For most of this Grade Aid the concept map activities will require you to provide the concepts, and acceptable answers will be provided for you. At other times, the answers will vary based on your own interpretations, and there may not be a single "correct" answer.

For this concept map no answers are being provided because each of your answers will be unique and individual.

For example, under the challenge of difficult predictions of behavior, you might say something like, "The same person might behave differently in one situation versus another situation."

CHAPTER 1
SCIENCE AND PSEUDOSCIENCE IN PSYCHOLOGY
SKILLS FOR THINKING SCIENTIFICALLY
IN EVERYDAY LIFE

BEFORE YOU READ ... CHAPTER PREVIEW

As you learned in the Prologue, psychology is the study of human and animal behavior and mental processes. Among the mental processes studied is how we reason about our experiences. Psychological research has shown that the ways of thinking that come natural and easy to us, although adaptive for simple tasks, are prone to biases and frequently result in our drawing inaccurate conclusions. For example, we often assume that things are what they appear to be. The safeguards provided by scientific methods help us avoid believing we have support for our claims until we have the kind of evidence that eliminates bias and alternative explanations.

The public often learns about psychology through media reports. Media sources, however, often blur distinctions between information, entertainment, and persuasion for profit. Although some psychological information provided by popular sources can be useful or at least harmless, some information provided by popular sources can be dangerous. Authors writing about experience either fail to recognize or ignore the problems inherent in casual observation. Without safeguards we can be convinced of the value of quick fixes and simple solutions that are actually ineffective.

The scientific process begins with an attitude. This attitude of communalism is the opposite of authoritarianism. Scientific knowledge is the result of shared discussion and evaluations of evidence. Although science strives to be objective, it acknowledges the difficulty inherent in being objective and takes an active role in reducing errors and biases.

Examples of common errors we make when observing casually include the confirmation bias and belief perseverance. The confirmation bias reflects our tendency to be biased collectors of information. Once we have a hypothesis or an expectation, we tend to seek evidence that confirms our expectation while ignoring contradictory evidence. Even when we do notice contradictions, we are able to maintain our belief by discounting the evidence. In contrast to these biased approaches to gathering information, the scientific approach forces us to look for disconfirming evidence. Although scientists certainly hope to confirm their predictions, failures to confirm predictions are viewed as important in that the information helps to correct the predictions and to ultimately make the predictions more successful.

Science is therefore an open process. Scientists are open to revising theories and open to new evidence. As a result, scientists avoid claiming that a particular theory has been proven. They are aware that additional evidence may arise that will require revision of a claim. The requirement that claims be supported by objective evidence and that claims be subject to criticism and revision, differentiates scientific claims from opinion. Valid scientific claims are those supported by the most and highest-quality evidence.

Because of its safeguards, scientific thinking is useful in everyday decision making. Everyday scientific thinking involves thinking critically about the claims one hears. Such critical thinking can help us examine evidence and determine which claims are most likely to lead to accurate predictions and conclusions. Although such critical thinking involves skepticism (asking questions), it is not the same as cynicism. The skeptic evaluates all claims based on their evidence and is willing to accept claims for which the evidence is convincing. The cynic rejects all claims that differ from his or her own and is unwilling to consider evidence. The text outlines six principles of critical thinking.

1. Extraordinary claims require extraordinary evidence: The more a claim contradicts what we already know, the more persuasive the evidence supporting it must be.
2. Falsifiability: For a claim to be meaningful it must at least be possible to show the claim false. A prediction such as "It will either rain or it will not" is meaningless because no event would show the statement false.
3. Occam's razor, or the principle of parsimony: The simplest explanation is preferred until the data suggest otherwise.
4. Replicability: Science is progressive and cumulative. No single study is held to be convincing because its outcome could reflect chance.
5. Ruling out rival hypotheses: Most psychological phenomena potentially have multiple explanations. In evaluating claims it is important to determine the degree to which alternative explanations have been accounted for.
6. Correlation is not causation: Perhaps the most common error in interpreting claims is the tendency to assume that because two factors occur together, one causes the other. In reality, observed covariation does not demonstrate causation because alternative explanations have not been ruled out.

Pseudoscience may sound scientific but it lacks scientific safeguards. Often people cannot tell that a claim is pseudoscientific because they do not have a clear understanding of the safeguards of science. Pseudoscience can be recognized by understanding seven warning signs that demonstrate how it differs from science. Pseudoscience avoids falsification by its overuse of ad hoc immunizing hypotheses. Without being able to falsify claims, pseudoscience lacks a self-corrective mechanism. Pseudoscience ignores Occam's razor in its exaggeration of claims. It fails to rule out alternative explanations, overrelying on anecdote and evading peer review. Finally, it resists being a part of a body of scientific evidence in its absence of connectivity and its psychobabble.

Despite the lack of supporting evidence, pseudoscientific claims persist because thinking with intuition and emotional reasoning comes more naturally than careful reasoning. We are motivated to see patterns in ambiguous data and to make sense out of the world. We lack the scientific literacy that would enable us to see logical fallacies. We believe that emotion is a guide to truth—if it makes us feel uncomfortable it must be wrong. We also assume that because everyone believes a claim it must be true (jump on the bandwagon). We think in an either–or manner—framing the question as if it has only two possible options. And we fall victim to the not-me fallacy, believing we are immune from error and don't need scientific safeguards.

Why are pseudosciences dangerous? The danger in believing in pseudoscience often lies in what is given up. People spend time and money on pseudoscientific options that are less likely to lead to successful outcomes that are more objectively evaluated. Pseudoscience can also lead to unnecessary tragedies, both for humans and other animals by causing actual harm. A lack of scientific understanding affects our ability to influence outcomes and make decisions that will benefit rather than harm our planet.

BEFORE YOU READ ... LEARNING OBJECTIVES

After reading Chapter 1 you should be able to:

1.1   Distinguish common from uncommon sense
1.2   Describe naive realism and its perils
1.3   Differentiate popular psychology information from misinformation
1.4   Describe the importance of science as a set of safeguards against biases
1.5   Identify the key features of scientific skepticism and distinguish it from pathological skepticism
1.6   Identify and explain six key principles of critical thinking that will be used throughout the text
1.7   Describe pseudoscience and its differences from science and metaphysics
1.8   Describe the prevalence of pseudoscientific beliefs
1.9   Identify seven key warning signs of pseudoscience
1.10   Describe the motivational factors that predispose us to pseudoscientific beliefs
1.11   Describe the role that scientific illiteracy may play in the public's acceptance of pseudoscience
1.12   Explain the importance of cognitive factors as contributors to pseudoscientific thinking
1.13   Identify key logical fallacies in psychological thinking that can predispose us to pseudoscientific beliefs
1.14   Describe the dangers of pseudoscience

BEFORE YOU READ ... TERM IDENTIFICATION

ad hoc immunizing hypothesis (p. 45)
apophenia (p. 52)
astrology (p. 35)
bandwagon fallacy (p. 55)
belief perseverance (p. 31)
bias blind spot (p. 55)
communalism (p. 29)
confirmation bias (p. 30)
connectivity (p. 47)
correlation–causation fallacy (p. 42)
critical thinking (p. 37)
disinterestedness (p. 29)
either–or fallacy (p. 55)
emotional reasoning fallacy (p. 54)
experiential thinking (p. 48)
falsifiable (p. 39)
hypothesis (p. 33)
logical fallacies (p. 54)
metaphysical claims (p. 44)

naïve realism (p. 25)
not-me fallacy (p. 55)
Oberg's dictum (p. 35)
opportunity cost (p. 56)
pareidolia (p. 51)
pathological skepticism (p. 35)
peer review (p. 47)
popular psychology industry (p. 24)
pseudoscience (p. 44)
rational thinking (p. 48)
replicability (p. 41)
risky prediction (p. 39)
scientific skepticism (p. 34)
scientific theory (p. 33)
terror management theory (p. 50)
third variable problem (p. 42)
transcendental temptation (p. 49)
variable (p. 42)

AS YOU READ ... PRACTICE ACTIVITIES

SCIENCE VERSUS POPULAR PSYCHOLOGY: COMMON VERSUS UNCOMMON SENSE

1. Take the test of popular psychology knowledge in your textbook on page 24. How did you do? If you missed any items, select the one you believed in most strongly or that you have heard the most often. Now look for evidence that supports the right answer. (LO 1.1)

2. Look at the proverbs and their opposites. Pick one pair and research which one of that pair has the better support in terms of both quantity and quality of evidence. Write up your findings here. (LO 1.2)

3. Examine any one of the Web sites that are listed in Table 1.1 in your textbook. Using the guidelines provided in the introductory chapter to this Grade Aid, note those aspects that support confidence in the good quality of the Web site you selected. Are there any aspects of this site, according to the guidelines, that lead you to be less than 100% confident in the site? (LO 1.3)

4. In your own words, describe how a hypothesis is different from a theory. (LO 1.4)

5. Why do scientific psychologists never claim that a theory is proven? Is this need to avoid the use of "proven" only true in psychology, or is it also true in other sciences? (LO 1.4)

CRITICAL THINKING: SORTING THE WHEAT FROM THE CHAFF

1. Compare confirmation bias with disconfirmation bias. Throughout this Grade Aid you will often be asked to compare two or more concepts with one another. Note that when you are asked to "compare" two concepts, you should think about the similarities *and* the differences. (LO 1.4 and 1.5)

2. Do you believe that critical thinking and scientific thinking are the same or different? Make a case for them being the same, and for them being different. (LO 1.4 and 1.6)

3. Take the case of ESP and apply three of the six critical thinking principles to cast doubt on the reality of ESP. (LO 1.6)

4. Using astrology as an example, briefly discuss one reason why people tend to believe in this pseudoscience, AND at least one reason why psychologists remain skeptical. (LO 1.6)

5. A student receives a bad grade on several tests and subsequently is treated for depression at the campus counseling center. Did the bad grades cause the student's depression? Explain three possible relationships that might actually exist in this situation. (LO 1.6)

PSYCHOLOGICAL PSEUDOSCIENCE: IMPOSTERS OF SCIENCE

1. Draw a relationship between the concepts of falsifiability, metaphysical claims, and pseudoscientific claims. (LO 1.6 and 1.7)

2. Read each of the following statements. Which ones ask a legitimate scientific question? Why or why not? (LO 1.6)

    a. People who believe in an afterlife are better adjusted than individuals who do not.

    b. Anxious individuals harbor unconscious sexual urges.

    c. Depressed individuals have sadder memories than do nondepressed individuals.

    d. After death our soul endures and is reborn in a new living being.

3. Many students have difficulty distinguishing statements that are not falsifiable from statements that are falsifiable, but likely to be false. Evaluate the following student's response to statement (c) in question 2. "This can be falsifiable because I know someone who is depressed and he is nothing like that. I know from experience that that statement is false or can be argued." (LO1.6)

4. In Table 1.3 your text provides the results of a large survey study of the prevalence of pseudoscientific beliefs. Before you accept these results as valid, what else might you want to know about this study and the people who were sampled? (LO 1.8)

5. Which of the 7 warning signs of pseudoscience do you see in the following claims? (LO 1.8)

    a. On our show today, we have 7 people. All are on our MegaVitamin Diet. All are running 5 miles a day. Their stories will prove our diet's effectiveness in boosting energy levels.

    b. The author of the national bestseller, *Men Are from Mars, Women Are from Venus*, John Gray, has never contributed to the body of research evidence in scientific psychology and many of his claims contradict those in the published literature. He does have a Ph.D., which he obtained with correspondence courses, but the institute he received his degree from is no longer accredited as a university.

    c. Author Rhonda Byrne, learned *The Secret* from experts in fields ranging from quantum physics to feng shui. "The Secret" is that your thoughts have an attracting influence on things around you. If you obsess on negative thoughts, you will draw negative energy. Believe in wealth and it will manifest itself to you (never mind those poor displaced people in Darfur or in drought-stricken and famine-stricken areas of the world). Oprah and John Gray agree.

6. Self-help books oversimplify, overgeneralize, lack connectivity, and lack peer review. Check out a "self-help" book from the library or peruse one in a bookstore. Is the author making a claim that applies to everyone? At all times? Is there any evidence of peer reviewed work supporting the claims? Does the author control for or recognize alternative explanations? (LO 1.9)

PSEUDOSCIENTIFIC BELIEFS: ORIGINS AND DANGERS

1. Why might conflicting news reports of research findings be particularly confusing for people with low scientific literacy? (LO 1.11)

2. Develop a relationship between illusory correlation (seeing a correlational relationship where none exists—e.g., between gender and how much a person talks) and apophenia. Provide an original example from your own life to support your argument. (LO 1.12)

3. Backward masking is an example of finding patterns in ambiguous auditory information. Playing words on a recording backward, the sounds have no meaning. Nevertheless, we try to make sense of what we hear. Once we hear a pattern, the confirmation bias takes over. You can listen to many examples at http://www.reversespeech.com/music_reversals.htm. Are you able to hear any of the messages in the backward audio files? (LO 1.12)

4. Have you ever been thinking of someone and suddenly, they call on the phone?
   How often has this happened in the last month?
   Why do you think this happened?

   Have you ever been thinking of someone and they did not suddenly call you on the phone?
   How often has this happened in the last month?
   Does this observation influence your perception of the first question?

   What cognitive biases does this activity demonstrate? (LO 1.12)

5.   Draw lines to match the following logical fallacies to their definitions and examples. (LO 1.13)

a. appeal to authority	1. making a decision without sufficient evidence	i) Some people who take Prozac commit suicide so no one should take it!
b. emotional reasoning	2. using emotions to guide evaluation of a claim	ii) Everyone I know who drives a Lexus loves it, so it must be a good car.
c. argument from antiquity	3. accepting a claim because many other people do	iii) You can't prove that subliminal messages don't influence me!
d. bandwagon	4. accepting a claim because it's been around a long time	iv) All cultures believe in an afterlife, so it must exist.
e. appeal to ignorance	5. seeing an issue as black or white, all-or-nothing	v) Astrology has been around since ancient times, so it must be valid.
f. either–or	6. assuming a claim is true because there is no hard evidence against it	vi) My doctor said so, so it must be true.
g. hasty generalization	7. accepting a claim because an authority made it	vii) As a devout Christian, I believe women who have abortions get depressed.

AS YOU READ ... CONCEPT MAP ACTIVITIES

ACTIVITY 1: Complete this concept map for the Basic Principles of Critical Thinking

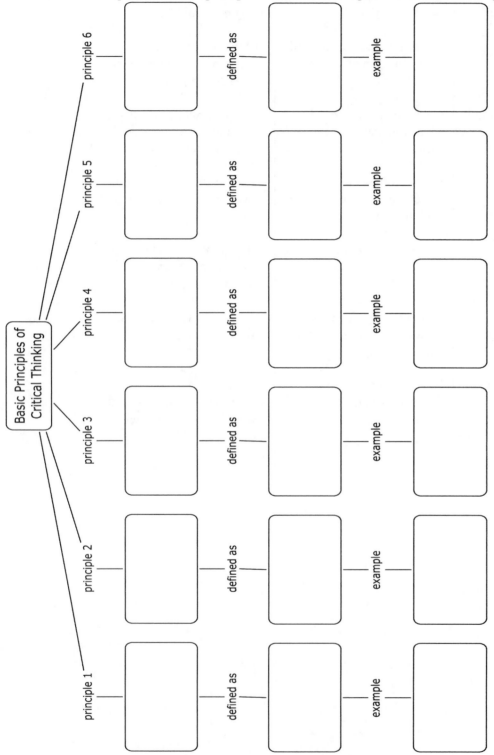

Author activity content supported by *IHMC Cmap Tools* Copyright ©1998-2007 Institute for Human & Machine Cognition

---

AS YOU READ ... MYTH OR REALITY?

Myth: Human behavior is more erratic during a full moon.

Reality: No evidence in terms of crime rates or hospitalizations indicate that human behavior is any more erratic during a full moon than it is during any other phase of the moon.

1. Develop an argument that people's false belief in the negative effects of the full moon can be attributed to confirmation bias.

Myth: People can bend spoons and walk across hot coals just using the power of their minds.

Reality: Of course these feats are not accomplished using the power of mind. People often pay large amounts of money to attend training sessions to help them unleash and connect with the power of their minds to accomplish such activities, but they are just being swindled.

1. Develop several hypotheses, drawing on the combined principles of scientific thinking, the seven warning signs of pseudoscience, and logical fallacies in scientific thinking to clearly reason through and provide alternative explanations for what might be happening during these and other sleights-of-mind.

AS YOU READ ... PUT YOUR CRITICAL THINKING SKILLS TO THE TEST

1. Your text points out in the first fictoid, that physicists and other "hard" scientists are no more skeptical than any other people, and less so than psychologists. Think of the reasons why this might be so. Consider what their education and training might (or might not) entail.

2. Psychological scientists always have a null hypothesis (a tacit statement of no differences between examined groups) that underlies each research hypothesis (an explicit statement of expected findings in a research study). How do you think the null hypothesis helps scientists to not fall prey to confirmation bias?

3. Were it not for Oberg's dictum, people would still have many false beliefs about physics, chemistry, our planet, and its place in the universe. Think of something you have previously learned about in school that was previously a cherished belief for decades or even centuries but that we now know to be false. (If you are stuck use a search to look for physics myths, chemistry myths, or astronomy myths). How do you think your life would be different today without Oberg's dictum?

4. Consider each of the six basic critical thinking principles. For each principle, note one belief that you seriously considered or held in the past, before you rejected it by applying the critical thinking principle.

5. According to L. Ron Hubbard, author of *Dianetics*, when the body dies, the spirit within will look for a new body. Often it will hang around pregnant women and enter the baby as it takes its first breath. How do you suppose Hubbard knows that events happen this way? What qualifies the claim as pseudoscientific?

6. As the text notes, scientific thinking is not limited to understanding psychology. An understanding of the interrelations among earth's systems as well as the ability to think about scientific data led to an important international agreement to protect the ozone layer, which is critical to protecting life on earth. The agreement resulted in banning substances that would deplete the ozone layer. Today, nations are finding it difficult to agree on the issue of global warming. How can psychological principles discussed in this chapter contribute to understanding the diversity of claims on this subject?

AS YOU READ ... MYPSYCHLAB CONNECTION

Science versus Popular Psychology: Common versus Uncommon Sense
To see how biased we can be in making decisions, complete the **explore** *Confirmation Bias*.

Critical Thinking: Sorting the Wheat from the Chaff
Review guidelines for **explore** *How to Be a Critical Thinker*.

Psychological Pseudoscience: Imposters of Science
Explore why astrology is considered a pseudoscience and how psychologists study it in *The Pseudoscience of Astrology*.

Pseudoscientific Beliefs: Origins and Dangers
Can you influence the outcome of a coin toss? Participate in the **explore** *Coin Toss* to learn when events do not predict subsequent outcomes.

AFTER YOU READ... PRACTICE TEST #1

Before beginning this practice test, estimate the percent you expect to get correct.
Anticipated percent correct: _____

1. The popular psychology industry refers to
   a. books written by psychological scientists.
   b. false information about psychology in the popular press.
   c. the combined everyday sources of information about human behavior.
   d. the workshops given nationwide in the large number of homegrown psychology networks.

2. What percentage of self-help books offer untested advice?
   a. 25%
   b. 50%
   c. 75%
   d. 95%

3. Janelle has suffered from depression ever since her late teens. She came across a Web site that sells a new herbal cure and is going to order her first month's supply for only $299.99. You tell Janelle
   a. you are happy she has finally found a way to cure her blues.
   b. she should be suspicious of anyone selling a "cure" rather than providing treatment.
   c. she needs to check a self-help book that evaluates herbal remedies before she spends so much money for a cure.
   d. she should have her doctor order the medication from a regular pharmacy, rather her ordering it from a Web site.

4. Science
   a. is an approach to evaluating evidence.
   b. refers to a body of established knowledge.
   c. is too rigid to help us to overcome preexisting biases in thinking.
   d. refers to what we call the complicated content of fields such as chemistry and biology.

5. Dr. Hansen is a psychologist who studies communication patterns in autistic children. She constantly reminds herself and her students to remain objective. Dr. Hansen thereby adheres to the principle of
   a. communalism.
   b. belief perseverance.
   c. disinterestedness.
   d. scientific humility.

6. Jesse believes he sometimes has ESP. For example, just last week he predicted there would be a pop quiz in class, so he studied extra hard, and sure enough, there was a pop quiz. Unfortunately, Jesse forgets about those times when he predicts a pop quiz and there is none. Jesse's behavior illustrates
   a. transcendental temptation.
   b. confirmation bias.
   c. Hume's dictum.
   d. hindsight bias.

7. Which of the following statements is TRUE regarding "scientific theories"?
   a. A theory is only proven to be a fact when all researchers accept it.
   b. A theory supported by the most and highest quality evidence is most likely to be accepted.
   c. It is difficult to determine which of several competing scientific theories is better because theories rely largely on personal opinion.
   d. It is difficult to determine which of several competing scientific theories is better because theories rely largely on the degree of authority of the researcher.

8. Scientific skepticism means scientists
   a. approach new findings in science with cynicism.
   b. reject ALL claims that fail to match their previous beliefs.
   c. approach ALL claims, even the most outrageous, with an open mind.
   d. reject scientific findings that contradict previously established scientific findings.

9. Pei-Shi believes that sugar causes hyperactivity in children because her aunt, who owns and operates a day care center, told her so. Pei-Shi's respect for _____ can lead to faulty thinking.
   a. Occam's razor.
   b. Hume's dictum.
   c. belief in authority.
   d. disconfirmation bias.

10. Which of these hypotheses can be falsified?
    a. People who believe in a soul live longer.
    b. Babies who die in infancy become angels.
    c. The spirits of our ancestors guide our present lives.
    d. How well we live today determines the life form we will return as in our future lives.

11. The major news media love to report new studies, especially when the findings contradict previous studies. Newscasters will often joke about not knowing what to believe anymore. In fact, people should know that
    a. even a good skeptic can accept a single, scientifically clean study.
    b. most of these studies need to be replicated before being accepted.
    c. when one study falsifies another study's results, this creates confusion even for scientists.
    d. when a study contradicts a prior study's findings, its results need to be supported by greater authority of the researchers.

12. Phillipe has noticed that every time he dreams about his psychology class, the next day the professor gives a pop quiz in class. Phillipe believes he has a type of ESP in which his dreams are predicting the future. Unfortunately, he has failed to
    a. rule out rival hypotheses.
    b. ask his friends if they would agree.
    c. consider using his ESP to predict other important events in his life.
    d. consult an expert authority on ESP and dreams, to see whether his conclusion could be possible.

13. According to the third variable problem, we often fail to notice
    a. that two variables are truly causally related.
    b. the statistical probability of a relationship between variables.
    c. when a third cause can result from a previous sequencing of cause and effect.
    d. another variable that could be leading two other variables to seem to be causally related.

14. Based on census data, the government finds that people who have more electrical appliances in their homes have fewer children. An "expert" therefore recommends that people who want smaller families should buy more electrical appliances. The expert has failed to consider that
    a. these same people may also believe in pseudoscientific beliefs.
    b. some appliances may be better for birth control than others.
    c. the data are probably based on anecdotes.
    d. correlation is not causation.

15. The problem with many pseudosciences is that
    a. just because they can't be falsified doesn't mean they aren't both valid and reliable.
    b. they "sound" scientific, and so fool people into thinking they are truly scientific.
    c. they are often misunderstood by scientists, who demand ridiculously rigorous tests of their scientific value.
    d. if too many people subscribe to them, too many people will develop superior skills and there are not enough jobs "at the top."

16. In a recent survey of average Americans, about _____ percent believed in ESP.
    a. 20%   c. 60%
    b. 40%   d. 80%

17. To support his case for the benefits of Vitamin C, George describes the changes in his health as a result of taking increased doses of Vitamin C. George is using _____ evidence.
    a. unambiguous   c. anecdotal
    b. correlational   d. scientific

18. The problem with using anecdotes as evidence is that
    a. they cannot be falsified.
    b. they take into account large amounts of data.
    c. peer-review of anecdotes is a time-consuming process.
    d. they are prone to bias, making them difficult to interpret.

19. Sometimes people have problems that traditional medicine and psychotherapy don't seem to help. They may then turn to pseudoscience because of its
    a. transcendental temptation.
    b. clear and rational explanations.
    c. strong base of empirical research evidence to support it.
    d. independence and lack of connectivity to other sciences.

20. When we see the "man in the moon" we exhibit
    a. pareidolia.   c. trichotillomania.
    b. apophenia.   d. triskaidekaphobia.

After completing the test, calculate your percent correct
(/ 20 =   ) x 100 = _____.

How accurate were your expectations? Does your performance suggest need for additional study? For the items you missed, go back and identify why the "correct" answer is the best answer.

AFTER YOU READ… PRACTICE TEST #2

Before beginning this practice test, estimate the percent you expect to get correct.
Anticipated percent correct: _____

1. According to naïve realism
   a. we perceive the world exactly as it is.
   b. reality can never be determined by its physical properties.
   c. our perception of the world comes from its objective properties.
   d. we cannot rely on common sense without risking a distorted view of reality.

2. Common sense
   a. is never accurate.
   b. is not "testable" using scientific methods.
   c. almost always contradicts research evidence.
   d. provides a good starting point for developing scientific hypotheses.

3. Popular psychology has led to an explosion of
   a. primarily correct information.
   b. primarily misinformation that can be harmful if followed.
   c. some correct information as well as much misinformation.
   d. a small amount of misinformation and, fortunately, much correct information.

4. Dr. Baron is a psychologist who often publishes his research findings or presents them to other psychological scientists at conferences so he can get feedback on his work. Dr. Baron exhibits
   a. perseverance.
   b. communalism.
   c. disinterestedness.
   d. confirmation bias.

5. A tendency to notice and remember instances in which events match our prior beliefs can strongly contribute to
   a. hindsight bias.
   b. placebo effects.
   c. confirmation bias
   d. illusory correlations.

6. Research shows that many students come into their first introductory psychology class with many misconceptions. Unfortunately, they leave the class with many of these same misconceptions. This illustrates
   a. disinterestedness.
   b. scientific thinking.
   c. scientific skepticism.
   d. belief perseverance.

7. When data from a test of a hypothesis based on scientific theory have been repeatedly obtained, the hypothesis is said to be
   a. true.
   b. a fact.
   c. proven.
   d. supported.

8. Annette has been criticized by her friends as living by the Missouri state motto, "Show me." As a skeptical scientist, Annette most likely
   a. takes this as an insult.
   b. takes this as a compliment.
   c. realizes she might need to change her attitude.
   d. decides to move to Missouri to live among people more like herself.

9. Sara has a strong belief in feng shui (the ancient Chinese practice of arranging space to achieve harmony with the environment). Her friends provide Sara with evidence that fails to confirm feng shui's validity but Sara insists she is simply keeping an open mind. You tell her,
   a. "At least you are following Occam's razor."
   b. "At least you are following Oberg's dictum."
   c. "Just be careful or you will fall prey to rational thinking."
   d. "There needs to be a limit to open-mindedness, before you reach the point of gullibility."

10. Marilise is convinced that because she sometimes wakes up with bruises on her body, that she has been abducted by aliens who performed tests on her while she is asleep. You tell her that
    a. if she really believes it, and has vivid memories of her abductions, it is probably true.
    b. her extraordinary claim really requires more evidence than waking up with bruises.
    c. her argument seems sufficiently rational to believe along with the evidence of the mysterious bruising.
    d. she probably needs to be hypnotized to help her remember more details of what was done to her by the aliens.

11. If you follow the belief that a simple answer to a problem is usually most accurate, you are using the principle of
    a. Occam's razor.   c. pareidolia.
    b. falsifiability.   d. apophenia.

12. A highly desirable feature of a scientific study is
    a. replicability.   c. having a third variable.
    b. ad hoc immunizing.   d. making a metaphysical claim.

13. Malia dreams about her old boyfriend Kimo, then sees him at the bookstore the next day. Malia is convinced her dream reflects a psychic experience. How confident should she be in her belief? Why?
    a. Very confident: Because it happened to her, she can be confident that the two events were related.
    b. Not very confident: Chance alone could explain the co-occurrence of events.
    c. Very confident: Other possible explanations seem unlikely.
    d. Not very confident: It would need to happen more than once for her to take it seriously.

14. Professor Taylor administered a test of learning strategies and a test of motivations for learning. She found a strong correlation between the two tests. She can now safely conclude that
    a. the use of learning strategies is related to the type of motivation a student has for learning.
    b. no relationship is evident between strategy use and motivations for learning.
    c. the particular motivation a student has for learning causes the student to use a particular strategy.
    d. the particular learning strategies that a student uses cause that student to adopt a certain motivation for learning.

15. Which of the following reflects a true scientific approach, as opposed to being largely a pseudoscience?
    a. Using lie detector machines to assess a person's honesty.
    b. Using hand-writing analysis to assess a person's personality.
    c. Using hypnosis to help a person recover repressed memories of early childhood sexual abuse.
    d. Using replication to show the correlation between watching violent TV programs and playground aggressiveness in elementary school children.

16. Ad hoc immunizing hypotheses take advantage of using
    b. facts rather than possibilities.
    b. legal loopholes rather than scientific loopholes.
    c. testimonial results rather than experimental results.
    d. what is possible rather than what has been demonstrated.

17. Claims about behavior that have lots of scientific-sounding language but are not based on scientific objective evidence are called
    a. psychobabble.
    b. peer-reviewed.
    c. emotional reasoning.
    d. psychological science.

18. People are often drawn to pseudoscience because it
    a. is based on rational thinking, and is more effortful to evaluate.
    b. is based on experiential thinking, and is less effortful to evaluate.
    c. follows Hume's dictum by providing extraordinary evidence for its extraordinary claims.
    d. follows Occam's razor by providing precise explanations for natural and supernatural phenomena.

19. Jeff has been treating his depression with herbal remedies because they are natural and his crystal-healing therapist recommended them. Because his depression is severe, Jeff has not been able to work in more than a year. Jeff's case illustrates
    a. blind spot bias.
    b. opportunity cost.
    c. confirmation bias.
    d. the bandwagon fallacy.

20. Pseudoscience
    a. not only prevents us from seeking proper care but can actually cause direct harm.
    b. is especially seductive because it uses scientific-sounding language and provides everyday evidence that even laypeople can understand without much effort.
    c. prevents people from applying a truly scientific approach to both large and small problems that face us as individuals and as a society.
    d. all of the above.

After completing the test, calculate your percent correct
(/ 20 =   ) x 100 = _____.

How accurate were your expectations? Does your performance suggest need for additional study? For the items you missed, go back and identify why the "correct" answer is the best answer.

AFTER YOU READ . . . PRACTICE TEST ANSWER KEYS

Practice Test 1.

1. c (p.24)
2. d (p. 27)
3. b (p. 28)
4. a (p. 29)
5. c (p. 29)
6. b (p. 30)
7. b (p. 33–34)
8. c (p. 34)
9. c (p. 36–37)
10. a (p. 39)
11. b (p. 41)
12. a (p. 41–42)
13. d (p. 42)
14. d (p. 42–43)
15. b (p. 44)
16. b (p. 45)
17. b (p. 46)
18. d (p. 46–47)
19. a (p. 49)
20. a (p. 51)

Practice Test 2.

1. a (p. 25)
2. d (p. 26)
3. c (p. 27)
4. b (p. 29)
5. c (p. 30)
6. d (p. 31)
7. d (p. 32)
8. b (p. 35)
9. d (p. 35)
10. b (p. 37–38)
11. a (p. 40)
12. a (p. 41)
13. b (p. 42–43)
14. a (p. 42–43)
15. d (p. 40–43)
16. d (p. 45)
17. a (p. 47–48)
18. b (p. 48)
19. b (p. 56)
20. d (p. 45–58)

AFTER YOU READ ... CONCEPT MAPPING ACTIVITY ANSWERS

ACTIVITY 1: Complete this concept map for the Basic Principles of Critical Thinking

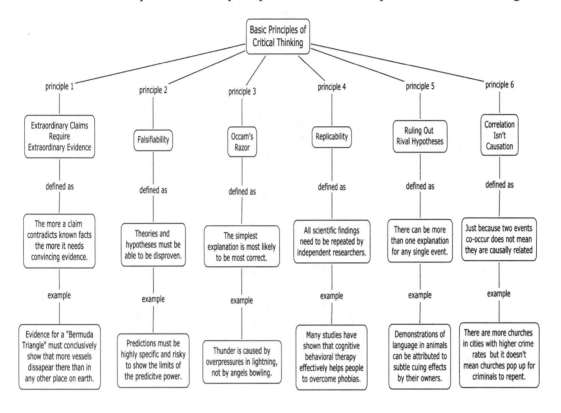

CHAPTER 2
RESEARCH METHODS
SAFEGUARDS AGAINST ERROR

BEFORE YOU READ ... CHAPTER PREVIEW

Students of psychology often wonder why they are expected to learn research methods when they "just want to learn about people." As you will discover in this text, thinking critically involves understanding that some things that seem to be true may not actually be true. Claims people make about behavior, or observations you may make yourself, may not hold up when looked at objectively. Your task is to learn to tell the difference between the claims that are most likely to be true and the claims that are probably not true. An understanding of research methods can help you with this task.

Although it is possible to learn many things about people from observation, human information processing involves the use of many shortcuts that can lead to biases. As a result, our biased observations can lead us to draw inaccurate and potentially harmful conclusions about human behavior.

Research methods provide tools to help us avoid being tricked by our own biases. For example, our observations can be biased by our tendency to look for what we expect to find (confirming evidence) rather than the unexpected (disconfirming evidence). Hindsight bias and overconfidence reflect our tendency to believe we "knew it all along" once an event occurs despite our inability to predict the event before it occurs. We oversimplify and look for what is easiest to see (the representativeness heuristic and the availability heuristic) and ignore what is more difficult to see (base rates). Scientific methods are designed to counter such tendencies to fool ourselves. Scientific methods permit us to systematically test a hypothesis (specific prediction) and to determine whether objective evidence exists to support our hypothesis. The system includes built in checks for bias and error. This self-correcting feature allows science to learn from its mistakes and as a result to grow and to develop. These features are not present in casual observation or pseudoscience, which can continue to promote ineffective or harmful hypotheses.

Research designs differ in the degree to which they maximize external validity (the degree to which they can generalize to the real world) versus internal validity (the degree to which they can make causal claims). Each design has advantages and disadvantages. Effective research programs include a variety of designs. Cases studies allow us to generate hypotheses but not test hypotheses. Correlational studies allow us to determine whether variables are systematically related to one another and allow us to make predictions but do not allow us to make causal claims. We cannot say that one of our variables causes the other because in a correlational study, we have not ruled out alternative explanations. The media are notorious for misinterpreting the meaning of correlational studies. Frequently the media will report correlations and suggest the findings imply causation when no such relation is supported by the data. This misinterpretation would be less likely to occur if people in the media and the public in general had a better understanding of research methods and statistics.

In order to rule out alternative explanations and be able to make causal statements, a true experiment must be conducted. A true experimental study is conducted in such a way as to assure that the independent variable (IV), and *only* the IV, caused the variability observed in the dependent variable (DV). To be able to make such a causal statement, the experiment must satisfy certain criteria. The experiment must have a true IV that is manipulated and must randomly assign participants to experimental and control conditions. Experimental control allows the experimenter to make sure everything in the experimental and comparison conditions are exactly the same in every way except in terms of the manipulation.

Even if the experimenter finds the expected effect, no single study would be taken as strong evidence for the hypothesis. Science looks at a body of evidence to provide support for its claims. Ideally this evidence comes from high-quality studies that use a variety of methods. Some studies will be high in internal validity; some studies will be high in external validity. If all of these studies together provide support, we can have general confidence in our claim.

An experiment is not easy to design and not all questions can be studied with experimental methods. Researchers must be cautious in designing studies. Challenges include avoiding the placebo effect and the Hawthorne effect, which make it appear that a treatment is effective despite it not having a real effect. Researchers must also be cautious to avoid their own biases. Biases can be avoided by conducting double-blind studies where neither the experimenter nor the participant is aware of which condition individuals are in. Another concern for researchers is the need to conduct studies with representative samples. That is, the researcher must randomly sample subjects from the population to which the research is expected to generalize. One must also attend to methods of measuring one's variables of interest. Meaningful measures must be both reliable (consistent) and valid (accurate) measures of the construct of interest.

Psychologists must attend to the rights of their research participants. Unfortunately, too many examples show how researchers in the past have put their research interest above the interests of the participants. Today, Institutional Review Boards review and approve all research with humans and other animals as participants and weigh the benefits of the research against any costs. Although debate continues, it is more likely today that the rights of the participants will be protected.

Much of the misunderstanding of psychology is the result of a failure to understand the way science works. This misunderstanding includes a misunderstanding of the role of statistics in research claims. Misunderstandings can involve simple descriptive statistics as well as inferential statistics. For example, although several measures of central tendency exist, many people don't realize the degree to which the mean is highly misleading when used to describe a skewed distribution. In terms of inferential statistics, the concept of significance is critical in knowing whether an observed difference reflects a real (not chance) difference in the population. At the same time, it is important to know that a difference may be significant but may still not have any practical value.

Failure to understand such concepts can contribute to the media's ability to lie with statistics. Advertisers and others attempting to persuade people that their claims are genuine, count on the public's lack of statistical understanding. Consumers of information must be critical in evaluating claims. Questions to ask include (1) Who is the source of the information? (2) Are there exaggerations in going from data to claim? (3) Is there balance in the reporting of evidence?

BEFORE YOU READ ... LEARNING OBJECTIVES

After reading Chapter 2 you should be able to:

2.1   Explain what research designs accomplish that we can't discover by intuition alone
2.2   Identify heuristics and biases that prevent us from thinking clearly about psychology
2.3   Distinguish the types of designs and conclusions that we can draw from each
2.4   Identify the potential pitfalls of each design that can lead to faulty conclusions
2.5   Explain the ethical obligations of researchers toward their research participants
2.6   Describe both sides of the debate on the use of animals as research subjects
2.7   Explain how to calculate measures of central tendency
2.8   Identify uses of various measures of central tendency and dispersion
2.9   Show how statistics can be misused for purposes of persuasion
2.10   Identify flaws in research design
2.11   Identify skills for evaluating psychological claims in the popular media

BEFORE YOU READ ... TERM IDENTIFICATION

availability (p. 68)
base rate (p. 68)
blind (p. 81)
case study (p. 72)
central tendency (p. 94)
cognitive biases (p. 69)
confound (p. 79)
control group (p. 78)
correlational design (p. 73)
demand characteristics (p. 84)
dependent variable (p. 79)
descriptive statistic (p. 94)
dispersion (p. 94)
double-blind (p. 82)
existence proofs (p. 72)
experiment (p. 78)
experimental groups (p. 78)
experimenter expectancy effect (p. 82)
external validity (p. 71)
file drawer problem (p. 80)
Hawthorne effect (p. 84)
heuristics (p. 67)
hindsight bias (p. 69)
illusory correlation (p. 75)

independent variable (p. 78)
inferential statistics (p. 94)
informed consent (p. 92)
internal validity (p. 72)
mean (p. 94)
median (p. 94)
meta-analysis (p. 80)
mode (p. 94)
naturalistic observation (p. 71)
nocebo effect (p. 82)
overconfidence (p. 70)
placebo effect (p. 81)
prefrontal lobotomy (p. 66)
random assignment (p. 78)
random selection (p. 85)
range (p. 94)
reliability (p. 86)
representativeness (p. 67)
response sets (p. 88)
scatterplot (p. 74)
standard deviations (p. 94)
statistics (p. 94)
validity (p. 86)

AS YOU READ ... PRACTICE ACTIVITIES

THE BEAUTY AND NECESSITY OF GOOD RESEARCH DESIGN

1. After reviewing 23 empirical studies on sugar and children, Dr. Mark Wolraich and colleagues concluded that sugar does not affect aggression, mood, motor skills, or cognitive skills (Wolraich, Wilson, & White, 1995). Yet many people claim that despite any research, they know there is a causal relation because they have *seen* it many times. (LO 2.1)

   Why are even multiple observations of children eating sugar and being active not good evidence supporting a causal connection?

   What alternative explanations exist for why one might observe children eating sugar and being active?

2. Students will argue that even if most psychics are fakes, the psychic they see is legitimate because their psychic gives accurate information. How might biases in thinking contribute to the illusion of accuracy? Read about the Forer Effect:

   http://www.skepdic.com/forer.html

   How does this effect illustrate the "but it works" illusion? (LO 2.1)

3. Maria likes classical music, wears glasses, and dresses plainly.
   Which is more likely?
   a. She is a librarian.
   b. She plays the piano.
   c. She is a librarian who plays the piano.

   Why did you answer as you did? Was your answer influenced by a stereotype you formed of Maria? If so, you may have relied on the representativeness heuristic and failed to consider base rates. Consider, is the likelihood of a and b together more or less likely than either a or b alone? (LO 2.2)

4. Our tendency to focus on stereotypes and to ignore base rates contributes to our misuse of the representativeness heuristic. We also ignore base rates when we misinterpret statements like the following: "Most accidents occur around the home." Although the statement is true, does it mean that the home is the most dangerous place to be? Why or why not? (LO 2.2)

5. Which is the more common cause of death in the United States, accidents, asthma, or tornadoes? (LO 2.2)

On what did you base your answer? If you used the availability heuristic you likely based your answer on the cause of death for which there was an easily retrieved image from memory. The answer, however, may not have provided such a memory. Asthma causes 16 times more deaths than accidents and 20 times more deaths than tornadoes.

6. Here is an anagram: OSTAT
   Here is the solution: TOAST
   On a scale from 1 to 10, how easy do you think it would be for someone to solve this anagram:

   Here is an anagram: AERTW
   On a scale from 1 to 10, how easy do you think it would be for someone to solve this anagram:

   Each of these anagrams is 5 letters, comes from a basic spelling list, and uses the same strategy to mix letters. Why do you think you rated the first as easier than the second? How does this example demonstrate hindsight bias? (LO 2.2)

7. Table 1.2 in Chapter 1 lists quotations from "highly intelligent people" in our past. These quotations seem surprising to us and even bizarre. How does the hindsight bias contribute to the difficulty we have understanding the perspective of people in previous eras? (LO 2.2)

8. Think for a minute: Why might the least skilled at a task be the least aware of their own lack of skill? Check out the research by Kruger and Dunning:

http://www.apa.org/journals/features/psp7761121.pdf

Is your explanation similar? (LO 2.2)

THE SCIENTIFIC METHOD: TOOLBOX OF SKILLS

1. Why do scientists never claim that a theory is proven? Is this need to avoid the use of *proven* only true in psychology, or is it also true in other sciences? Did you know astronomers at the beginning of the twentieth century believed the entire universe consisted of the Milky Way? (LO 2.3)

2. Complete this table comparing the types of designs, their advantages, disadvantages, and types of conclusions we can draw from them. (LO 2.3)

	Advantages	Disadvantages	Conclusions
Naturalistic Observation			
Case Studies			
Correlational Design			
Experimental Design			

3. Research in Taiwan finds a significant positive correlation between the number of appliances in the home and whether a couple uses birth control (known as the toaster method of birth control). What does this correlation mean? Can you predict whether a couple uses birth control from knowing how many appliances they own? Why or why not? (LO 2.3)

4. Create a scatterplot from the following data set (plot the scores). (LO 2.3)
   What type of correlational relationship do the data suggest?

Cups of Coffee/Day	GPA
1	3.5
2	3.0
3	2.5
4	2.0

5. As the text indicates, illusory correlations occur because we are poor judges of the degree to which events occur together. We attend to confirming evidence and ignore disconfirming evidence. What are people making the following claims ignoring? (LO 2.3)

   a. Every time I wash my car it rains!

   b. My joints hurt when it rains.

6. A bathroom scale that is 5 pounds off can be reliable (consistent) but is it valid? Can a measure be valid but not reliable? Why is reliability so important when we are trying to make predictions? (LO 2.4)

7. Dr. See teaches statistics and biological psychology. Students see these classes as hard and Dr. See as a hard teacher. When they finally have an opportunity to interact with Dr. See outside of class, they find she is really funny and a nice person and they are SHOCKED. What "effect" discussed in the text would explain the students' surprise? (LO 2.4)

8. In the original research on the effect of listening to Mozart's music on abilities, the researcher randomly assigned college students to one of three conditions. Group A listened to 10 minutes of Mozart's piano sonata in G major. Group B listened to a relaxation tape. Group C listened to silence. Group A performed better than group B and C on a task of spatial reasoning when measured immediately after they listened but not when measured 10 minutes after listening. (LO 2.4)

   What is the independent variable?

   What is the dependent variable?

   Based on the sample, the IV, and DV, what could the researchers *appropriately* conclude?

9. Why are participants randomly assigned to research conditions in an experiment? What is the purpose of a control (comparison) group? (LO 2.4)

10. Research suggests that 80% of drug effects can be attributed to the placebo effect. Why might the placebo effect be even greater when the placebo produces side effects? (LO 2.4)

ETHICAL ISSUES IN RESEARCH DESIGN

1. What is informed consent? Why is it critical to protecting rights of research participants? (LO 2.5)

2. What is "deception"? When is the use of deception justified in a psychological study? (LO 2.5)

3. What is a "debriefing"? If you have participated in a psychological study as part of your introductory psychology course, were you given such a debriefing? (LO 2.5)

4. Introductory psychology students often participate in research studies. Acacia, an introductory psychology student, shows up for a study and is given a questionnaire about sibling relationships. Her brother was killed in Iraq a year ago and she gets emotional when she thinks about him. She does not want to complete the questionnaire. The researcher tells her she has to complete the form because it is required for her introductory psychology class. Evaluate this scenario in terms of ethical guidelines for research. (LO 2.5)

5. What critical question must a researcher answer if his or her study using animals is to be considered justified? (L.O. 2.6)

6. Research with animals is both critical and controversial. Think about your beliefs about such research. Are there types of research you find acceptable? Are there types of animals you find to be acceptable as subjects? Are there types of regulations that make animal research acceptable? Much of what we know about the function of the neuron has been learned from the study of the squid. Is a squid an acceptable subject of study? Research with invertebrates is not regulated. Should it be? (L.O. 2.6)

STATISTICS: THE LANGUAGE OF PSYCHOLOGICAL RESEARCH

1. Calculate the mean, median, and mode for the following distributions. (LO 2.7, 2.8)

In a community of 9 households, the annual incomes are as follows:

$ 20,000
25,000
30,000
30,000
40,000
45,000
50,000
100,000
1,000,000

_____

mean =
median =
mode =

Women's shoes are sold as follows:

5
5 1/2
6
7 1/2
8
8
8
8
10

_____

mean =
median =
mode =

Which measure of central tendency would be most appropriate for someone trying to describe the distributions? Why?

2. In comparing distributions, why is it important to know about their central tendency *and* to know about the dispersion? (LO 2.8)

3. For the following claims, identify the information being "left out." (LO 2.9)

a. No other product is more effective than ours.

b. Brand X toothpaste users have 27% fewer cavities.

c. There are more plane accidents today than in 1911.

4. An advertisement claims, "People rate our beer higher than any other beer!" and provides the following graph. Evaluate their claim and the evidence. (LO 2.9)

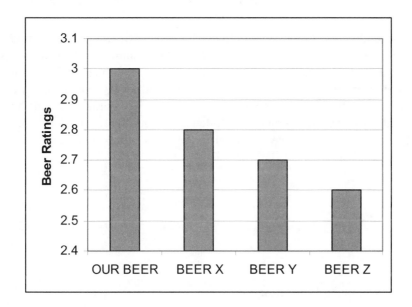

BECOMING A PEER REVIEWER OF PSYCHOLOGICAL RESEARCH

1. Dr. Concoctor is interested in the effect of computer games on young boys' aggressive behavior. He randomly assigns a group of young boys to play either a simple ping-pong type computer game or an action-packed combat type computer game for 30 minutes. He then observes the boys' behavior on the playground.

What type of design is this study? (LO 2.10)

Is there an independent variable? If so, what is it?

Is there a dependent variable? If so, what is it?

Do you see any problem(s) with this study? If so, what? Can you think of a way to fix the problem(s)?

2. A marriage counselor notices that quite a few of the couples she works with are opposites of one another in a variety of ways. She wonders whether "opposites attract." She gives personality inventories to her clients and finds that in fact, the majority are opposites. She writes a book to show how we are attracted to people who are our opposites. How would you evaluate her study and her claim? (LO 2.10)

3. Mrs. Zeebarth is enthusiastic about the use of technology to teach math. She believes that compared with students taught math with traditional methods, students taught math supported by technology will be more enthusiastic about learning math. Mrs. Zeebarth teaches math with technology, and Mr. Kaminski in the next classroom teaches math traditionally. Mrs. Zeebarth interviews the children in her class and the children in Mr. Kaminski's class about how much they like math. She finds her students are enthusiastic about math and Mr. Kaminski's students are not. Mr. Kaminski is not convinced and tells Mrs. Zeebarth her study is flawed. Identify the flaws Mrs. Zeebarth needs to correct to strengthen her study and her conclusions. (LO 2.10)

4. Evaluate the information on the following Web sites:
    http://mozarteffect.com
    http://faculty.washington.edu/chudler/neurok.html

Go to Explore … then The Musical Brain … then Music & Memory
How credible are the sites? What are the author's claiming? On what evidence are their claims based? How confident should you be in the Mozart Effect? (L.O. 2.11)

AS YOU READ ... CONCEPT MAP ACTIVITIES

ACTIVITY 1: Review some of the ways research participants' rights are protected by completing this map.

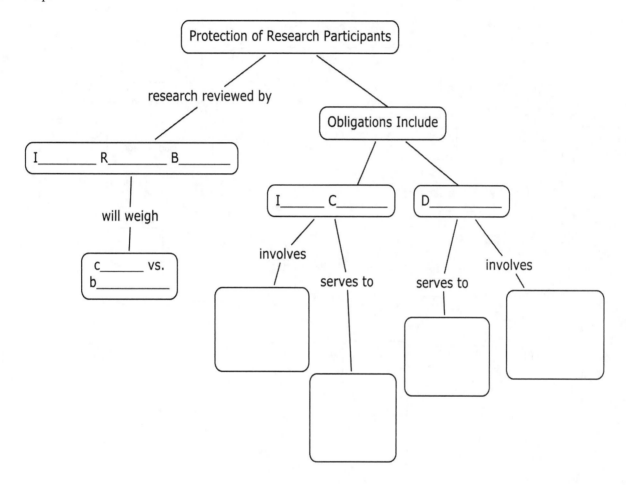

Chapter 2 Research Methods

ACTIVITY 2: Try to complete this concept map by referring to the types of research design described in the text and summarized in the table you created for an earlier activity. Compare the ways of summarizing, Table vs. Map. Which do you prefer?

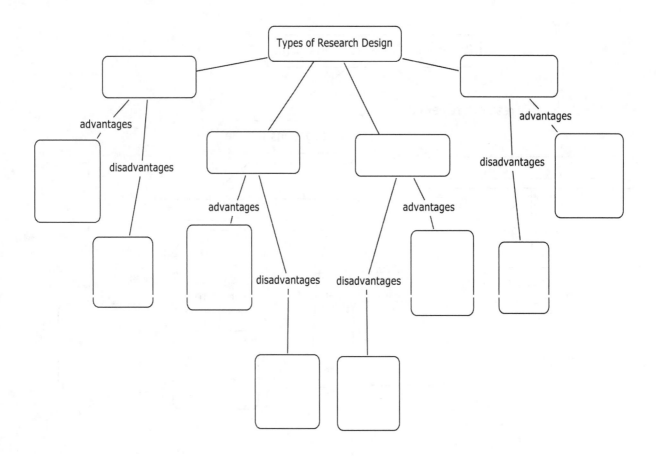

Author activity content supported by *IHMC Cmap Tools* Copyright ©1998-2007 Institute for Human & Machine Cognition

---

AS YOU READ … MYTH OR REALITY?

Myth: Sugar causes hyperactivity in children.
Reality: Although many believe they have observed a causal relation between children's consumption of sugary food and high activity level, objective research suggests any carbohydrate would give the same level of energy and "no one has heard of a rice high or potato buzz."

1. What cognitive biases contribute to this misconception?

Myth: 50% of all marriages end in divorce.
Reality: No credible evidence supports the statement that half of all marriages end in divorce. The overall divorce rate is on the decline.

1. Why is this misconception so pervasive?
2. Take a look at this website for some discussion about how a misreading of statistics is likely to have contributed to the misconception.
   http://www.truthorfiction.com/rumors/d/divorce.htm

Myth: Homework for children boosts academic learning and teaches responsibility.
Reality: Homework in elementary school shows virtually no relation to performance.

Although educators will insist on the benefits of homework for young children, the empirical data do not support the claim. Harris Cooper, the major homework researcher, has shown that limited amounts of homework may contribute to performance in older children, no effect has been shown for young children. In addition, large amounts of homework contribute to negative attitudes toward school. A brief summary of this research can be found at this site:
http://www.slate.com/id/2149593/

a. If the evidence fails to support an effect, why do you think educators cling to their beliefs?

AS YOU READ … PUT YOUR CRITICAL THINKING SKILLS TO THE TEST

---

1. The *Journal of American Pediatrics* reports a link between TV watching and obesity. Does this link imply a causal relation? What alternative explanations can you think of?

2. In the book, *How We Know What Isn't So*, Thomas Gilovich (1991) makes the following claim: Thus by their very nature, many of the social sciences provide helpful practice in thinking clearly and rigorously about the phenomena of everyday life. . . . This may be one of the reasons why fewer psychologists believe in the existence of ESP than their colleagues in the natural sciences or humanities.
   a. Why might this be the case? How would you study this question among college students of various majors?

3. As your text suggests, statistics describe general tendencies that can be true in most cases even if not true for every case. That is, a claim can be made, based on statistical evidence that is true on average even though exceptions exist. Despite this probabilistic nature of statistics, the exceptional case can sometimes be made to look more persuasive than the typical case. This persuasive technique of misusing "an example" is sometimes called the "man who . . . statistic."
   a. When is the use of examples appropriate and when is it inappropriate? (*Hint*: Think of the difference between reasoning by anecdote and illustrating with anecdote.)
   b. Does your psychology instructor ever use examples? Are they used appropriately?
   c. How do politicians and advertisers use examples? Listen carefully to the next speech or testimonial you hear.

As You Read ... MyPsychLab Connection

The Scientific Method: A Toolbox of Skills

Why can't we draw conclusions about cause and effect from correlational studies? **Explore** *Correlations Do Not Show Causation* to find out why.

Ethical Issues in Research Design

How ethical would you be as a psychological researcher? Use the **simulation** *Ethics in Psychological Research* to test your knowledge about research ethics.

Statistics: The Language of Psychological Research

How do we know what conclusions we can and cannot draw from data? Practice with this hands-on **simulation**, *Doing Simple Statistics*.

Becoming a Peer Reviewer of Psychological Research

Impress your friends as you apply your skills to critiquing psychological articles in the news by **listening** to *Reviewing Reports of Psychology in the News*.

AFTER YOU READ ... PRACTICE TEST #1

Before beginning this practice test, estimate the percent you expect to get correct.
Estimated percent correct _____

1. A new book has just come out called *Get Your Brain Fit, Now!* The author, a former Mr. Universe, claims that just as you can get your body in shape, you can get your brain fit through a series of "mental exercises." He describes these exercises and provides evidence for their effectiveness by describing in detail the stories of four people. Each of the four stories tells of a person who felt dull and boring before "getting fit" and creative and exciting after "getting fit." The author claims that his exercises helped these people and will help you too. Why would you be skeptical of this claim?
   a. The author's claim is based on testimonial evidence.
   b. It is clear that these four people did not really improve.
   c. The improvement described may be the result of the placebo effect.
   d. Both a and c.

2. A researcher wants to see whether caffeine will effect problem solving in rats. One group of rats is fed rat chow containing caffeine. Another group is fed their regular rat chow. In this experiment, the type of rat chow (caffeinated vs. noncaffeinated) fed to the rats is the
   a. control group.   c. independent variable.
   b. dependent variable.   d. extraneous variable.

3. In the experiment described above, the rats who ate the regular, noncaffeinated rat chow are the
   a. control group.   c. experimental group.
   b. independent group.   d. the sleepy group.

4. When psychologists say that their results are statistically significant, they mean that the results
   a. have important practical applications.
   b. have important implications for scientific theory.
   c. are unlikely to be due to the fluctuations of chance.
   d. are positively correlated.

5. A study of college students reports finding a strong correlation between coffee consumption and grade point averages, with those drinking more coffee getting lower grades. A possible explanation for this finding is that
   a. high coffee consumption causes students to get lower grades.
   b. getting lower grades causes students to drink more coffee.
   c. a third variable could be causing both high coffee consumption and low grades.
   d. all of the above are possible explanations.

6. The correlation between coffee consumption and grades reveals
   a. a positive relationship.   c. zero (no linear) relationship.
   b. a negative relationship.   d. an indefinable relationship.

7. Which of the following conclusions is suggested by the findings reported in question 5?
   a. You can predict that if a student is a heavy coffee drinker, it is likely that s/he is getting poor grades.
   b. The correlation coefficient is probably about +.75.
   c. If you observe a good student drinking a lot of coffee, it is evidence that the correlation is wrong.
   d. There is a significant difference between coffee drinking and grades.

8. "Brand X toothpaste users have 27% fewer cavities." The problem with a statement such as this one is that it doesn't give information about
   a. how many cavities an average person has.
   b. who made up the comparison group.
   c. the definition of cavity.
   d. whether there were response sets.

9. Anatol is convinced his dreams can tell the future. Just the other night he dreamt of his wife and when he awoke, there she was sleeping next to him. Anatol's belief is an example of
   a. an illusory correlation.
   b. the stereotype effect.
   c. the ability of certain people to have prophetic dreams.
   d. hindsight bias.

10. Why do researchers randomly assign participants in experiments to experimental and control (comparison) conditions?
    a. To eliminate negative correlations in the research.
    b. In attempt to make equivalent groups that differ only in terms of the independent variable.
    c. To avoid doing unethical research in which some participants get preferential treatment.
    d. To keep people from guessing the research question.

11. The effects of fatigue play a role in an estimated two-thirds of road accidents. Yet we fear drunk drivers and rarely think of sleepy drivers. This example of selective attention reflects
    a. subjective attention.
    b. overconfidence.
    c. the availability heuristic.
    d. hindsight bias.

12. "Why do I need to know statistics and research methods? I just want to help people!" How would you answer this question?
    a. We can only prove our claims by providing statistics.
    b. A failure to subject therapies to objective evaluations can harm those the therapy is trying to help.
    c. Statistics are important in conducting research, but clinical observation is important in evaluating the effectiveness of therapies.
    d. Although most psychologists don't use statistics, it is a traditional part of their training.

13. A school district superintendent compares an affluent high school that does not have a full health services center with an inner city high school that does have a full health services center. He finds that when compared with the students in the inner city school, students in the affluent school are statistically healthier. He argues that this study provides evidence that school health service centers play no role in student health and that the district does not need to provide such centers on its school campuses. His conclusions are not really supported because
    a. students' family income is likely confounded with school provision of health services.
    b. providing health services serves a basic need regardless of statistical findings.
    c. this study did not involve random assignment or the manipulated independent variable.
    d. both a and c.

14. Which of the following statements about ethics in psychological research is TRUE?
    a. In contrast to many other countries, the United States has never conducted studies that violated participants' right to informed consent.
    b. Milgram's study would be approved today because of the knowledge gained.
    c. In the debriefing, participants are informed about the purpose of the study.
    d. Deception is no longer allowed in psychological studies.

15. Jane Goodall was the first to observe demonstrations of tool use and homicide among chimpanzees in their natural environment. The observational method she used is generally considered to be
    a. high in external validity.
    b. high in internal validity.
    c. subject to demand characteristics.
    d. difficult to interpret because of the Hawthorne effect.

16. Before participating in a psychological study, Lenita signed an "informed consent," which means
    a. she was told the purposes and hypotheses of the study.
    b. she was told that deception would not be used in the study.
    c. she was given an accurate picture of the risks involved in the research before agreeing to participate.
    d. both a and b.

17. For which of the following distributions would the MEAN be an appropriate measure of central tendency?
    a. 2, 3, 5, 6
    b. 2, 3, 4, 10
    c. 0, 1, 1, 1, 1
    d. 2, 8, 9, 10, 11

18. Which of the following statements about animal research in psychology is TRUE?
    a. Ethical issues are of little concern with animals because animals do not have feelings.
    b. Animal researchers must weigh carefully the benefits and costs of such research.
    c. Animals are rarely used in psychological research now that we have computer models.
    d. Recent reports show that the majority of labs using animals in research are violating ethical standards.

19. A report in the media claims "EATING CHOCOLATE CRITICAL FOR GOOD HEALTH." In evaluating this claim you would
    a. want to know more about the study on which the article is based.
    b. try it out for yourself.
    c. accept the findings as long as the article is not written by a candy company.
    d. accept the article as long as it is balanced by a view of the reasons to avoid chocolate.

20. A university administrator wants to demonstrate that the tutoring centers on campus are ineffective. He provides evidence showing that the GPAs of students who receive tutoring are lower than the GPAs of students who do not receive tutoring. Do these data support his claim?
    a. Yes, the averages scores are different.
    b. No, the students are likely to differ in ways other than in their obtaining tutoring.
    c. Yes, because he has a comparison group, he can claim to support his claim.
    d. No, he did not identify the type of tutoring the students received.

After completing the test, calculate your percent correct
$$(\quad / 20 = \quad) \ x \ 100 = \underline{\hspace{1cm}}.$$

How accurate were your expectations? Does your performance suggest need for additional study? For the items you missed, go back and identify why the "correct" answer is the best answer.

AFTER YOU READ ... PRACTICE TEST #2

Before beginning this practice test estimate the percent you expect to get correct.
Esitmated percent correct: _____

1. A researcher measured how much time children spent on their homework and their standardized test scores. The researcher found that as the amount of homework increased, the performance on the standardized test increased. The type of relation observed was
   a. a positive linear relation.
   b. a negative relation.
   c. no relation.
   d. impossible to tell from this description.

2. In question 1, the research method described is a
   a. true experiment.
   b. case study.
   c. correlational study.
   d. meta-analysis.

3. Based on the homework research, which of the following would be an appropriate conclusion?
   a. Increasing homework will increase test scores.
   b. Knowing how much time a student spends on homework allows one to predict test scores.
   c. All children should be given more homework.
   d. a and c are true.

4. A new medication is given to individuals who experience frequent tension headaches. The researchers in this study should include a placebo group in order to
   a. control for alternative explanations.
   b. save money on medication.
   c. avoid the experimenter expectancy effect.
   d. avoid the nocebo effect.

5. During the debriefing period of an experiment, participants
   a. are told about the purpose of the study.
   b. are questioned by the Institutional Review Board about the study.
   c. are paid for their participation.
   d. sign an informed consent.

6. In an experiment, the control group is characterized by all of the following EXCEPT
   a. It provides a standard against which the changes in the other groups can be measured.
   b. It differs from the experimental group only in terms of the independent variable.
   c. It is required to make a statement of cause and effect.
   d. It is part of all research designs.

7. Mako's parents came to visit him at college and it rained all weekend. Now he is convinced it always rains on weekends so he misses class during the week in order to entertain visitors. Mako's reasoning reflects
   a. inferring cause from correlation.
   b. a belief in an illusory correlation.
   c. hindsight bias.
   d. the representativeness heuristic.

8. Ceci and Bronfenbrenner's study, "Don't forget to take the cupcakes out of the oven," assigned children to either bake cupcakes or to charge a motorcycle battery. Half did the task in their own homes and the other half did the task in the lab. Children were told to monitor the time and remove the cupcakes or battery cables in exactly 30 minutes. The results showed that children as young as 10 are able to use a complex strategy to remember future events but are more likely to do so in their own home environment compared with an unfamiliar laboratory environment. This study is an important demonstration of researchers' need to attend to
   a. external validity.   b. the file drawer problem.
   b. experimenter expectancy effects.   d. the nocebo effect.

9. Wolfgang is convinced that piano training improves school performance of children. He compares the school performance of his students with the children living in his apartment who do not take piano lessons. He finds his students are getting better grades in school compared with the children in his apartment. He concludes that he is correct in believing the difference is because of the piano training. Is his conclusion warranted?
   a. Yes, he has an independent variable and a control group.
   b. No, the difference demonstrated only applies to his students not to piano training in general.
   c. Yes, musical training teaches discipline.
   d. No, his groups were not randomly assigned, differences other than piano training exist.

10. Alejandro thinks he is quite a good comedian despite most people thinking his jokes are far from funny. According to the cognitive skills discussed in the chapter, Alejandro's judgment demonstrates
   a. the Great Fourfold Table of Life.
   b. that people overestimate their level of skill at a task.
   c. that there are individual differences in humor.
   d. the availability heuristic.

11. Which of the following is an important recommendation made about statistical reasoning?
   a. When looking at statistical graphs, read the scale labels and note scale ranges.
   b. Be aware of the influence of base rates on statistics.
   c. Because you can be tricked by statistics, it is important to rely on your own observations.
   d. Both a and b.

12. Which of the following is TRUE?
   a. The processes that lead to heuristics are generally maladaptive.
   b. A correlation of -.80 is just as high as a correlation of +.80.
   c. Statistically significant findings are important and large in size.
   d. Mode and standard deviation are both measures of dispersion.

13. The primary justification for using deception in a study is that
   a. deception never causes psychological stress.
   b. subjects who are unaware of the real purpose of the study will act more naturally.
   c. debriefing participants is inefficient.
   d. both b and c.

14. _____ are useful for generating hypotheses but limited in terms of testing hypotheses.
   a. Experimental studies   c. Meta-analyses
   b. Case studies   d. Correlational studies

15. Sample #1: 80, 85, 95, 95, 220
    Sample #2: 95, 95, 98, 99, 100
    Although these two distributions have the same _____, they are likely to have different _____.
    a. means ; modes
    b. modes ; standard deviations
    c. medians; standard deviations
    d. standard deviations; modes

16. The College Vegans want to show the administration how concerned the campus is with the cafeteria's selling of animal products. They survey their organization and find 100% of the students do not want animal products sold on campus. The administration isn't impressed with their findings because
    a. no attempt was made to obtain a random selection of students on campus.
    b. the Vegans need to conduct a true experiment to support their point.
    c. their results are correlational.
    d. they did not have random assignment.

17. Alana is failing Spanish. She comes across several Web sites describing the value of various audio CDs for learning language. She should evaluate the sites in terms of
    a. how quickly she needs to improve and how quickly the sites claim they can produce
        results.
    b. how many people have said the CDs have worked for them.
    c. what types of evidence is used to support the claims being made.
    d. whether the CDs are described as reflecting a "scientific breakthrough."

18. Joowan just took a personality test in a magazine and found out she was a "Rocker." In reading the descriptions of personality types identified by the test, she remembers she took the same test in another magazine last week and was identified as a "Slacker." With such different results, it is likely this test
    a. is low in validity and low in reliability.
    b. is high in demand characteristics.
    c. is low in reliability but high in validity.
    d. is both b and c.

19. Looking over evaluations of communication professors at his college, Ray notices that Dr. Lin has good scores on all measures and is rated HOT! Dr. Smith also has good ratings but is not rated hot. Ray assumes this means Dr. Lin is a better professor than Dr. Smith. One potential influence on Ray's assumption
    a. is the Hawthorne effect.   c. is the horns effect.
    b. is the halo effect.   d. is the Clever Hans effect.

20. Gunter began to feel a stomachache after drinking a beer before dinner and wine with dinner. What factor was responsible for Gunter's stomachache?
    a. Mixing liquors
    b. The cumulative effect of liquors
    c. The food served
    d. You cannot tell the cause of his stomachache from this observation

After completing the test, calculate your percent correct
(/ 20 =   ) *x 100 = _____ .*

How accurate were your expectations? Does your performance suggest need for additional study? For the items you missed, go back and identify why the "correct" answer is the best answer.

AFTER YOU READ ... PRACTICE TEST ANSWER KEYS

Practice Test 1.

1. d (p. 73, 81)
2. c (p. 78)
3. a (p. 78)
4. c (p. 96)
5. d (p. 77)
6. b (p. 73)
7. a (p. 77)
8. b (p. 78)
9. a (p. 76)
10. b (p. 78–79)
11. c (p. 68–69)
12. b (p. 65)
13. d (p. 78–79)
14. c (p. 91–92)
15. a (p. 71)
16. c (p. 92)
17. a (p. 94)
18. b (p. 93)
19. a (p. 100)
20. b (p. 78–79)

Practice Test 2.

1. a (p. 73)
2. c (p. 73)
3. b (p. 77)
4. a (p. 81)
5. a (p. 92)
6. d (p. 78–79)
7. b (p. 75–76)
8. a (p. 71)
9. d (p. 78–79)
10. b (p. 70)
11. d (p. 96–98)
12. b (p. 73)
13. b (p. 92)
14. b (p. 72)
15. b (p. 94)
16. a (p. 85)
17. c (p. 98–101)
18. a (p. 86)
19. b (p. 88)
20. d (p. 75–78)

AFTER YOU READ ... CONCEPT MAPPING ACTIVITY ANSWERS

ACTIVITY 1

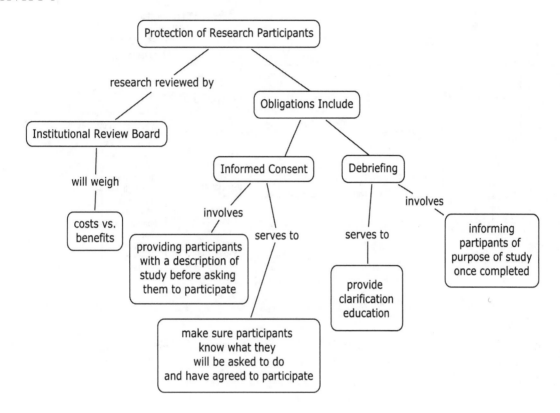

Chapter 2 Research Methods

ACTIVITY 2: Here are some of the most important advantages and disadvantages of the various research designs.

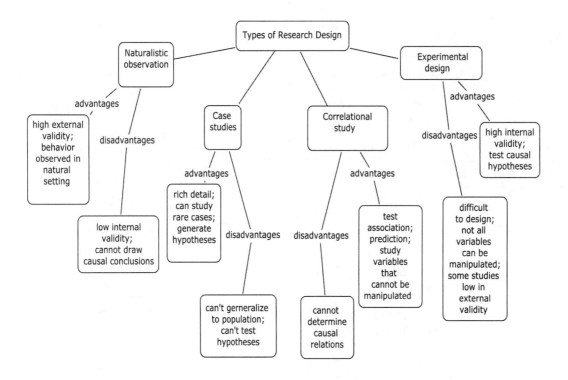

CHAPTER 3
BIOLOGICAL PSYCHOLOGY:
THE BRAIN-BODY COMMUNICATION SUPERHIGHWAY

BEFORE YOU READ ... CHAPTER PREVIEW

The nervous system is the most complex of human organ systems. It is composed of many parts, any one of which is capable of astonishing feats. Although the information in this chapter may seem daunting, it is included early because of its importance in understanding the mental processes and behavior of human beings.

Any discussion of biological psychology requires an understanding of the major parts of the nervous system. The central nervous system is composed of the brain and spinal cord and the peripheral nervous system is composed of the somatic and autonomic nervous systems. The brain is composed of the forebrain, or cerebral cortex, the midbrain and hindbrain. The cortex is divided into two hemispheres, connected by the corpus callosum. Each hemisphere is further divided into lobes, including the frontal lobe, responsible for executive functions, with the motor cortex at its back margin. The area in front of the motor cortex is the prefrontal cortex, which initiates many executive functions, and includes Broca's area, a language production area. Next is the parietal lobe, behind the frontal lobe, with a somatosensory area that corresponds to, and is directly behind, the motor cortex. The parietal lobe integrates sensory inputs, and maintains attention. The temporal lobe, located below the parietal and prefrontal areas, is specialized for sound perception and contains Wernicke's area, a language area responsible for speech perception. The temporal lobe is also important for memory formation. Finally, the occipital lobe, at the back of the head, is specialized for visual perception.

Buried beneath the forebrain are the basal ganglia, which help to control movement and where dopamine is secreted, as well as the basal forebrain, where acetylcholine is secreted. Connected to the forebrain and going toward the spinal cord is the brain stem, which contains the thalamus, a set of nuclei through which pass messages into and out of the nervous system. This midbrain area includes the reticular activating system, which controls arousal. Finally, the hindbrain, directly behind the midbrain, contains the cerebellum, the pons, and the medulla, which is an important area for sustaining life functions such as breathing and heartbeat. Separating the two hemispheres are hollow areas, the cerebral ventricles, filled with cerebrospinal fluid, which provides nutrients and cushions the brain.

The spinal cord contains neurons that carry messages from the brain to the extremities, the efferent or motor neurons, neurons that carry message from the extremities to the brain, the afferent or sensory neurons, as well as neurons within the spinal cord called interneurons, which allow for a rapid connection of sensory to motor neurons to produce reflex responses.

The peripheral nervous system has two parts, the somatic nervous system, which connects the CNS to muscles throughout the body, and the autonomic nervous system, which connects directly to the limbic system, a set of interconnected subcortical areas responsible for emotion and memory, connected to the endocrine system. The limbic system includes the hypothalamus, responsible for homeostasis, the amygdala, responsible for emotion, the cingulate cortex, modulating social behaviors, and the hippocampus, critically important for the formation of new memories. The endocrine system is responsible for controlling hormones, through a series of glands, including the pituitary gland, which controls many of the body's other glands, the adrenal glands, which produce both adrenaline, a neurotransmitter, as well as cortisol, a stress-related hormone, and sex hormones, including estrogen and testosterone. The autonomic nervous system is divided into two parts. The sympathetic nervous system activates the nervous system for "flight-or-fight" and the parasympathetic nervous system restores functions suited to rest and digestion.

Activity in the nervous system occurs by the activity of nerve cells, neurons, and glial cells. Glial cells are more numerous and provide supportive functions for the neurons, including producing myelin, a fatty cover for axons, that helps to speed neural transmission. Neurons are specially designed for communicating with one another, and consist of a cell body, dendrites for receiving messages, axons for sending messages, and axon terminals, where neurotransmitters are released. Messages connect between neurons through a microscopic space, called a synapse. Neurotransmitters released from the axon terminals of one neuron are picked up by the dendrites or cell bodies of the next neuron. Neurons communicate in two ways: electrically and chemically. Electrically, all neurons have a resting potential that is negatively charged. As messages come into the cell, some of them are excitatory and some are inhibitory, but all are added together. When a sufficiently high level is reached an action potential occurs, sending a message down the axon to release its neurotransmitter and send a message to subsequent neurons. At this point the message changes from an electrical message to a chemical message, as neurotransmitters are released into the synapse. Some drugs, called psychoactive drugs, either mimic or enhance a neuron's activity, called agonists, and others decrease a neuron's activity, called antagonists.

But how do we get from mind to brain? Recent technological developments have helped scientists to understand how mind and brain interact in situations where they can stimulate parts of the brain, or examine the effects of various brain damage on behavior, or simply observe the normal brain in action. These techniques include the EEG, which represents electrical activity in the brain using surface electrodes; various scanning techniques, which allow a clearer pictures of anatomical structures, including CT scans and MRI images; and functional imaging techniques, which allow scientists to see the brain in action, including PET scans, fMRI, and TMS. At least one interesting aspect of this work has been to debunk several myths, including the notion that we only use 10% of our brains, or are primarily left-brained or right-brained. Neuroimaging techniques have allowed a clearer picture of those functions that are localized, such as language, and those that are widely distributed. Furthermore, scientists know that some functions are preferentially performed by one hemisphere or the other, but that most human behaviors require the ongoing activity of both hemispheres in concert.

Another important consideration regards genetics. With the completion of the human genome project we now know most everything we can about human genetics. One important distinction is made between genotype, each person's genetic makeup, and phenotype, how that genetic makeup expresses itself in terms of dominant and recessive genes. Studies of behavioral genetics and heritability allow scientists to evaluate the effects of environment on genetics. Much of this information has come from studies of families, of twins, and of adoptions of twins into different families. The hope is that as genetic markers of disease are uncovered, the transmission of such disorders may be limited. This new information also holds hope for treating CNS damage. Scientists now know that the brain has greater plasticity—the ability to change—that was previously thought. Scientists have discovered that brains change as we learn, with new synapses forming and old ones becoming inactive. Similarly, new studies are showing greater plasticity following injury and degeneration. Stem cell treatments are also offering the promise of recovery following neurodegenerative diseases.

BEFORE YOU READ ... LEARNING OBJECTIVES

After reading Chapter 3 you should be able to:

3.1	Identify the parts of the nervous system that play a role in sensation and perception
3.2	Track the parts of the nervous system that play a role in motor functions
3.3	Clarify the relationship between the nervous system and the body
3.4	Identify the parts of the brain that play a role in emotion
3.5	Clarify how the autonomic nervous system works in an emergency and in everyday situations
3.6	Describe what hormones are and how they affect behavior
3.7	Distinguish the parts of neurons and what these parts do
3.8	Describe electrical responses of neurons and what makes them possible
3.9	Explain how neurons use neurotransmitters to communicate with each other
3.10	Describe the relationship between mind and brain
3.11	Identify the different brain stimulating, recording, and imaging techniques
3.12	Evaluate results demonstrating the brain's localization of function
3.13	Describe genes and how they result in observable traits
3.14	Explain the concept of heritability and the misconceptions surrounding it
3.15	Recognize when the brain changes most and when it changes least

---

BEFORE YOU READ ... TERM IDENTIFICATION

---

absolute refractory period (p. 126)
acetylcholine (p. 114)
action potential (p. 126)
adoption studies (p. 141)
adrenal gland (p. 122)
amygdala (p. 119)
aphasia (p. 111)
association cortex (p. 113)
autonomic nervous system (p. 120)
axons (p. 125)
basal forebrain (p. 114)
basal ganglia (p. 113)
blood-brain barrier (p. 125)
brain stem (p. 114)
Broca's area (p. 110)
central nervous system (CNS) (p. 108))
cerebellum (p. 115))
cerebral cortex (p. 108)
cerebral hemispheres (p. 110)
cerebral ventricles (p. 116)
chromosomes (p. 137)
computed tomography (CT) (p. 132)
corpus callosum (p. 110)
dendrites (p. 125)
dominant genes (p. 137)
dopamine (p. 113)

electroencephalography (EEG) (p. 131)
endocrine system (p. 120)
endorphins (p. 128)
family studies (p. 140)
fitness (p. 138)
forebrain (p. 108)
frontal lobe (p. 110)
functional MRI (fMRI) (p. 132)
genes (p. 137)
genotype (p. 137)
glia (glial cells) (p. 125)
heritability (p. 139)
hindbrain (p. 115)
hippocampus (p. 120)
hormone (p. 120)
hypothalamus (p. 119)
interneurons (p. 116)
lateralization (p. 134)
lesion (p. 130)
limbic system (p. 118)
magnetic resonance imaging (MRI) (p. 132)
magnetoencephalography (p. 132)
medulla (p. 115)
midbrain (p. 114)
motor cortex (p. 110)
myelin sheath (p. 125)

natural selection (p. 138)

neurogenesis (p. 145)

neurons (p. 108)

neurotransmitter (p. 125)

occipital lobe (p. 112)

parasympathetic division (p. 120)

parietal lobe (p. 111)

peripheral nervous system (PNS) (p. 108)

phenotype (p. 137)

pituitary gland (p. 121)

plasticity (p. 142)

pons (p. 115)

positron emission tomography (PET) (p. 132)

prefrontal cortex (p. 110)

receptor sites (p. 127)

recessive genes (p. 137)

reflex (p. 116)

resting potential (p. 126)

reticular activating system (p. 115)

reuptake (p. 127)

sensory cortex (p. 112)

somatic nervous system (p. 116)

split-brain surgery (p. 134)

stem cells (p. 144)

sympathetic division (p. 120)

synapse (p. 116)

synaptic cleft (p. 125)

synaptic vesicles (p. 125)

temporal lobe (p. 112)

thalamus (p. 114)

threshold (p. 126)

transcranial magnetic stimulation (TMS) (p. 132)

twin studies (p. 140)

Wernicke's area (p. 112)

AS YOU READ ... PRACTICE ACTIVITIES

THE BRAIN AND BEHAVIOR: NETWORKED WITH THE SOMATIC NERVOUS SYSTEM

1.   Differentiate between the central nervous system (CNS) and the peripheral nervous system (PNS). (LO 3.1)

2.   Which is the primary structure that makes up the forebrain, and what is its function? (LO 3.2)

3.   On this silhouette of the brain, indicate each of the four major lobes of each cerebral hemisphere and note the specializations associated with each. Then name each of the two major speech centers in the brain and note their locations in the drawing. Finally, add in the locations of motor and somatosensory cortex. (LO 3.2)

4.   An airline "hub" is a transfer point where passengers change planes en route to a distant destination. Develop an analogy between the function of airline hubs and the functions of the thalamus. (LO 3.3)

5.   Complete this table by filling in the specific action or sensory function associated with each structure. (LO 3.3)

Regions of the CNS	Areas with Action and Arousal Functions	Areas with Sensory and Perception Functions
Forebrain	*Basal ganglia*	*Neocortex*
	Basal forebrain	*Limbic system (cingulate cortex, hippocampus, and amygdala)*
	Hypothalamus	*Thalamus*
Midbrain	*Substantia nigra*	*Superior colliculus*
	Reticular activating system (RAS)	*Inferior colliculus*
Hindbrain	*RAS*	
	Pons	*Cerebellum (cerebellar cortex)*
	Medulla	
Spinal Cord	*Motor neurons*	*Sensory neurons*

(Brain Stem spans the Midbrain, Hindbrain, and Spinal Cord regions)

6.   At http://www.med.harvard.edu/AANLIB/home.html you can have some fun navigating around the whole brain atlas and looking at all of the structures you've been reading about! (LO 3.3)

7.   At http://thebrain.mcgill.ca/flash/a/a_01/a_01_m/a_01_m_fon/a_01_m_fon.html you can navigate about the Web site at several different levels from social to molecular, and from beginner to advanced. (LO 3.3)

8. If you suffer damage to your cerebellum, how might your behavior be affected? (LO 3.3)

THE BRAIN AND EMOTION: NETWORKED WITH THE AUTONOMIC NERVOUS SYSTEM

1. On this silhouette of the brain, note the location of the corpus callosum (as a reference structure) and then draw and label the four limbic system structures. Note the functions of each. (LO 3.4)

2. Complete this table for the autonomic nervous system's activities. (LO 3.4)

Autonomic Nervous System

Sympathetic Nervous System		Parasympathetic Nervous System	
Organ	**Action**	**Organ**	**Action**
_____	_____	_____	_____
_____	_____	_____	_____
_____	_____	_____	_____
_____	_____	_____	_____
_____	_____	_____	_____

3.   Now, imagine that you are being chased by a large, angry dog. Go over the various sympathetic nervous system changes that occur and note how these might be quite practical in the need to either flee or stay and fight. (LO 3.5)

4.   How does the hypothalamus affect the pituitary gland? (LO 3.6)

5.   How is the action of growth hormone different from that of other pituitary hormones? (LO 3.6)

6. Compare the activities of cortisol to those of adrenaline. (LO 3.6)

NERVE CELLS: COMMUNICATION PORTALS

1.   Draw a neuron and label the major structures within the neuron. Then list the function of each structure. (LO 3.7)

2.   You are a glial cell, seldom recognized for all the important work you do. You have an opportunity to be interviewed by a newspaper reporter. Convince him to write up a special report of all the important things that you do. (LO 3.7)

3.   Go to http://faculty.washington.edu/chudler/ap.html and watch an action potential. (LO 3.8)

4.   Compare (remember that "compare" in this case means you should note how things are similar and also how they are different) a graded potential with an action potential. (LO 3.8)

5.   Compare the actions of agonists and antagonists and give an example of each. (LO 3.9)

6.   Complete the following table of neurotransmitters. Rely on the text, NOT on Table 3.2. (LO 3.9)

Neurotransmitter	Selected Roles	Drugs That Interact with the Neurotransmitter System
Glutamate		
Gamma-Aminobutyric Acid (GABA)		
Norepinephrine (NE) (Adrenaline)		
Dopamine		
Serotonin		
Endorphins		
Anandamide		

MAPPING THE MIND TO UNDERSTAND OUR ACTIONS

1.   Describe the three sources of evidence we use to map brain activity to mind. (LO 3.10)

2.   Complete the following table. (LO 3.11)

Technique	Type (Structure or Function)	What It Can Tell Us
Electroencephalograph (EEG)		
Computed tomography (CT scans)		
Magnetic resonance imaging (MR)		
Positron emission tomography (PET)		
Functional MRI (fMRI)		

3.   Discuss the problems with using phrenology for assessing localization of function. Also explain phrenology's greatest "virtue." (LO 3.12)

4.   Even though this Web site at http://faculty.washington.edu/chudler/image.html is titled, "Neuroscience for Kids," it is definitely appropriate for all age groups. Enjoy surfing around some of the links with more information and more images. (LO 3.12)

5.   Before reading your text, how much of your brain did you believe you were using on a regular basis? Describe the evidence that we use more than 10% of our brains. Why do you think that people are willing to believe such misconceptions surrounding limited use of our brain's resources? (LO 3.12)

6.   You are having a bite to eat at your favorite diner when the person next to you strikes up a conversation. You mention you are studying psychology, to which this person immediately replies, "I am so right-brained!" Although you may want to get up and run away from this half-brained person, describe some of the arguments that favor and counter the belief that we are "right-brained" versus "left-brained." Convince your new friend that we use our whole brain all of the time. (LO 3.12)

7.   Complete this table for scientifically verified specializations of the hemispheres. (LO 3.12)

Side of Brain	Specialized Function
Right	
Left	

NATURE AND NURTURE: DID YOUR GENES—OR PARENTS—MAKE YOU DO IT?

1.   Compare heredity to heritability. Be sure to consider dominant and recessive genes. (LO 3.13)

2.   Describe three major misconceptions about heritability and note the evidence that disconfirms each misconception. (LO 3.14)

3.   In terms of behavioral genetics, what can (or cannot) each of the following tell us about the heritability of a trait: (a) family studies; (b) studies of identical (monozygotic) twins; and (c) studies of fraternal (dizygotic) twins? (LO 3.14)

4.   Speculate on what we can learn from adoption studies of twins raised together or apart. Then go to http://www.psych.umn.edu/psylabs/mtfs/special.htm. Compare your speculative answers with known findings. (LO 3.14)

5.   Should all children be tested for known genetic markers of disease? What could be the potential effects of knowing about potentially genetically transmitted disease? What could be the potential effects of not knowing about potentially genetically transmitted disease? (LO 3.14)

6.   Go to http://stemcells.nih.gov/info/basics/. Note at least three new things you learned about stem cells. Note at least one misconception you might have had for which you now have correct information after reading through this Web site. (LO 3.15)

AS YOU READ ... CONCEPT MAP ACTIVITIES

ACTIVITY 1: Complete the following concept map of the divisions of the nervous system.

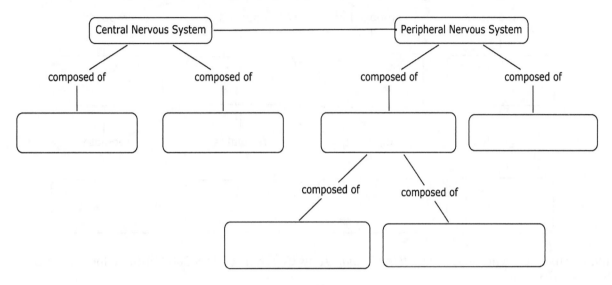

Author activity content supported by *IHMC Cmap Tools* Copyright ©1998-2007 Institute for Human & Machine Cognition

ACTIVITY 2: Complete this concept map for a typical reflex response, such as what happens when you step on a nail.

Author activity content supported by *IHMC Cmap Tools* Copyright ©1998-2007 Institute for Human & Machine Cognition

Chapter 3 Biological Psychology

ACTIVITY 3: Complete the following concept map of limbic circuits.

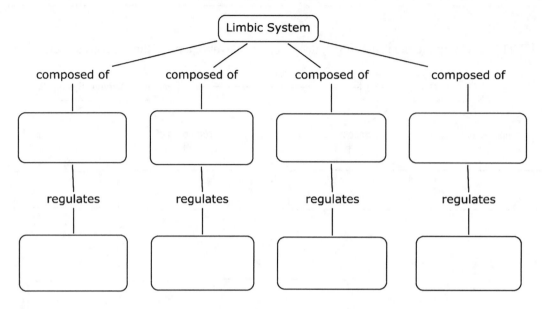

Author activity content supported by *IHMC Cmap Tools* Copyright ©1998-2007 Institute for Human & Machine Cognition

ACTIVITY 4: Complete the following concept map of the endocrine system.

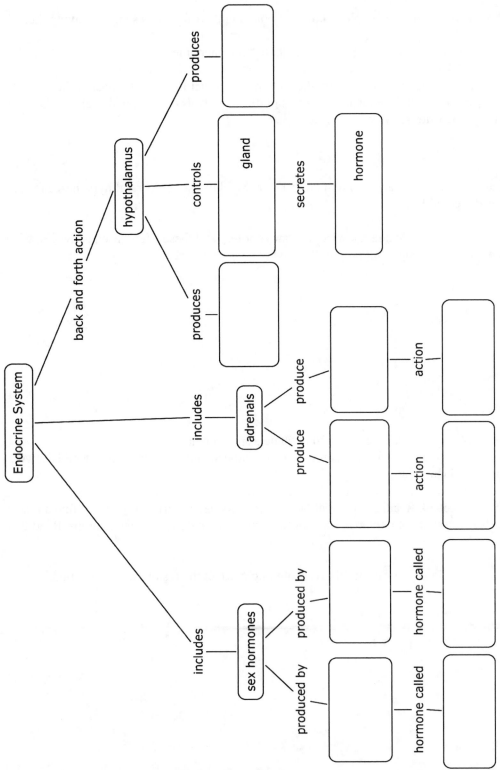

AS YOU READ ... MYTH OR REALITY?

Myth: We can revive people in comas by playing their favorites songs or saying their names.

Reality: No clear scientific evidence exists for this phenomenon.

1.   At http://www.aiemme.it/english/mt8.htm, the authors assert that listening to music is beneficial to patients in a coma. Critique their findings in terms of significance levels of statistical analyses. Do you agree with the authors' conclusions? Why or why not?

2.   The article at http://in.news.yahoo.com/060620/139/65825.html suggests rival hypotheses for the girl's awakening. Read it carefully.

3.   Now, based on your accumulated knowledge from your text and these Web-based activities, what is the reality? Why might some people fall prey to this myth?

Myth: As adults, we lose about 100,000 neurons each day.

Reality: Although we do lose neurons each day, the actual number is considerably lower, perhaps one tenth of that. (Juan, 2006)

1.   At http://www.dsrf.co.uk/Reading_material/New_braincells/newbrain1.htm you will find a report of recent studies that suggest that not only may the loss be small, but we do regenerate neurons. Read this carefully.

2.   Discuss how the findings reported at this Web site might affect the restoration of function following stroke.

As You Read … Put Your Critical Thinking Skills to the Test

1.   In your book you read about Phineas Gage and the effects of frontal lobe damage that he suffered in a work-related accident. What do you think would be the effects of a frontal lobotomy? Frontal lobotomies had a brief popularity in the 1940s and 1950s. Search the Internet for information on the typical effects of frontal lobotomies and compare them to the effects of Phineas Gage's accident and to what you expected to find.

a.   Were you correct?

b.   How were your expectations correct, and how were they incorrect?

c.   How do the descriptions of people who have had a lobotomy compare to the effects of Phineas Gage's accident?

d.   Can you find more recent examples on the Internet?

2.   While you are watching TV, you decide you need a snack, but you want to wait for a commercial to come on before heading out to the kitchen. Describe the activity of your somatic nervous system in helping you to get up and get a snack from the kitchen, and then get back to watching TV. Be sure to consider that you want to inhibit going to the kitchen until the commercial comes on, that you then want to navigate over to the kitchen and remember that you went there to get a snack, and return to the TV room before the commercials are over, and that you finally want to be able to pick up the story on the TV program when you return.

3.   An analogy is often made between action potentials and the flushing of a toilet. Develop that analogy here and think of the ways that the two function in common. Be sure to consider all aspects of neural transmission of messages.

4.   While still an undergraduate student, one of the co-authors of this study guide had the wonderful experience of taking art lessons at California State University, Long Beach, from Betty Edwards (see http://www.drawright.com). She makes a living on promoting her program of "Drawing on the Right Side of the Brain." Knowing what you know about how the hemispheres function together and apart, critique her program.

5.   Your text comments on the fact that in the 1800s employers sometimes demanded that potential employees "have their heads examined" by phrenologists before hiring them. This practice relates to modern day use of personality inventories or lie detector tests before hiring potential employees. Go to http://www.skepdic.com and read about lie detectors, as well as personality tests, particularly the Myers-Briggs Temperament Inventory (be sure to click the link to the Forer Effect), which is frequently used by human resources departments. Using the critical thinking skills you developed in Chapter 1, decide whether we have come very far in this type of pre-employment testing, since the 1800s.

As You Read ... MyPsychLab Connection

The Brain and Behavior: Networked with the Somatic Nervous System
Test your knowledge of the endocrine and limbic systems by completing the *Autonomic Nervous System*, *Endocrine System,* and *Limbic System* **explores**. Apply your knowledge of how the brain affects everyday behaviors with the **simulation** *Physiological Bases of Behavioral Problems*. For a personal look at neuronal damage and behavioral problems, **watch** *Connie: Head Injury* and *ALS Lost Nerve Power*. These videos review some behavioral problems associated with neuronal damage resulting from head trauma and degenerative diseases.

Nerve Cells: The Body's Communication Portals
For an interactive visual of how neurotransmission and receptor binding works, review the **explores** *Structure of a Neuron, The Action Potential, Neuronal Transmission, The Nerve Impulse, Afferent and Efferent Neurons*, and *The Synapse*. To see the effects of drugs on neurotransmitter binding and the brain, review the **simulation** *General Model of Drug Addiction*. Learn more about brain communication and neurotransmission by **watching** the videos *Brain Building* and *Exercise Your Brain*.

Mapping the Mind to Understand Our Actions
To see how the brain processes sensory information, such as vision, complete the **explore** *The Visual Cortex*. To receive a hands-on learning experience of hemispheric functioning and split-brain studies, check out the **simulations** *Hemispheric Experiments* and *Split-Brain Experiments*. How do scientists map the brain? Find out by **watching** the video *MKM and Brain Scans*.

Nature and Nurture: Did Your Genes—or Parents—Make You Do It?
For an interactive visual on genetics and DNA, utilize the **explores** *Dominant and Recessive Traits* and *Building Blocks of Genetics*. For further insight to genetics and DNA, **watch** the videos *Junk DNA, How the Human Genome Map Affects You,* and *Genetic Time Clock*. Interested in stem cell research and cloning? **Watch** *Cloned Child* and *Human Cloning—The Ethics*.

AFTER YOU READ ... PRACTICE TEST #1

Before beginning this practice test, estimate the percent you expect to get correct.
Anticipated percent correct: _____

1.   The central nervous system is composed of
a.   the autonomic and somatic nervous systems.
b.   the right and left hemispheres of the brain.
c.   the brain and spinal cord.
d.   neurons and glial cells.

2.   John suffers from severe epilepsy that did not respond to drug therapy. Doctors have proposed surgery to disconnect the hemispheres of his brain by severing the band of fibers called the _____ that connects the two hemispheres.
a.   corpus callosum   c.   hippocampus
  b.   myelin sheath   d.   thalamus

3.   Al, who is strongly right-handed, suffered a stroke in Broca's area of his left hemisphere. Al most likely now suffers from
a.   anosagnosia.   c.   acalculia.
  b.   alexithymia.   d.   aphasia.

4.   Michael J. Fox suffers from Parkinson's disease, which results from
        a.   a deficit in acetylcholine production in the basal forebrain.
        b.   a deficit in dopamine production by the substantia nigra.
        c.   a deficit in adrenaline production by the renal cortex.
        d.   a deficit in serotonin release in the synapses.

5.   The hindbrain is composed of
        a.   the pons, cerebellum, and medulla.
        b.   the hippocampus, amygdala, and hypothalamus.
        c.   the prefrontal cortex, Broca's area, and motor strip.
        d.   the autonomic, sympathetic, and parasympathetic nervous systems.

6.   You are driving along the freeway when another driver suddenly cuts you off, leading you to feel angry and upset with the other driver. This emotional response is mediated by
    a.   the thalamus.   c.   pituitary hormones.
        b.   the limbic system.   d.   the lymphatic system.

7.   A gazelle is being chased by a hungry lion in the wild. It is quite likely that there is activation of the gazelle's
a.   Broca's area.   c.   sympathetic nervous system.
        b.   endocrine system.   d.   parasympathetic nervous system.

8.   The _____ is called the "master" gland.
a.   thyroid   c.   pituitary
        b.   adrenal   d.   endocrine

9.   Gina suffers from an illness in which the myelin sheath surrounding neurons has deteriorated. She is most likely suffering from

    a.   schizophrenia.
    b.   multiple sclerosis.
    c.   Alzheimer's disease.
    d.   Parkinson's disease.

10.   Action potentials send messages from one neuron to another. The progression of an action potential within a single neuron occurs in the following sequence.

    a.   Axon, cell body, dendrites, axon terminals
    b.   Axon terminals, axon, cell body, dendrites
    c.   Dendrites, axon, cell body, axon terminals
    d.   Dendrites, cell body, axon, axon terminals

11.   Action potentials move more quickly along myelinated fibers because

a.   depolarization can jump the spaces between nodes and does not need to fire the entire length of the axon.

b.   myelin is a fatty substance and the depolarization occurs more quickly in fat than in watery substances.

c.   myelin contains salts that can transmit the message for depolarization more quickly down the axon.

d.   depolarization depends on the presence of glial cells to support the movement of ions within the axon.

12.   A frequent analogy used for understanding the transmission of neural signals across a synapse is that of a lock and key mechanism. This analogy arises from the finding that

a.   reuptake is limited to specific neurotransmitters within the synapse.

b.   only specific neurotransmitters can bind to specific postsynaptic membranes.

c.   glial cells can act as a locksmith to prevent confusion in transmitting messages.

d.   the neurotransmitter unlocks the ability of the neuron to generate a new action potential.

13.   Agonists work to _____ a neuron's activity, whereas antagonists work to _____ a neuron's activity.

    a.   enhance; reduce
    b.   reduce; enhance
    c.   block; reduce
    d.   reduce; block

14.   The EEG has

    a.   poor temporal resolution but great spatial resolution.
    b.   good temporal resolution but poor spatial resolution.
    c.   neither good temporal nor good spatial resolution.
    d.   both good temporal and spatial resolution.

15.   The PET scan depends on

    a.   recording metabolic activity related to oxygen metabolism.
    b.   recording metabolic activity related to glucose metabolism.
c.   noninvasive measures of electrical activity on the surface of the scalp.
    d.   noninvasive measures of metabolic activity on the surface of the scalp.

16.   What is the danger of relying too much on neuroimaging tests?
a.   We will give up using traditional psychological tests for assessing brain functions.
b.   We may focus too much on activity in areas that are not traditionally thought to be specialized for a particular function.
c.   We run the risk of assigning narrowly defined functions to brain regions, rather than remembering that most functions are distributed.
d.   We will pay too much attention to how different parts of the brain work together rather than focusing on individual parts and how they function.

17.   Your friend, Kutali, says he is definitely a left-brained person because he excels in his math classes but performs miserably in his language classes. You tell him
a.   indeed scientific evidence supports some specialization across hemispheres so he must have greater activation of one hemisphere compared to the other if his school grades support his premise.
b.   no scientific evidence supports this type of hemispheric asymmetry for complex tasks, and actually the two hemispheres function together.
c.   he has it backwards: if he likes math but dislikes languages he must be right-brained.
d.   he needs to also assess his handedness before reaching this conclusion.

18.   Andrea has brown eyes, but all of her children have blue eyes, which means that
a.   Andrea probably adopted her children, because brown eye color is dominant and her natural children would all have brown eyes.
b.   Andrea's recessive genes combined with her husband's dominant genes to determine eye color in her children.
        c.   Andrea's dominant traits are expressed in her children.
        d.   Andrea's phenotype does not reflect her genotype.

19.   Which of the following is NOT a misconception concerning heritability?
        a.   Heritability is a fixed number.
        b.   Heritability tells us whether a trait can be changed.
        c.   Heritability is a statistic that applies only to groups of individuals.
d.   Heritability applies to a single individual rather than to differences among individuals.

20.   When rats are raised in an enriched environment their brains show
        a.   larger neuronal cell bodies.
        b.   a reduced need for myelination.
        c.   increased size, as determined by weight.
        d.   increased branching of neuronal dendrites.

After completing the test, calculate your percent correct
(/ 20 =   ) x 100 = _____.

How accurate were your expectations? Does your performance suggest the need for additional study? For the items you missed, go back and identify why the "correct" answer is the best answer.

AFTER YOU READ ... PRACTICE TEST #2

Before beginning this practice test, estimate the percent you expect to get correct.
Anticipated percent correct: _____

1.   The peripheral nervous system helps us to
   a.   think, talk, and reason.
   b.   make decisions and use language.
   c.   analyze sensory information and think.
   d.   control behavior and experience emotion.

2.   The frontal lobe of the cortex is responsible for
   a.   motor function, executive function, and language.
   b.   transferring short-term to long-term memories.
   c.   primary processing of auditory inputs.
   d.   somatosensory processing.

3.   The parietal lobe of the cortex is responsible for
a.   many kinds of perception, including spatial perception.
b.   relaying messages to and from the extremities.
c.   storage of autobiographical memories.
d.   coordination of motor movements.

4.   The thalamus can be thought of as
a.   the end of the line of a train station—this is where all trains end up.
b.   an airline hub, with most flights coming and going through the hub.
c.   a map, showing where various nuclei are located relative to one another.
d.   a parking garage, where vehicles are left for a temporary amount of time.

5.   The development of "bionic" artificial limbs provides a nice example of how we can discriminate science from pseudoscience because
a.   doctors can completely explain how the arm works.
b.   if it were pseudoscientific it would not function for very long.
c.   scientific limbs are developed quickly and efficiently.
d.   only a scientific arm could perform the fine motor tasks that are possible with such an arm.

6.   In the film *Memento*, the main character, Lenny, compensates for his inability to form new memories by taking Polaroid pictures of important people and objects. Lenny clearly has damage to his
   a.   amygdala.   c.   hippocampus.
   b.   frontal lobe.   d.   cingulated cortex.

7.   _____ are secreted into the blood stream directly, in order to affect behavior.
a.   Neurotransmitters   c.   Chromosomes
b.   GABA molecules   d.   Hormones

8.	You notice smoke coming out of a house and hear a child crying inside. As you run inside to save the child your heart muscle contracts, your pupils dilate, and airways open up. All of these effects are probably the result of the release of _____ into your bloodstream.
a.	oxytocin
b.	adrenaline
c.	endorphins
d.	testosterone

9.	If glial cells were up for an academy award, the category they would be nominated in would be
a.	best actor.
b.	best director.
c.	best visual effects.
d.	best supporting actor.

10.	Graded potentials differ from action potentials in that
a.	graded potentials are like a gun being fired, whereas the action potential depends on excitatory and inhibitory inputs cancelling each other out.
b.	during graded potentials the electrical charge within the neuron changes but during action potentials it remains constant.
c.	an action potential occurs only after the graded potential reaches a certain threshold of excitation.
d.	a graded potential is an all-or-nothing response, and the action potential is not.

11.	During neurotransmission,
a.	the absolute refractory period is lengthened.
b.	action potentials are continuously generated.
c.	neurotransmitter is released into the synaptic cleft.
d.	enzymes are required to activate muscle receptors.

12.	Your friend Joe is a serious runner. He always runs until he feels a good burn in his legs and his chest works hard to provide his body with oxygen. In fact, Joe runs several times a day because he says a good hard run gives him a "runner's high." Which neurotransmitter system is probably responsible for Joe's runner's high?
a.	GABA
b.	Serotonin
c.	Endorphin
d.	Acetylcholine

13.	Your friend Mike wants to go see a phrenologist. You tell him to save his money because
a.	phrenology still needs to be falsified.
b.	your friend could learn much more about himself by visiting an astrologer.
c.	enlarged areas on the outside of the head are only accurate in determining vanity, friendliness, and happiness.
d.	bumps on the outside of the head have not been shown to correspond to any known personality traits or abilities.

14.	The major drawback of CT scans and MRI images is that they both
a.	only provide information about structures, not functions.
b.	carry the risk of overexposure to radioactivity.
c.	do not allow a view of inner brain structures.
d.	are invasive.

15.   Evidence against the 10% myth (we only use 10% of our brains) comes from
        a.   the general success of courses to improve our brain power.
        b.   the effectiveness of self-help books to increase mental capacity.
        c.   neuroimaging studies, which fail to find any consistently silent areas.
        d.   psychics who are able to perform extraordinary feats of mental powers.

16.   Jillian has had her corpus callosum severed. When the sentence "Stand up" Is presented to her right visual field-left hemisphere, she will
        a.   read the words out loud.
        b.   stand up but claim she doesn't know why.
        c.   stand up, but not be able to read the words.
d.   be able to read the words but won't understand the words or carry out the command.

17.   Genotype refers to _____, whereas phenotype refers to _____.
a.   a person's observable traits; that which is passed on from parents to offspring.
b.   a person's expressed traits; recessive and dominant traits in combination.
c.   a person's actual genetic makeup; a person's observable traits.
d.   recessive traits; dominant traits.

18.   Behavioral genetics allows us to study
        a.   only the effects of genetics on behavior.
        b.   the differences in genetic makeup within a single individual.
        c.   the interaction of nature and nurture in the expression of a trait.
        d.   behavioral traits, but cannot tell us about the heritability of diseases.

19.   The logic underlying twin studies that seek to increase our understanding of the heritability of disorders is that
a.   twins must be separated at birth for the results to be meaningful.
b.   monozygotic twins are more genetically alike than dizygotic twins.
c.   monozygotic twins share the same embryonic sac and, therefore, share more environmental factors than do dizygotic twins.
d.   monozygotic and dizygotic twins have unequal environmental experiences because MZ twins are often dressed alike, but DZ twins are not.

20.   An important aspect of enhancing neural plasticity following spinal cord injury is
        a.   enhancing axon growth.   c.   enhancing myelination of axons.
        b.   decreasing physical activity.   d.   inhibiting glial cell overgrowth.

After completing the test, calculate your percent correct
(/ 20 =   ) x 100 = _____.

How accurate were your expectations? Does your performance suggest the need for additional study? For the items you missed, go back and identify why the "correct" answer is the best answer.

AFTER YOU READ . . . PRACTICE TEST ANSWER KEYS

Practice Test 1.

1. c (p. 109)
2. a (p. 110)
3. d (p. 110)
4. b (p. 113)
5. a (p. 115)
6. b (p. 118)
7. c (p. 120)
8. c (p. 121)
9. b (p. 125)
10. b (p. 126)
11. a (p. 127)
12. b (p. 127)
13. a (p. 128)
14. b (p. 131)
15. b (p. 132)
16. c (p. 133)
17. b (p. 135)
18. d (p. 137)
19. c (p. 139)
20. d (p. 143)

Practice Test 2.

1. d (p. 109)
2. a (p. 110)
3. a (p. 111)
4. b (p. 114)
5. a (p. 118)
6. c (p. 120)
7. d (p. 120)
8. b (p. 122)
9. d (p. 125)
10. c (p. 126)
11. c (p. 127)
12. c (p. 128)
13. d (p. 130)
14. a (p. 132)
15. c (p. 133)
16. a (p. 135)
17. c (p. 137)
18. c (p. 139)
19. b (p. 141)
20. a (p. 144)

AS YOU READ ... CONCEPT MAPPING ACTIVITY ANSWERS

ACTIVITY 1:

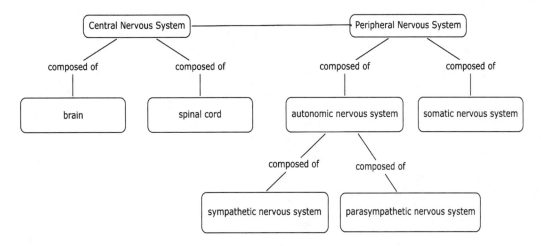

ACTIVITY 2:
You should have entered the terms: *afferent neurons*, *interneurons*, and *efferent neurons* in that order going across the nodes.

ACTIVITY 3:

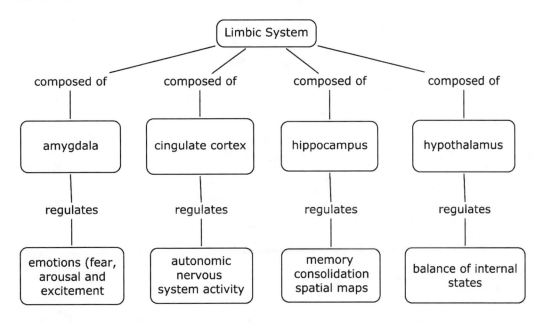

ACTIVITY 4:
Alphabetical list of terms you might have included:

adrenaline	ovaries	vasopressin
boosts energy	oxytocin	
cortisol	regulates cardiac function	
estrogen	testes	
growth	testosterone	

CHAPTER 4
SENSATION AND PERCEPTION:
HOW WE SENSE AND CONCEPTUALIZE THE WORLD

BEFORE YOU READ ... CHAPTER PREVIEW

Sensation is the detection of a physical energy by means of specialized sense organs, whereas perception is the organization and interpretation of these sensory inputs. Transduction is the process by which a physical stimulus becomes a psychological reality. Sensation requires a minimum amount of intensity of stimulation, called an absolute threshold. The smallest difference in intensity that can be detected is called a just noticeable difference (JND). The change in stimulus intensity needs to be greater, the stronger the original stimulus. Sometimes perception occurs in a background of other stimuli, and signal detection can go wrong. Of course, we cannot consciously perceive a stimulus at all if it is well below threshold, or subliminal. Although strong evidence exists for subliminal or unconscious perception, the evidence for subliminal *persuasion* is meager at best; no clear evidence indicates that people can be subliminally persuaded to perform certain behaviors. Perception depends on bottom-up processing sensory memory and top-down processing. Perception also depends on context, and on constancy of shape, size, and color. In fact, most things we perceive are composed of many smaller sensations that bind together to form a single perception. For perception to occur we need to selectively attend to stimuli. When many things are going on around us it is difficult to focus on only one thing; focusing on more than one thing leads to a quick deterioration of perceptual quality. Some people claim to have ESP and claim to be able to perceive sensations that are outside of the usual sensation. Although belief in ESP is pervasive, scientific evidence for ESP is lacking. People tend to believe in ESP because of the confirmation bias and the fallacy of positive instances.

In terms of vision, we respond to a very narrow range of wavelengths of light as they reflect off surfaces in the environment. Brightness is the intensity of the light that reaches our eyes, and hue is the color of light. We're sensitive to three primary colors of light— red, green, and blue. Different parts of the eye have specific functions in transmitting light. The iris, the colored part of the eye, is a set of muscles controlling an opening that modifies the amount of light permitted through the pupil, an opening allowing light into the eye. The cornea is a curved, transparent layer covering the iris and pupil. The lens is transparent, and changes shape to focus light on the back of the eye through a process called accommodation. The retina is a thin membrane at the back of the eye that contains receptor cells. The fovea is the central part of the retina. The two types of receptor cells are rods and cones. Rods are long and narrow, used in low light, and to see basic shapes and forms. Cones are used in high light and give us color and detailed vision. Ganglion cells, the last cells in the retinal circuit, contain axons that leave the eye as the optic nerve, creating a small blind spot at their exit point. The optic nerve travels to the brain, half splitting at the optic chiasm to travel to the same hemisphere and half crossing to the other side. The optic tracts send most of their axons to the primary visual cortex, V1, but some go to the superior colliculus in the midbrain and on to arousal centers.

Perception is more complicated. We have feature detector cells in V1 that respond to external stimuli based on specific orientation or motion, allowing us to see lines, edges and corners. Several principles, first articulated by the Gestalt psychologists, help us to perceive objects in space, including subjective contours, proximity, similarity, good continuation, closure, symmetry, and figure-ground. Face recognition is especially important for humans and cells located in the temporal lobe are specialized for this task. Motion perception is especially complex, involving the organization of separate, changing images, into a single, flowing perception. For color perception, three different types of cones each respond to a different light wavelength. If one of these receptors is faulty, then color blindness occurs. Another aspect of color perception involves the opposite pairing of colors at the ganglion cell and thalamus levels, and explains why afterimages are of different colors than the actual stimulus. Depth perception is complicated because we can perceive depth using either both eyes, based on the different message that each eye receives, and how the eye muscles move to focus moving images on the retina, or on using just one eye. Monocular depth cues include relative size, texture gradients, interposition, linear perspective, height in plane, light and shadow, and motion parallax. When perception fails to operate as it should we experience optical illusions, including the moon illusion, the Ames room, the Müller-Lyer illusion, the Ponzo illusion, the horizontal-vertical illusion, and the Ebbinghaus-Tichener illusion. Blindness is the inability to see or perceive either anything at all or very clearly at all. Evidence as to whether blind individuals' other senses take over to compensate for the loss of vision is inconclusive. Some evidence shows that somatosensory areas, especially for touch, do spread out and take up more space.

Sound results from waves, which have pitch and amplitude. Pitch corresponds to the wave frequency with fast waves producing a higher pitch and slow waves producing a lower pitch. The amplitude or height of the sound wave corresponds to loudness. The outer ear has the simplest function for processing sound as it funnels sound waves onto the eardrum. From the middle ear, sound is transmitted to the cochlea, in the inner ear, where vibration is transduced into neural activity. The cochlea is filled with a thick fluid. Waves travel through the spiral-shaped cochlea, bending hair cells embedded in a thin basilar membrane running down its middle. The hair cells convert acoustic information into action potentials, sending their axons as the auditory nerve to auditory cortex in the temporal lobe. Pitch is perceived because different areas of primary auditory cortex respond selectively to different frequencies of sound waves, which excite hair cells in different areas of the basilar membrane—at least for high-pitched sounds. For low-pitched sounds an additional mechanism causes hair cells fire at the speed at which the sound waves arrive. Furthermore, we can localize sound because binaural information reaches the brain at a slightly offset time frame. Monaural cues can be used to localize sound based on clarity and intensity of the sound. Sound illusions can occur, similarly to visual illusions. Often these are based on our expectations built up from prior experiences or from a dissociation between visual and auditory cues. Deafness can occur for several reasons, most commonly because of damage to the auditory nerve, or if the ossicles malfunction.

Smell results when odors (airborne chemicals) interact with receptors in the lining of our nasal passages. Odors have a lock-and-key mechanism for smell perception and humans have possibly thousands of specific odors they can detect. Once the receptors are activated, then the information goes to the olfactory cortex and on to the limbic system. We're sensitive to five basic tastes— sweet, salty, sour, bitter, and umami. Fat is being investigated as a sixth basic taste. The "tongue map" for tastes, which many students learn about in elementary and high school is a misconception—all tastes are spread out throughout the taste buds on our tongue. From the taste buds, messages are sent to the gustatory and somatosensory cortex, and also on to the limbic system. To a great extent taste is strongly influenced by odors.

We have three body senses. The somatosensory system responds to stimuli applied to the skin, such as touch, pain, or temperature, primarily via free nerve endings. Free nerve endings send their messages to the spinal cord, to the brain, to the somatosensory cortex. Proprioception keeps track of body position via two types of receptors: stretch detectors in muscles and force detectors in tendons. This information also eventually goes to the somatosensory cortex and even to the motor cortex if quick movement is necessary. Finally, the vestibular sense is our sense of balance. The semicircular canals, attached to the cochlea, send information on motion and orientation. The sense receptors are similar to those for hearing but their message is sent via the brainstem to the cerebellum, as well as the somatosensory cortex.

BEFORE YOU READ ... LEARNING OBJECTIVES

After reading Chapter 4 you should be able to:

4.1   Identify the basic principles that apply to all senses
4.2   Track how our minds build up perceptions
4.3   Analyze the scientific support for and against ESP
4.4   Explain how the eye starts the visual process
4.5   Identify the different kinds of visual perception
4.6   Describe different visual problems
4.7   Explain how the ear starts the auditory process
4.8   Identify the different kinds of auditory perception
4.9   Identify how we sense and perceive tastes and odors
4.10   Describe the three different body senses
4.11   Explore how pain perception differs from touch perception

---
BEFORE YOU READ ... TERM IDENTIFICATION
---

absolute threshold (p. 153)
accommodation (p. 165)
acuity (p. 165)
audition (p. 177)
basilar membrane (p. 178)
binocular depth cues (p. 170)
blind spot (p. 166)
brightness (p. 163)
cochlea (p. 178)
cornea (p. 165)
color blindness (p. 170)
cones (p. 166)
depth perception (p. 170)
extrasensory perception (p. 159)
fovea (p. 165)
gustation (p. 180)
hue (p. 163)
just noticeable difference (JND) (p. 154)
lens (p. 165)
monocular depth cues (p. 170)

olfaction (p. 180)
organ of Corti (p. 178)
perception (p. 152)
perceptual constancy (p. 157)
phantom pain (p. 186)
pheromones (p. 182)
proprioception (p. 184)
retina (p. 165)
rods (p. 165)
selective attention (p. 158)
semicircular canals (p. 188)
sensation (p. 152)
sense receptor (p. 153)
somatosensory (p. 184)
taste buds (p. 181)
timbre (p. 177)
transduction (p. 153)
trichromatic theory (p. 170)
vestibular sense (p. 184)

AS YOU READ ... PRACTICE ACTIVITIES

TWO SIDES OF THE COIN: SENSATION AND PERCEPTION

1. Differentiate between sensation and perception. Use an original example to illustrate the difference. (LO 4.1)

2. Differentiate between subliminal perception and subliminal persuasion. Based on your reading of the text, do you believe that you could be subliminally persuaded by an advertiser to purchase a product? Why or why not? (LO 4.1)

3. Provide an original example from your everyday life of both size constancy and of color constancy. (LO 4.2)

4. Think of a time, or ask a friend about an instance, when a personal coincidence just seemed too weird to have occurred by chance or coincidence. How might you explain it in terms of the fallacy of positive instances? (LO 4.3)

5. Draw an analogy between the psychics' use of multiple end points, and the Barnum effect. If you are not yet familiar with the Barnum effect you can read about it in Chapter 14, Personality, or you can go online to http://www.skepdic.com and find information about it. (LO 4.3)

SEEING: THE VISUAL SYSTEM

1. Using the following silhouette of the eyeball, label the cornea, pupil, iris, lens, retina, fovea, and blind spot. (LO 4.4)

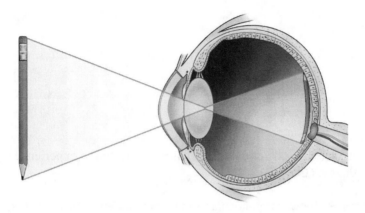

2. Briefly note the function of each of the structures you have labeled in the drawing in question 1. (LO 4.4)

3. Compare the many functions of rods and cones. Remember to discuss both the similarities and differences between them. Does their distribution along the retina make sense to you? (LO 4.4)

4. Go to http://desktoppub.about.com/od/gestalt/Gestalt.htm and explore different ways that Gestalt principles are used in everyday life in various public media, such as advertising and developing company logos. (LO 4.5)

5. Draw a simple, but original picture or line drawing to illustrate the following Gestalt principles: (LO 4.5)

    a. proximity

    b. similarity

    c. closure

6. Go to http://www.michaelbach.de/ot/col_lilacChaser/index.html to experience a great example of opponent process theory. (LO 4.5)

7. What are the differences between monocular and binocular depth cues—that is, what does each depend on? (LO 4.5)

8. Make a line drawing of a landscape, even if you can only make stick figures and geometrical shapes. Incorporate the following aspects of depth perception into your drawing: relative size, texture gradient, interposition, linear perspective, light and shadow, and height in plane. Draw a line to, and label, each of these elements in your drawing. (LO 4.5)

9. Go to http://www.exploratorium.edu/exhibits/depth_spinner/index.html and enjoy the motion-related visual illusions. (LO 4.5)

10. According to microscopic studies of the retina, some dog species appear to lack one of the three types of cones. What do we call this type of color blindness, and how would it affect vision in those animals? (LO 4.6)

HEARING: THE AUDITORY SYSTEM

1. Label the parts of the ear designated by the letters A, B, C, D, and E. Note a function of each part. (LO 4.7)

A _____

B _____

C _____

D _____

E _____

2. Timbre is the most difficult sound quality to understand. What makes the definition of timbre different from the definitions of loudness and pitch? (LO 4.7)

3. Compare place theory of pitch perception with frequency theory of pitch perception. When would one be more likely to dominate perception over the other? (LO 4.8)

4. Just as monocular and binocular cues aid in visual perception of space, monaural and binaural cues contribute to perception of auditory cues. What are the different ways we use monaural and binaural auditory cues? (LO 4.8)

5. Your text discusses both blindsight and echolocation as separate explanations for why some blind people don't bump into objects more often than they do. How do you believe the input from different sensory systems might interact to help the blind? (LO 4.8)

SMELL AND TASTE: THE SENSUAL SENSES

1. You may have noticed that when you have a cold and a sore throat you can taste sweet or salty tastes but not much else. For example, if you have some popsicles to soothe your sore throat they probably all taste the same. Why do you think this happens? (LO 4.9)

2. At some time in school you may have heard about the "tongue map"—that map that shows which parts of your tongue are sensitive to which of the basic tastes. If the tongue map were correct then you should only be able to taste sweet things with the tip of your tongue and salty things with an area along the sides about one-third of the way up from the tip towards the base of your tongue. Try this. (LO 4.9)

   a. Put your head back and place some sugar way back on the base of your tongue. Did you taste anything? What? Why?

   b. Place some salt on the very tip of your tongue. Did you taste anything? What? Why?

   c. Has this experiment convinced you that the tongue map is not accurate? Why or why not?

3. Buy a small box of flavorful jelly beans (Jelly Bellies work well). Now, shut your eyes and reach into the package. With your eyes shut, hold your nose tightly shut with the other hand and put the jelly bean into your mouth. Try not to breathe so that air is not pushed up the backside of your nasal passages. Chew up the jelly bean. What flavor was it? How sure are you? Was it easy to tell what the flavor was? Why or why not? (LO 4.9)

4. What do you think about including "fat" as a basic taste? Do you believe it is a taste that is affected by smell? Do you believe that you can taste "fat"? If not, then how would you describe what you experience when you taste something that has fat in it, versus something that does not, such as fat-free yogurt compared to a creamy yogurt? (LO 4.9)

OUR BODY SENSES: TOUCH, BODY POSITION, AND BALANCE

1. You've stepped on a tack. List all of the places to which the message goes. (LO 4.10)

2. Go back to Chapter 3 and review what happens during a spinal reflex (withdrawal reflex). Why is a faster turnaround time for the motor response more important than the psychological realization of what is happening? Have you ever been consciously aware of this time difference? If so, explain what happened. (LO 4.10)

3. Describe the ways proprioception and the vestibular system work together to help you maintain balance. (LO 4.10)

4. Motion sickness results from a mismatch between the messages sent by two sensory systems. Surf the Web on your own and find information on which two sensory systems are most likely to be implicated, and explain in your own words what causes motion sickness. If you ever go on a cruise, what could you do to minimize this effect? (LO 4.10)

5. Think of where you most often see tattoos on people's bodies. Do these areas correspond to areas of high or low density of free nerve endings? (LO 4.11)

6. Go to http://faculty.washington.edu/chudler/pain.html and read about the gate-control theory of pain. Based on the information at this Web site, what could you do to at least minimize pain perception when you know in advance that something painful will happen to you? (LO 4.11)

AS YOU READ ... CONCEPT MAP ACTIVITIES

ACTIVITY 1: See how well you can fill in this fairly complicated map of the sensory systems.

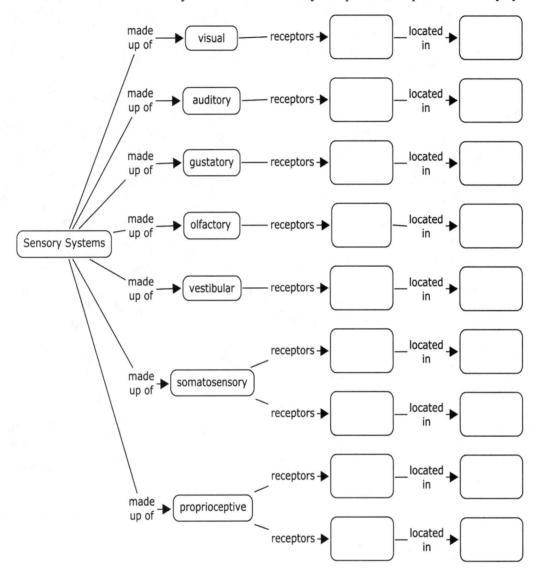

Author activity content supported by *IHMC Cmap Tools* Copyright ©1998-2007 Institute for Human & Machine Cognition

ACTIVITY 2: This map shows the visual system and should simplify your understanding of the complexities of both sensation and perception in vision.

As You Read … Myth or Reality?

Myth: People can be persuaded to buy certain products by subliminally hiding sexual messages in the product's labeling or advertising.

Reality: Being frequently exposed to the labeling or advertising might make a person feel more comfortable with the product and that could lead to increased purchasing (the mere exposure effect). However, by definition, if something is *sub*liminal, people will not be consciously aware of the presence and meaning of the sexual symbols and thus will not be persuaded to buy the products.

1. Explore the following four sites:
    http://www.planetperplex.com/en/img.php?id=308
    http://www.snopes.com/disney/films/lionking.htm http://www.planetperplex.com/en/item277
    http://www.planetperplex.com/en/item265

    How convinced are you that people can really "see" sexual innuendos in any of these ads on a normal day-to-day basis?

2. In some of them, such as the Pepsi ad, the image is more blatant if the cans are positioned just right. Do you believe it is still, then, "subliminal"?

Myth: Vision occurs because our eyes emit a light that interacts with objects outside of ourselves.

Reality: No evidence supports this belief.

1. Read a summary of early beliefs about vision.
    http://findarticles.com/p/articles/mi_m0PAL/is_509_159/ai_n6153266/
    Early master painters, such as Leonardo da Vinci believed that vision occurs because of a ray emitted by the eyes. It was not until Helmholtz (who developed the trichromatic theory of color vision you have read about) that scientists understood how vision works.
2. In addition, http://en.wikipedia.org/wiki/History_of_scientific_method provides a discussion of the scientific method. Read one of the nice examples of how the scientific method was able to lead scientists to the correct conception of vision: that objects reflect light, not that the eyes emit light.

3. Finally, if you go to
   http://www.cartage.org.lb/en/themes/sciences/Physics/Optics/briefhistory/briefhistory.htm you will notice that even early Greek philosophers argued back and forth about how vision works: light waves into the eyes or light waves out of the eyes. However, by the early 1800 scientific doubt had been eliminated.

4. So, if science has conclusively shown since the 1800s that vision occurs because of light waves reflected INTO the eye, why do you think some people still persist in believing that vision occurs because of light rays emitted from the eyes?

AS YOU READ ... PUT YOUR CRITICAL THINKING SKILLS TO THE TEST

---

1. Signal detection theory is applied to a variety of psychological phenomena, including recognition memory, and diagnosis of psychopathology.
    a. Go to http://epsych.msstate.edu/deliberate/sig_det/index.html. Read the explanatory text and do the exercise. How did you do relative to what the theory would predict? If your results are not as predicted where did they differ? Why do you think this happened—be honest!
    b. Now provide a hypothesis based on signal detection theory of what should happen with the diagnosis of psychopathology. For which disorders would you shift the criterion more so than for other disorders?

2. Psychic readings are sleight of mind (much like we talk about "magic" tricks as "sleight-of-hand") using a technique called "cold reading." Your text describes several cold reading techniques.
    a. Go to http://www.youtube.com/watch?v=saTR3r297ys
        Watch a few minutes' worth of the video—no need to watch all 10 minutes. Were you convinced by the reading? Why or why not?
    b. Go back over the list of cold reading techniques in your text and find a few of the techniques that you saw used in this video.
    c. Now go to http://www.youtube.com/watch?v=dkbkkkT6ejA for an alternative viewpoint.
    d. Finally, go to http://www.comedycentral.com/motherload/?lnk=v&ml_video=75230 and enjoy!

3. Go to http://www.youtube.com/watch?v=voAntzB7EwE and watch the video. Do not look ahead at the questions.
    a. What did you notice the first time?
    b. What did you fail to notice the first time?
    c. Based on this exercise what can you conclude about eyewitness accuracy? Remember that in addition to any normal viewing conditions, eyewitness events are witnessed in a context of emotional upset, occur very quickly, and our attention is often diverted by other important events, such as the presence of a weapon.

Two Sides of the Coin: Sensation and Perception
To better understand top-down processing, complete the **explore** *Top-Down Processing*, which presents a visual re-creation of classic methodologies on this topic. In the **simulation** *Ambiguous Figures*, you can see how visual perception and sensation work together and sometimes how one overrides the other. **Listen** to the podcast *Sensation and Perception,* which contains a lively conversation between two psychologists to help you better understand how these processes work together to help you see, hear, smell, and taste.

Seeing: The Visual System
Explore your knowledge of different types of visual illusions with *Five Well-Known Illusions*. Review how the optical system processes light waves with the **explore** on *Light and the Optic Nerve*, which presents a visual simulation of how light is processed through the eye. For more on how light is processed through the retina **explore** *Receptive Fields*. **Explore** *Normal Vision, Nearsightedness*, to see what causes the need for corrective lenses. Your stereotypes about the way the world works or even expectancies that you have can influence what you see. Participate in a visual **simulation** on *Perceptual Sets* that demonstrates how what we see can be influenced by what other people say or do with perceptual sets. *Gestalt Laws of Perception* is another **simulation** that will help you review the Gestalt principles. *Distinguishing Figure-Ground Relationships* **simulation** provides you with an opportunity to test your ability to not succumb to visual illusions. Can you tell the difference between two images? If you think you can, try the **simulation** *Methods of Constant Stimuli*.

Hearing: The Auditory System
Explore different sound waves with *Frequency and Amplitude of Sound Waves*. Test yourself on all the structures of the ear with the interactive **explore** *Major Structures of the Ear*.
Watch the following four video clips on how the brain processes auditory information: *Cochlear Implants, Ear Ringing, Listening to Blues Test*, and *Noise and the Brain*.

Our Body Senses: Touch, Body Position, and Balance
Watch the *Brain Pain* to see how distraction in virtual reality games can decrease how much pain patients report and result in fewer pain signals in the brain.

Smell and Taste: The Sensual Senses
Watch *Alzheimer's Smell Test* to see how a decline in sensitivity to smell may signal onset of the disease Alzheimer's. **Watch** *Aromatherapy* to see how odors, such as vanilla, modify your emotions.

AFTER YOU READ ... PRACTICE TEST #1

Before beginning this practice test, estimate the percent you expect to get correct.
Anticipated percent correct: _____

1. Sensation is to perception as
    a. global is to specific.
    b. complex is to simple.
    c. normal is to abnormal.
    d. physical is to psychological.

2. Sense receptors are
    a. more numerous in people with extrasensory perception.
    b. specialized cells that transduce physical inputs into neural activity.
    c. hairs in your ears and nose that improve hearing and smell, respectively.
    d. undifferentiated across sensory modalities; visual receptors look just like auditory ones.

3. According to signal detection theory, if you are an air traffic controller
    a. a "miss" is preferred to a "hit."
    b. a "false alarm" is preferred to a "hit."
    c. a "false alarm" is preferred to a "miss."
    d. a "miss" is preferred to a "false alarm."

4. Caroline is sitting in a lab with stereo headphones on, and hears two different stories playing simultaneously in the right and left channels. Caroline is probably a participant in a study of
    a. dichotic listening.
    b. sensory adaptation.
    c. perceptual constancy.
    d. subliminal persuasion.

5. Anika has blue eyes; Jose has brown eyes. The difference in eye color is the result of different pigments in the
    a. cornea.
    b. pupil.
    c. lens.
    d. iris.

6. The process by which the shape of the lens changes to focus on things that are either close by or far away is called
    a. laxity.
    b. constriction.
    c. assimilation.
    d. accommodation.

7. Rods are specialized for _____, whereas cones are specialized for _____.
    a. low light; color vision
    b. color vision; negative afterimages
    c. bright light conditions; dark adaptation
    d. detecting details; detecting overall shapes

8. Hubel and Weisel earned a Nobel Prize for their lifetime work on defining feature detector cells in cats, which
    a. are cells in the retina that fire in response to specific features in the environment.
    b. correspond to human ganglion cells, showing early perceptual decoding in the eye.
    c. detect specific lines and edges, responding to specific length, orientation, and motion.
    d. are clusters of cells distributed in somatosensory cortex that only respond to specific stimuli.

9. The Gestalt principles of organization
   a. are rules that help us to organize elements into something that is complete.
   b. are binocular cues for perceiving three-dimensional objects.
   c. help us to understand the perception of different colors.
   d. illustrate how illusions lead to inaccurate perceptions.

10. If you stand at the edge of a cornfield, the stalks will look coarse close to you and finer if you look into the distance. This phenomenon is called
    a. relative size.
    b. relative motion.
    c. texture gradient.
    d. linear perspective.

11. A person who is blind in one eye uses more _____ cues than _____ cues.
    a. disparity; size
    b. monocular; binocular
    c. convergence; texture
    d. memory; perceptual

12. Depth perception develops
    a. at birth.
    b. as soon as children start to walk.
    c. about the age children start kindergarten.
    d. about the same age as toddlers begin to crawl.

13. In regards to pitch, fast waves produce a _____-pitched sound, and slow waves produce a _____-pitched sound.
    a. high; low
    b. loud; soft
    c. true; fuzzy
    d. deep; shallow

14. The auditory sensory receptor cells are located in the
    a. cochlea.
    b. ossicles.
    c. oval window.
    d. tympanic membrane.

15. As the decibels of a sound increase, the
    a. amplitude increases.
    b. frequency increases.
    c. amplitude decreases.
    d. frequency decreases.

16. A chemical released by one animal that changes the social behavior or another animal is called a
    a. steroid.
    b. pheromone.
    c. testosterone.
    d. photopigment.

17. Katie is going out tonight with a guy she just met and is interested in romantically. To assure herself that he will also be attracted to her, Katie bought a bottle of a new perfume, "FER-O-MOAN," advertised to excite a man's sexual instincts.
    a. Smart Katie. This is a sure way to make this new guy at least show a sexual interest in her.
    b. Silly Katie. Just because she uses the perfume doesn't mean his sexual excitation will be toward her.
    c. Silly Katie. No scientific evidence indicates that pheromone molecules actually "work" with humans.
    d. Smart Katie. Good evidence shows that all mammals, including humans, respond to pheromones.

18. Dennis is sitting in the dentist's chair. As he receives an injection of lidocaine, the dentist jiggles and pulls his cheek near the gum area. The dentist probably does this because
    a. touch messages, sent faster than pain messages, reach the brain first, and reduce the pain messages from the injection.
    b. the anesthetic will spread out more evenly to numb the desired area more quickly.
    c. the anesthetic will spread out and cover a larger area so that less is needed overall.
    d. he wants to distract Dennis from what he is doing, so he will not clench his jaws.

19. Which of the following structures is related to our sense of balance?
    a. Ossicles
    b. Otoliths
    c. Semicircular canals
    d. Basilar membrane

20. Wanda recently had a spell during which she could not keep her balance and kept throwing up. She thought she had food poisoning and went to the Emergency Room. The doctor told her that she had
    a. a middle ear infection—the ossicles could not move freely to transmit messages within the ear.
    b. an outer ear infection and that her ear canal had filled with fluid, putting pressure on the tympanic membrane.
    c. an inner ear infection—her semicircular canals were filled with excess fluid and the otoliths could not respond.
    d. an inner ear infection causing the fluid in her semicircular canals to be spinning wildly out of control.

After completing the test, calculate your percent correct
(/ 20 =   ) x 100 = _____.

How accurate were your expectations? Does your performance suggest the need for additional study?
For the items you missed, go back and identify why the "correct" answer is the best answer.

AFTER YOU READ ... PRACTICE TEST #2

Before beginning this practice test, estimate the percent you expect to get correct.
Anticipated percent correct: _____

1. Amelia is watching TV. When listening to the show, hearing the various sounds of the actors' words would be _____. Interpreting the meaning of these words is an example of _____.
   a. sensation; perception
   b. perception; sensation
   c. assimilation; accommodation
   d. accommodation; assimilation

2. The absolute threshold is
   a. the highest level of perception that can be tolerated.
   b. the highest level of perception that can be responded to.
   c. the lowest level of stimulation that is detected only 50% of the time.
   d. the lowest level of stimulation that can be detected nearly 100% of the time.

3. You are watching an old movie when the sound track offsets from the visual track. The lip movements of the speakers lag behind the words you hear. This is bothersome for you because of
   a. echolocation.
   b. the tritone illusion.
   c. the octave illusion.
   d. the McGurk Effect.

4. Because we organize information into perceptual sets,
   a. we see something like A13C as A-B-C, and not as A-13-C.
   b. we see things as constantly changing in size and color, until it stops moving.
   c. we primarily use incoming sensory information to interpret the world around us.
   d. we can separate our biases and expectations from the processing of a physical stimulus.

5. Antwon is at a family picnic at the beach talking to his cousins near the water's edge. He hears his mother say his name in conversation with her sisters, although she is up by the picnic tables cooking hamburgers. This ability to pick up unattended but personally important information exemplifies the
   a. Ganzfield effect.
   b. cocktail party effect.
   c. von Restorff effect.
   d. illusory placebo effect.

6. The problem with ESP studies is that
   a. people with pure ESP are seldom aware of their ability, and so we miss testing the right people.
   b. ESP has never been documented under strict testing conditions.
   c. laboratory conditions disrupt the flow of psychic energies.
   d. scientists are so skeptical, that they miss the signs of ESP.

7. Hue is simply a more technical name for
   a. color.
   b. intensity.
   c. reflection.
   d. brightness.

8. Visual acuity is sharpest when images are focused on the fovea, which has a high concentration of
   a. rods.
   b. cones.
   c. bipolar cells.
   d. ganglion cells.

9. Light waves are entering your eye. As they do so, they proclaim, "Here we come,
   a. through the pupil, past the lens, through the vitreous, and on to the retina!"
   b. past the lens and through the pupil, through the vitreous and on to the sclera!"
   c. from the retina, through the vitreous, out the lens and the cornea, to freedom, back outside!"
   d. from the ganglion cells, out the vitreous, escaping through the lens, look out world, here we come!"

10. Although the visual sensory receptors are _____, the optic nerve is made up of the axons of the _____.
    a. ganglion cells; fovea
    b. in the lens ; the retina
    c. rods and cones ; ganglion cells
    d. at the blindspot ; rods and cones

11. The point at which the optic nerve exits the eye is the _____ of the eye.
    a. fovea
    b. cornea
    c. blind spot
    d. basilar membrane

12. Kim just put up her Christmas tree and meticulously arranged the lights to form star shapes when they flash sequentially. She steps back in delight to watch the individual lights flash on and off to make the patterns of stars. This kind of motion reflects
    a. motion parallax.
    b. subjective contours.
    c. the psi phenomenon.
    d. the phi phenomenon.

13. The idea that we have three different types of cone cells, each responding to a different wavelength of light, is called
    a. trichromatic theory.
    b. opponent-process theory.
    c. feature detection theory.
    d. RYB (red/yellow/blue) theory.

14. Because of the difference in the images that reach each eye, we receive two slightly different views of the world. This phenomenon is known as
    a. accommodation.
    b. binocular disparity.
    c. interposition.
    d. convergence.

15. _____ is to the frequency of sound waves, as _____ is to the frequency of visually perceived waves.
    a. Pitch; hue
    b. Pitch; timber
    c. Timbre; intensity
    d. Loudness; saturation

16. The primary function of the ossicles is to
    a. assemble sensations into perceptions.
    b. transform sound waves into impulses.
    c. gather sound waves and send them into the middle ear.
    d. pass sound waves from the ear drum to the oval window.

17. Jimmi is walking down the street when she hears someone behind and slightly to her right call her name. She turns and sees her friend waving at her. How did Jimmi know where to look?
    a. Jimmi's past experiences (top-down processing) told her where to look.
    b. Jimmi first saw the waving out of the corner of her eye and then associated the sound with it.
    c. The sound of her name arrived at each ear at slightly different times because of how they are separated on her head.
    d. As sound waves bounce off objects in the environment, they created echoes that Jimmi used to help her locate the sound.

18. Humans can detect
    a. slightly more smells than tastes.
    b. VERY MANY more tastes than smells.
    c. VERY MANY more smells than tastes.
    d. about the same amount of smells and tastes.

19. Smell and taste perception come together when messages from both the olfactory cortex and the gustatory cortex are sent on and reach
    a. the thalamus.
    b. the limbic system.
    c. association cortex.
    d. somatosensory cortex.

20. The vestibular system detects the
    a. chemicals in the air.
    b. pressure on the skin.
    c. position of the head.
    d. direction and distance of sounds.

After completing the test, calculate your percent correct
(/ 20 =   ) x 100 = _____ .

How accurate were your expectations? Does your performance suggest the need for additional study?
For the items you missed, go back and identify why the "correct" answer is the best answer.

AFTER YOU READ . . . PRACTICE TEST ANSWER KEYS

Practice Test 1.

1. d (p. 152)
2. b (p. 153)
3. c (p. 154)
4. a (p. 158)
5. d (p. 163)
6. d (p. 165)
7. a (p. 165-166)
8. c (p. 167)
9. a (p. 168)
10. c (p. 170)
11. b (p. 170-171)
12. d (p. 171)
13. b (p. 176)
14. a (p. 178)
15. a (p. 177)
16. b (p. 182)
17. c (p. 182)
18. a (p. 185)
19. c (p. 188)
20. c (p. 188)

Practice Test 2.

1. a (p. 152)
2. c (p. 153)
3. d (p. 155)
4. a (p. 157)
5. b (p. 159)
6. b (p. 159)
7. a (p. 163)
8. a (p. 163-165)
9. b (p. 165)
10. c (p. 165-166)
11. c (p. 166)
12. d (p. 169)
13. a (p. 170)
14. b (p. 171)
15. a (p. 163, 176)
16. d (p. 178)
17. c (p. 179)
18. c (p. 181)
19. b (p. 182)
20. c (p. 184)

AFTER YOU READ ... CONCEPT MAPPING ACTIVITY ANSWERS

ACTIVITY 1: Here is a list of terms in alphabetical order that you might have included in this concept map.

basilar membrane	muscles	semicircular canals
eye	nasal receptors	skin
free nerve endings	nose	stretch receptors
force detectors	otoliths	tendons
inner ear	papillae	tongue
mechanoreceptors	retina	

ACTIVITY 2: Here is a possible completed concept map.

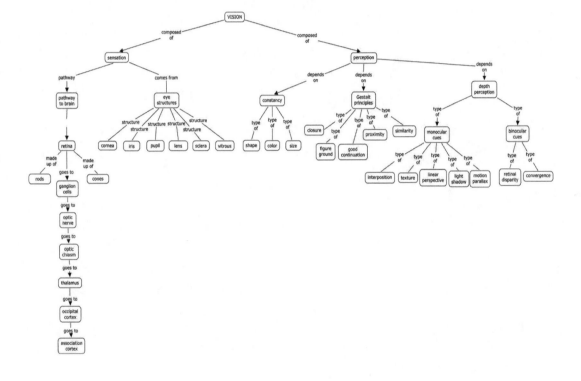

CHAPTER 5

CONSCIOUSNESS
EXPANDING THE BOUNDARIES OF
PSYCHOLOGICAL INQUIRY

BEFORE YOU READ ... CHAPTER PREVIEW

This chapter will introduce you to many different states of consciousness. About a third of our lives is spent asleep, driven by an internal biological clock and reflecting a circadian rhythm. Most young adults, up through about age 25, need an average of 9 hours of sleep per night. After that, adults still need about 7 hours of sleep per night. Many adults don't get the required amount of sleep, and suffer from sleep deprivation and sleep debt, which has many serious mental and physical health risks. Research using electrical recording devices, such as EEG, EOG, and EMG, shows that sleep progresses through a series of five stages. Stage 1 occurs when you first fall asleep, followed by Stage 2, which is a light sleep state in which we spend most of our time asleep. Stages 3 and 4 represent increasingly deep sleep stages that are necessary to feel rested the next day. Stage 5 represents paradoxical or REM sleep, during which we dream. When deprived of sleep, we get to this stage the fastest and spend the most time in. It is a time of elevated brain activity (the brain does *not* rest during sleep); however, muscles may become paralyzed. Various aspects of dreams are consistent across cultures and genders and evidence indicates that even blind people dream—although not with visual imagery if a person has been blind since birth. Most dreams are in color and tend to be more negative than positive. In addition, there are several types of dreams. For example, in lucid dreaming a person becomes aware of the dream and can take control of its outcome. Sleep can be disrupted by various disorders. Insomnia, the most common sleep disorder, is characterized by an overall lack of sleep. It can be caused by many things, such as depression or restless leg syndrome. Short-term psychotherapy including behavioral techniques offers the best treatment; sleeping pills do not. Other sleep disorders include narcolepsy, sleep apnea, night terrors, and sleepwalking.

Several theories and hypotheses try to account for why we dream. The oldest is Freud's theory of wish fulfillment. Freud suggested that dreams have an obvious, manifest content and a hidden, latent content. Research evidence has failed to support Freud's theory. Another theory is called activation-synthesis and suggests that dreams start out as random brain activation that we weave into a meaningful interpretation. Evidence supporting this theory is that particular brain areas are highly active, whereas others are inactive during dreaming, and some neurotransmitters surge, while other shut down. PET scans also show the prefrontal cortex is very active. Another theory of dreaming is called neurocognitive and suggests that our cognitive capacities shape what we dream about. In terms of content, many dreams are associated with emotional concerns and everyday preoccupations. About 50–80% of people report recurrent dreams. Despite the disagreements among scientists, they generally agree an intimate connection occurs between brain activity and dreaming, that acetylcholine turns on REM sleep, and that the forebrain plays an important role in dreams. What scientists don't know is why we dream. We do know that dreams are involved in processing emotional memories, in integrating new experiences with established memories, in learning new strategies and ways of doing things, in simulating threatening events so we can better cope with them in everyday life, and in reorganizing and consolidating memories.

Consciousness is complicated by other findings, such as out-of-body experiences. About 25% of college students report sensations of seeing their bodies from outside of themselves. These experiences appear to be instances of fantasizing, with a momentary loss of connection to the physical self. Similarly, near-death experiences occur in an average of about one-fourth of people who were near death. The reports are often similar, consisting of the sense of a bright light and of floating upward, although some people report negative experiences. People often think it is a mystical experience, but scientists are now able to replicate it in the lab. The bright light and sense of floating apparently results from a release of endorphins when certain brain areas become oxygen starved, and for this reason the experiences have so much in common. Another insight into consciousness comes from déjà vu. More than 66% of all people claim to have had this experience. Another insight into consciousness comes from research into meditation. Of the several types of meditation, all seem to have many positive effects. Related to meditation is what happens during hypnosis. There are many misconceptions about hypnosis. It is a technique to increase suggestibility across a variety of feelings, beliefs, and behaviors. It is not a "trance state" in which "amazing" behaviors can be performed, nor is it unique. It is not a sleeplike state in which people are not aware of their surroundings and forget what happened; and most importantly, it does NOT improve memory—in fact, evidence suggests it may actually lead to false memories. Some researchers believe the hypnotic state occurs because of the expectation that it will occur. The best use of hypnosis has been in clinical practice where it has been shown to help with pain control, but other legitimate uses are questionable.

Psychoactive drugs alter consciousness by changing chemical processes in neurons. As with hypnosis and meditation, there seems to be an expectation effect that either magnifies or reduces the effects of these drugs. Stimulant drugs such as tobacco, cocaine, and amphetamines, including methamphetamine, excite the nervous system. Depressant drugs, which are categorized as either sedative or hypnotic, depress the nervous system. Alcohol is probably the oldest psychoactive drug and is a depressant drug, but can be a stimulant at low doses. Alcohol abuse provides a good example of addiction. Individuals require more and more to reach the same level of intoxication, a condition called "tolerance." When the drug is stopped, individuals suffer from uncomfortable symptoms, called "withdrawal," which can be eliminated by ingesting more alcohol. Furthermore, people who have taken the drug for a long time will experience delirium tremens during withdrawal, a state of disorientation and agitation. Other sedative-hypnotic drugs include the barbiturates, nonbarbiturates, and benzodiazepines. Another category of psychoactive drugs include the opiate narcotics: heroin, morphine, and codeine. These drugs are very effective for controlling pain, but are highly addictive. A final category of drugs includes the psychedelic drugs—drugs that alter perception, mood, and thought. These drugs include marijuana, which has sedative and hypnotic qualities, and is a mild hallucinogen. A more potent hallucinogen is LSD. Even tiny amounts alter our perceptions and consciousness. Although the effects may be simply curious, they can also be extremely unpleasant, producing psychosis-like symptoms.

BEFORE YOU READ ... LEARNING OBJECTIVES

After reading Chapter 5 you should be able to:

5.1 Identify the different stages of sleep and the neural activity and dreaming behaviors that occur in each
5.2 Identify the features and causes of sleep disorders
5.3 Determine how Freud's theory of dreams relate to research evidence on dreaming
5.4 Explain how theories of brain activation attempt to account for dreaming
5.5 Determine how scientists explain seemingly "mystical" alterations in consciousness
5.6 Evaluate the benefits of meditation
5.7 Distinguish myths from realities concerning hypnosis
5.8 Distinguish different types of drugs and their psychological effects on consciousness

---

BEFORE YOU READ ... TERM IDENTIFICATION

activation–synthesis theory (p. 205)
alcohol hallucinosis (p. 221)
biological clock (p. 197)
circadian rhythm (p. 197)
consciousness (p. 196)
déjà vu (p. 210)
delirium (p. 221)
dissociation theory (p. 217)
hallucinogenic (p. 223)
lucid dreaming (p. 201)
insomnia (p. 202)
hypnosis (p. 213)
hypnotic (p. 218)
meditation (p. 212)
mystical experience (p. 225)
narcolepsy (p. 203)
narcotics (p. 223)

near-death experience (NDE) (p. 208)
night terrors (p. 204)
non-REM sleep (p. 199)
out-of-body experience (OBE) (p. 208)
past life regression therapy (p. 215)
psychoactive drugs (p. 218)
rapid eye movements (REM) (p. 198)
REM sleep (p. 199)
restless leg syndrome (p. 203)
sedative (p. 218)
sleep apnea (p. 203)
sleep paralysis (p. 196)
sleepwalking (p. 204)
sociocognitive theory (p. 216)
stimulants (p. 221)
tolerance (p. 220)
withdrawal (p. 220)

AS YOU READ ... PRACTICE ACTIVITIES

THE BIOLOGY OF SLEEP

1.   Consciousness is probably one of the most fundamental human experiences. Without consciousness we'd have little or no cognitive activity. Describe, in your own words, what "consciousness" means to you. (LO 5.1)

2.   What is commonly called the "biological clock" is really a nucleus of neurons. (LO 5.1)

a.   Where is it located?

b.   How many neurons typically make up this nucleus?

c.   Go back to Chapter 3 and remind yourself how many neurons are typically present in the human brain. Calculate the percentage of neurons that are dedicated to maintaining consciousness.

d.   What is the importance of your biological clock being located in the structure you've named, relative to the action of melatonin—and what IS melatonin?

3.   Keep a sleep log for the next week then come back to this item. Answer each question fully, not with a simple "yes" or "no." (LO 5.1 and LO 5.2)

a.   How many hours per night did you sleep?

b.   Did you sleep through the night, or wake up and go back to sleep again?

c.   Was this a typical week for you?

d.   Are you in sleep deprivation?

e.   Are you in sleep debt? (Make sure you know the difference.)

f.   How might this affect your day-to-day life?

g.   Develop a plan of what you will do the next time you find yourself unable to sleep, giving yourself several options. Write out this plan on an index card and place it by your bed.

4.   REM sleep is interesting because of the paradoxical activities that occur. Describe several here and note the reasons why scientists believe these events occur. Were you familiar with some of them before reading your text? Which ones? Were some of the paradoxical events new to you? Which ones? (LO 5.1)

5.   Complete this table for the sleep stages. (LO 5.1)

	Lasts	**Characterized by**
Stage 1		
Stage 2		
Stages 3, 4		
Stage 5		

6.   Go to http://www.sleepnet.com/sleeptest.html where you can take a sleep disorders test. Go ahead and take it! Then you can also play around with different symptoms and see what the test results show. You will see that most sleep disorders do follow closely along the lines described in your text. (LO 5.2)

7.   Complete this table for the disorders of sleep. Describe each disorder in the space provided. (LO 5.2)

Insomnia	
Narcolepsy	
Sleep Apnea	
Night Terrors	
Sleepwalking	

THEORIES AND PSYCHOLOGY OF DREAMS

1.   In Chapter 1, "Introduction," and Chapter 4 "Sensation and Perception," you read about how people have an innate tendency to create order from chaos, for example, seeing images of faces in random patterns, such as the "man in the moon." Which theory of dreaming picks up this theme? Note specific aspects that lead you to this conclusion. (LO 5.3)

2.   Map out the pathway of acetylcholine activation during REM sleep. Note the various brain structures that are involved and how all of this might lead to the experience of a "dream." (LO 5.3)

3.   Different brain areas have been found to be activated during REM sleeping, using different approaches to studying the brain. List the brain areas that are activated and the evidence to support that activation. (LO 5.4)

4. How are children's dreams different from adult dreams in terms of both content and overtones? (LO 5.4)

5. Your text lists several functions of dreams. Summarize them here. (LO 5.4)

OTHER ALTERATIONS OF CONSCIOUSNESS AND UNUSUAL EXPERIENCES

1. Evaluate the quality of the evidence that out-of-body experiences (OBEs) are a "real" experience. (LO 5.5)

2. True or False? All near-death experiences (NDEs) are described as spiritual and pleasant. What is the evidence for your answer? Explain some of the brain's biochemical events that could explain several typical NDE elements, following severe trauma. (LO 5.5)

3. Your text discusses four testable explanations for the déjà vu experience. Summarize them, in your own words, here. (LO 5.5)

4. Compare the two types of meditation described in your text. (LO 5.6)

5. In your own words, list the six commonly held misconceptions about hypnosis. Then briefly suggest evidence that contradicts each misconception. In addition, some known benefits to hypnosis are legitimate. List a few of them here, as well as some cautions about hypnosis. (LO 5.7)

6. Compare the two most accepted models of hypnosis: the sociocognitive and the dissociative. Which model do you favor? Why? (LO 5.7)

DRUGS AND CONSCIOUSNESS

1. Complete this table with the four drug types. For the "Effects" include more details than are included in the table in your text—note specific effects. (LO 5.8)

Drug Type	Effect	Examples

2. Compare the actions of different stimulant drugs. (LO 5.8)

3. Compare the actions of different depressant drugs. (LO 5.8)

4. Using alcohol as a model, describe the signs and symptoms of addiction. (LO 5.8)

5. Table 5.4 lists a number of alcohol-related misconceptions. Which of these have you heard of? Which of these did you believe in? Pick the one you most believed in, then surf the Internet for evidence to disconfirm your belief. Summarize the information from the Web site in your own words. Be sure to include the URL here, as well as a brief review of the quality of the Web site. (LO 5.8)

As You Read ... Concept Map Activities

ACTIVITY 1: This comprehensive map covers many of the basic ideas of the entire chapter. Of course, it could include many more links, and you should feel free to draw in more nodes and label your links after you have completed the existing nodes and links.

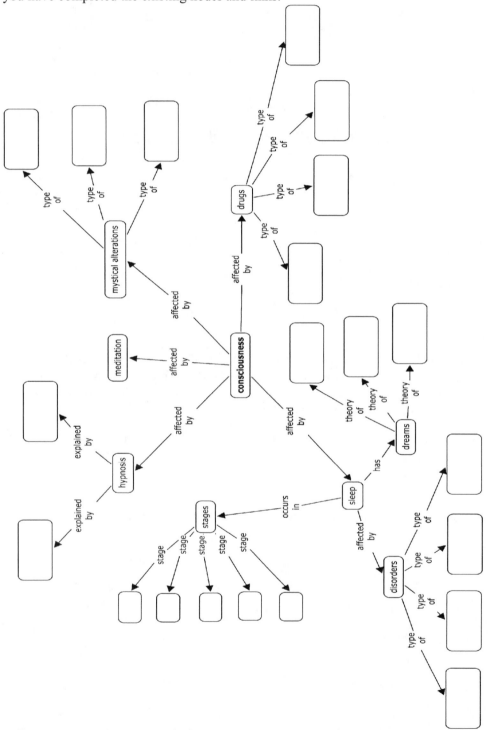

Author activity content supported by *IHMC Cmap Tools* Copyright ©1998-2007 Institute for Human & Machine Cognition

AS YOU READ ... MYTH OR REALITY?

Myth: Some people don't dream.
Reality: All people dream, probably every night, they just don't remember their dreams.

1. We have all met people who tell us they don't dream. Do you know anyone who makes this claim? This statement contradicts the research evidence, starting with an important study by Dement (1978). He noted that all people show REM sleep at various times during the night. Indeed, when he woke people up during REM sleep they consistently reported that they were dreaming.
a. Surf the Internet on your own. You will find a wealth of Web sites devoted to discussions of dreaming. Be sure you review your critical thinking principles and Web-evaluation criteria!
b. Make an argument for why people might not remember their dreams. Although this issue probably has no completely "correct" answer, many hypotheses are certainly available—some better than others.

Myth: Mixing different types of alcoholic beverages, for example, drinking beer and then switching to whiskey, will give you a greater hangover than if you just stick with one type of alcoholic beverage.
Reality: It makes no difference what you are drinking or how you mix your alcohols together. What matters is the overall alcohol content—the more you drink the greater the hangover.

1. Go to http://health.ninemsn.com.au/article.aspx?id=113108 and http://healthlibrary.epnet.com/GetContent.aspx?token=dce59228-1023-4705-b1c7-b407be7b4fc6&chunkiid=156993 and read all about it.

2. Develop an argument you could use to convince your friends, the next time they tell you that mixing different alcoholic beverages, or drinking them in a particular sequence will give you a worse hangover.

AS YOU READ ... PUT YOUR CRITICAL THINKING SKILLS TO THE TEST

1.   Many people believe in biorhythms—the cycling of your physical, emotional, and intellectual well-being. Biorhythm charts can illustrate this concept. Some people monitor the highs and lows of these cycles and plan their lives around them.
a.   Find a Web site where you can calculate your biorhythm chart. Go ahead and calculate it! What did you find out about yourself?
b.   Now evaluate the Web site using the criteria in the start of this Grade Aid. What can you conclude about the overall quality of the Web site?
c. Go to http://skepdic.com/biorhyth.html and read this critique of biorhythms. Does your assessment of the Web site quality, taken together with the skepdic.com entry influence your belief in the accuracy of your "biorhythms"?

2.   Young adults, generally between the ages of 15 and 23, undergo a phase shift in their circadian cycle, called the "Circadian Shift." During this time, young adults are at their peak performance from later in the morning until later at night, compared to other age groups. However, the need for total sleep hours is increased, averaging about 9.2 hours per night.
a.   You can read more about circadian phase shifts and their effects on behavior:
http://www.apa.org/monitor/oct01/sleepteen.html
http://www.sleepfoundation.org/site/pp.aspx?c=huIXKjM0IxF&b=2419155&printmode=1
b.   Keep track of the times of day when you feel you are at your best, and the times of day when you feel you are slowing down. Does your behavior reflect a circadian shift? However, how does your life schedule affect your overall sleep deficit? Do you have early morning classes? Are you able to fall asleep early enough to get your 9 hours of sleep before you get up for school, ON A REGULAR BASIS? If not, what could you do to rearrange your schedule?

3.   In Chapter 1 you read about six principles of critical thinking. Put these skills to the test. Here are three different Web sites with three slightly different, albeit somewhat overlapping, interpretations of what it means to dream about guns. How can you reconcile the differences? Consider the three theories of dreaming presented in your text.
http://www.dreamloverinc.com/g.htm#Guns
http://dreammoods.com/cgibin/searchcsv.pl?method=exact&header=dreamsymbol&search=gun
http://www.dreamhawk.com/dyd-g2.htm#gun

AS YOU READ … MYPSYCHLAB CONNECTION

The Biology of Sleep
Watch the video *Lucid Dreaming*, which covers the physiology of lucid dreaming and how scientists have learned to induce lucid dreaming in a laboratory setting. To review topics such as sleep disorders, **watch** *Robert: Insomnia* the real case of a man suffering from a sleep disorder.

Theories and Psychology of Dreams
Gain a better understanding of the various theories of dreams by utilizing the **explore** *Theories of Dreaming*. Through this explore you can learn more about the psychodynamic, cognitive, and physiological theories of dreams.

Other Alterations of Consciousness and Unusual Experiences
Learning about hypnosis? Check out the **simulation** *Hypnosis*, where you can experience an induction method used in hypnosis. Not only will you receive hands-on experience on how one is inducted into the hypnotic state, but this activity will also help dispel the myths of hypnosis by allowing you to think critically about what actually constitutes the hypnotic state. So why do people become hypnotized? In trying to understand hypnosis, you may also wish to **watch** the video *Hypnosis*.

Drugs and Consciousness
When reviewing how drugs and alcohol affect consciousness and behavior, check out the **explore** *Behavioral Effects Associated with Various Blood Alcohol Levels*. When learning about drugs and consciousness, **watch** the video *Kathy: Substance Abuse*. This video features a real case study of a woman who has a history of abusing substances and talks about the deleterious effects that the substances have had on her everyday life.

AFTER YOU READ ... PRACTICE TEST #1

Before beginning this practice test, estimate the percent you expect to get correct.
Anticipated percent correct: _____

1. On average, about _____ of college students experience sleep paralysis, accompanied by feelings of anxiety or terror, feeling vibrations, or hearing humming noises.
    a. 10% to 25%   c. 60% to 75%
    b. 33% to 50%   d. 75% to 90%

2. Surveys show that on average, college students only sleep about _____ hours per night, accumulating a 3-hour per night sleep deficit.
    a. 6   c. 9
    b. 7   d. 11

3. Sleep deprivation can lead to
    a. weight loss.   c. poor learning in school.
    b. excess non-REM sleep.   d. increased risk of low blood pressure.

4. Hypnagogic imagery refers to
    a. the dream-like images of stage 1 sleep.
    b. the vivid images of stage 5 (REM) sleep.
    c. images induced during hypnosis.
    d. the images present in lucid dreaming.

5. The most important sleep stage, so you wake up feeling rested the next day, includes
    a. stages 1 and 2.   c. stages 3 and 4.
    b. stage 2.   d. stage 5 (REM).

6. The most important sleep stage, from another perspective seems to be
    a. stage 1 sleep because deprivation makes it difficult to fall asleep, so less time is spent in any of the other sleep stages.
    b. stage 5 (REM)—when animals or people are sleep-deprived they get into REM sleep more quickly and spend more time in REM sleep than they would otherwise.
    c. stage 2 (light sleep)—when sleep-deprived, humans and animals spend almost all of their time in Stage 2 sleep, maybe only going through the full cycle once, after several hours.
    d. stage 3 or 4 deep sleep—when animals or people are sleep-deprived they get into Stages 3 and 4 sleep more quickly and spend more time in deep sleep than they would otherwise.

7. Many dreams have negative and aggressive themes, so researchers train people to control dream content during times that they are aware of dreaming. This awareness of dreaming is called
    a. light dreaming.   c. aware dreaming.
    b. lucid dreaming.   d. awake dreaming.

8. Milana recently traveled to a wedding 7 time zones from her home, and when she got back her boyfriend broke up with her. She is now having trouble sleeping. Because you are her good friend you advise her to
a. take a brisk run around the block to tire herself out.
b. turn up the thermostat so the room is nice and warm, or even hot.
c. get up and sit in a chair and read a novel until she really can't stay awake any more.
d. have a cup of hot coffee or tea because the warm liquid in her stomach will help her fall asleep.

9. REM dreams differ from non-REM dreams in that non-REM dreams
a. are more thought-like and repetitive.
b. are more illogical.
c. show more "plot" shifts.
d. are more emotional.

10. Jose's wife complains that his snoring and frequent turning over in his sleep are keeping her awake at night. Yet Jose insists that he sleeps well, despite often feeling tired in the morning. Jose probably suffers from
a. insomnia.
b. narcolepsy.
c. night terrors.
d. sleep apnea.

11. According to Freud, dreams have two aspects. The actual content of the dream is called _____ content, and the hidden, underlying meaning is called the _____ content.
a. outer; inner
b. overt; covert
c. manifest; latent
d. external; internal

12. While asleep, Kendra's brain is busy. As acetylcholine surges, and activates brain stem areas, random messages are sent to the thalamus and relayed throughout the cortex. As she enters Stage 5 sleep, Kendra has a dream of talking to friends in class. This process reflects the _____ theory of dreaming.
a. neurocognitive
b. wish fulfillment
c. dream protection
d. activation-synthesis

13. Near-death experiences (NDEs) are not a purely biological phenomenon because evidence shows that
a. they are spiritually bound.
b. they are influenced by culture.
c. they have never been reported by neither agnostics nor atheists.
d. they provide a glimpse into the afterlife, suggesting a religious component.

14. John was in an accident and was seriously injured. He tells his friends that he felt his consciousness leave his body, and he watched from above as the doctors worked on him. He saw his deceased grandparents were there, smiling at him and the pain went away. Then, as the doctors finished working on him his consciousness returned to his body. John experienced a(n)
a. NREM dream.
b. déjà vu experience.
c. hypnotic regression.
d. near-death experience.

15. Reports of déjà vu experiences are
a. very rare, about 5%.
b. very common, about 85%.
c. somewhat uncommon, about 35%.
d. more common than not, about 65%.

16. You are a movie reviewer for a local newspaper and just saw a film in which stage show volunteers were given specific posthypnotic suggestions to rob jewelry stores and mail the jewels to the hypnotist. You title your review,
a. "Entertaining, and Realistic!"
b. "Plot Follows Known Research Evidence."
c. "Entertaining, But Goes Against the Known Facts."
d. "A 'How-To' for Getting Rich Quickly and Safely."

17. One problem for sociocognitive theories of hypnosis is that they
a. fail to specify the role of the "hidden observer."
b. can't explain why a belief in reincarnation interferes with past life regression.
c. fail to account for why some people are simply not responsive to hypnotic suggestions.
d. can't explain why people's level of suggestibility is unresponsive to changes in attitudes and beliefs about hypnosis.

18. Alcohol is primarily a
a. psychedelic.
b. stimulant.
c. anesthetic.
d. depressant.

19. The most powerful natural stimulant is
a. cocaine.
b. alcohol.
c. amphetamine.
d. methamphetamine.

20. Jasmine says she will never smoke marijuana because it leads to the use of other stronger and more addictive drugs. You tell Jasmine that
a. she is right. Good research evidence suggests that marijuana is a gateway drug.
b. she might be right, but the direction of cause and effect has not been established; and other reasons perhaps explain why some people start out with marijuana and move on to more potent drugs.
c. she is wrong. The research evidence clearly contradicts Jasmine's beliefs; in fact, in studies of addicts, the direction of progression was TO marijuana, not FROM it.
d. she is right. Even though you know that no research evidence supports Jasmine's belief, you figure it's best if Jasmine doesn't take any chances that way.

After completing the test, calculate your percent correct
(/ 20 =   ) x 100 = _____.

How accurate were your expectations? Does your performance suggest the need for additional study? For the items you missed, go back and identify why the "correct" answer is the best answer.

AFTER YOU READ ... PRACTICE TEST #2

Before beginning this practice test, estimate the percent you expect to get correct:
Anticipated percent correct: _____

1. Janelle has recently started therapy because she believes that she has been visited by aliens who held her down and examined her, usually right after she fell asleep, or just before she woke up. Her therapist, who is a scientific psychologist, explains that
a. she probably suffers from night terrors.
b. she probably suffers from sleep paralysis.
c. she was in a state of paradoxical sleep and dreamed it.
d. she was probably sexually abused by a family member.

2. As a young adult college student, to function at your best, you should be getting _____ hours of sleep per night to be fully alert each day.
a. 6
b. 7
c. 9
d. 11

3. During stage 1 sleep many people experience a sudden feeling of falling. Research shows
a. most people who die in their sleep experience this falling sensation but fail to wake before they "land."
b. it is a normal muscle contraction event present in stage 1 sleep.
c. these people are more suggestible and hypnotizable.
d. it is strongly associated with sleep apnea.

4. We spend most of our time asleep, about _____ %, in stage 2 sleep.
a. 25
b. 45
c. 65
d. 85

5. We spend the least time in REM sleep _____ in an entire night's sleep cycle, and more _____ in the sleep cycle.
a. early and late; midway
b. midway; early and late
c. late; early
d. early; late

6. Whether a person is dreaming in San Diego or Moscow or anywhere else they are likely to have
a. dreams that are more negative than positive.
b. dreams that are more positive than negative.
c. more aggressive dreams if they are men, but more positive dreams if they are women.
d. more aggressive dreams if they are women, but more positive dreams if they are men.

7. Sophie is having trouble falling sleep, and once she does, she often wakes up after a couple of hours and can't get back to sleep. Sophie most likely suffers from
a. insomnia.
b. narcolepsy.
c. night terrors.
d. prefrontal lobe dysfunction.

8. People with narcolepsy
a. usually fall asleep if they remain calm for too long.
b. go directly into REM sleep, suggesting their sleep cycle is disordered.
c. will fall asleep for about an hour at a time but then wake up feeling refreshed.
d. have a good response to caffeine, and can stave off attacks during working hours by taking caffeine pills.

9. If someone is sleepwalking you should
a. wake them up and tell them to go back to bed.
b. NEVER wake them up because doing so can be dangerous.
c. suggest psychotherapy because it is a sign of underlying problems.
d. ask them what they are dreaming about because REM sleep triggers acting out the dreams.

10. Research tests of Freud's wish fulfillment and dream protection explanations of dreams failed to find
a. negative content; most people's dreams are primarily positive.
b. much sexual content—only 10% of dreams are sexual in nature.
c. frequent nightmares, which Freud predicted should occur regularly.
d. common events; about 90% of dreams reflect bizarre themes in disguise.

11. According to PET scan studies, the _____ can be important for dreaming; whereas studies of brain damaged patients suggest the _____ can be important.
a. forebrain; limbic system
b. brainstem areas; frontal cortex
c. prefrontal cortex; parietal lobes
d. deep frontal areas; occipital lobes

12. Reports of out-of-body experiences are
a. very rare (about 2%).
b. very common (about 90%).
c. more common than not (about 60%).
d. slightly more uncommon than common (about 35%).

13. As finals approach, Kareem has been studying day and night. He is under intense pressure to raise his grades to keep his scholarship. He tells you how earlier, while in the library studying, he felt himself "float" over himself and "saw" himself studying. This experience frightened him, but you tell him not to worry
a. at least 90% of the population reports experiencing an OBE.
b. he can now develop this ability and will be able to have astral projections.
c. as long as he doesn't "fall" while he is above himself, he will be in no danger during such experiences.
d. high stress, such as he is under right now, is related to increased reports of out-of-body experiences (OBEs).

14. Near-death experiences (NDEs) are really misnamed because they can also occur with
a. alcohol intoxication.
b. NREM state dreams.
c. electrical stimulation of the temporal lobes.
d. rapidly rising to the surface from a deep underwater dive.

15. River wants to increase his creativity and sense of tranquility. To achieve this state, he has enrolled in a course of transcendental meditation that costs $125. You advise River that
a. it is a great investment in his future! You get what you pay for in this case.
b. research suggests he can achieve these benefits, but he doesn't need to lay out $125 for a specific course—he can do it himself.
c. no scientific evidence shows that meditation can help with creativity and a sense of tranquility, so he should save his money.
d. although he might achieve some tranquility, he can do the same thing for free by sitting quietly; however, no evidence indicates that his creativity can be enhanced.

16. Hypnosis can be accurately portrayed as
a. a sleep-like state.
b. an altered state during which amazing feats are possible.
c. increasing people's confidence for memories recalled under hypnosis.
d. an aid to increasing memory accuracy for repressed traumatic events in the past.

17. The psychoactive drug that has probably been used for the longest time by humans is
a. alcohol.
b. cocaine.
c. marijuana.
d. mescaline.

18. Omar, who is 6' tall and weighs 200 pounds, and Deolinda, who is 5'2" and weighs 110, are at a bar. They each drink 3 beers in an hour. Who is drunker?
a. Deolinda; because BAC is affected by body mass, and Deolinda simply has less of it.
b. Omar; because he has less lean body mass, and will not metabolize the alcohol as well.
c. Omar; because beer has less effect on women, who are more sensitive to hard liquor.
d. Deolinda; because women's expectations result in their becoming drunk on smaller amounts of alcohol.

19. Mary bought some white powder from a friend and "snorted" it. Soon afterwards she felt a calm, pleasant feeling. This effect can probably be attributed to
a. the psychoactive effects of the drug producing her feeling.
b. her mental set probably overriding the psychoactive properties of the drug.
c. any psychoactive effects of the drug along with her expectations of how she will feel.
d. her friend substituting something else because snorting a white powder should have resulted in a stimulant buzz.

20. Cocaine is legitimately used as a(n)
a. hallucinogen.
b. anesthetic.
c. narcotic.
d. sedative.

After completing the test, calculate your percent correct
(/ 20 =   ) x 100 = _____.

How accurate were your expectations? Does your performance suggest the need for additional study? For the items you missed, go back and identify why the "correct" answer is the best answer.

AFTER YOU READ . . . PRACTICE TEST ANSWER KEYS

Practice Test 1.

1. b (p.196)
2. a (p. 198)
3. c (p. 198)
4. a (p. 199)
5. c (p. 199)
6. b (p. 200)
7. b (p. 202)
8. c (p. 202)
9. a (p. 200–201)
10. d (p. 203)
11. c (p. 205)
12. d (p. 206)
13. b (p. 209–210)
14. d (p. 209)
15. d (p. 210)
16. c (p. 213–214)
17. c (p. 216–217)
18. d (p. 218)
19. a (p. 221)
20. b (p. 224)

Practice Test 2.

1. b (p. 196)
2. c (p. 198)
3. b (p. 199)
4. c (p. 199)
5. a (p. 199–200)
6. d (p. 201)
7. a (p. 202)
8. b (p. 203)
9. a (p. 204)
10. b (p. 205)
11. c (p. 206)
12. d (p. 208)
13. d (p. 209)
14. c (p. 209–210)
15. b (p. 212)
16. c (p. 215)
17. a (p. 218)
18. a (p. 219)
19. c (p. 219–220)
20. b (p. 221)

AFTER YOU READ ... CONCEPT MAPPING ACTIVITY ANSWERS

ACTIVITY 1: For this map you should have included the following terms, listed here in alphabetical order.

activation-synthesis	neurocognitive	sociocognitive
depressants	night terrors	stimulants
déjà vu	opiates	1
dissociation	out-of-body experiences	2
dream protection	psychedelics	3
insomnia	REM	4
narcolepsy	sleep apnea	
near-death experiences	sleep walking	

CHAPTER 6
LEARNING
HOW NURTURE CHANGES US

BEFORE YOU READ ... CHAPTER PREVIEW

Learning is defined as a change in an organism's behavior or thoughts as a result of experience. It is fundamental to everything else we do. Habituation is the simplest form of learning. It allows us to keep from becoming overloaded with stimulation from the environment and is seen in the most basic life forms. Eric Kandel, who won a Nobel Prize for his work with a very simple organism, the sea slug *Aplysia,* discovered much of what we know about learning, including habituation, and its opposite, sensitization.

The British Associationists were the first to systematically examine learning. They noted that stimuli come to be connected together. In modern times, this association is best seen in the work of the Russian physiologist, Ivan Pavlov, who studied digestion in dogs. He noticed that the dogs often started to salivate before being fed. The process by which the dogs learned to anticipate food is now called classical conditioning. A neutral stimulus comes to elicit a conditioned response (CR)—a response that is similar to a naturally occurring, unconditioned response (UCR). Thereby, the neutral stimulus becomes a conditioned stimulus (CS) when it is paired with an unconditioned stimulus (UCS) that naturally elicits a UCR. Many classically conditioned responses help assure our survival; for example, with taste aversion we learn to avoid certain foods that make us sick. A CR becomes extinguished when we stop pairing the CS with the UCS, so that the connection between the two is lost. Spontaneous recovery of the CR can occur, however, when we are again put in the situation in which the original conditioning occurred. However, without continued pairing of the CS and UCS, it will quickly reextinguish. Sometimes a CR occurs to a stimulus that is very similar to the original CS, a process called stimulus generalization. At other times the CS is seen as clearly distinct from other stimuli and therefore the CR occurs only to that CS, and not to other stimuli in the environment, a process called discrimination. A new CS can also be created by pairing an old CS with a new CS. This process is called higher-order conditioning because it goes beyond the initial ordering of events of the CS predicting the UCS. A good example can be seen in addictive behaviors, where just being in a situation in which a behavior, such as smoking, was frequently engaged in, will elicit the craving for a cigarette, although seeing cigarettes in other situations will not do so. Many additional applications of classical conditioning to everyday life include the acquisition of fears and phobias (as seen in the classic case of "Little Albert"), in disgust reactions, and in advertising.

Another type of conditioning is called operant conditioning. Instead of depending on a stimulus that naturally elicits a reflex response, operant conditioning depends on the consequences of behaviors. Positive consequences strengthen behavior, and negative consequences weaken it. Although classical conditioning depends on natural responses of the nervous system, with operant conditioning, almost any behavior can be learned and maintained. A prominent psychologist, important to the history of operant conditioning, was B. F. Skinner. Using a Skinner Box, he recorded the behaviors of animals following different consequences. Reinforcement always increases behavior, and can be a reward or the taking away of something unpleasant. This action is different from punishment, which involves either giving an unpleasant stimulus or taking away something pleasant. Research shows that reinforcement is more effective than punishment for changing behavior. Acquisition, extinction, spontaneous recovery, and stimulus generalization and discrimination are all found in operant conditioning. Stop rewarding or punishing a behavior and the conditioning effect will wane. Use similar reinforcers, and generalization will occur; discrimination will occur to dissimilar reinforcers. Reinforcement can be continuous or partial, and can be given consistently based either on time or on the number of times a behavior is performed, or it can be given inconsistently, on average over a set amount of time or the average of a number of times a behavior is performed. These different schedules of partial reinforcement result in different patterns of responding. One last aspect of acquisition is that behaviors need to be shaped, and do not occur spontaneously, as with classical conditioning. The principles of operant conditioning can help you be a better student. For example, instead of doing something you like to do often and a lot, first do what you would rather not be doing (such as studying) and then reward yourself with the more desirable activity. Another good everyday example is that operant conditioning can explain superstitious behaviors: you did something that was followed by a positive outcome, and now you repeat the initial behavior, anticipating again the positive outcome. So called "token economies" take advantage of using secondary reinforcers, such as tokens, or stars, which a person can accumulate to earn desired rewards. Finally, applied behavior analysis is used with many disabilities in which reward systems are set up to encourage desired behaviors. In considering how operant and classical conditioning differ, one interesting new finding is that they are each mediated by different brain areas. Also notable is that often BOTH operant and classical conditioning work together to maintain behaviors, especially unwanted behaviors such as phobias, where a physiological reflex response accompanies the external presentation of a stimulus, and which is diminished by escaping or avoiding the phobic stimulus.

Cognitive models of learning are also important to consider. Whereas strict models of conditioning are called stimulus-response (S-R) models, cognitive models are often called S-O-R models because they take into account the organism's assessment of a stimulus. An early challenge to S-R models came from Edward Tolman, who talked about "latent learning," learning that can't be demonstrated to come from a specific stimulus. A second type of learning is called observational learning because it occurs from simply watching others do a task, or from watching the consequences others receive for a particular behavior. An early researcher in this area was Albert Bandura who showed that children can learn to act aggressively by watching others act aggressively. In more recent years similar studies have examined the effects of media violence on real-world aggression with similar conclusions. Another type of learning documented by Wolfgang Kohler, a Gestalt psychologist, involves insight—the sudden "aha" feeling when a solution to a problem suddenly comes to us after other strategies have failed.

In recent years, a focus has been on the biological influences on learning. For example, in "conditioned taste aversion" we learn to strongly dislike foods whose eating is followed by illness—even if the food itself was safe and clean. Such a strong form of learning often occurs after just one instance of illness and remains for a long time. This taste aversion has been a problem for patients undergoing chemotherapy, for example. Another important biological aspect of conditioning concerned preparedness—a predisposition to respond a certain way to some stimuli. Preparedness is also related to the concept of instinctive drift, which is characterized by great difficulty in trying to operationally condition some behaviors based on an organism's predisposition to respond in certain ways to environmental stimuli.

Finally, it is important to consider learning fads. One such fad is "sleep-assisted learning" where learning is supposed to occur during sleep. Not only have scientific studies shown that this kind of learning is not possible, but if it were possible, it would have a long history of helping us to learn. Another fad concerns "accelerated learning" where a number of diverse techniques are supposed to help people learn more quickly. As with sleep-assisted learning, the scientific studies have not supported any of these methods. In educational circles "discovery learning" has been promoted. It requires students to teach themselves deep scientific principles based on their own inquiries. An assessment of discovery learning shows that the solutions to problems that students generate in this way are more often incorrect than correct, and are never corrected by the teacher, leading to life-long misconceptions. A final area to consider is that of "learning styles." Here again, the research evidence is clear: no scientific evidence supports the notion that students learn better when provided with one type of material versus another and furthermore, might delay students' effective learning in a different mode.

BEFORE YOU READ ... LEARNING OBJECTIVES

After reading Chapter 6 you should be able to:

6.1   Describe examples of classical conditioning and discriminate conditioned stimuli and responses from unconditioned stimuli and responses

6.2   Explain how conditioned responses are acquired, maintained, and extinguished

6.3   Explain how complex behaviors can result from classical conditioning and how they emerge in our daily lives

6.4   Describe how behaviors are acquired through operant conditioning

6.5   Identify the similarities and differences between operant and classical conditioning

6.6   Describe reinforcement and its effects on behavior

6.7   Distinguish negative reinforcement from punishment as influences on behavior

6.8   Outline the evidence that supports learning in the absence of conditioning

6.9   Explain how learning can occur through observation

6.10   Identify evidence of insight learning

6.11   Explain how biological predispositions can facilitate learning of some associations

6.12   Evaluate popular techniques marketed to enhance learning

6.13   Determine whether individuals' learning ability depends on how well the instructional style matches their learning styles

---

BEFORE YOU READ ... TERM IDENTIFICATION

acquisition (p. 236)

classical (Pavlovian or respondent) conditioning (p. 234)

cognitive maps (p. 257)

conditioned response (CR) (p. 235)

conditioned stimulus (CS) (p. 234)

discriminant stimulus (S_dA) (p. 247)

equipotentiality (p. 262)

extinction (p. 236)

fetishism (p. 240)

fixed interval (FI) schedule (p. 248)

fixed ratio (FR) schedule (p. 248)

habituation (p. 233)

higher-order conditioning (p. 238)

insight (p. 244)

instinctive drift (p. 264)

latent inhibition (p. 238)

latent learning (p. 256)

law of effect (p. 244)

learning (p. 232)

learning styles (p. 267)

mirror neurons (p. 261)

negative reinforcement (p. 244)

observational learning (p. 257)

operant conditioning (p. 242)

partial reinforcement (p. 248)

phobias (p. 237)

positive reinforcement (p. 244)

Premack principle (p. 251)

preparedness (p. 263)

primary reinforcers (p. 253)

pseudoconditioning (p. 241)

punishment (p. 245)

reinforcement (p. 244)

renewal effect (p. 237)

schedule of reinforcement (p. 248)

secondary reinforcers (p. 253)

shaping by successive approximations (shaping) (p. 250)

Skinner box (p. 244)

spontaneous recovery (p. 237)

stimulus discrimination (p. 237)

stimulus generalization (p. 237)

unconditioned response (UCR) (p. 235)

unconditioned stimulus (UCS) (p. 235)

variable interval (VI) schedule (p. 249)

variable ratio (VR) schedule (p. 249)

AS YOU READ ... PRACTICE ACTIVITIES

CLASSICAL CONDITIONING

1.   Discriminate between habituation and sensitization. What do these processes suggest about learning? (LO 6.1)

2.   Go to http://nobelprize.org/educational_games/medicine/pavlov/ and condition a dog to salivate. Did you earn your certificate? (LO 6.1)

3.   Provide an original example of how a behavior could be classically conditioned—do not use one from your text or lecture. Show all the steps of how the conditioning occurs and identify the unconditioned stimulus, conditioned stimulus, unconditioned response, and conditioned response. (LO 6.1)

4.   Compare and contrast acquisition with spontaneous recovery. (LO 6.1)

5.   Draw an analogy between the predictive nature of a conditioned response in eliciting a conditioned response, to the nature of a positive correlation between two variables. (LO 6.1)

6.   Your text discusses the difficulty of backward conditioning. Develop a hypothesis of why this might be, and suggest a way to test your hypothesis. (LO 6.2)

7.   Beer commercials often show people having a good time.
   a.   Discuss how the marketing companies are taking advantage of higher-order conditioning.

   b.   Discuss how their plan could fail on account of latent inhibition. (LO 6.3)

8.	In the famous case of Little Albert, Watson and Reyner (1920) showed how phobias can be classically conditioning. Describe this study in terms of the following criteria. (LO 6.3)

Design

Findings

Lesson learned

OPERANT CONDITIONING

1.	Describe the critical aspect of operant conditioning, and provide an original example that highlights that aspect of the conditioning process. (LO 6.4)

2.	Go to https://pantherfile.uwm.edu/johnchay/PL06/OC/OC.html and have some fun conditioning a pigeon. Examine the effects of different schedules of reinforcement and be sure to extinguish your pigeon's pecking behavior before you leave! (LO 6.4)

3.	Complete this table to help distinguish between classical and operant conditioning. (LO 6.5)

	Classical Conditioning	Operant Conditioning
Target behavior is		
Reward is		
Behavior is produced because		

4.   Describe Thorndike's original study on the law of effect. (LO 6.5)

Design:

Findings:

Lesson learned:

5.   Complete the following table. Be sure to use your own, ORIGINAL example from your everyday life. (LO 6.6)

	Definition	Effect on Behavior	Original Example
Positive Reinforcement			
Negative Reinforcement			

6.   Match each scenario to the type of consequence. (LO 6.7)

Students come to class unprepared to discuss assigned readings. The professor cancels class and sends them to the library to read. The rest of the semester they show up prepared for discussions.

a.   negative reinforcement

You forget to replace the batteries in your smoke alarm. As the batteries start to drain the smoke alarm goes off with an ear-splitting buzzer. You subsequently replace the batteries every time you change your clocks for daylight savings time.

b.   positive reinforcement

You spend hours in the library researching original sources for your term paper, rather than limiting yourself to the ones you can easily access online. Your teacher is impressed with the depth of your review and assigns you an A on the paper. You now do in-library research for all your papers.

c.   punishment

d.   punishment

Your roommate leaves his/her dirty underwear lying around in the common bathroom in your dorm suite. You throw it away in disgust. Your roommate now takes the dirty underwear back to his/her room.

7.   Complete this table with important concepts in both classical and operant conditioning. Make sure your definitions can fit either classical or operant conditioning and that your examples are original and indicate whether it is drawn from classical or operant principles of conditioning. (LO 6.4)

Term	Definition	Example
Acquisition		
Extinction		
Spontaneous Recovery		
Stimulus Generalization		
Stimulus Discrimination		

8.   Describe one of your own superstitious behaviors you have now, or have engaged in, in the past. Discuss how that behavior might have been reinforced. (LO 6.4)

9.   Differentiate between primary and secondary reinforcers. Which do you think will maintain a behavior for a longer time, and why? (LO 6.4)

10.   Complete this table indicating the effect on behavior of each partial reinforcement schedule. (LO 6.6)

	RATIO	INTERVAL
FIXED		
VARIABLE		

11.   The first year after negotiating a high salary contract, many athletes have an "off year" in their sport, leaving many fans criticizing the high salary. Explain the athlete's behavior in terms of the effects of a fixed interval reinforcement schedule on behavior. (LO 6.6)

12.   How does the gambler's fallacy explain the reasoning behind why people tend to buy many lottery tickets as the jackpot goes up? (LO 6.6)

COGNITIVE MODELS OF LEARNING

1.   Discuss how Tolman's (1932) studies on latent learning opened the door for "thinking" to be considered essential to learning by addressing the following aspects of his study. (LO 6.8)

Design:

Findings:

Lesson learned:

2.   Discuss these important aspects of Albert Bandura's studies of observational learning of aggression. (LO 6.9)

Design:

Findings:

Lesson learned:

3.   The evidence linking aggression and the amount of time spent watching violent TV is primarily correlational. Despite this evidence, many psychological scientists believe the link is a causal one. Discuss the reasons for this belief. (LO 6.9)

4.   Insight learning is often accompanied by the "aha" feeling when the solution to a problem you have been unable to solve for a while finally comes to you. Describe such an occurrence in your own life. (LO 6.10)

BIOLOGICAL INFLUENCES ON LEARNING

1.   What are the three ways in which conditioned taste aversion differs from other types of classical conditioning? (LO 6.11)

2.   Consider each of the three ways that conditioned taste aversion differs from other types of conditioning in terms of their survival benefits. (LO 6.11)

3.   Connect the concepts of "equipotentiality" and "belongingness." (LO 6.11)

4.   Your text suggests that dog phobias cannot be completely explained in terms of classical conditioning and therefore probably have a genetic component. Think of an alternative explanation, based on experience, that might foster a dog phobia in some people, and not in others. (LO 6.11)

LEARNING FADS: DO THEY WORK?

1.   In considering sleep-assisted learning, accelerated, and discovery learning, why do you believe people are willing to spend their time and money on trying such programs? Consider several biases in decision making when answering this question. (LO 6.12)

2.   What is a major confound that has not been considered in studies of sleep-assisted learning? How could you control for this confound? (LO 6.12)

3.   Most students have experienced some form of "discovery learning" in their classes. Think of an example from your own education in which a teacher allowed you to come up with your own conclusions. Did the teacher also provide direct instruction along with the discovery learning to help you reach a correct solution? (LO 6.12)

4.   Do you find the distinction between analytic and holistic approaches to learning to be very clear? In what ways is it clear and in what ways would you like to know more? (LO 6.13)

As You Read ... Concept Map Activities

ACTIVITY 1: Complete this concept map as an overview of different learning and conditioning models.

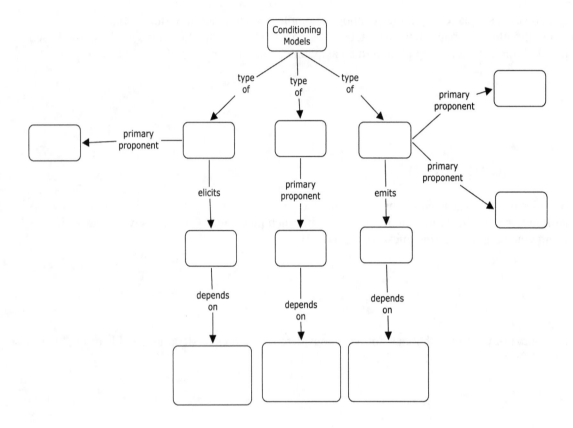

Author activity content supported by *IHMC Cmap Tools* Copyright ©1998-2007 Institute for Human & Machine Cognition

ACTIVITY 2: Complete this concept map for classical conditioning with an example from your own life.

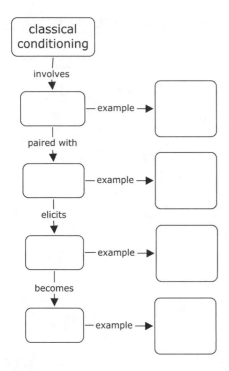

Author activity content supported by *IHMC Cmap Tools* Copyright ©1998-2007 Institute for Human & Machine Cognition

Chapter 6 Learning

ACTIVITY 3: Complete this concept map for operant conditioning reinforcement schedules.

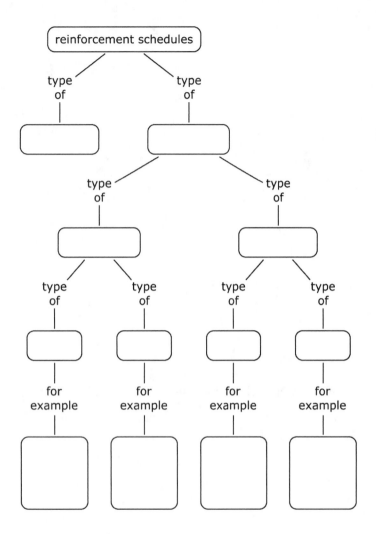

AS YOU READ ... MYTH OR REALITY?

Myth: Spare the rod and spoil the child.
Reality: Punishment is not as effective at long-range behavior change, as is reinforcement.

Many people believe that punishment is almost necessary for raising children properly. Others believe that any form of physical punishment, no matter how mild, constitutes abuse and creates a potential for future aggression in the child.
1.   Reread page 246 in your text and synthesize the arguments both in favor of and against physical punishment.
2.   Which side are you more inclined to side with? Why?

Myth: People have distinct learning styles, such as auditory, visual, or kinesthetic, and it is best if they tailor their learning environments to match their style.
Reality: No scientific evidence supports this hypothesis, and, in fact, because students have to interact in a world that is multifaceted, it is to their advantage to learn by all the different possible styles.

1.   First write down what you honestly believe to be your primary learning style: Auditory learners prefer to learn through hearing the spoken word. Kinesthetic learners prefer to learn through doing, touching, and interacting. Visual learners prefer to learn by examining images, demonstrations, and body language.
2.   Go to the following three Web sites and complete each learning style inventory and note your style in terms of verbal, auditory, or kinesthetic—you may need to surf around the Web site for some of them to find how to "translate" your scores into these criteria:

http://www.usd.edu/trio/tut/ts/style.html
Resulted in learning style _____

http://www.calstatela.edu/faculty/jshindl/plsi/taketest.htm
Resulted in learning style _____

http://www.vark-learn.com/english/page.asp?p=questionnaire
Resulted in learning style _____

3.   How did you do? Did you get the same analysis from each Web site? If not, why do you think that might be so? Did your answer to question 1 match the analysis in question 2? If not, why do you that what you intuitively thought about yourself did not match what the questionnaires suggested?

AS YOU READ ... PUT YOUR CRITICAL THINKING SKILLS TO THE TEST

---

1.   You have a close friend who is having trouble with test anxiety. Although she studies hard and knows the material, she often performs poorly on exams. How can you help your friend to overcome her test anxiety and really perform to the best of her ability?
a.   By examining the classically conditioned responses that maintain her test anxiety
b.   By examining the law of effect and the principles of operant conditioning that maintain her test anxiety in terms of schedules of reinforcement and both primary and secondary reinforcers
c.   By examining cognitive models of learning

2.   Drugs, such as Antabuse, are often used to help people with a substance abuse disorder, in this case, alcohol abuse, stop drinking. These drugs act by inducing severe vomiting whenever alcohol is consumed. Consider how the effects of such drugs might continue long after the drugs have been stopped, in helping people to avoid drinking alcohol.

3.   Central to understanding everyday applications of conditioning models is an understanding of several practical aspects of conditioning. To help you better understand this concept:

a.   Develop a relationship between the concepts of "preparedness" and "instinctive drift." In some ways these two concepts overlap, and other ways they are distinct. Think of an original example for each.
b.   Each of these concepts also provides evidence against the assumption of equipotentiality. Develop these lines of evidence.

As You Read ... MyPsychLab Connection

Classical Conditioning

Explore *Classical Conditioning of Little Albert* to see how this classic study used the principles of conditioning to learn a phobia. Review the process of classical conditioning with the **explore** *Three Stages of Classical Conditioning*. Once an organism learns to have a response to one stimulus, will they respond that way to similar stimuli? Find out by reviewing the **explore** *Process of Stimulus Generalization and Stimulus Discrimination in Classical Conditioning*. To see how classical conditioning can lead to the same conditioned response to new stimuli, complete the **explore** *Higher-Order Conditioning*. Can you unlearn a response? Find out by **exploring** *Process of Extinction and Spontaneous Recovery*.

Operant Conditioning

Watch the video *B. F. Skinner Biography* to learn more about B. F. Skinner, what led up to his research on operant conditioning, and to see a Skinner Box in action. **Explore** *Stimulus Generalization and Stimulus Discrimination in Operant Conditioning* to see how pigeons in a Skinner Box can learn to respond to red lights but not to green lights. If you have ever wondered how animal trainers condition the animals to perform, check out the **explore** *Dolphins at Sea World* to see how the technique of shaping is used with dolphins. Try your hand at gambling and see how different schedules of reinforcement affect your response with a **simulation** titled *Schedules of Reinforcement*.

Cognitive Models of Learning

Explore, *Banduras Study on Observational Learning*, provides visual animations to describe a classic study on modeling and its implications. Complete the simulation *Latent Learning* to experience learning that occurs but is not observable until some incentive or reinforcer is present. How would you define media violence? Test your critical thinking skills by completing the **simulation** *Media Violence*, which allows you to provide your interpretation of different studies on aggression. **Watch** *Banduras Bobo Doll Experiment*, a re-creation of the widely known experiment, in which you can see the actual stimulus, the Bobo Doll, in action and witness how children model an adult's violent behavior. **Listen** to the podcast *Mirror Neurons*, which was first introduced in Chapter 3, "Biopsychology," and think about how these cells may affect learning.

Biological Influences on Learning

The **explore**, *Taste Aversions, examines how conditioned taste aversions affect cancer patients undergoing chemotherapy.*

Learning Fads: Do They Work?

Can you really speed up the process of learning that some products claim? Evaluate these claims in the **explore** *Accelerated Learning*.

AFTER YOU READ ... PRACTICE TEST #1

Before beginning this practice test, estimate the % you expect to get correct.
Anticipated % correct: _____

1. Learning results from
a. nature.
b. spontaneous recovery.
c. preparedness.
d. experience.

2. Habituation occurs to
a. stimuli we conclude are safe.
b. any stimulus with equal likelihood.
c. stimuli that are dangerous and irritating.
d. loud and painful stimuli, as a protective mechanism.

3. Learning, as the association of one stimulus with another, was first systematically studied by
a. Gestalt psychologists.
b. the British Associationists.
c. William James, the "father of American psychology."
d. structuralists, such as Wilhelm Wundt, the "father of psychology."

4. Brandi feeds her dog, Spot, canned food every day. Whenever Brandi's mom opens a can, Spot comes running. Spot has been conditioned to
a. eat in the kitchen.
b. expect dog food to be in every can that is opened.
c. the smell of the food in the can, no matter what it is.
d. connect his master's love for him to the sound of the can opener.

5. Jane wants to use classical conditioning to teach her dog to wag his tail whenever he hears the house phone ring. She plans to pet her dog, which always makes his tail wag, and then immediately call the house phone with her cell phone. How successful will she be?
a. Very successful; this is a correct pairing of events.
b. Very successful, as long as she varies the interval between petting the dog and ringing the house phone.
c. Not very successful at all; tail wagging to a sound cannot be conditioned.
d. Not very successful at all; this describes backwards conditioning.

6. Carina is trying to get over her fear of large spiders, starting with tarantulas. To do this, she has successfully trained herself to breath deeply and relax whenever she sees a tarantula. However, yesterday Carina saw a scorpion and became very fearful. This is probably due to
a. stimulus renewal.
b. spontaneous recovery.
c. stimulus generalization.
d. stimulus discrimination.

7. Operant conditioning is also called
a. classical conditioning.
b. cognitive conditioning.
c. two-process conditioning.
d. instrumental conditioning.

8. When a behavior occurs as an automatic reflex, it is called _____ but when it occurs as a voluntary behavior it is called _____.
a. illicit; emetic
b. elicited; emitted
c. intentional; automatic
d. generalized; discriminant

9. Every time you eat chocolate you enjoy the taste and feel great afterwards—your mood improves and you have more energy. You often eat chocolate in the afternoon. This situation best illustrates
a. latent inhibition.
b. a conditioned response.
c. the law of effect.
d. an occasion setter.

10. Negative reinforcement ALWAYS _____ a target behavior; whereas punishment ALWAYS _____ a target behavior.
a. inhibits; enhances
b. increases; decreases
c. removes; establishes
d. helps acquisition of; helps extinction of

11. When Ana's children misbehave in the store, she often tells them, "Wait until we get home!" as which time she always remembers to punish them. What does the research evidence suggest about her discipline strategy?
a. Delayed punishment is seldom effective.
b. Severity of punishment is more important than the length of delay.
c. The length of delay and the effectiveness of punishment are positively correlated.
d. Allowing the child to think about the undesired behavior and upcoming punishment is the best strategy when using punishment.

12. Once a behavior is established, the best way to maintain it for the long run is to reinforce it
a. often.
b. never.
c. always.
d. occasionally.

13. You are a sportscaster announcing a race between people reinforced on different schedules. You announce, "With a rapid rate of response, difficult to extinguish, the person with the highest rate of response is going to be
a. Granny, playing slot machines."
b. Hildegard, going to church every Sunday."
c. Samantha, going to the movies a couple of times each month."
d. Jones, accumulating frequent flyer miles for a free airfare ticket."

14. Joachim's mother is potty training him. At first she praises him when he approaches his potty chair, and then only when he sits on it. Next she praises him if he "goes" in the potty chair, even. Finally, she only praises him if he goes in the potty chair, and keeps his diaper dry. Joachim's mother is using

a. shaping.
b. habituation.
c. preparedness.
d. the Premack Principle.

15. Brana always wears a religious medal around her neck on exam days because she believes the spirits help her to perform well. You think to yourself,
a. "Good for her, she is sure to do better!"
b. "Geez, Brana will never be a well-educated person with this type of belief."
c. "Well, on some past exam Brana must have performed well while wearing that medal."
d. "Brana must also be an athlete, because athletes are known for such superstitious behaviors."

16. Two-process theory explains the persistence of some phobias as a combination of operant and classical conditioning in which the feared stimulus
a. causes a person to emit a classically conditioned response, whereas avoidance becomes an operantly conditioned response.
b. elicits positive reinforcement for the feared item, followed by a return to homeostasis of the autonomic nervous system.
c. elicits a classically conditioned autonomic response, and an operantly conditioned negative reinforcement to removing one's self from the target stimulus.
d. is feared less in the long run (classical conditioning effect), but more in the short term (operant conditioning effect).

17. Early behaviorists, who developed the models of conditioning
a. did not believe that thinking played a role in this type of learning.
b. considered thinking to be a special class of behaviors, unrelated to learning.
c. denied "thinking," but accepted "emotion" as an important contributor to learning.
d. believed that "thinking" only applied to human learning, and so they only studied animals.

18. A critical component of observational learning is that it occurs
a. in just a single trial.
b. without reinforcement.
c. only with partial reinforcement.
d. only with continuous reinforcement.

19. Behaviorists believed that the study of mental events, such as imagery, were unworthy of study. Modern neuroimaging studies of _____ show brain activity in the same areas when we watch activities as when we participate in them.
a. mirror neurons
b. instinctive drift
c. primary reinforcers
d. pseudoconditioning

20. Sometimes a solution to a problem suddenly comes to us. This event is called
a. trial-and-error.
b. latent learning.
c. insight learning.
d. instinctive learning.

After completing the test, calculate your percent correct
(/ 20 =   ) x 100 = _____.

How accurate were your expectations? Does your performance suggest the need for additional study?
For the items you missed, go back and identify why the "correct" answer is the best answer.

AFTER YOU READ ... PRACTICE TEST #2

Before beginning this practice test, estimate the % you expect to get correct.
Anticipated % correct: _____

1. When Jill first got glasses they felt uncomfortable around her nose and behind her ears, and she was constantly aware of having them on. Now, weeks later, she doesn't even know she has them on. Jill has _____ to wearing her glasses.
   a. habituated
   b. generalized
   c. become sensitized
   d. become conditioned

2. Pavlov's primary research interest was in
   a. digestive processes in dogs.
   b. pecking behavior in pigeons.
   c. bar-pressing behavior in rats.
   d. taste aversion training in dogs.

3. For something to become a CS, it be must be
   a. directly meaningful in its context.
   b. preferably at a subliminal level of stimulation.
   c. easily perceived but meaningless in its original context.
   d. very specific and distinct (i.e., louder or brighter than other things in its context).

4. Every time Annette drops her son, Jay, at school, he says "Good-bye!" and then slams the car door. Now whenever Jay says, "Good-bye!" Annette winces. How can you explain this?
   a. Jay has a loud booming voice that hurts Annette's ears.
   b. Annette knows that she is going to miss her son all day.
   c. Because the original CS-UCS pairing was intermittent, it resulted in a higher-order conditioning.
   d. Wincing has become a conditioned response to the prior pairings of hearing Jay say "Good-bye!" and then slam the car door.

5. Dasan has trained his dog, Speck, to drool to the sound of the cell phone ring tone. However, Dasan has noticed that Speck also drools whenever the house phone rings, probably because of
   a. the renewal effect.
   b. spontaneous recovery.
   c. stimulus generalization.
   d. stimulus discrimination.

6. Shanaya has successfully quit smoking. However, whenever she goes to a nightclub, her cigarette cravings return because the nightclub comes to act as a(n)
   a. renewal stimulus.
   b. aversive stimulus.
   c. backward stimulus.
   d. higher-order stimulus.

7. In pseudoconditioning
   a. the CR actually triggers the CS.
   b. the CS directly triggers a UCR.
   c. the UCS fails to trigger the UCR.
   d. the backwards pairing of UCS-CS elicits the CR.

8. Every time Chris went ice-skating he fell hard on his backside, sometimes even hitting the back of his head on the ice. Because of this experience, Christ no longer goes ice-skating. This situation is a good example of
a. latent inhibition.
b. an occasion setter.
c. the law of effect.
d. a conditioned response.

9. The advantage of using a Skinner Box when studying operant conditioning in rats is that
a. the studied animals cannot escape, as they could in Thorndike's puzzle box.
b. it accurately records all behaviors on its own, so you can do other things at the same time.
c. the floor can be electrocuted so you can readily punish undesired behaviors during training.
d. it provides constant food and water so you don't have to attend to the animals over the weekend.

10. By definition, negative reinforcement ALWAYS acts to
a. provide rewards.
b. provide punishment.
c. increase target behavior.
d. decrease target behavior.

11. Cha believes that if you spare the rod, you spoil the child, so she spanks her children when they misbehave. You convince her to stop spanking because
a. punishment in general has been shown to actually increase unwanted behaviors.
b. this type of punishment lets them know that a behavior is wrong, but doesn't show them what they should be doing instead.
c. her child will stop the behavior in the long run but in the short run, behavior will be much worse.
d. she is classically conditioning her children to elicit the unwanted behavior when she isn't looking.

12. When Shane's dog was a puppy he always gave him a treat if he only used a specific part of the backyard for his bathroom. Shane eventually ran out of treats and the puppy started using the entire backyard as his bathroom. This change in behavior can be attributed to
a. stimulus generalization.
b. stimulus discrimination.
c. acquisition of the new behavior.
d. extinction of the original behavior.

13. If your professor gives you 5 quizzes over the course of a 15-week semester, your diligent studying is best reinforced if the professor uses a _____ schedule of reinforcement.
a. fixed ratio
b. variable interval
c. fixed interval
d. variable ratio

14. An important thing to understand about operating conditioning is that
a. shaping is rapid and can lead to unintended behaviors.
b. shaping is best applied to applications of the Premack Principle.
c. shaping can result in superstitious behaviors if the trainer is not careful.
d. shaping can take a long time and requires great patience on the part of the trainer.

15. According to the Premack principle
a. a more frequent behavior can reinforce a less frequent behavior.
b. educated people are less likely to engage in superstitious behaviors.
c. higher-order conditioning is more difficult in some species than in others.
d. superstitious behaviors that are operantly conditioned are more difficult to extinguish.

16. Chuck's teacher gives him a gold star every time he reads a book and turns in a book report. The top three readers in the class will earn a gift certificate to a toy store. Chuck's teacher is using
a. a token economy.
b. pseudoconditioning.
c. classical conditioning.
d. applied behavior analysis.

17. The best evidence so far, that classical and operant conditioning are distinct processes comes from
a. brain imaging studies that show different areas of activation for each type of conditioning.
b. the qualitative differences between elicited versus emitted responses.
c. the quantitative differences between elicited versus emitted responses.
d. some phobias can only be explained by classical conditioning, and others can only be explained by operant conditioning.

18. The "O" in S-O-R psychology stands for
a. original.
b. orienting.
c. organism.
d. organized.

19. A husband who observes his wife in pain during labor will exhibit some of the brain activity she is showing. This best illustrates the functioning of
a. preparedness.
b. mirror neurons.
c. instinctive drift.
d. insight learning.

20. A close friend is about to undergo chemotherapy. She is worried about the side effects, including the nausea and vomiting that will surely occur. You advise her to
a. avoid eating anything at all.
b. eat only the foods she likes the best.
c. eat foods she doesn't like, just as she starts the chemo.
d. eat foods she doesn't like, after she starts to feel nauseous.

After completing the test, calculate your percent correct
(/ 20 =   ) x 100 = _____.

How accurate were your expectations? Does your performance suggest the need for additional study?
For the items you missed, go back and identify why the "correct" answer is the best answer.

AFTER YOU READ . . . PRACTICE TEST ANSWER KEYS

Practice Test 1.

1. d (p. 232)
2. a (p. 233)
3. b (p. 234)
4. b (p. 235)
5. a (p. 236)
6. c (p. 237)
7. d (p. 242)
8. b (p. 242)
9. c (p. 243)
10. b (p. 244–245)
11. a (p. 247)
12. d (p. 248)
13. a (p. 248–249)
14. a (p. 250)
15. c (p. 252)
16. c (p. 254)
17. a (p. 255)
18. b (p. 257)
19. a (p. 259–260)
20. c (p. 261)

Practice Test 2.

1. a (p. 233)
2. a (p. 234)
3. c (p. 234–235)
4. d (p. 235)
5. c (p. 237)
6. d (p. 238)
7. b (p. 241)
8. c (p. 243)
9. b (p. 244)
10. c (p. 244)
11. b (p. 246)
12. d (p. 247)
13. b (p. 249)
14. d (p. 250)
15. a (p. 251)
16. a (p. 253)
17. a (p. 254)
18. c (p. 256)
19. b (p. 260–261)
20. c (p. 262)

AFTER YOU READ . . . PRACTICE TEST ANSWER KEYS

AFTER YOU READ ... CONCEPT MAPPING ACTIVITY ANSWERS

ACTIVITY 1:

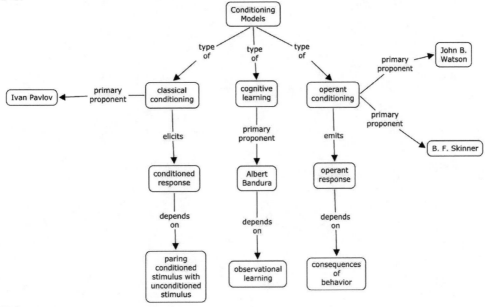

ACTIVITY 2:
conditioned stimulus (ex: metronome sound)
unconditioned stimulus (ex: gun shot)
unconditioned response (ex: eye blink)
conditioned response (ex: gun shot)

ACTIVITY 3:

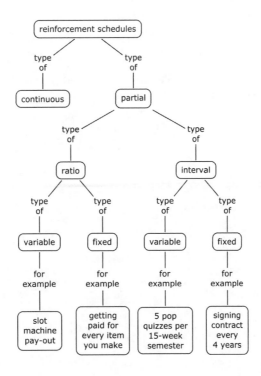

CHAPTER 7
MEMORY
CONSTRUCTING AND RECONSTRUCTING OUR PASTS

BEFORE YOU READ ... CHAPTER PREVIEW

Memory is defined as the retention of information over time. The paradox of memory is that it can be excellent sometimes, with individuals showing remarkable feats of memory; and it can be extremely poor at other times, even resulting in memory illusions—false but forceful memories. The evidence strongly supports the reconstructive nature of memory. It is not reconstructive like a tape or video recording. Memory has three stores. Sensory memory holds incoming information for less than half a second and if the information is attended to it passes to short-term memory. STM holds 7 ± 2 chunks of information for less than half a minute, and if the information is further encoded it passes to long-term memory. The serial position effect—the increased likelihood of remembering items at the beginning (primacy effect) and the end (recency effect) of a list of items—provides insight into differences in short-term and long-term memory. Long-term memory can be partitioned into explicit and implicit memory. Explicit memory consists of declarative memories, which are composed of semantic and episodic memory. Implicit memory is composed of procedural memory, priming, conditioning, and habituation.

For information to be remembered, it passes through a series of stages that include encoding, storage, and retrieval. Mnemonic techniques are associated with encoding. Mnemonics, such as peg-word method, are used to help us remember more information, more accurately, and for a longer time. Schemas are helpful with storage. Schemas are frameworks we develop based on past experiences that help us to interpret and store new information with similar, old information, so that later we can access it more readily. Retrieval gets at the heart of memory: determining whether some information from the past made it through the encoding and storage processes and, if so, whether it can be accessed as needed.

Memory retrieval is difficult to study because it's nearly impossible to determine whether the memory is there but inaccessible, or whether the information is simply not there. Recall is usually harder than recognition because it requires generating information from memory, and then, just as for recognition, a conscious recognition of the information as being "correct." Another way of testing memory, called relearning, was first developed by Hermann Ebbinghaus in the 1880s. In this testing, you learn some information, time passes until you have "forgotten" the information, and then you are asked to relearn it. The speed with which you can relearn is thought to be a measure of "savings" from the first learning episode. Relearning may be a more sensitive measure of memory, but the way we test it may be confounded with the use of distributed practice—learning spread out over several sessions. This approach is in contrast to massed practice, where information is learned in one sitting—cramming! Research evidence consistently shows that distributed practice is superior for long-term retention, whereas massed practice is superior for short-term retention. The tip-of-the-tongue phenomenon, which occurs when we know that we know some information, but cannot immediately remember it, provides useful insights into memory. Usually a hint will immediately elicit the correct information showing that the information was available but not accessible. Another factor that affects retrieval is encoding specificity: the match between learning and retrieval conditions and operations. The evidence is strong that memory is enhanced when external environments match, when a person's internal states match, and when moods match.

Over the past century there have been many attempts to localize memory in the brain. In the 1920s Karl Lashley looked for the "engram," a physical trace of memory. He was unable to find specific areas devoted to memory, but rather concluded memory was distributed throughout the brain. More recently, researchers have focused on long-term potentiation (LTP): a phenomenon in which the stimulation of single cells leads to the activation of other cells. Studies of LTP (as well as other sources of evidence) point to the hippocampus as being an important brain structure for the formation of memory. Other insights into memory come from studies where memory is severely lacking, a condition called amnesia, of which there are two types, retrograde amnesia and anterograde amnesia. Many amnesia myths tend to be perpetuated by movie-makers, but case studies have shown consistencies in amnesia types based on the type of event that caused the amnesia and which part of the brain was damaged. These studies support the importance of the hippocampus in memory consolidation, and point to an important role of the amygdala. Finally, serious memory loss, as seen in Alzheimer's-type dementia provides insights into normal memory functioning.

So how does memory develop? Children's memories develop increasing sophistication from about 3 years old through 12 years old. But we know that even 2-month-old infants have memory, as found from their responses to items in their environment, such as a mobile. We remember little from our early lives because of infantile amnesia, which is attributed to several causes. First, the hippocampus is not fully developed before age 2 or 3. Second, we don't develop a sense of self until after the age of 18 months. A final problem involves increased suggestibility. Children's schemas are more malleable and it is easier to misguide their memory.

So how do researchers examine memory accuracy? One line of evidence comes from the study of flashbulb memories, which are vivid memories of how we learned of emotional events, such as 9/11. At one time these types of memories were thought to be exemplarily accurate, but over time we have learned that these vivid memories, in which people have complete confidence, are distorted over time, the same way as any other memories. We also tend to forget which elements of a memory came from individual sources. A good example of a source memory error is cryptomnesia, where a person unwittingly plagiarizes another's work. Another finding concerning memory accuracy is that it is relatively easy to distort memory, or to implant a completely false memory intentionally. Studies of eyewitness testimony have provided a wonderful source of information on false memories because they tend to be for events that are brief, emotionally charged, and often filled with threatening stimuli, which may distract attention from more relevant information. Finally, we all make some common memory errors, including absentmindedness, suggestibility, bias, blocking, transience, persistence, and misattribution.

BEFORE YOU READ ... LEARNING OBJECTIVES

After reading Chapter 7 you should be able to:

7.1   Identify the ways that memories do and do not accurately reflect experiences
7.2   Explain the function, span, and duration of each of the three memory systems
7.3   Differentiate the subtypes of long-term memory
7.4   Determine methods for connecting new information to existing knowledge
7.5   Distinguish ways of measuring memory
7.6   Describe how the relation between encoding and retrieval conditions influences remembering
7.7   Describe the role of long-term potentiation in memory
7.8   Explain how amnesia helps to clarify the distinction between explicit and implicit memory
7.9   Distinguish different types of amnesia and the relevance of amnesia to the brain's organization of memory
7.10   Identify the key impairments of Alzheimer's disease
7.11   Identify how children's memory abilities change with age
7.12   Examine why we fail to remember experiences from early childhood
7.11   Explain how suggestions can shape children's memories
7.12   Identify factors that influence people's susceptibility to false memories and memory errors

BEFORE YOU READ ... TERM IDENTIFICATION

anterograde amnesia (p. 299)
chunking (p. 282)
context-dependent learning (p. 295)
cryptomnesia (p. 307)
decay (p. 280)
distributed versus massed practice (p. 294)
duration (p. 278)
echoic memory (p. 279)
elaborative rehearsal (p. 283)
encoding (p. 288)
encoding specificity (p. 295)
episodic memory (p. 286)
explicit memory (p. 286)
flashbulb memories (p. 304)
iconic memory (p. 278)
implicit memory (p. 286)
infantile amnesia (p. 302)
interference (p. 280)
levels of processing (p. 283)
long-term memory (p. 284)
long-term potentiation (p. 296)
Magic Number (p. 281)
maintenance rehearsal (p. 283)
memory (p. 275)
memory illusion (p. 276)
meta-memory (p. 301)
mnemonic (p. 288)

misinformation effect (p. 307)
permastore (p. 284)
primacy effect (p. 285)
priming (p. 286)
proactive inhibition (p. 281)
procedural memory (p. 286)
recall (p. 292)
recency effect (p. 285)
recognition (p. 292)
rehearsal (p. 282)
relearning (p. 292)
retrieval (p. 292)
retrieval cues (p. 292)
retroactive inhibition (p. 281)
retrograde amnesia (p. 299)
schema (p. 291)
semantic memory (p. 286)
sensory memory (p. 278)
serial position curve (p. 285)
short-term memory (p. 279)
source monitoring (p. 305)
span (p. 278)
state-dependent learning (p. 295)
storage (p. 291)
suggestive memory technique (p. 276)
tip of the tongue (TOT) phenomenon (p. 294)
von Restorff effect (p. 285)

AS YOU READ ... PRACTICE ACTIVITIES

HOW MEMORY OPERATES: THE MEMORY ASSEMBLY LINE

1. Look up the words *fallible* and *malleable* in a dictionary. How do their definitions fit with the notion of memory being prone to error? (LO 8.1)

2. Compare iconic and echoic memory. Think of an original everyday example for each. (LO 8.2)

3. Describe Sperling's study of sensory memory. (LO 8.2)

   Design:

   Findings:

   Lesson learned:

4. *Short-term memory* and *working memory* are two names for essentially the same memory store. Each of these ways of naming this memory process suggests something unique about the process. Discuss what each of the names tells us about the function of this memory store. (LO 8.2)

5. Why do you think Peterson and Peterson (1959) asked their participants to count backwards by threes during the interval between hearing three letters and recalling them? (LO 8.2)

6. Compare proactive interference effects and retroactive interference effects. Provide an original example of each from your own life. (LO 8.2)

7. Compare maintenance and elaborative rehearsal. Provide original examples of how each of these types of rehearsal might be the best technique to use in a specific situation. (LO 8.2)

8. Complete this table for the three memory systems. (LO 8.2)

	Sensory Memory	Short-Term Memory	Long-Term Memory
Coding			
Duration			
Capacity			
Forgetting Mechanism			

9. What are serial position effects? Describe the different component effects. What does each effect tell us about memory? (LO 8.2)

10. Compare explicit and implicit memory. To which subtypes of long-term memory are they related? (LO 8.3)

THE THREE STAGES OF MEMORY

1. How do "stages" of memory differ from "systems" of memory? (LO 8.4)

2. Go to http://www.exploratorium.edu/memory/dont_forget/playing_games_3.html. After completing the exercise there, use the method of loci to create a path to help you remember the following terms: proactive interference, retroactive interference, episodic memory, semantic memory, and procedural memory. Why is this task for 5 concepts so MUCH more difficult than the task for 20 terms on the Web site? (LO 8.4)

3. What is your classroom schema? Write it out and compare notes with several of your classmates. Which elements were most often shared? How do you think having a classroom schema affected your classroom behavior on your first day of college? (LO 8.4)

4. Relearning is seldom used these days to test memory. Think of some reasons why recall and recognition are favored as measures of memory. (LO 8.5)

5. Complete the following table by providing an example of how you could apply each of these memory concepts to your own study needs. (LO 8.6)

Memory Concept	Application
Distributed vs. Massed Practice	
Elaborative Retrieval	
Levels of Processing	
Mnemonic Devices	
Encoding Specificity	
Context-Dependent Learning	
State-Dependent Learning	

THE BIOLOGY OF MEMORY

1. It has been difficult to localize memory in any specific brain area. Instead, various aspects of memory seem to be widely distributed throughout our brains. What do you think might be the advantages and disadvantages of such a distribution of function? (LO 7.7)

2. Compare anterograde and retrograde amnesia. (LO 7.7)

3. Go to http://www.youtube.com/watch?v=coZK-t7lbp8 and think about the kind of life that Clive Wearing lived. Compare what you learn about Clive to what you can learn about another patient with similar brain damage at http://ahsmail.uwaterloo.ca/kin356/episodic/LifewithoutEP.htm What can you conclude about memory systems from these case studies? (LO 7.8)

4. Many older adults develop dementia for a variety of reasons. For example, older adults who develop depression may seem to be losing their mental abilities. In addition, older adults often take medication to control high blood pressure, which has a side effect of the loss of sodium and potassium. As you should remember from Chapter 3, these minerals are important for neural transmission. Thus, loss of these minerals can also lead to dementia-type symptoms. Why do you believe it is important to clearly reject other diagnostic possibilities in older adults who seem to be less mentally sharp? (LO 7.10)

THE DEVELOPMENT OF MEMORY: ACQUIRING A PERSONAL HISTORY

1. Memory abilities change with development from childhood through adulthood. Discuss three reasons why for this change. (LO 7.11)

2. Describe research evidence that infants have implicit memory. (LO 7.11)

3. Discuss some of the evidence that speaks in favor of infantile amnesia and against the notion of good memory back to early infancy. (LO 7.12)

4. Think about one of your earliest memories. Is it likely that this memory is completely accurate? Why or why not? (LO 7.13)

5. True or False. Adults should always believe a child's description of abuse. Explain your answer. (LO 7.13)

WHEN GOOD MEMORY GOES BAD: FALSE MEMORIES

1. Write down your flashbulb memory for 9/11. Check with the people you believe can verify the accuracy of your memory. Remember, the "flashbulb" is an episodic memory including elements such as who told you the news, where, when, what you were doing, what you and others were wearing, the weather at the time, etc. This is distinct from what by now is your semantic memory of the actual event of 9/11. (LO 7.14)

2. Go to http://www.estripes.com/article.asp?section=104&article=40909&archive=true to read more about new efforts to develop a pill that can reduce the emotional burden of past traumatic events, which often lead to posttraumatic stress disorder. These pills may not erase the actual memory, but do erase memory for the emotions that accompanied the events. What are the pros and cons of such a pill? Do you think it is a good idea? Why or why not? (LO 7.14)

3. List three conditions under which eyewitness testimony is likely to be faulty, and provide an original example of each to illustrate the effect of these on memory. (LO 7.14)

4. Go to http://www.exploratorium.edu/exhibits/wig/index.html and have fun playing around and learning more about eyewitness memory. (LO 7.14)

5. List Schacter's (2001) "Seven Sins of Memory" and provide an original example from your own life to illustrate each one. (LO 7.14)

AS YOU READ ... CONCEPT MAP ACTIVITIES

ACTIVITY 1: Complete the following concept map for the stages of memory:

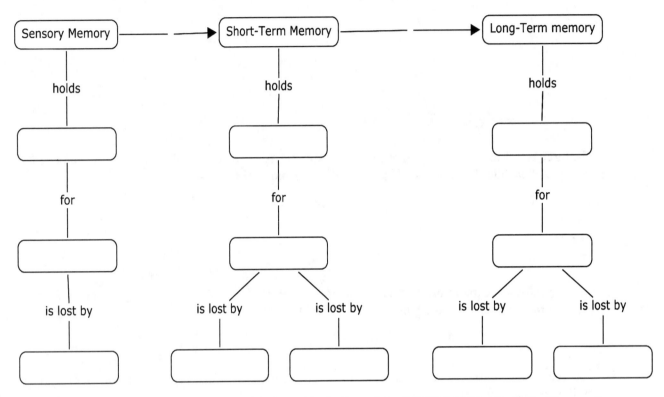

Author activity content supported by *IHMC Cmap Tools* Copyright ©1998-2007 Institute for Human & Machine Cognition

ACTIVITY 2:   Complete this concept map for the organization of long-term memory.

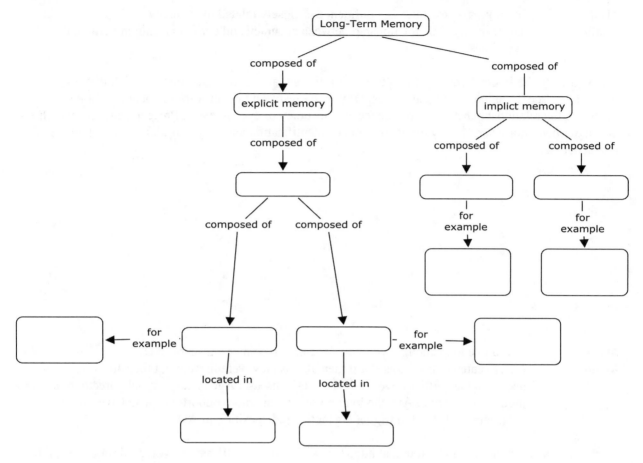

Author activity content supported by *IHMC Cmap Tools* Copyright ©1998-2007 Institute for Human & Machine Cognition

---

AS YOU READ ... MYTH OR REALITY?

Myth: In criminal eyewitnesses, confidence is closely related to accuracy.
Reality: There is very little relationship between accuracy and confidence among criminal eyewitnesses.

1. If you go to the Internet you can find dozens of articles that explain situations in which this is particularly true. Imagine that you are an expert witness testifying in court for the benefit of a jury regarding the relationship between confidence and accuracy of eyewitnesses. Present a case for why line-ups, in particular, are particularly prone to errors of identification and why confidence should *not* be taken into account.

Myth: If you live long enough, you will develop Alzheimer's disease (AD).
Reality: Many centenarians are as sharp mentally as they were throughout their lives, yet some people in their fifties develop Alzheimer's disease. Age is not so much directly related, as indirectly related to AD: the longer you live the more opportunity you have for an environmental event to trigger a genetic predisposition to AD.

A great explanation of AD can be found at http://www.alz.org/brain/01.asp As you go through the slide show you should be aware of the constant comparisons that are made between the brain of a person with AD and the brain of a healthy, normal older adult. What are some of the changes that occur with AD? Make sure to also read through the myths about AD at http://www.alz.org/alzheimers_disease_myths_about_alzheimers.asp.
Not only is it NOT the case that AD is inevitable if you live long enough, but this site can dispel many other myths.

1. Do you know anyone with AD? In what ways are you better able to understand their condition now?

AS YOU READ ... PUT YOUR CRITICAL THINKING SKILLS TO THE TEST

1. At some fundamental level, both the depth of processing framework and the encoding specificity effect are conceptually similar. Consider the elements of processing that connect these two processing effects.

2. The text presents a wealth of evidence that memory is reconstructive.
    a. How then might you explain the extraordinary accuracy with which actors learn long parts, especially in stage plays?
    b. Think of another example where memory is primarily reproductive rather than reconstructive.

3. At http://abcnews.go.com/GMA/story?id=2596305 and at http://www.cbsnews.com/stories/2006/11/02/national/main2143883.shtml you will find the story of a man who was identified as an amnesia victim, found wandering in Denver. The man was actually missing from western Canada, near the U.S. border. In the end, the man most probably was not an amnesia victim, but suffered from a dissociative amnesia.
    a. Find information on dissociative amnesia and differentiate between dissociative amnesia and the type of amnesia suffered by people such as Clive Wearing and H. M.

As You Read ... MyPsychLab Connection

How Memory Operates: The Memory Assembly Line
When reviewing the capacity of short-term memory, participate in the **simulations** *Digit Span, How Good Is Your Memory for Stories?* and *Delay and Interference on Short-Term Memory*. To learn more about the levels-of-processing approach, complete the **simulation** *Depth Processing*. Learn more about the serial position effect by completing the **simulations** *Serial Position Effect* and *The Serial Position Curve*.

The Three Stages of Memory
Explore *Key Processes in Stages of Memory and Encoding* and *Storage and Retrieval in Memory* to learn more about the key processes of memory. Scared of the dentist? You are not alone.

The Biology of Memory
To learn about an experiment conducted on the biology of Alzheimers, **watch** *What Happens with Alzheimers?*

The Development of Memory: Acquiring Personal History
It is often difficult to believe in the suggestible nature of memory. In order to learn about this phenomenon, **watch** *Memory: Elizabeth Loftus* and see several of these experiments conducted. The results may surprise you!

When Good Memories Go Bad: False Memories
When reviewing how false memories are created, review the **simulation** *Creating False Memories* and see if you are tricked!

AFTER YOU READ ... PRACTICE TEST #1

Before beginning this practice test, estimate the percent you expect to get correct.
Anticipated percent correct: _____

1. Salvador Dali created a classic painting of memory titled, "The Persistence of Memory" in which images of time-pieces are stretched and distorted. This image of memory is correct in as much as
   a. all memories are time-locked to their acquisition.
   b. memories become somewhat distorted over time.
   c. memory accurately represents events at the time of their formation.
   d. memories are often so distorted and stretched as to be "unreadable," as are the clocks in this painting.

2. Katy is studying for a history exam. As Katy reads her textbook and tries to memorize important dates, visual information she picks up from her textbook flows from her
   a. iconic memory to short-term memory to long-term memory.
   b. iconic memory to long-term memory to short-term memory.
   c. short-term memory to long-term memory to iconic memory.
   d. short-term memory to iconic memory to long-term memory.

3. Information loss in short-term memory is attributed to
   a. primarily decay.
   b. exclusively decay.
   c. primarily interference.
   d. exclusively interference.

4. Many ice hockey players play roller hockey in the summer. Although the basic game skills are similar, stopping on ice versus stopping on wheels requires a different technique. When making the transition from ice to wheels, some players end up spinning in circles on. This is probably a result of
   a. poor motor memories.
   b. proactive inhibition.
   c. retroactive inhibition.
   d. anterograde interference.

5. John just met a girl whom he finds attractive. Unfortunately he doesn't have a pen handy and will have to remember her phone number. Which method would be most effective?
   a. Rote rehearsal
   b. Repetitive rehearsal
   c. Elaborative rehearsal
   d. Maintenance rehearsal

6. The serial position curve reflects the operation of
   a. sensory, short-term, and long-term memory systems.
   b. long-term memory, seen in the recall of a distinctive item, called the von Restorff effect.
   c. long-term memory, seen in the recency effect, and short-term memory, seen in the primacy effect.
   d. long-term memory, seen in the primacy effect; and short-term memory, seen in the recency effect.

7. While you are at home, sick, you call your best friend to bring you a few things from the store. Your friend is driving and cannot write down your items which you read from a list, "tissues, a newspaper, gelatin, cough syrup, chicken soup, apple juice, aspirin, ginger ale, ice pops, Sudafed, menthol rub, and the TV Guide." Which items is your friend most likely to forget?
   a. Menthol rub and the TV Guide.
   b. Tissues, a newspaper, gelatin, cough syrup
   c. Chicken soup, apple juice, aspirin, ginger ale
   d. Ice pops, Sudafed, menthol rub, and the TV Guide

8. Mnemonics help primarily to aid in
   a. recall.
   b. storage.
   c. retrieval.
   d. encoding.

9. If Jessie remembers the errands she needs to run today by imagining a grocery store in the shape of a large bun, a gas pump shaped like a tennis shoe, with the laces acting as a hose, and clothes hanging from a tree in dry-cleaner plastic bags, she is using
   a. the method of loci.
   b. a pegword method.
   c. the keyword method.
   d. an "external" memory aid.

10. Linda believes that all cheerleaders are thin, pretty, energetic, and promiscuous. When she notices from a distance that her boyfriend is talking to a cheerleader, she later remembers that the distance between him and the cheerleader was
    a. closer than it really was because encoding was biased by her schema.
    b. closer than it really was because her encoding was disrupted once her emotions kicked in.
    c. greater than it really was because she stored the memory based on a distorted visual perception.
    d. greater than it really was because her cheerleader schema stored the memory along with her baseball schema, where individuals are usually located far apart.

11. Marcus is studying for his history final by using a mnemonic of connecting the actual contours of the numbers to a pictorial representation of the event that occurred on that date. Later, during the test, when he needs to remember the events, the dates can act as
    a. states.
    b. TOTs.
    c. engrams.
    d. retrieval cues.

12. According to the classic Ebbinghaus forgetting curve
    a. how much we remember is strongly based on wide individual differences.
    b. much of what we learn is forgotten very shortly after learning it for the first time.
    c. how quickly we forget depends on how long we know we will need to remember it.
    d. much of what we learn we remember for a relatively long time, and then we forget it.

13. Elaborative rehearsal is often recommended as a good study habit because
    a. it reduces source confusion for new information.
    b. it makes rote memorization of facts much easier.
    c. it creates connections between new and old knowledge.
    d. it keeps information active in short-term memory for a longer time.

14. Encoding specificity is the basis for the study habit advice that you
    a. relax yourself before you study, so you can improve encoding.
    b. study in as many different places as possible for each class.
    c. study only in the classroom in which your class is held, at times when it is not in use.
    d. study consistently in a single place, and then imagine yourself in that place when taking a test.

15. Generalized amnesia
    a. is extremely rare.
    b. usually shows rapid recovery
    c. includes a loss of memory about one's self.
    d. is limited to procedure knowledge but spares episodic memory.

16. Children's memory improves with age, probably due to
    a. better meta-memory—knowledge of their own memory ability.
    b. increasing use of rote repetition.
    d. the increasing development of their sense of self.
    c. an increasing ability to remember events from early infancy.

17. Infantile amnesia
    a. is greatest in children who fail to recognize themselves in a mirror at a younger age.
    b. shows some individuals can remember events as early as birth.
    c. is rare, and often due to psychological repression of traumatic events early in life.
    d. probably occurs because brain structures such as the hippocampus are not yet sufficiently developed.

18. In source monitoring confusion
    a. we might confuse our dreams with our actual experiences.
    b. our memory for earlier learned information dominates our memory for later learned information.
    c. our memory for later learned information dominates our memory for earlier learned information.
    d. we discriminate whether information was obtained from an electronic medium, such as a computer, or from a print medium, such as a book.

19. According to the misinformation effect
    a. we remember false information more readily than true information.
    b. people readily confuse the source of information, even mistaking dreams as factual events.
    c. we sometimes truly fail to recognize someone else's ideas, and confuse them as being our own.
    d. inaccurate information received after an event can become incorporated into the original memory.

20. According to Schacter's (2001) "seven sins of memory," even memory errors have a practical side in that
    a. absentmindedness frees up our attention to focus on other things.
    b. blocking might prevent us from saying something embarrassing.
    c. suggestibility allows us to remember our inferences about events.
    d. transience is practical because remembering everything we've ever experienced would be burdensome.

After completing the test, calculate your percent correct
(/ 20 =   ) x 100 = _____.

How accurate were your expectations? Does your performance suggest the need for additional study?
For the items you missed, go back and identify why the "correct" answer is the best answer.

AFTER YOU READ ... PRACTICE TEST #2

Before beginning this practice test, estimate the percent you expect to get correct.
Anticipated percent correct: _____

1. As Janice helps her daughter prepare for her senior prom, she describes the events of her own senior prom. Her memory is likely to reflect
   a. reproduction: Janice's memory is much like a photocopy or snapshot of what occurred, and once activated, Janice can "read it out."
   b. reproduction: Janice can retrieve her memory of her own senior prom much like one downloads and opens a stored document on a computer.
   c. reconstruction: Janice uses the experiences of helping her daughter to prepare for senior prom to create a memory for Janice's own senior prom.
   d. reconstruction: Janice can retrieve some information and then fills in the missing information with probable details, so as to provide a coherent story.

2. The different stages of memory differ in terms of two dimensions. These dimensions are
   a. span and scan.
   b. span and duration.
   c. scan and forgetting mechanisms.
   d. duration and forgetting mechanisms.

3. You are a participant in a memory study in which you hear three letters, followed by a 3-digit number, and must immediately start counting backwards by threes from this number. After counting backwards for 3 seconds, you are likely to remember _____ of the numbers, and after 30 seconds you are likely to remember _____ of the numbers.
   a. most; none
   b. most; most
   c. none; most
   d. none; none

4. Joe Montana, a football Hall of Fame member, would probably recall a briefly presented video image of football players lined up for a play, better than would Tony Gwynn, a baseball Hall of Fame member. This difference is probably accounted for by differences in
   a. chunking.
   b. athleticism.
   c. interference.
   d. visual memory.

5. You have an important test tomorrow. As you review your notes you find you don't remember a few of the concepts. Your best strategy to memorize this information is to
   a. try to keep the information "alive" as long as possible.
   b. extend the duration of short-term memory until test time.
   c. repeat the information over and over and over to yourself.
   d. connect these new concepts to other ones already firmly in your memory.

6. You are exposed to a word list and are asked to determine whether the words, individually, evoke an emotional reaction. Your friend is exposed to the same words and is asked to note whether the words are presented in black or blue ink. Later, when asked to recall the words
   a. you recall more words than your friend because you processed them more deeply to begin with.
   b. you recall more words than your friend because the encoding and recall conditions are more alike.
   c. your friend recalls more words than you do, because your friend processed them more deeply to begin with.
   d. your friend recalls more words because the emotional overtones inhibit your ability to encode the words very well.

7. You jump into a car with a stick shift for the first time. You remember your dad telling you to just gently let up on the clutch while simultaneously depressing the gas pedal. You follow his directions exactly but stall the engine several times before getting going. The problem is that driving a stick shift requires you to develop a(n) _____ memory, so the verbal instructions are not very helpful.
    a. explicit
    b. episodic
    c. semantic
    d. procedural

8. The three important processes of memory are
    a. encoding, storage, and retrieval.
    b. priming, encoding, and retrieval.
    c. attention, elaboration, and storage.
    d. perception, attention, and elaboration.

9. The drug propranolol has been found to be effective in
    a. increasing overall memory for a traumatic event.
    b. decreasing overall memory for a traumatic event.
    c. decreasing the strong emotions associated with traumatic memories.
    d. increasing distortion of the emotional aspects of a traumatic memory.

10. Storage is enhanced by our schemas because
    a. nature has given us natural ways of storing information most economically.
    b. we can toss our new memories in quickly, and sort them out later, when we need them.
    c. they help us encode new information so it becomes associated with related, old information.
    d. they are like a filing cabinet, with no ambiguity about which "drawer" to use for filing new information.

11. During recognition, a person only needs to confirm that the presented information is "correct," but with recall a person
    a. also needs to decide if it is "incorrect."
    b. needs a cue to trigger memory for the information.
    c. needs to see how long it takes to relearn the material.
    d. must first generate previously stored information, and can then confirm that the generated information is "correct."

12. "Sensitivity" of memory measures from most sensitive (most likely to truly accurately detect a memory), to least sensitive (most likely to miss accurately detecting a memory) goes from
    a. recall, to recognition, to relearning.
    b. relearning, to recognition, to recall.
    c. recognition, to recall, to relearning.
    d. recognition, to relearning, to recall.

13. You and your roommate, who are both taking the same introductory psychology class, are studying for the next exam. This course has a cumulative final. You distribute your practice sessions over several days, whereas your roommate crams the night before the exam. How will this affect your and your roommate's learning of the course material?
    a. You should perform better on both the next exam and on the final.
    b. Your roommate should perform better on both the next exam and on the final.
    c. Your roommate should perform just slightly better on the next exam but you should perform much better on the final.
    d. You should both perform equally well on the final, but you roommate should perform much better on the next exam.

14. According to encoding specificity
    a. recognition is always easier than recall.
    b. encoding and retrieval processes are clearly distinctive and independent.
    c. learning is an activity independent of the conditions under which it occurs.
    d. recall can be easier than recognition, if cues present at learning are also present at recall.

15. Loss of memory for past events is called _____; whereas the inability to form new memories is called _____.
    a. proactive amnesia; retroactive amnesia
    b. retroactive amnesia; proactive amnesia
    c. retrograde amnesia; anterograde amnesia
    d. anterograde amnesia; retrograde amnesia

16. Infants' memory is often tested by examining how much they kick in response to a familiar versus a new toy, such as a mobile. This behavior is governed by principles of
    a. operant conditioning.   c. classical conditioning.
    b. social learning theory.   d. hippocampal development.

17. Dementia is the progressive decline of cognitive/mental functions and
    a. is always irreversible once it begins.
    b. can occur for many reasons, one of which is Alzheimer's disease.
    c. typically begins in all people around an average age of 65.
    d. begins with distance memories and then progresses to affecting more recent memories.

18. Flashbulb memory—memory for the events surrounding our reception of important, surprising information—is
    a. vivid, and usually stable and accurate.
    b. vivid, but no more accurate that standard memory.
    c. like a permanent snapshot of the event, captured by a flash on a camera.
    d. so strongly tied to the facts of the event, that we remember both very well.

19. If you believe in the "weapon focus effect" you are also likely to believe that
    a. memory for the details of a criminal's description are likely to be enhanced.
    b. the stress of the situation heightens arousal, therefore leading to greater eyewitness accuracy.
    c. eyewitnesses to a crime involving a weapon are less likely to be trusted for the accuracy of their recall.
    d. repression—the added stress of a crime plus the use of a weapon can lead to a complete failure of the retrieval process.

20. The controversy responsible for the "memory wars" stems from
    a. the negative effect of line-ups on identification of criminals.
    b. whether cryptomnesia is a case of plagiarism versus source monitoring confusion.
    c. courtroom battles over jury instructions regarding memory accuracy versus fallibility.
    d. our inability to differentiate between recovery of repressed, traumatic memories, versus false memories of trauma.

After completing the test, calculate your percent correct
(/ 20 =   ) x 100 = _____.

How accurate were your expectations? Does your performance suggest the need for additional study? For the items you missed, go back and identify why the "correct" answer is the best answer.

AFTER YOU READ . . . PRACTICE TEST ANSWER KEYS

Practice Test 1.

1. b (p. 276)
2. a (p. 278)
3. c (p. 280)
4. b (p. 281)
5. c (p. 283)
6. d (p. 284–285)
7. c (p. 285)
8. d (p. 288)
9. b (p. 289)
10. a (p. 291)
11. d (p. 292–293)
12. b (p. 293)
13. c (p. 294)
14. d (p. 294–295)
15. a (p. 298)
16. a (p. 302)
17. d (p. 303)
18. a (p. 305)
19. d (p. 307)
20. d (p. 311)

Practice Test 2.

1. d (p. 277–278)
2. b (p. 278)
3. a (p. 280)
4. a (p. 282)
5. d (p. 283)
6. a (p. 283–284)
7. d (p. 286)
8. a (p. 287)
9. c (p. 306)
10. c (p. 291)
11. d (p. 293)
12. b (p. 294)
13. c (p. 294)
14. d (p. 294–295)
15. c (p. 298)
16. a (p. 302)
17. b (p. 300)
18. b (p. 304–305)
19. c (p. 309)
20. d (p. 310)

AFTER YOU READ ... CONCEPT MAPPING ACTIVITY ANSWERS

ACTIVITY 1: Complete the following concept map for the stages of memory.

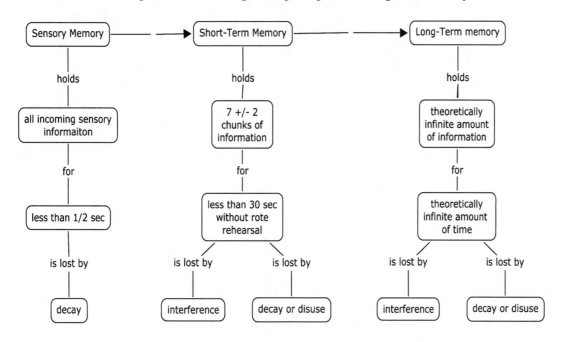

ACTIVITY 2: Complete this concept map for the organization of long-term memory.

The following terms, listed in alphabetic order, should appear in your concept map along with your own original examples for episodic, semantic, and procedural memories and priming.
cerebellum
cerebrum
episodic memory
priming
procedural memory
semantic memory

CHAPTER 8
LANGUAGE, THINKING, AND REASONING
GETTING INSIDE OUR TALKING HEADS

BEFORE YOU READ ... CHAPTER PREVIEW

Language plays a critical role in much of what makes us human. Language is involved in the maintenance of social relationships as well as in the organization of experience. We can think about language at four levels. At the simplest level are phonemes, followed by morphemes, syntax, and extralinguistic information. Scientists continue to debate how and why a complex language system evolved. Language permits the communication of elaborate thought, but requires a long learning period, a large brain, and complex physiology. Although language is characterized by arbitrariness, this arbitrariness contributes to the flexibility of language.

Research on language acquisition suggests that language development begins early and follows a regular sequence. Humans appear to be able to tune into the melody and rhythm of their native language before birth. Although first sounds reflect unintentional vocalizations (cries, burps), increased control of the vocal tract leads to intentional vocalizations such as cooing and later, babbling. Children produce their first words around their first birthday and begin to combine words by their second birthday. Theories of language acquisition tend to differ in their emphasis on nature versus nature. Each may reflect only part of the picture. Errors children make in learning language tell us the process is generative—not entirely the result of modeling. But children need to hear language and to interact with users in a meaningful context.

Although nonhuman animal species use communication systems primarily in the contexts of mating and aggression, some exchange other types of information. Efforts to teach language to nonhumans suggest that the basics of language can be taught, but the language never reaches the syntactic complexity of a three-year-old human. Misconceptions regarding the system of sign language are numerous. It is a linguistic system, not "just gestures." In acquiring sign language, children follow the same developmental trajectory as do children learning all languages. Bilingual children may experience some delays in syntactical development, but delays are offset by metalinguistic insight and proficiency. Children appear to be more proficient in second language use when they are exposed to the language before age seven. Proficiency in acquiring a second language drops off gradually after age seven, suggesting the acquisition period is not a strict critical period.

Linguistic determinism is the view that no thought is possible without language. Evidence against this view includes findings that children can perform complex tasks before language. The more moderate view of linguistic relativity suggests that language shapes rather than determines thought. Linguistic relativity may be true for some but not all aspects of cognition.

Learning to read requires mastery of both whole word recognition and phonetic decomposition. Before children can learn to read, they must master prereading skills. For example, they must learn that printed words have meaning. Proficient readers tend to be both faster at reading and better at comprehending than poorer readers but reading speed doesn't cause comprehension.

Thinking can be defined as any mental activity or processing of information. Although the mind has been compared with a computer, human information processing is more flexible and creative than computer processing. Humans also tend to use thinking shortcuts, or heuristics, to increase efficiency.

Techniques to streamline processing include top-down processing and the use of categories and schemata. These techniques impose order on information by relying on previous experience. Intuition and snap judgments can enable us to extract useful information from small bits of information. However, heuristics and biases in the way we process information can also lead to cognitive errors. The scientific method is an important remedy for the errors in judgment that result from these cognitive biases. Problem solving involves generating a strategy to accomplish a goal. Four hurdles in problem solving are the salience of surface similarities, mental sets, functional fixedness, and context and consequence effects.

BEFORE YOU READ ... LEARNING OBJECTIVES

After reading Chapter 8 you should be able to:

8.1	Describe the four levels of analysis that comprise language
8.2	Discover the developmental trajectory of language acquisition in children
8.3	Compare human and nonhuman animal communication
8.4	Determine how sign language in deaf individuals relates to spoken language acquisition in hearing people
8.5	Identify the pros and cons of bilingualism
8.6	Identify the ways in which our language may influence our thinking
8.7	Describe the challenges associated with reading and reading strategies
8.8	Identify the skills required to learn to read
8.9	Analyze the relationship between reading speed and reading comprehension
8.10	Identify types of cognitive economy and the pros and cons of economizing
8.11	Describe the challenges that humans face when attempting to solve problems or make decisions

BEFORE YOU READ ... TERM IDENTIFICATION

anomia (p. 318)
artificial intelligence (p. 341)
babbling (p. 324)
bilingual (p. 323)
categories (p. 343)
covert speech (p.334)
cryptophasia (p. 333)
dialects (p. 321)
extralinguistic (p. 320)
functional fixedness (p. 347)
generative (p. 327)
holophrases (p. 326)
homesign (p. 334)
language (p. 319)
language acquisition device (p. 327)
linguistic determinism (p. 334)

linguistic relativity (p. 337)
mental set (p. 347)
metalinguistic (p. 332)
morphemes (p. 320)
nativist (p. 327)
phonemes (p. 320)
phonesthemes (p. 323)
phonetic decomposition (p. 338)
problem solving (p. 345)
sign language (p. 330)
social pragmatics (p. 327)
syntax (p. 320)
thinking (p. 341)
transcranial magnetic stimulation (p. 336)
whole word recognition (p. 338)

AS YOU READ ... PRACTICE ACTIVITIES

HOW DOES LANGUAGE WORK?

1. List the levels of speech analysis from the smallest to the largest unit, then match the level of speech analysis with its description. (LO 8.1)

Phoneme   elements of communication context
Extralinguistic information   grammatical rules of language
Syntax   smallest unit of meaningful speech
Morpheme   sounds of language

	Levels of Speech	Description
Smallest	1._____	_____
	2._____	_____
	3._____	_____
Largest	4._____	_____

2. Look at the examples of ambiguous headlines and sentences with multiple meanings in Table 8.1 of the text. Can you make up some others? How do these examples illustrate the complexity of our linguistic system? What are the pros and cons of such a complex linguistic system? (LO 8.1)

3. For each language achievement, give an example, then note the order of development (1st, 2nd, 3rd). (LO 8.2)

Order	Achievement	Example
_____	Two-word speech	_____
_____	Babbling	_____
_____	Holophrastic speech	_____

4. Language development is a process—it doesn't happen all at once. Look at the development progress of the children described here. Would any of these observations concern you? Why or why not? (LO 8.2)

    Yara is a 13-month-old who does not yet comprehend any spoken words, including her name.

    Alicia is a 2-year-old who uses the word *duck* to refer to all birds.

    Mako is almost 3 and still says "poon" for *spoon*.

5. For each of these theories of language development, identify the "main point," whether the theory emphasizes the source of language as nature or nurture, and the major criticism of the theory. (LO 8.2)

	Main Idea	Source	Criticism
Imitation			
Nativist			
Social Pragmatics			
General Cognitive Processing			

6. What are the similarities and differences in human and nonhuman animal communication? (LO 8.3)

7. How is the learning of sign language for a deaf child similar to language learning by a hearing child? (LO 8.4)

8. Although some evidence indicates that bilingual children experience some delay in each of their languages relative to their monolingual counterparts, bilingualism offers some advantages. List at least two advantages. (LO 8.5)

DO WE THINK IN WORDS? THE RELATION BETWEEN LANGUAGE AND THOUGHT

1. Using your own words, briefly describe the idea of "linguistic determinism." (LO 8.6)

2. Had you heard the claim that Eskimos (Inuits) have 1,000 different words for snow? Give at least two reasons to doubt this view. (LO 8.6)

3. How does the idea of linguistic relativity differ from linguistic determinism? (LO 8.6)

4. Some claim that conceptual categories create metaphors that influence our thinking. For example, thinking about love as madness results in thinking of "being crazy in love," and "going mad over him." Can you think of other examples of metaphors that influence our thinking about a concept? (L.O. 8.6)

5. What makes cross-cultural research on language and thinking challenging? (*Hint*: Remember confounds?) (L.O. 8.6)

READING: RECOGNIZING THE WRITTEN WORD

1. Try out the Stroop effect at
    http://faculty.washington.edu/chudler/words.html
     Why is it difficult? (LO 8.7)

    Why is the Stroop effect greater for adults than for children?

    Would the Stroop effect hold for a bilingual adult? Would it be greater for one
    language than another?

2. What are the prereading skills a child needs to master before learning to read? Why do you think these
    skills are important? (LO 8.8)

3.   Phonological awareness is important in the development of reading as well as in the development of
     spelling. As young children learn to spell, they will often represent all of a word's phonemes in the
     spelling. For example, what might this child be trying to say about "ways to travel"? (LO 8.9)

        "u kan tak a kar or chran or chip."

4. Proficient readers tend to be both faster at reading and better at comprehending than poorer readers.
    Does this finding imply that faster reading speed causes better comprehension? Explain your answer.
    (LO 8.9)

THINKING AND REASONING

1. Without looking back at the book, how would you define *thinking*?

Now check the text's definition.
Did your definition capture the essence of *thinking* as defined by the text? (LO 8.10)

2. Many people have compared the human brain with a computer. But despite their similarities, they also have differences. Give two ways human brains differ from computers. (LO 8.10)

3. What are the benefits of cognitive economy? (LO 8.11)

4. Complete this table of heuristics/biases by filling in the descriptions and examples. (LO 8.11)

Heuristic/Bias	Description	Example
Availability Heuristic	assessing probability based on ease of generating examples	
Confirmation Bias kids eat candy they are all hyper."		"Every time I've seen
Correlation = Causation Fallacy		
Hindsight Bias known that kid would snap. Look at all of		"They should have the evidence!"
Ignoring Base Rates into account	failing to take the base likelihood of an event	

5. How does the "scientific method" help us avoid errors in thinking? (LO 8.11)

6. Functional fixedness involves seeing objects in their usual way and not being able to see alternative functions, even when the alternatives would be practical and useful. Can you think of a time when you "suffered from" or "overcame" functional fixedness? If not, try to create an example. (LO 8.11)

7. College students often claim that they used memorization successfully in high school and are reluctant to give up this low-level strategy despite finding it to be an ineffective way of studying in college. Why might students have difficulty giving up an ineffective strategy? (LO 8.11)

8. OK … you probably heard this one as a kid: Ask someone to spell the word *joke*. Then ask him to spell *folk*. Next ask him to spell *poke*. Finally ask him to spell the white of an egg. He will probably spell "y-o-l-k." But the yolk is the yellow part of an egg. The white part is called albumin. What problem-solving hurdles discussed in your text make this question tricky? (LO 8.11)

AS YOU READ ... CONCEPT MAP ACTIVITIES

ACTIVITY 1: Complete the following concept map for reading.

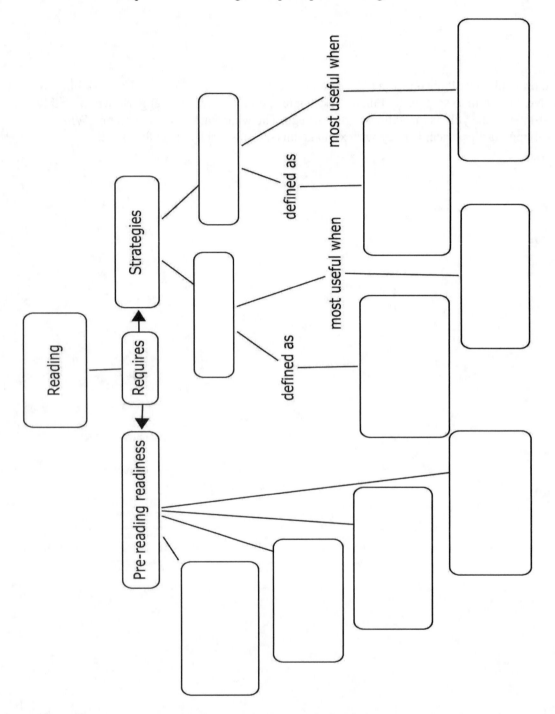

Author activity content supported by *IHMC Cmap Tools* Copyright ©1998-2007 Institute for Human & Machine Cognition

ACTIVITY 2: Create your own concept map in the space provided below by organizing the following concepts from the chapter. Be sure to include superordinate terms, links, and examples that may not be included in the list but are necessary to make the map meaningful.

Theories of Language Development: Imitation, Nativist, Social Pragmatic, General Cognitive Processing.
Language Development: Course, Prelinguistic abilities, Babbling, Single words, Holophrases, Two-word combinations.
Features of Language: Four Levels of Analysis, Phonemes, Morphemes, Syntax, Extralinguistic information.

AS YOU READ ... MYTH OR REALITY?

Myth: Dyslexia is a perceptual problem caused by children making reversal
              errors when they read (e.g., reading *was* for *saw*).

Reality: All children reverse letters when learning to read. Dyslexic children make more reversal
              errors than other children because they make more overall reading errors.

1. In drawing the conclusion that reversal errors cause the dyslexia, what errors in thinking are
    occurring? (*Hint*: The observation that dyslexic children make reversal errors is missing what
    important element of the scientific method?)

Myth: Learning difficult subjects such as Latin has broad effects on thinking.

Reality: Little evidence shows that we can develop "mental muscle" by learning difficult subjects.

1. Rather than developing general skills, people seem to learn things that are more specific. What
    concepts discussed in this chapter support the claim that transfer of learning across context is
    difficult? (*Hint*: Transfer between initial and later learning depends not only on the similarity of
    elements across the two experiences but on the individual noticing the similarity.)

AS YOU READ ... PUT YOUR CRITICAL THINKING SKILLS TO THE TEST

1. Teaching hearing infants to use sign language has become popular recently. Try using Google to search for Internet sites on "Baby Sign Language." Review a few of these sites.
   a. What are the claims they are making?
   b. What is their support?
   c. Now look at one of the articles below by Johnston, Durieux-Smith, and Bloom. How are the conclusions these authors draw different from the Internet sites? Why?
   http://fla.sagepub.com/cgi/content/abstract/25/2/235
   http://www.cllrnet.ca/Docs/Programs/GraduateStudentResearchReviews/2003/CRR.pdf

2. If some is good, is *more* necessarily better? Based on the text's description of factors contributing to reading development, which of the following do you think would be a better choice for a preschool-aged child and why?

A copy of the book, *Read Aloud Rhymes for the Very Young* (Prelutsky & Brown, 1986) for $13.57. Or *The Hooked on Phonics Pre-K Kit* with 3 CD ROMS, Audio CD, 6 workbooks, Bingo Cards, 5 sets of Flashcards, and Progress Poster for $99.95.

AS YOU READ ... MYPSYCHLAB CONNECTION

How Does Language Work?

Have you ever wondered how slips of the tongue occur? Participate in this brief **simulation** on *Lexical Bias in Slips of the Tongue* to show how slips of the tongue can be artificially created.

If you would like to see how we learn language, **watch** *Stimulating Language Development* and *Language Learning*. Have you ever wondered what it might be like to learn in a bilingual environment? **Watch** *Teaching in a Bilingual Classroom* and *Bilingual Education* to find out. To learn more about how other animals communicate, **watch** *Birds and Language*. Are gestures intentional? What is the purpose of gestures? **Watch** *Hand Gesturing Study* to learn about research on gesturing.

Do We Think in Words? The Relation between Language and Thought

How does advertising really work? To understand the theory of linguistic relativity and see how words influence the impressions you form of products, news, other students, and so on, engage in the **simulation** *Power of Words*.

Reading: Recognizing the Written Word

Want to incorporate a fun activity into your learning? Check out the **simulation** *Experiencing the Stroop Effect*. This activity will demonstrate how interference affects your speed of processing information.

Thinking and Reasoning

Are you creative enough to solve a problem that seems as if it has no solution? Try the **explore** *The Two-String Problem*, to find out. Psychologists tap into how your mind organizes information in this classic reaction-timed **simulation** called *The Mind's Organization of Conceptual Knowledge*.

AFTER YOU READ ... PRACTICE TEST #1

Before beginning this practice test, estimate the percent you expect to get correct.
Anticipated percent correct: _____

1. _____ is the view that all thought is represented verbally and that thinking is limited by language.
   a. Linguistic relativism
   b. Covert speech
   c. Linguistic determinism.
   d. The verbal-thought theory

2. The levels of speech analysis from smallest to largest unit are
   a. morpheme, phoneme, extralinguistic information, syntax.
   b. phoneme, morpheme, syntax, extralinguistic information.
   c. morpheme, syntax, extralinguistic information, phoneme.
   d. phoneme, morpheme, extralinguistic information, syntax.

3. _____ are variations within a language used by a group of people who share geographic proximity or ethnic background.
   a. Holophrases
   b. Dialects
   c. Phonetic decompositions
   d. Morphemes

4. Misunderstandings can occur in phone conversations and e-mails because _____ information is missing from the communication.
   a. extralinguistic
   b. syntax
   c. morphemes
   d. phonemes

5. The theory of language that puts the greatest emphasis on innate sources focuses on
   a. imitation.
   b. social pragmatics.
   c. the language acquisition device.
   d. both a and b.

6. The theory of language development that would be the most difficult to falsify is the
   a. nativist theory.
   b. general cognitive processing theory.
   c. social pragmatics theory.
   d. both b and c.

7. Although chimpanzees can learn to communicate with sign language they never really master
   a. syntax.
   b. vocabulary.
   c. the use of signs to make requests.
   d. responding to rewards.

8. One-year-old Lenita says "cookie" while pointing to a cookie just out of reach. She is demonstrating
   a. overgeneralization.
   b. syntax.
   c. a holophrase.
   d. babbling.

9. When children reach the "two-word" stage of language development
   a. they are usually a year old.
   b. they rarely combine words in the correct order.
   c. they understand more about syntax than they can produce.
   d. they rely on holophrases to communicate.

10. The learning of sign language for a deaf child is similar to the learning of spoken language by a hearing child. Which of the following is NOT one of the ways these processes are similar?
    a. Both language systems have the same linguistic features and complexity.
    b. Acquisition follows a similar developmental sequence beginning with babbling.
    c. Sign language use activates the same brain areas as those involved in spoken language.
    d. Both hearing and deaf children learn language from native speakers.

11. Two-year-old Pippa is growing up in a bilingual family—her parents speak both English and Spanish with her. Some evidence indicates that, as a bilingual child, Pippa will
    a. experience significant delays in vocabulary acquisition.
    b. have the advantage of greater metalinguistic awareness.
    c. will only develop proficiency in one language.
    d. will only be able to learn both languages because she is under the age of seven.

12. Of the two major reading strategies, _____ is more efficient when reading familiar words, and _____ is critical for less-familiar words.
    a. linguistic relativity; linguistic determinism
    b. whole word recognition; phonetic decomposition
    c. linguistic determinism; linguistic relativity
    d. phonetic decomposition; whole word recognition

13. You are an avid reader and want your child to develop her reading skills. Which of the following would best prepare a child for reading?
    a. Use flashcards displaying whole words.
    b. Have the child sit on your lap while you read nursery rhymes.
    c. Show the child lots of children's videos.
    c. Have the child hear lots of different people speaking.

14. Several students from your Introductory Psychology class are looking at an ad for a speed reading course and debating its claims. Which of the following statements about reading speed is actually TRUE?
    a. Learning to speed read will improve your comprehension.
    b. Proficient readers tend to be both faster at reading and better at comprehending than poorer readers.
    c. Subvocalizing is critical to comprehension.
    d. Reading speed cannot be increased.

15. For several months following 9/11, thousands of people stopped flying. This response was probably because of heightened fear due to
    a. the availability heuristic.   c. hindsight bias.
    b. correlation is causation belief.   d. confirmation bias.

16. Bianca could not find a vase for the rose Mic brought her. Her failure to realize that her water bottle would have served the purpose is an example of
    a. salience of surface similarities.   c. availability heuristic.
    b. functional fixedness.   d. the consequence effect.

17. Students' failure to realize that memorization techniques that worked in high school may not help them understand material at the college level may be thought of as an example of the problem-solving hurdle known as
    a. salience of surface similarities.
    b. correlation is causation.
    c. mental set.
    d. the consequence effect.

18. Which of the following children would be of greatest concern to you?
    a. Nico at 12 months can comprehend several words, but does not yet speak.
    b. Rubin at 18 months calls all gray-haired men "grandpa."
    c. Mato at 13 months does not recognize his name.
    d. All of these children are experiencing significant delays.

19. Intuition, snap judgments, and heuristics
    a. free us to engage in tasks of greater complexity.
    b. have not been studied empirically.
    c. are usually more accurate than careful analysis.
    d. are accurate only in rare situations.

20. A major reason it is difficult to draw conclusions from research on cross-cultural differences in language and thought is because
    a. cross-linguistic comparisons are correlational rather than experimental.
    b. language and culture are nearly always confounded.
    c. there is no thought without language.
    d. both a and b are true.

After completing the test, calculate your percent correct
(*/ 20 =*   *) x 100 = _____.*

How accurate were your expectations? Does your performance suggest the need for additional study? For the items you missed, go back and identify why the "correct" answer is the best answer.

AFTER YOU READ ... PRACTICE TEST #2

Before beginning this practice test, estimate the percent you expect to get correct.
Anticipated percent correct: _____

1. The complexity of human language
   a. contributes to its flexibility.
   b. requires an extended learning period.
   c. holds true only for certain languages.
   d. applies to both a and b.

2. Which of the following statements about phonemes is TRUE?
   a. Phonemes are categories of sounds that our vocal apparatus produces.
   b. A one-to-one correspondence occurs between individual letters of the alphabet and the phonemes in the language.
   c. All languages use the same phoneme categories.
   d. Phonemes include the smallest units of meaning in a language.

3. Syntax
   a. is a set of rules that is rarely violated in spoken language.
   b. is universal across languages.
   c. includes morphological markers that change the meaning of existing words.
   d. reflects the speaker's nonverbal cues.

4. People have begun to use signs such as ☺ and ;-) in their e-mails as partial compensation for
   a. a lack of syntactical information.
   b. a lack of extralinguistic information.
   c. confirmation biases.
   d. availability heuristics.

5. The nativist account of language acquisition
   a. claims that children come into the world knowing how to speak.
   b. proposes a specific human organ for language acquisition.
   c. makes claims that are largely unfalsifiable.
   d. both b and c.

6. Research suggests that, before birth, infants
   a. cannot hear inside the womb.
   b. can learn to read if read to regularly.
   c. can learn about the melody and rhythm of their native language.
   d. can hear but cannot make out characteristics of language.

7. Babbling
   a. refers to unintentional vocalization.
   b. evolves over the first year of life.
   c. initially includes only sounds of an infant's native language.
   d. is not dependent on control of the vocal tract.

8. Chimpanzee and human infant language learning are both similar and different. Which of the following statements is FALSE?
    a. Human babies get better and faster at word learning; chimpanzees do not.
    b. Chimpanzees require thousands of trials of paired associations with rewards; human children do not.
    c. Human children use words to request food and other pleasurable activities; chimpanzees do not.
    d. Chimpanzees never fully master syntax; human children combine words to form complex sentences.

9. A child who is learning a second language
    a. will develop greater proficiency if exposed to the second language before age 7.
    b. will experience delays in learning the vocabulary of each of his/her languages.
    c. will never learn the syntax of the second language if first exposed after age 8.
    d. will perform more poorly on language tasks compared with monolingual children.

10. Research on the relation between language and cognition
    a. suggests that language shapes all aspects of perception, thought, and memory.
    b. finds that some aspects of thinking are more vulnerable to language influence than others.
    c. finds that cultures that have only two "color" words, dark and bright, cannot distinguish other colors.
    d. finds that language cannot affect thinking.

11. The reading strategy that involves sounding out words by drawing correspondences between printed letters and sounds is known as
    a. phoneme identification.
    b. word decomposition.
    c. phonetic decomposition.
    d. whole word recognition.

12. Many factors are critical in children developing the ability to read. Which of the following statements about reading is FALSE?
    a. In learning to read children must learn to recognize whole words.
    b. In learning to read children must learn to recognize how printed letters correspond to sounds.
    c. In learning to read children must learn that written words are meaningful.
    d. In learning to read children must listen to books read in utero.

13. The social pragmatics account of language acquisition
    a. holds that children learn language by being directly reinforced by their parents.
    b. holds that children infer word meanings from the context of social interaction.
    c. is a nativist account of language development.
    d. is unfalsifiable.

14. Once a child is labeled dyslexic, teachers and parents notice the reversal errors the child makes in his/her reading (e.g., reading *was* for *saw*), but fail to notice that all children make reversal errors when learning to read. This tendency to see the dyslexic child's errors is an example of
    a. mental set.
    b. confirmation bias.
    c. functional fixedness.
    d. salience of surface similarity.

15. Which of the following statements regarding children's errors in language use is TRUE?
    a. Children rarely make errors they do not hear.
    b. Children's errors are not part of normal development and require speech therapy.
    c. Using the word *grandpa* for any gray-haired man is an example of an undergeneralization.
    d. Errors tell us children are generating language from their understanding of its rules.

16. Which of the following statements about sign language is TRUE?
    a. Deaf people don't need sign language because they can lip-read.
    b. Learning to sign impedes a deaf child's ability to learn to speak.
    c. American Sign Language is English translated word-for-word into signs.
    d. Deaf babies pass through the same stages in language acquisition as do hearing babies.

17. The Stroop effect naming task
    a. requires attending to both printed words and their printed color.
    b. demonstrates that reading is automatic
    c. is more difficult for young children who are just learning to read.
    d. is a task in which it is easier to read words than to name the color in which the word is written.

18. Top-down processing
    a. is an example of a cognitive error in information processing.
    b. uses preexisting knowledge to help streamline information processing.
    c. begins with the analysis of sensory data.
    d. both b and c.

19. Searching for a hammer and not thinking of using your shoe is an example of
    a. functional fixedness.   c. consequence effect.
    b. availability heuristic.   d. confirmation bias.

20. Sarah believes that sugar causes hyperactivity. She has frequently noticed that her daughter gets excited when eating ice cream at Ben & Jerry's. Sarah has failed to notice, however, that her daughter also gets excited when eating French fries at McDonald's. Sarah's differential attention best illustrates
    a. functional fixedness.   c. confirmation bias.
    b. the availability heuristic.   d. hindsight bias.

After completing the test, calculate your percent correct
(/ 20 =   ) x 100 = _____.

How accurate were your expectations? Does your performance suggest the need for additional study? For the items you missed, go back and identify why the "correct" answer is the best answer.

After You Read . . . Practice Test Answer Keys

Practice Test 1.

1. c (p. 334)
2. b (p. 320)
3. b (p. 321)
4. a (p. 320)
5. c (p. 327)
6. a (p. 327)
7. a (p. 329)
8. c (p. 326)
9. c (p. 326)
10. d (p. 331)
11. b (p. 332)
12. b (p. 338)
13. b (p. 339)
14. b (p. 340)
15. a (p. 345)
16. b (p. 347)
17. c (p. 346)
18. c (p. 325)
19. a (p. 342–344)
20. d (p. 328)

Practice Test 2.

1. d (p. 322)
2. a (p. 320)
3. c (p. 320)
4. b (p. 320)
5. d (p. 327)
6. c (p. 323)
7. b (p. 324)
8. c (p. 329)
9. a (p. 323)
10. b (p. 337)
11. c (p. 338)
12. d (p. 338–340)
13. b (p. 327)
14. b (p. 345)
15. d (p. 325–327)
16. d (p. 330)
17. b (p. 338)
18. b (p. 343)
19. a (p. 347)
20. c (p. 345)

AFTER YOU READ ... CONCEPT MAPPING ACTIVITY ANSWERS

ACTIVITY 1: Complete the following concept map for reading.

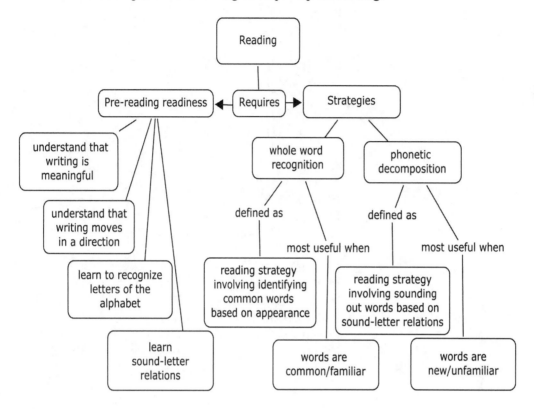

CHAPTER 9
INTELLIGENCE AND IQ TESTING
CONTROVERSY AND CONSENSUS

BEFORE YOU READ ...CHAPTER PREVIEW

Is intelligence one thing or many? The answer depends on your level of specificity. The various abilities that demonstrate intelligent behavior show modest positive correlations. The correlations suggest that the abilities vary together (they have something in common), but they also vary independently from one another (each ability is in some way unique). So although most theorists agree that intelligence involves comprehending and adapting to the environment, theories differ in the degree to which they focus on the commonalities versus the differences among the various abilities reflecting intelligence. Spearman was interested in what is common among intellectual abilities and proposed a single capacity underlying intelligence he called "g" (general intelligence). Other theorists emphasize how the correlations among the abilities form clusters. Cattell and Horn, for example, proposed a distinction between fluid intelligence (the mechanics of solving novel problems) and crystallized intelligence (the accumulation of knowledge). Validity for this distinction comes from evidence that fluid intelligence tends to decline with age while crystallized intelligence can continue to increase in healthy adults. Some theorists have proposed multiple "intelligences" that are distinct from one another. Criticism of these theories include observations that many of these so called "separate" intelligences are in fact positively correlated and some of these intelligences are more appropriately seen as talents. Search for neural correlates of intelligence suggests that "brainy" people tend to have somewhat larger brains, although the cause and effect are unclear. Intelligent people do have more efficient brains. The activity related to intelligence seems to be within the prefrontal cortex, an area involved in planning.

Intelligence was measured before most of these theories were proposed. In 1905, Binet and Simon had a practical problem: to identify school children who may be in need of educational assistance. They developed a battery of tests that would predict school success. The early form of the intelligence quotient was calculated as mental age/chronological age x 100. Because of problems with this index, today IQ reflects where a person's measured intelligence falls within the normal distribution. Scores are distributed normally along a bell curve. A score of 100 reflects the average for people at that age. Ninety-five percent of people score between 70 and 130. Scores below 70 reflect mental retardation; scores above 130 reflect giftedness. Mental retardation may result from a variety of influences including genetic errors (e.g., Down syndrome) and teratogens (e.g., FAS). The environment after birth also plays a role, particularly in influencing the mild forms of retardation. Among the classification of mental retardation, most individuals fall within the mild category and can be mainstreamed into normal classrooms. Terman's study of gifted children dispelled several myths including the idea that gifted individuals are physically fragile, "burn out" at an early age, and are predisposed to mental disorders.

Once those in business and politics became users of IQ tests, misinterpretations led to misuse and abuse. Tests were given to populations for which they were not designed and were used to label and to sort people. The eugenics movement took sorting to extremes, encouraging people with high IQs (and supposedly good genes) to reproduce and those with low IQs to be sterilized. The movement is an example of how abuses can result from misinterpretations of science.

The sources of IQ include both genetics and environment. Researchers have observed that IQs of identical twins correlated at about .75 and the IQs of fraternal twins correlate about .35. This observation suggests genetic influences on IQ because identical twins are more alike than fraternal twins; and suggests environmental influences because the correlation among IQs of identical twins is less than 1.00. Adoption studies also suggest the influence of genetics on intelligence because adopted children's IQs are more similar to their birth mothers compared with their adopted mothers; they also suggest the influence of environment because children adopted from deprived environments into enriched environments show higher IQs. Environmental influences on IQ are difficult to disentangle but likely include nutrition and poverty. The puzzling Flynn effect reflects the finding that the average IQ has been rising steadily. Most psychologists assume the effect reflects environmental factors such as improved nutrition.

More variability can be found in IQ scores among members of the same sex than between members of opposite sexes. The few sex differences in IQ scores that do exist include higher performance on some verbal measures for females and higher performance on some spatial measures for males. Although average group differences do appear among races, substantial overlap is present in the distributions. Most research suggests that environmental factors such as poverty, social discrimination, and characteristics of the testing situation rather than genetic differences underlie racial differences.

Psychologists generally require creative accomplishments to be both novel and successful. Creativity has been measured by tests of divergent thinking (e.g., the capacity to generate many solutions to a problem), but creativity also involves convergent thinking (e.g. finding the best answer to a problem). It also appears that "…the best predictor of the *quality* of a person's creative accomplishment is the *quantity* of that person's output." The personality trait, "openness to experience," is moderately positively correlated with crystallized intelligence. Because the observation is correlational, several explanations are possible for this relation. Emotional intelligence refers to the ability to understand one's own and other emotions. Despite its popularity, the concept does not predict variability between individuals beyond general intelligence and basic personality measures. One reason "smart" people may come to believe strange things is the ideological immune system—the tendency to defend against views that contradict one's own. Wisdom has been defined as an application of one's intelligence for the common good. Wise people balance their own and others' interests. Wisdom does not necessarily come with age.

BEFORE YOU READ … LEARNING OBJECTIVES

After reading Chapter 9 you should be able to:

9.1   Identify different models and types of intelligence
9.2   Describe the neural correlates of intelligence
9.3   Determine how psychologists calculate IQ
9.4   Explain the history of misuse of intelligence tests in the United States
9.5   Distinguish the unique characteristics of mental retardation and genius
9.6.   Explain how genetic influences can be determined from family studies
9.7   Identify ways in which the environment affects IQ measures
9.8   Identify the similarities and differences in mental ability between men and women
9.9   Evaluate the evidence concerning racial differences in IQ
9.10   Explain why evidence regarding group differences in IQ does not imply inherent
       superiority or inferiority of one group relative to another
9.11   Show how creativity and personality relate to intelligence
9.12   Evaluate scientific research on emotional intelligence and wisdom

---

BEFORE YOU READ ... TERM IDENTIFICATION

---

abstract thinking (p. 356)
association fallacy (p. 365)
bell curve (p. 371)
between-group heritability (p. 385)
convergent thinking (p. 388)
crystallized intelligence (p. 358)
culture-fair IQ test (p. 367)
deviation IQ (p. 364)
divergent thinking (p. 388)
emotional intelligence (p. 390)
eugenics (p. 364)
fluid intelligence (p. 358)
Flynn effect (p. 379)
g (general intelligence) (p. 357)

ideological immune system (p. 391)
intelligence quotient (p. 354)
intelligence test (p. 356)
mental age (p. 364)
mental retardation (p. 372)
multiple intelligences (p. 358)
s (specific abilities) (p. 357)
Stanford-Binet IQ Test (p. 367)
stereotype threat (p. 386)
test bias (p. 384)
triarchic model (p. 359)
Wechsler Adult Intelligence Scale (WAIS) (p. 366)
wisdom (p. 391)
within-group heritability (p. 385)

AS YOU READ ... PRACTICE ACTIVITIES

WHAT IS INTELLIGENCE? DEFINITIONAL CONFUSION

1. Most psychologists would agree that intelligence has something to do with higher mental processes. What are the four abilities generally believed to demonstrate intelligence behavior? (LO 9.1)

2. The first intelligence test developed in 1905 by Binet and Simon was designed to solve what practical problem? (LO 9.1)

As you read through the chapter, keep track of the outcomes that are related to modern IQ scores and those that tend not to be related to IQ scores.

Related to IQ	Not Related to IQ

3. Intelligence tests include a variety of items tapping mathematical ability, verbal ability, spatial reasoning, and verbal reasoning. Despite this variety, items tend to correlate positively with one another. Does this finding suggest that intelligence is one thing or many? Could it be both? Explain your answer. (LO 9.1)

4. Carol Dweck and others study people's beliefs about the nature of intelligence and how these beliefs relate to behavior. (LO 9.1)

   According to this research, how does the behavior of people who believe in a fixed (unchanging) intelligence tend to differ from the behavior of people who believe intelligence is flexible?

   Do you tend to see intelligence as fixed or flexible? Do you see the same relation between your belief and your behavior as the relations observed by Dweck?

5. Gardner proposes that multiple intelligences are different from and independent from one another. (LO 9.1)

   Complete the following statements.
           Gardner's claims are based on evidence from…

Despite popular appeal, researchers remain critical of Gardner's claims because…

6. What is the main lesson of Kruger and Dunning's work on how well we know whether we know? (LO 9.1)

What implications does this work have for studying in college? (*Hint*: What do we ask you before and after each quiz?)

7. Sternberg proposes three domains of intelligence in his triarchic model. List and give an example of these domains. (LO 9.1)

   1. _____

   Example_____

2. _____

Example_____

3. _____

Example_____

Criticism of his claims include:

8. Research on the biological basis of intelligence and information processing suggests at least some validity to the idea that people who are intelligent are "quick minded." What sort of evidence supports this view? (LO 9.2)

A moderate correlation can be demonstrated between brain size and IQ. What does this correlation mean?

INTELLIGENCE TESTING: THE GOOD, THE BAD, AND THE UGLY

1. What was Wilhelm Stern's original formula for calculating IQ? (LO 9.3)

Modern IQ scores indicate where a person's measured intelligence falls in the normal distribution. Describe what this means and how it avoids a flaw in the original formula. (LO 9.3)

2. Draw a bell curve to describe the normal distribution of IQ scores. Label the following: (LO 9.3)
→   The point representing the average IQ score in the population.
→   The point representing the usual distinguishing point for mental retardation.
→   The part of the distribution representing the 95% of people who have IQs between 70 and 130.

3. Fill in this outline describing the most commonly used IQ test today. (LO 9.3)

The _____ _____ _____ (or WAIS)

        Yields three scores
           Verbal Scale
                consisting of

           Performance Scale
                consisting of

           Full Scale
                combining

4. Misuses of IQ testing followed the development of the "testing business." Explain the misinterpretation of the IQ measure that underlies this misuse. (LO 9.4)

5. Terman's study of exceptional individuals with IQs above 135 dispelled several myths about individuals with high IQs. List the myths and the realities. (LO 9.3)

      Myths:

      Realities:

      Research on genius also provided evidence that becoming a genius in one's chosen field takes ….

6. "IQ-type" assessments taken in the first few years of life *do not* correlate with later IQ, yet measures of speed of habituation *do* show moderate correlations with later IQ. (LO 9.5)

      Why do you think early IQ measures do not predict later IQ measures but a measure of information processing does predict later IQ?

7. The Raven's Progressive Matrices is considered a "culturally fair test." What does this mean? (LO 9.5)

8. The chapter brings up the standardized test, the SAT, at several points. Summarize these findings by answering the following questions: (LO 9.5)

      How are SAT scores affected by training courses?

      Are SAT scores correlated with first year college grades?

      Are SAT scores correlated with later college grades?

      What factors might explain these observed relations?

GENETIC AND ENVIRONMENTAL INFLUENCES ON IQ

1. Complete this sentence: Studies of the correlations between IQs of twins show that identical twins' IQs are generally [higher/lower] compared with correlations between IQs of fraternal twins. (LO 9.6)

These observations suggest that IQ is genetically influenced because…

These observations also suggest that IQ is environmentally influenced because…

2. Findings from adoption studies include the following: (LO 9.6)
    a. Adopted children tend to be more similar to their _____ parents.

    b. Resemblance to adoptive parents _____ with age.

    c. Contributions of the environment are suggested by the observation that adoptive children from deprived environments show _____ IQ when adopted into enriched environments.

What conclusions can be drawn from these studies?

How do adoption studies allow us to separate genetic from environmental influences? (LO 9.6)

3. **T or F**: Later-born children tend to have slightly *lower* IQs than earlier-born children. Explain. (LO 9.7)

4. What evidence supports the claim that schooling influences intelligence? (LO 9.7)

5. Discuss ways poverty might influence children's IQ scores. (LO 9.7)

6. What is the Flynn effect? (LO 9.7)

What possible explanations for the effect have been proposed?

Can you think of others?

GROUP DIFFERENCES IN IQ: THE SCIENCE AND THE POLITICS

1. Complete this sentence, and then draw and label overlapping bell curves (i.e., men, women) to reflect your answer. Finally, check your answer and drawing with Figure 9.16.

Although gender differences [do/do not] appear in average IQ scores, more [men/women] are at both the low and the high ends of the IQ bell curve. (LO 9.8)

2. Men and women tend to score at the same level on most intellectual tasks. However, women tend to score higher on tasks involving _____, and men tend to score higher on tasks involving _____. (LO 9.8)

3. Complete this sentence, then *explain* your answer.
    The variability [within/between] races tends to be greater than the variability [within/between] races. (LO 9.9)

4. Herrnstein and Murray's book, *The Bell Curve*, contributed to a controversy because it claimed … (LO 9.9)

Evaluate the evidence that contradicts the book's claim.

1. Test bias

2. Misinterpretation of heritability

3. Stereotype threat

5. **T or F:** Heredity may contribute to individual differences in intelligence but not necessarily to group differences. Explain your answer. (LO 9.10)

THE REST OF THE STORY: OTHER DIMENSIONS OF INTELLECT

1. Differentiate divergent and convergent thinking and link each with its example. (LO 9.11)

_____ thinking is . . .

An example question would be "How many ways could you use a paper cup?"

_____ thinking is . . .

An example question would be "What is the area of a 3 x 5 rectangle?"

2. Evaluate the following statement: "The best predictor of the quality of a person's creative accomplishment is the quality of that person's output." (LO 9.11)

3. The personality trait, "openness to experience," is moderately positively correlated with crystallized intelligence. The observation is correlational, which means that several explanations are possible for the relation. Describe at least two possible explanations. (LO 9.12)

4. Emotional intelligence refers to … (LO 9.12)

Despite its popularity, the concept does not predict variability between individuals beyond …

5. Why might "smart" people nevertheless believe strange things? How is the ideological immune system involved? (LO 9.12)

6. What are the three characteristics of wisdom? Do you know someone you would consider wise? What is it about this person that reflects the characteristic of wisdom? (LO 9.12)

AS YOU READ ... COGNITIVE MAP ACTIVITIES

ACTIVITY 1: The various components of intelligence can be summarized by what is called the "hierarchy of mental abilities." Try to describe such a hierarchy. Start with *g* at the top, include the "clusters" or "facets," and then give an example of "specific abilities."

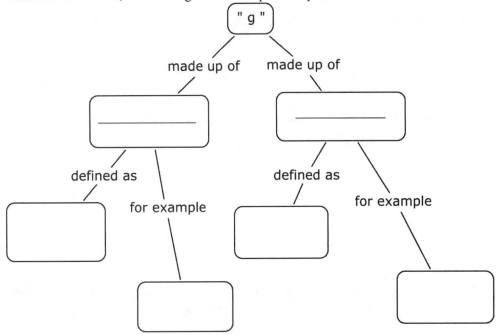

ACTIVITY 2: Summarize the criteria and categorize for classifying the degrees of mental

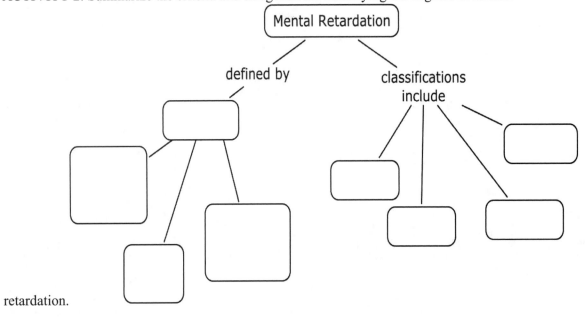

retardation.

Author activity content supported by *IHMC Cmap Tools* Copyright ©1998-2007 Institute for Human & Machine Cognition

AS YOU READ … MYTH OR REALITY?

Myth: Fifty percent of a child's intelligence is acquired by age 4.
Have you heard this claim? Have you ever thought about what it "means"? When you do,
do you still think it makes sense?
Reality: Not only does the brain remain malleable throughout life, some abilities continue to develop well into late adulthood.

1.   The 50% claim is partly based on a misinterpretation of "mental test data." As the text notes, developmental tests before the age of 4 tend to have low reliability and to be unrelated to (poor predictors of) later IQ scores. By age 4, however, you can predict with about 50% accuracy what a child's IQ test score will be at age 17. Why does this statistical finding not translate to the claim as stated?

This 50% myth relates to anther myth of infant intellectual development that you will read more about in Chapter 10.

Myth: Highly stimulating early environments are critical for infant intellectual development.
Reality: Most normal environments provide adequate stimulation for infant development.

1.   Like the 50% misconception, infant stimulation claims are partly based on a misinterpretation of research. Research does show a negative effect of deprived environments on intelligence. However, adding *more* stimulation to already normal environments is an overextrapolation of the findings. It is the overextrapolation that seems to dominate the market for infant products. Look for websites marketing "infant stimulation" products. How have these marketers misinterpreted the scientific research?

Myth: Teaching students according to their preferred learning style will positively influence their
           learning.
Reality: Little evidence supports the claim that learning styles actually differentiate students, can be reliably measured, or that "teaching" to student's learning styles facilitates learning.

1.   You may have heard the claim that students' preferred style of learning (auditory, visual, etc.) influences their learning. Learning styles are popular among teachers despite a lack of supporting evidence (http://www.aft.org/pubs-reports/american_educator/fall99/DiffStrokes.pdf). If so little research supports learning styles, why do you think the concept remains so popular with teachers?

As You Read ... Put Your Critical Thinking Skills to the Test

---

1. The Flynn effect reflects the observation that average IQ scores have been rising. Based on your understanding of the factors influencing IQ, is it possible "We are getting less dumb" rather than "We are getting smarter"? What evidence would support such an interpretation?

2. If Dweck's work on the relations between perceptions of ability and effort are correct, why might the current obsession with performance and testing students be undermining their learning?

3. As the text notes, early intervention programs result in positive effects such as lower high school dropout rates but do not produce lasting increases in IQ. Reflecting on these findings, Brooks-Gunn stated, "It is unrealistic, given our knowledge of development, to expect short-term early interventions to last indefinitely, especially if children end up attending poor quality schools. It is magical thinking to expect that if we intervene in the early years, no further help will be needed by children in the elementary school years and beyond." http://www.srcd.org/Documents/Publications/SPR/spr17-1.pdf

How do concepts presented in Chapter 9 support this statement?

As You Read ... MyPsychLab Connection

What is Intelligence? Definitional Confusion
To become familiar with and to compare non-traditional methods of intelligence **explore** *Gardner's multiple intelligences* and *Sternberg's triarchic model of intelligence*.

Intelligence Testing: The Good, the Bad and the Ugly
Watch Robert Guthrie, author of Even the Rat Was White discuss the validity of intelligence tests and what they measure in *Are Intelligence Tests Valid: Robert Guthrie*.

Genetic and Environmental Influences on IQ
What's more important when it comes to intelligence – nature or nurture? To find some clues, **explore** *Correlations between IQ Scores of Persons of Varying Relationships*. How well do you understand the influences on IQ? Test yourself by **exploring** *Factors Affecting Intelligence*.

Group Differences in IQ: The Science and the Politics
Try the **simulation** *Mental Rotation*, which explains how spatial abilities are tested and allows you to participate. Did you know that knowledge of a stereotype has been shown to impact scores on tests? **Listen** to the podcast *Stereotype Threat* to find out how.

The Rest of the Story: Other Dimensions of Intellect
Do you think "out of the box?" Test yourself with the **simulation** *Creativity*.

AFTER YOU READ ... PRACTICE TEST #1

Before beginning this practice test, estimate the percent you expect to get correct.
Anticipated percent correct: _____

1. In general, experts agree intelligence is demonstrated by
a.   social, emotional, verbal, and artistic ability.
b.   abstract reasoning, adaptive learning, knowledge acquisition, and the ability to
learn from experience.
c.   the sensory capacities: visual, auditory, gustatory, and olfactory.
d.   practical, analytical, emotional, and creative ability.

2. The first intelligence test developed in 1905 by Binet and Simon was designed to solve what practical problem?
a.   To determine which military recruits would serve as officers and which would
serve on the front lines.
b.   To identify those who were from "good stock."
c.   To identify school children in need of educational assistance.
d.   To predict career success.

3. According to Dweck and others who have studied people's beliefs about intelligence, people who believe that intelligence is a fixed entity tend to
a.   become energized after failure.
b.   believe that effort contributes to the development of knowledge.
c.   persist on difficult tasks.
d.   avoid challenging tasks.

4. Which of the following statements about Gardner's theory of multiple intelligences is NOT true?
a.   He has demonstrated that the eight forms of intelligence are independent from one another.
b.   His claims are partly based on evidence from people with brain damage.
c.   Critics claim that several of his intelligences reflect nonmental talents.
d.   He believes the ability to recognize, identify, and understand animals is an intelligence.

5. Which of the following reflects crystallized intelligence?
a.   Your ability to solve a puzzle you've never seen
b.   Your ability to answer the question "What's the population of the United States?"
c.   Your ability to "size up" people you've just meet
d.   Your reaction time

6. Brain volume correlates positively (between .3 and .4) with measured intelligence. What can you say based on this finding?
a.   It's likely that brain size has nothing to do with thinking.
b.   Large brain volume is necessary for high intelligence.
c.   A third variable underlies the observed relation.
d.   We don't know whether these findings reflect a direct causal relation.

7. Modern IQ scores
a.　　are calculated as MA/CA x 100.
b.　　rely on a statistic called deviation IQ.

c. reflect simple mental age.
d. = CA/MA.

8. Abdul is considered a child genius with an IQ of 145. Based on the research with people with exceptional abilities, which of the following is likely to be TRUE?
a.　　He is above average in physical health.
b.　　He is likely to develop severe psychopathology in adulthood.
c.　　He will achieve brilliance with little effort.
d.　　He will burn out and become "average" by age 25.

9. Of those classified as having mental retardation, 85% fall into the _____ category.
a.　　mildly retarded
b.　　moderately retarded

c.　　severely retarded
d.　　profoundly retarded

10. Although "IQ-type" measures from the first few years of life do not correlate with later IQ, _____shows moderate correlations with later IQ.
a.　　age at which the infant reaches motor-milestones
b.　　age at which the child speaks his/her first words
c.　　speed of habituation
d.　　visual acuity

11. IQ studies of adopted children find
a.　　adopted children tend to be more similar to their adoptive parents compared with their biological parents.
b.　　adopted children's resemblance to their adoptive parents decreases with age.
c.　　children adopted from deprived environments are unaffected by their enriched adoptive environments.
d.　　IQs of unrelated adopted children, raised in the same family, are highly correlated

12. Which of the following statements is TRUE?
a.　　Later-born children tend to have slightly higher IQs than earlier-born children.
b.　　Heredity may contribute to individual differences in intelligence but not necessarily to group differences.
c.　　Intelligence and creativity are highly related.
d.　　Intelligence and personality are entirely independent.

13. Although _____ gender differences are found in average IQ scores, more _____ are at both the low and the high ends of the IQ bell curve.
a.　　no; men.
b.　　no; women.

c.　　some; men.
d.　　some; women.

14. Which of the following statement about heritability is TRUE?
a.　　The variability between races tends to be greater than the variability within races.
b.　　Because IQ is heritable, differences between groups are the result of genetic differences.
c.　　Because IQ is heritable, racial difference in IQ are heritable.
d.　　Within-group heritability doesn't necessarily imply between-group heritability.

15. Herrnstein and Murray's book, *The Bell Curve*, contributed to a controversy because it claimed
a.   the dominate culture had created tests that were biased against subcultures.
b.   the media had a tendency to misinterpret the concept of heritability racial differences.
c.   intelligence was the result of genetic differences between races.
d.   observed racial differences in IQ were really the result of stereotype threat.

16. Research on group differences in intelligence show that
a.   men and women are more similar in levels of intelligence than they are different.
b.   women are better than men on mathematical analysis.
c.   more women than men fall at the high and low ends of the IQ distribution.
d.   men tend to get lost because they have poor spatial abilities.

17. Which of the following ideas do you think psychologists would consider creative?
a.   Washing your car by driving it into a lake
b.   Developing a liquid paper to cover mistakes in typing
c.   Killing flies with darts
d.   Both a and c

18. Which of the following individuals demonstrates LOW levels of emotional intelligence?
a.   Lupe can tell from a distance when her husband is angry.
b.   Alicia goes for a walk when stressed by work.
c.   Mikhail ignores his mother when she is angry because he feels she gets angry for no reason.
d.   Anna knows her father will be mad if she leaves a mess in the kitchen.

19. Which of the following reflects the text's discussion of "smart" people?
a.   Smart people are immune to the belief in strange things.
b.   The strength of the ideological immune system is negatively related to IQ.
c.   People with high IQs are vulnerable to the sense of knowing everything.
d.   The higher the IQ, the more likely one is to consider alternative explanations.

20. What are the three characteristics of wisdom?
a.   Concern for self, concern for others, and concern for society
b.   Practical intelligence, analytic intelligence, and creative intelligence
c.   Age, IQ, and creativity
d.   Verbal ability, social concern, and emotional intelligence

After completing the test, calculate your percent correct
(/ 20 =   ) x 100 = _____.

How accurate were your expectations? Does your performance suggest the need for additional study?
For the items you missed, go back and identify why the "correct" answer is the best answer.

AFTER YOU READ ... PRACTICE TEST #2

Before beginning this practice test, estimate the percent you expect to get correct.
Anticipated percent correct: _____

1. Which of the following is TRUE?
a.	Although some abilities cluster together, little evidence indicates a "general intelligence."
b.	Correlations among the variety of items assessing intelligence prove that a single common factor underlies individual differences in IQ.
c.	Our ability to solve spatial problems is due to our general problem-solving ability and also to our specific spatial ability.
d.	The finding that items on intelligence tests do not correlate supports the notion of multiple intelligences.

2. Fluid intelligence
a.	increases steadily through adulthood.
b.	reflects the accumulation of information.
c.	is uncorrelated with crystallized intelligence.
d.	is measured by items such as the ability to solve novel puzzles.

3. Which of the following is one of Sternberg's proposed three domains of intelligence?
a.	practical intelligence, or "street smarts."
b.	*g,* or global intelligence.
c.	spatial intelligence, or the ability to think about objects in three dimensions.
d.	emotional intelligence, or the ability to understand and control emotion.

4. What is the main lesson of Kruger and Dunning's work on how well we know whether we know?
a.	Most people are able to accurately estimate their own level of intelligence (IQ).
b.	People with low levels of skill in a given domain may overestimate their performance because they don't know that they don't know.
c.	People who perform poorly on a job are clearly aware of their poor level of performance.
d.	Both a and c.

5. Research on the biological basis of intelligence and information processing suggests at least some validity to the idea that people who are intelligent are "quick minded." What sort of evidence supports this view?
a.	Measured intelligence correlates negatively with reaction time.
b.	A moderate correlation is evident between brain volume and measure of intelligence.
c.	Most items on intelligence tests tend to be intercorrelated.
d.	Psychologists refer to thinking as information processing.

6. The distribution of IQ scores in the population approximates a normal distribution (bell curve), which means that 95% of people have IQs between

a.	100 and 200.	c.	70 and 130.
b.	80 and 100.	d.	75 and 100.

7. Terman and others who study exceptional individuals have found that children with high IQs
a.   demonstrate exceptional abilities with little effort.
b.   burn out at an early age.
c.   suffer from poor physical health.
d.   demonstrate normal mental health.

8. The Raven's Progressive Matrices test
a.   is considered a "culturally fair test."
b.   provides both verbal and performance scores.
c.   includes questions such as "How is a dog and a rose alike?"
d.   assesses memory for lists of digits.

9. According to the text's discussion of the standardized test,
a.   SAT scores are uncorrelated with IQ scores.
b.   SAT scores are uncorrelated with first-year college grades.
c.   SAT scores are strongly correlated with later college grades.
d.   SAT scores' modest improvement with prep courses is likely due to practice effects.

10. Poverty can influence children's IQ scores
a.   by influencing quality of nutrition.
b.   by influencing degree of exposure to toxins.
c.   because poverty is influence by genetic factors.
d.   both a and b.

11. What is the Flynn effect?
a.   The finding that earlier-borns score higher on tests of intelligence compared with later-borns.
b.   The finding that the least competent are likely to have the most confidence in their competence.
c.   The finding that average intelligence scores have been rising over time.
d.   The finding that crystallized intelligence can increase throughout adulthood.

12. Which of the following statements about gender differences in IQ is TRUE?
a.   Men and women tend to score at the same level on most intellectual tasks.
b.   Women tend to score higher on tasks requiring spatial abilities.
c.   Men tend to score higher on tasks requiring verbal abilities.
d.   More women fall at the lower end and more men fall at the higher end of the IQ distribution.

13. IQ tests have been shown to be good predictors of _____, but NOT good predictors of_____.
a.   school performance; crime-proneness
b.   health literacy; health-related outcomes
c.   job performance; school performance
d.   school performance; creativity

14. Which of the following family members would likely be the MOST similar in IQ?
a.   Mother and father   c.   Identical twins
b.   Mother and biological child   d.   Fraternal twins

15. Which of the following findings provides evidence that the family environment influences the development of intelligent behavior?
a.   Identical twins are more similar in IQ than fraternal twins.
b.   Siblings reared together are more similar in IQ than are siblings reared apart.
c.   Identical twins reared apart are more similar in IQ than are siblings reared together.
d.   Adopted children are more similar in IQ to their biological mother than to their adopted mother.

16. Which piece of research provides the strongest evidence that schooling exerts an influence on IQ?
a.   Number of years in school correlates .60 with IQ.
b.   Individuals with high IQ scores enjoy taking classes more than individual with low IQ scores.
c.   When comparing children of the same age who differ in years in school, children who've attended an extra year of school tend to have higher IQs.
d.   Children's IQs increase significantly during the summer months.

17. The eugenics movement
a.   was based on careful redesign of childhood IQ tests to make them appropriate for use with adults.
b.   recommended but never required the sterilization of low IQ individuals.
c.   was an effort to improve a population's "genetic stock."
d.   both a and b.

18. Avery is developing a measure of creativity. Which of the following questions would she be likely to include in her assessment?
a.   You have 2 pair of black and 2 pair of brown socks in a drawer. The room is pitch black. How many socks to you need to pull out to be sure you have at least one pair?
b.   7,695 x 15,480 = ?
c.   How many uses can you think of for a shoe?
d.   In order to duplicate this pattern [   ]   [] , what shape would come next?

19. The personality trait, "openness to experience," is moderately positively correlated with crystallized intelligence, which indicates that
a.   intellectually curious people expose themselves to more knowledge and learn more.
b.   people who know more find learning easier and more enjoyable.
c.   with only a moderate correlation, no real link is likely between the trait and intelligence.
d.   either a or b is possible.

20.   Although Yolanda is 8 years old, she has some difficulty dressing herself. Recently she received a score of 68 on a Wechsler Intelligence Test for Children. Which of the following is likely to be true?
a.   She is considered profoundly mentally retarded.
b.   She will likely be mainstreamed into a regular classroom.
c.   She is unlikely to develop adaptive functioning abilities by adulthood.
d.   Both a and c.

After completing the test, calculate your percent correct
(/ 20 =   ) x 100 = _____ .

How accurate were your expectations? Does your performance suggest need for additional study? For the items you missed, go back and identify why the "correct" answer is the best answer.

AFTER YOU READ ... PRACTICE TEST ANSWER KEYS

Practice Test 1.

1. b (p. 356)
2. c (p. 356)
3. d (p. 355)
4. a (pp.358–359)
5. b (p. 358)
6. d (p. 362)
7. b (p. 364)
8. a (pp. 373–374)
9. a (p. 372)
10. c (p. 369)
11. b (p. 376)
12. b (pp. 377, 385)
13. a (pp. 380–381)
14. d (pp. 383–385)
15. c (pp. 383–386)
16. a (pp. 381–382)
17. b (p. 387)
18. c (p. 390)
19. c (pp. 390–391)
20. a (p. 391)

Practice Test 2.

1. c (p. 357)
2. d (p. 358)
3. a (pp. 359–360)
4. b (p. 361)
5. a (p. 362)
6. c (p. 371)
7. d (p. 373)
8. a (p. 367)
9. d (pp. 368–369)
10. d (p. 378)
11. c (p. 379)
12. a (p. 380)
13. d (pp. 370, 388)
14. c (p. 375)
15. b (pp. 375–376)
16. c (p. 377)
17. c (p. 364)
18. c (p. 387)
19. d (p. 389)
20. b (p. 372)

AFTER YOU READ ... CONCEPT MAPPING ACTIVITY ANSWERS

ACTIVITY 1: In this hierarchy of mental abilities, several "examples" of abilities are possible.

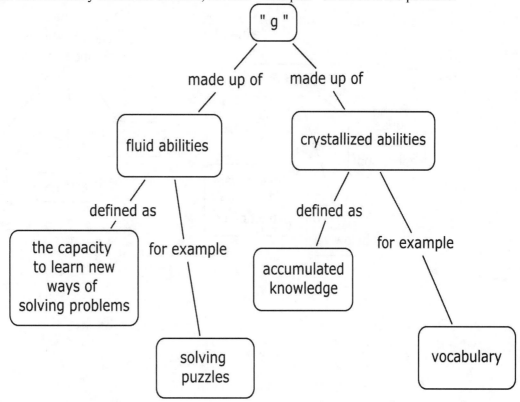

ACTIVITY 2: Summarize the criteria and categorize for classifying the degrees of mental retardation.

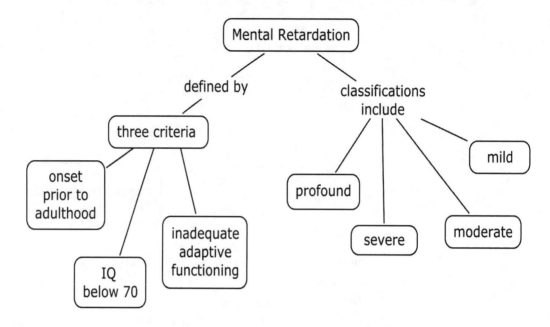

CHAPTER 10
HUMAN DEVELOPMENT
HOW AND WHY WE CHANGE

BEFORE YOU READ ... CHAPTER PREVIEW

Developmental psychology is the study of how behavior changes over time. It is a particularly complex division of psychology. One of the challenges we face is that of avoiding the post hoc fallacy—the belief that because one event preceded another the two are causally related. A second important consideration is to realize that human development is bidirectional. Parents may influence their children's behavior but children also influence parents' behavior. Our failure to understand that we are often biased in the interpretation of our observations contributes to a variety of misconceptions regarding child development. Two important misconceptions are the ideas of infant determinism and childhood fragility.

Recognizing the difficulties in studying development, researchers must draw conclusions cautiously. Cross-sectional methods, comparing different individuals of different ages measured at the same point in time, can tell us about age differences but not changes with age. The comparisons are between different people (different cohorts) who may differ in ways other than age. Looking longitudinally at the same people over time can tell us that the people we observed changed over time.

Although an old question, the nature or nurture question today generally asks *how* these two factors go together in influencing development. It is likely that the two influence development in many ways. The effect of genes may depend on the environment; gene expression may influence the environment; and the environment may influence the expression of genes.

Understanding child development begins with an understanding of prenatal development. Here nature and nurture are already interacting. During the three stages of prenatal development (blastocyst, embryo, and fetus), the process of cell generation, differentiation, and development follow genetic paths but can be derailed by genetic errors and environmental influences (teratogens). A full-term pregnancy lasts 40 weeks and a full-term baby weighs 7.5 pounds. Babies born before 36 weeks are considered premature and babies weighing less that 5.5. pounds are considered low birth weight.

Babies are born with big heads but little motor control. Motor coordination present at birth includes reflexes that play survival roles. Self-initiated motor movement develops over time. The age of acquisition of motor milestones varies but the sequence is generally uniform. The prenatal brain produces more neurons than it will ever need. Brain development continues after birth with synaptic generation, mylenization, and pruning.

Cognitive development refers to the study of how children develop the ability to think, reason, and remember. Piaget's contributions to our understanding of cognitive development include the idea that children are active participants in their acquisition of knowledge about their world. He believed that individuals progress through qualitatively different stages in cognitive development. The final stage of development involves the ability to reason logically about abstract problems. Although Piaget made an enormous contribution to the study of cognitive development, his view of domain-general stages of development has been criticized.

Vygotsky also saw children as active participants in the acquisition of knowledge, but emphasized the role of the social environment in cognitive development. He identified the zone of proximal development as a level of performance the individual is capable of achieving with assistance. As skills are mastered, the assistance (scaffold) may be removed. Current views of cognitive development see development as continuous rather than stage-like and specific rather than general.

It is difficult to determine the meaning of children's performance on cognitive tasks because performance can be influenced by task demands, such as language demands. However, infants appear to have some rudimentary knowledge of physical objects but basic knowledge becomes more refined and elaborated with experience. By age four, children begin to develop a theory of mind—the understanding that one person can know something another does not. In human history, counting is a relatively recent cognitive skill and may not be an inevitable consequence of development.

Infants are predisposed to develop social relationships. They prefer human faces and voices and are motivated to develop attachments to caregivers. The attachment bond appears to be based on contact comfort. Researchers have identified patterns of attachment styles (secure, insecure-avoidant, insecure-anxious, and disorganized). These patterns depend on both caregiver responsiveness and infant temperament.

Temperament reflects an infant's basic emotional style and is believed to be largely genetic in origin. Individual differences in temperament can predispose individuals to develop certain behaviors (e.g., shyness). Infants' temperament can influence the parent's ability to be responsive and therefore can influence attachment style and parenting.

In assuming child behavior is monodirectional, much parenting advice seems to be at odds with developmental research. Psychological observations of parenting styles find optimal development among children whose parents are authoritative rather than permissive, uninvolved, or authoritarian. It is important to recognize that the parenting style may be qualified by culture and that other influences act on children in addition to their parents. The power of the parent is only one of several misconceptions regarding development.

Developmental researchers also look at how children's cognitive development influences social development. Children's initial concepts of morality are based largely on fear of punishment but over time become more sophisticated and based on intentions and consequences. Kohlberg studied moral reasoning by analyzing responses to moral dilemmas. His work has been influential despite criticism. Researchers have also studied how children's gender identities appear to be influenced by both nature and nurture.

Adolescence may be a period of stress including greater conflict with parents over limits and expectations; but on balance, stress and unhappiness are not more pronounced in adolescence than during other developmental periods. Multiple changes do occur during adolescence including physical, social, and cognitive changes. Cognitive development continues through adolescence and into adulthood as the individual develops the ability to realize that real-world problems do not have simple answers. Although some researchers, such as Erikson, propose stage theories of development, change in adulthood follows a variety of trajectories as adults deal with issues involving careers, marriage, parenting, and aging. Claims of midlife transitions and empty nest syndromes seem to be overstated. Change for older adults depends on physical health and social support. Although some cognitive decline is inevitable, some improvement may also occur, particularly in crystalline intelligence.

BEFORE YOU READ ... LEARNING OBJECTIVES

After reading Chapter 10 you should be able to:

10.1   Identify ways to think critically about developmental findings
10.2   Clarify how nature and nurture can contribute to development
10.3   Track the trajectory of prenatal development and identify barriers to normal development
10.4   Describe how infants learn to coordinate motion and achieve major motor milestones
10.5   Understand major theories of the mechanisms by which children learn
10.6   Explain the processes by which children acquire knowledge in important cognitive domains
10.7   Describe how and when children establish emotional bonds with their caregivers
10.8   Explain the environmental and genetic factors contributing to the social style in children
10.9   Determine how children's understanding of morality and important social concepts like gender develop
10.10   Determine the physical, emotional, and cognitive changes that take place during the transition from childhood to adulthood
10.11   Identify developmental changes during major life transitions in adulthood
10.12   Summarize the nature of age-related declines in physical, social, and cognitive domains

---

BEFORE YOU READ ... TERM IDENTIFICATION

---

accommodation (p. 408)
adolescence (p. 430)
assimilation (p. 408)
attachment (p. 418)
average expectable environment (p. 423)
blastocyst (p. 403)
cognitive development (p. 406)
cohort effects (p. 400)
concrete operations stage (p. 410)
conservation (p. 410)
constructivist theory (p. 408)
contact comfort (p. 420)
cross-sectional design (p. 400)
developmental psychology (p. 399)
egocentrism (p. 409)
embryo (p. 403)
empty-nest syndrome (p. 436)
fetus (p. 403)
formal operations stage (p. 410)
gender identity (p. 429)
gender roles (p. 429)
gene expression (p. 402)
gene-environment interaction (p. 402)
group socialization theory (p. 424)
identity (p. 433)

imprinting (p. 418)
longitudinal design (p. 400)
menarche (p. 432)
menopause (p. 439)
midlife crisis (p. 436)
mono-operation bias (p. 421)
motor behaviors (p. 406)
nature via nurture (p. 402)
object permanence (p. 408)
post hoc fallacy (p. 399)
prenatal (p. 403)
preoperational stage (p. 408)
primary sex characteristics (p. 431)
psychosocial crisis (p. 433)
scaffolding (p. 411)
secondary sex characteristics (p. 432)
self-control (p. 426)
sensorimotor stage (p. 408)
spermarche (p. 432)
stranger anxiety (p. 418)
temperament (p. 421)
teratogens (p. 404)
theory of mind (p. 415)
zone of proximal development (p. 411)
zygote (p. 399)

AS YOU READ ... PRACTICE ACTIVITIES

SPECIAL CONSIDERATIONS IN HUMAN DEVELOPMENT

1. What is the post hoc fallacy? Why do we need to be particularly attentive to this fallacy when studying development? (LO 10.1)

2. Describe the following myths and realities: (LO 10.1)

   Myth: Infant determinism

   Reality:

   Myth: Childhood fragility

   Reality:

3. Why should we be particularly cautious in drawing conclusions from developmental designs? (LO 10.1) (*Hint*: Is either the longitudinal or cross-sectional design a "true experiment"?)

4. List three ways nature and nurture can interact. Give an example of how nature and nurture can have reciprocal (bidirectional) effects. (LO 10.2)

THE DEVELOPING BODY BEFORE AND AFTER BIRTH: PHYSICAL AND MOTOR DEVELOPMENT

1. Match the stage of prenatal development with its description. (LO 10.3)

    a. blastocyst   _____ period during which limbs, feature, and organs take form

    b. embryo   _____ ball of identical cells that have not yet begun to take on specific functions

    c. fetus   _____ period of physical maturation of organs

2. Why might teratogens have their greatest effect on the development of major structures if exposure occurs during the embryonic period? (LO 10.3)

3. T or F: Studying the effect of teratogens on infant development is challenging because it's difficult to find a perfect control group. Explain your answer. (LO 10.3)

4. A full-term baby is born at _____ weeks and weighs about ____ pounds. A baby weighing less than ____ pounds is considered low birth weight. A baby born at less than _____ weeks has not reached the age of viability and is unlikely to survive. (LO 10.3)

5. Make a list of preventative steps one can reasonably take to reduce the risk of abnormalities in pregnancy. (LO 10.3)

6. Motor movements at birth include the following reflexes. (LO 10.4)

_____

_____

_____

7. T or F: Children tend to achieve motor milestones in the same order even though the age of acquisition may vary. Explain your answer (i.e., the factors that might contribute to this statement being true or false). (LO 10.4)

8. T or F: Infants' brains produce only as many neurons as they need. Explain your answer. (LO 10.4)

COGNITIVE DEVELOPMENT: CHILDREN'S LEARNING ABOUT THE WORLD

1. Complete this chart of the Piagetian Stages of Cognitive Development with their primary achievement. (LO 10.5)

Stage	Age	Primary Way of Thinking
		Thinks in terms of physical interactions with objects
		Thinks in terms of representations Does not understand that objects retain identity despite transformation
		Operates on physical representations Cannot operate on the abstractions
		Can reason in terms of the hypothetical and abstract; thinks systematically

2. Use the following terms to complete this chart comparing the similarities and differences between Piaget's and Vygotsky's theories of cognitive development.
   (LO 10.5)

Claims: active learner; social environment key; physical environment key; ZPD; domain-general development; domain-specific development; stages of cognitive development

Piaget claims	Both claim	Vygotsky claims

3. Give an example of how you would scaffold a child learning to brush her teeth. (LO 10.5)

4. Why would Vygotsky suggest that playing with a child would do more to foster cognitive development than would playing Mozart music or showing a *Baby Einstein* video? (LO 10.5)

5. Discuss the concept of "theory of mind." What is it? How is it assessed? Why do you think the structure of the assessment affects the child's performance? (LO 10.6)

6. Of the cognitive achievements described in the text, the one *least* likely to be innate is _____. Provide evidence to support your answer. (LO 10.6)

SOCIAL AND MORAL DEVELOPMENT: CHILDREN'S RELATIONS WITH OTHERS

1. Contact comfort rather than nourishment appears to underlie the attachment relationship. What implication does this finding hold for fathers? (LO 10.7)

2. T or F: Stranger anxiety demonstrates a problem in the attachment relationship. Explain your answer. (LO 10.7)

3. What are the patterns of attachment? How is the attachment relationship generally studied? Why is it important to understand the method by which attachment is studied in order to understand the limitations of the claims made from these studies? (LO 10.7)

4. T or F: Infants differ from one another at birth. Explain your answer. (LO 10.8)

5. Match the parenting "style" with its example. (LO 10.8)

    a. Authoritative   _____ "You will do it because I told you to!"

    b. Authoritarian   _____ "Sure honey, you can stay up as long as you want."

    c. Permissive   _____ "We want you to call if you will be late because we worry about the irresponsible drivers out there."

    d. Uninvolved   _____ "I don't care what you do. Just leave me alone!"

6. Authoritative parents tend to have competent children. Because this finding is correlational, the parents may not be the cause or the only cause of child behavior. What other factors are likely to account for the observed relation? (Don't forget bidirectional influences.) (LO 10.8)

7. Describe the basic sequence of moral development. How does Kohlberg study moral development? Why might this method underlie most of the criticism that can be made of his theory? (LO 10.9)

DEVELOPMENT DOESN'T STOP: CHANGES IN ADOLESCENCE AND ADULTHOOD

1. How are teens different from adults? (LO 10.10)

2. T or F: The teenage brain is a work in progress. Explain your answer. (LO 10.10)

3. Why is adolescence stressful for teens? Why is it stressful for their parents? (LO 10.10)

4. Development in childhood is often described as age related whereas development in adulthood is described as transition related. Discuss the major life transitions confronted during adulthood. (LO 10.11)

5. Discuss each of these myths of adult development and their reality. (LO 10.11)

Myth: Most men experience a midlife crisis in which they try to regain their youth.
Reality:

Myth: Menopause is a period of increased depression for women.
Reality:

Myth: Depression in mothers follows "flight of their children" and their empty nest.
Reality:

Myth: Mental decline in all cognitive domains is inevitable with old age.
Reality:

6. List the characteristics that are likely to decline with age. (LO 10.12)

7. List the characteristics that tend to remain stable or increase, particularly in healthy adults. (LO 10.12)

AS YOU READ ... COGNITIVE MAP ACTIVITIES

ACTIVITY 1:

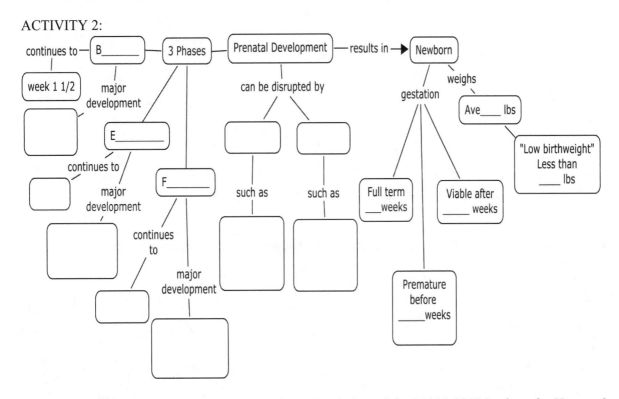

Developmental Research Designs

Longitudinal — compares — _____ individuals over _____

Longitudinal — advantages include

disadvantages include

Cross-sectional — disadvantages include

Cross-sectional — advantages include

Cross-sectional — compares — _____ individuals at same _____

Author content activity supported by *IHMC Cmap Tools* Copyright ©1998-2007 Institute for Human & Machine Cognition

ACTIVITY 2:

continues to — B_____ — 3 Phases — Prenatal Development — results in → Newborn

week 1 1/2

B_____ — major development

E_____

continues to — E_____ — major development

F_____

continues to — F_____ — major development

Prenatal Development — can be disrupted by — such as

can be disrupted by — such as

Newborn — gestation — Full term ___weeks

gestation — Viable after ____ weeks

gestation — Premature before ____weeks

Newborn — weighs — Ave____ lbs

Ave____ lbs — "Low birthweight" Less than ____ lbs

Author content activity supported by *IHMC Cmap Tools* Copyright ©1998-2007 Institute for Human & Machine Cognition

---

AS YOU READ... MYTH OR REALITY?

Myth: Mozart music increases the intelligence of infants.

Reality: Music may influence performance by influencing arousal but has no demonstrated, lasting effect on intelligence.

A good brief description of the original research may be found at http://faculty.washinton.edu/chudler/. Look at the researchers' operational definition of variables, the research design, and the sample studied. How do the claims go way beyond the data?

Myth: Many children have been killed by poisons or dangerous objects put into their Halloween candy.

Reality: Few documented injuries have been caused by Halloween candy.

As the discussion of the availability heuristic in Chapter 2 suggested, we tend to worry about the wrong things because our attention is grabbed by the dramatic or the memorable. For example, compare the number of deaths per year from Halloween candy with the number of deaths due to diarrhea. Why do you think we pay more attention to Halloween candy?

http://www.livescience.com/strangenews/051025_halloween_candy.html
http://www.time.com/time/magazine/article/0,9171,901061016-1543876,00.html
http://rehydrate.org/

As You Read … Put Your Critical Thinking Skills to the Test

1. Extraordinary claims require extraordinary evidence. The following claims are made in *Child Genius Magazine*. Check out the website and evaluate whether the claims have empirical support. http://www.internationalparentingassociation.org/BrainDevelopment/mobility1.html

How would the average reader know whether these claims are actually supported? For example, this passage comes from the website:

> The moment a child is conceived is not too early to start focusing on the child's vast learning potential. In the fetus, the brain is developing rapidly. The right hemisphere is highly active while the left hemisphere is relatively dormant. In this manner, the soul of the child is endowed with extrasensory perception, which is carried out through the phenomenal fetal right brain in connection with every single cell of the fetal body—the cells themselves being ESP receptors.

2. The site also claims that crawling is not only essential for brain development but that promoting early crawling can promote intellectual development, or super babies. How do the following claims reflect a misunderstanding and an overgeneralization from correlational data?

> It is important to understand that these … areas of child development are related … if a child improves in one area, such as hearing, [one] would find some improvement in all the other areas as well. This demonstrates how physical achievement is associated with mental achievement. The amount of crawling and creeping a baby does will have an effect on how well that child can see and hear and how well he will be able to speak and read.

AS YOU READ ... MyPsychLab CONNECTION

Special Consideration in Human Development
To become a better consumer of developmental research, **explore** *Cross-Sectional and Longitudinal Research Designs*, which explains the advantages and disadvantage of each design. **Listen** to the podcast *Research Designs*, an interactive conversation about the conclusions we can draw from cross-sectional and longitudinal designs.

The Developing Body before and after Birth: Physical and Motor Development
Learn how brain development occurs with the **explore** *Dendritic Spreading: Forming Interconnections in the Brain*. After learning about embryonic development, **explore** *The Embryonic Period: a Critical Period of Human Development* to see what changes occur during this stage. Test your own knowledge of different stages and corresponding ages with the **explore** *Life Stages and Approximate Ages in Human Development: Prenatal*. To examine what an infant should be doing developmentally, **explore** *Infants Perceptual & Cognitive Milestones*. There are many videos that illustrate key concepts in fetal development. **Watch** *Period of the Zygote* to see the cells after fertilization and *Brain Development and Nutrition* to see how brain growth is affected by diet. What reflexes do newborns have? **Watch** *Reflexes: Babinski, Reflexes: Moro, Reflexes: Palmar Grasp, Reflexes: Sucking* and *The Newborns Reflexes* to learn about and see the reflexes in action. Is motor development a progressive series of stages? **Watch** *Motor Development in Infants and Toddlers: Karen Adolph* to find out. The **simulation** *Teratogens and Their Effects* allows you to role-play a physician in diagnosing what medication, chemical, or environmental agent has interfered with normal development.

Cognitive Development: Children's Learning about the World
To grasp Piagetian concepts, **explore** *Piaget's Stages of Cognitive Development* then **watch** *The Sensorimotor Stage, Conservation of Liquids,* and *The Preoperational & Concrete Operational Stage*.

Social and Moral Development: Children's Relations with Others
Test your knowledge of attachment styles with the **simulation** *Attachment Classifications in the Strange Situation*. *Kohlberg's Stages of Moral Reasoning* provides another interactive test of children's responses on the Heinz moral dilemma task.
A set of videos demonstrate different temperaments of infants: **watch** *Temperament: Difficult* and *Temperament: Easy*. There are also two videos that illustrate attachment and separation issues of infants: **watch** *Stranger Anxiety* and *Separation Anxiety*. *Early Gender Typing* recreates research by Patricia Bauer, showing that children as young as two prefer gender type toys.

Development Doesn't Stop: Changes in Adolescence and Adulthood
Explore Erikson's theory with *Erikson's First Four Stages of Psychosocial Development* and *Erikson's Last Four Stages of Psychosocial Development*. For a summary of physical and cognitive changes, **explore** the interactive table in *Major Changes in Important Domains of Adult Functioning*.

AFTER YOU READ ... PRACTICE TEST #1

Before beginning this practice test, estimate the percent you expect to get correct.
Anticipated percent correct: _____

1. An ad for an infant computer program claims it provides important early stimulation for your infant because "The first three years of life are the most critical for brain development." This ad reflects
   a. the belief in childhood resilience.
   b. the empirical research on infant brain development.
   c. the myth of infant determinism.
   d. the average expectable environment claim.

2. If we wanted to know whether aggressive 10-year-old boys will grow up to be aggressive 15-year-old teenagers, we would most likely conduct
   a. a clinical study.
   b. a true experiment.
   c. a cross-sectional study.
   d. a longitudinal study.

3. Which of the following occurs during the embryonic period?
   a. Fertilization of the ovum
   b. Development of the heart and lungs
   c. Cell division
   d. Final maturation of the organs

4. Which of the following is characteristic of the full-term newborn?
   a. She must be taught how to suck efficiently.
   b. She is born at 32 weeks gestation.
   c. She is likely to weigh 7.5 pounds.
   d. Both b and c.

5. According to Piaget's theory, cognitive development
   a. proceeds through a series of qualitatively different stages.
   b. is dependent on the sociocultural context in which the child is embedded.
   c. is characterized as a passive process of behavior acquisition.
   d. moves through the zone of proximal development.

6. Research on attachment suggests that
   a. the source of attachment is contact comfort.
   b. those who provide nourishment for the infant become primary attachment figures.
   c. temperament can influence the attachment relationship.
   d. both a and c.

7. "We want you to be in by midnight or call and tell us you will be late. We worry about you because we know that there can be many irresponsible drivers on the roads at night." This statement demonstrates what Baumrind characterized as _____ parenting.
   a. permissive
   b. authoritative
   c. authoritarian
   d. restrictive

8. Children often change their environment by acting in ways that influence their parents to respond differently from how they might have otherwise. This is an example of
    a. unidirectional effects.
    b. infant determinism.
    c. bidirectional effects.
    d. group socialization effects.

9. Children tend to achieve motor milestones in the same order even though the age of acquisition may vary. Which of the following statement is the *best* description of what underlies motor development?
    a. Motor development is the result of an innate and inflexible motor program.
    b. Motor development is the result of physical maturation of body.
    c. Motor development is the result of physical maturation and environmental factors.
    d. Motor development is the result of parental practices that encourage or discourage exploration.

10. The preoperational stage of cognitive development is an advance over the sensorimotor stage because now the preschool-aged child can think in terms of
    a. representations.
    b. operations.
    c. the hypothetical.
    d. the here-and-now.

11. Temperament
    a. seems to have genetic and prenatal origins.
    b. is the result of parental responsiveness.
    c. refers to the observation that most babies are temperamentally challenging.
    d. is unrelated to later personality.

12. Which of the following would be an example of a scaffold?
    a. Allowing a child to explore a set of graduated size blocks on his/her own
    b. Helping a child solve a puzzle by suggesting he first find all the edge pieces
    c. Reinforcing a child with praise when she brushes her teeth
    d. Using flashcards to teach a child math facts

13. Which of the following reflects research based on Kohlberg's theory of moral development?
    a. Moral level seems to have a low correlation with moral behavior.
    b. The assessment of moral reasoning is uncorrelated with verbal intelligence.
    c. People pass through Kohlberg's stages in different orders in different cultures.
    d. Studies clearly show that men perform at higher moral levels compared with women.

14. One advantage of the cross-sectional design over the longitudinal design is
    a. one doesn't have to worry about the cohort effect confound.
    b. it is simpler to conduct than the longitudinal design.
    c. it allows the researcher to observe individuals change over time.
    d. both and c.

15. Arnold expects obedience from his children. He often says, "You will do it because I told you to!" According to Baumrind, Arnold's parenting style is
    a. authoritative.
    b. permissive.
    c. authoritarian.
    d   neglectful.

16. Research indicates that one way the average 17-year-old teenager differs from the average adult is
    a. the teen is in a stage of role confusion while the adult is in a stage of integrity.
    b. the teen is experiencing the most stressful period of the lifespan.
    c. areas of the teen's brain involved in reasoning are not fully mature.
    d. the teen has not yet reached sexual maturity.

17. Adult development differs from child development in that
    a. physical maturation plays a greater role in adulthood compared with childhood.
    b. the course of development in adulthood reflects greater variety in trajectories and in the timing of transitions.
    c. adulthood involves stability while childhood involves change.
    d. adult development is characterized by decline while childhood is characterized by progression.

18. If you wanted to assess the readiness of older adults to retire, it would be appropriate to use
    a. biological age.
    b. social age.
    c. chronological age.
    d. functional age.

19. Which of the following students is at the highest level of understanding according to Perry?
    a. "I appreciate professors who help me see the right answers."
    b. "Everyone has a right to his or her own opinion."
    c. "Some opinions are supported by better arguments and evidence."
    d. "If I say the right things, then I'll get a good grade."

20. Which of the following accurately reflects cognitive changes with age?
    a. Compared with younger adults, older adults perform worse on tests of analogies and vocabulary but perform better on tests that require memory for a random list of words.
    b. Elderly people's hearing, sight, and other senses decline but their reaction times are the same as those of younger adults.
    c. Older adults show significant declines in both free recall and cued recall.
    d. Many of the changes associated with ageing are actually due to diseases that are correlated with age.

After completing the test, calculate your percent correct
(/ 20 =   ) x 100 = _____ .

How accurate were your expectations? Does your performance suggest the need for additional study? For the items you missed, go back and identify why the "correct" answer is the best answer.

AFTER YOU READ... PRACTICE TEST #2

Before beginning this practice test, estimate the percent you expect to get correct.
Anticipated percent correct: _____

1. Vygotsky and Piaget agreed that
   a. mental tools facilitate human activity.
   b. individuals are active in the construction of knowledge.
   c. culture plays a role in cognitive development.
   d. development occurs in four qualitatively different stages.

2. A full term baby is born at _____ weeks and weighs about _____ pounds.
   a. 30; 8
   b. 40; 7.5
   c. 22; 5.5
   d. 32; 6

3. Which of the following statements is a valid example of the nature via nurture concept?
   a. Most children exposed to severe stress grow up with severe psychological problems.
   b. Research suggests that highly fearful children tend to seek out environments that protect them from their anxieties.
   c. Children raised in almost total isolation during the first year of life will suffer significant delays through adulthood.
   d. Children with both the low MAO gene and a history of maltreatment are at heightened risk for antisocial behaviors.

4. Which of the following statements regarding early brain development is TRUE?
   a. The fetus ends up manufacturing many more neurons than it will need as an infant.
   b. Neurons do not sort themselves out and move into their final position until well after birth.
   c. Mylenization, pruning, and synaptogenesis are completed by the 36th week of gestation.
   d. Because the brain has a long period of maturation, it is the organ least vulnerable to teratogens.

5. Studies of the effects of teratogens on prenatal development
   a. involve exposing pregnant women to various substances.
   b. are true experiments.
   c. are difficult because of the trouble finding a matched control group.
   d. are cross-sectional studies.

6. You conduct a study comparing the computer game–playing skill of 10-year-old, 30-year-old, and 50-year-old participants. You find the 10-year-olds outperform the 30-year-olds who outperform the 50-year-olds. Although skill could decline with age, an alternative explanation for your finding is
   a. the post hoc fallacy.
   b. conservation.
   c. the cohort effect.
   d. the habituation effect.

7. Why might teratogens have their greatest effect on the development of major structures if exposure occurs during the embryonic period?
    a. Major organs are developing during this period.
    b. Fertilization occurs during this period.
    c. Cell division and differentiation occur during period.
    d. Neurons are sorting and organizing themselves during this period.

8. Based on problems with physical science, such as the pendulum problem, Piaget concluded that adolescents can
    a. problem solve, but only with trial and error.
    b. manipulate abstract ideas and think systematically.
    c. understand that despite the relativity of much knowledge, it is possible to commit to an answer.
    d. solve problems, but with lower levels of formal reasoning compared with adults.

9. One of the criticisms made of Piaget's claims is that
    a. his observations of children's performance on tasks seems to be influenced by task demands.
    b. his theory reflects a passive child.
    c. development seems to be more stage-like than he proposed.
    d. development seems to be more general across domains than he proposed.

10. Compared with sensorimotor infants, the preoperational child can
    a. understand the permanence of objects.
    b. perform conservation tasks.
    c. think in terms of representations.
    d. both a and c.

11. Vygotsky would likely recommend
    a. providing lots of toys for your infant because the physical environment promotes cognitive development.
    b. playing with your infant because social interaction promotes cognitive development.
    c. buying stimulating toys for your infant because early brain stimulation is critical for later brain development.
    d. playing Mozart music for your infant because music promotes intellectual development in infants.

12. The ability called "theory of mind"
    a. is key in perspective-taking.
    b. does not seem to develop until age 7 or 8.
    c. appears to be innate.
    d. depends on the child's cognitive level and not how researchers structure the task.

13. The attachment relationship is influenced by
    a. infant temperament.
    b. relationships with peers.
    c. parental responsiveness.
    d. both a and c.

14. Kagan's studies of temperament found that infants categorized as behaviorally inhibited
    a. were at a heightened risk for shyness and anxiety disorders in childhood.
    b. were at increased risk for impulsive behaviors in later childhood.
    c. account for about 40% of infants.
    d. both b and c.

15. Which of the following claims regarding parenting appears to be TRUE according to developmental research?
    a. Parents are the most powerful influences on child development.
    b. Parental quality matters most for children with strong genetic predispositions toward behavior problems.
    c. Parents don't really have an influence on child behavior.
    d. Parents and peers each account for 50% of the variability in child behavior.

16. The development of counting _____ across cultures, whereas stranger anxiety _____ across cultures.
    a. varies greatly; appears identically
    b. appear identically; varies greatly

17. _____ appears to underlie the attachment relationship.
    a. Nourishment   c. Contact comfort
    b. Imprinting   d. Reinforcement

18. According to Perry's studies of how people understand the concept of "knowledge," college freshmen
    a. enter college with a realistic understanding of knowledge.
    b. see knowledge as relative—there are no right or wrong answers.
    c. develop their views of knowledge over the course of their college years.
    d. find it easy to accept that answers will often depend on the situation.

19. Which of the following statements about the study of moral development is TRUE?
    a. When evaluating moral dilemmas, the answers the person gives are less important than the reasoning.
    b. Compared with individualist cultures, cultures that favor communalism are more likely to demonstrate postconventional morality.
    c. An individual who believes that speeding is only bad when cops are around is at the conventional stage of moral development.
    d. A strong positive correlation is evident between moral level and moral behavior.

20. Which of the following is supported by evidence?
    a. Most men experience a midlife crisis in which they try to regain their youth.
    b. Menopause is a period of increased depression for women.
    c. Depression in mothers follows "flight of their children" and their resulting "empty nest."
    d. Older adults experience declines in their information-processing speed.

After completing the test, calculate your percent correct
(/ 20 =   ) x 100 = _____.

How accurate were your expectations? Does your performance suggest the need for additional study? For the items you missed, go back and identify why the "correct" answer is the best answer.

After You Read ... Practice Test Answer Keys

Practice Test 1.

1.   c (p. 401)
2.   d (p. 400)
3.   b (p. 403)
4.   c (p. 405)
5.   a (pp. 408–411)
6.   d (pp. 419–422)
7.   b (p. 423)
8.   c (p. 399)
9.   c (pp. 406–407)
10. a (pp. 409–410)
11. a (p. 421)
12. b (p. 411)
13. a (pp. 427–428)
14. b (p. 400)
15. c (p. 423)
16. c (p. 432)
17. b (p. 435)
18. d (pp. 437–438)
19. c (p. 433)
20. d (pp. 438–439)

Practice Test 2.

1.   b (pp. 410–411)
2.   b (p. 405)
3.   b (p. 402)
4.   a (p. 404)
5.   c (p. 404)
6.   c (p. 400)
7.   a (p. 404)
8.   b (p. 410)
9.   a (p. 410)
10. c (pp. 409–410)
11. b (p. 411)
12. a (p. 415)
13. d (p. 421)
14. a (p. 422)
15. b (p. 424)
16. a (pp. 416, 418)
17. c (pp. 419–420)
18. c (p. 433)
19. a (pp. 427–428)
20. d (pp. 438–439)

AFTER YOU READ ... CONCEPT MAPPING ACTIVITY ANSWERS

ACTIVITY 1:

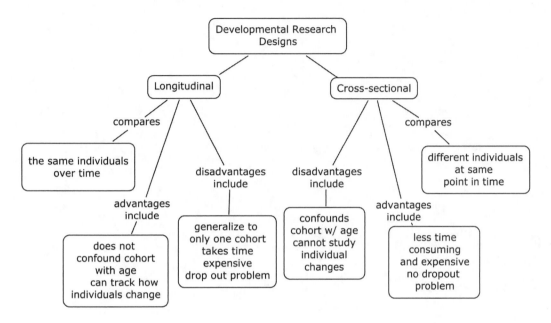

ACTIVITY 2:
The Prenatal Map should include the following terms and concepts:
Blastocyst: cell differentiation, implantation
Embryo: eight week; organogenesis
Fetus: physical maturation
Teratogens: alcohol
Genetic disruptions: Down syndrome
Gestation: full-term at 40 weeks; viable at 25 weeks; premature before 36 weeks
Weighs: average 7.5 lbs; low birth weight less than 5.5 lbs

CHAPTER 11
EMOTION AND MOTIVATION
WHAT MOVES US

Although emotion and reason are often portrayed as opposites, reasoning in the everyday world requires access to our emotional responses to experience. Theories of emotion describe the relation between emotion and thinking differently, but all note the interaction. In the James-Lange theory, emotions result from our bodily reactions to stimuli—we are afraid of the bear because we are running. Cannon and Bard proposed that the emotion-provoking event triggers a bodily reaction and emotional reaction simultaneously—we are afraid and we are running at the same time. The Schachter two-factor theory suggests that events trigger arousal but we look to the situation to label the arousal with the appropriate emotion—I'm aroused ... it must be because of that bear.

Current theories of emotion emphasize the evolution of emotional expression. Discrete emotions theory proposes that humans are biologically programmed to experience a set of emotions-behavior links. For example, disgust motivates us to avoid substances perceived as harmful; fear motivates us to be vigilant. Ekman believes a set of primary emotions are universal and can be recognized across cultures through facial expressions. This universality as well as brain imaging studies and physiological measures show some support for the theory. Cultures however do differ in display rules of emotion—that is, they differ in how and the when emotions are expressed.

Evidence also suggests that unconscious influences act on emotion. For example, the mere exposure effect reflects the finding that we are more likely to *like* stimuli we are exposed to repeatedly. The facial feedback effect suggests we are more likely to feel emotions corresponding to facial features— smile and you'll feel happier.

Nonverbal expressions of emotion are more valid indicators of emotion than are words. Because we are less aware of these nonverbal cues to our emotions, they are more difficult for us to conceal. Some people are able to use nonverbal cues to tell whether a person is lying. Most of us, however, are not very good at detecting lies. The polygraph is also not as good at detecting lies as its proponents believe. It is better at detecting arousal. Arousal however can result from reasons other than lying. The polygraph, therefore, is biased against the innocent. An alternative, the guilty knowledge test, seems more promising.

Positive psychology emphasizes human strengths, including resilience, copying, and happiness. Like the emphasis on wellness in general, these strengths can help people avoid distress. Happiness predicts longevity and broadens thinking and problem solving. Popular theories of happiness reflect many misconceptions. How we react to life events is a better indicator of our happiness than the actual events we experience. Self-esteem does not cause happiness and even the old are happy. Happy people do tend to be married, have friends, are religious, and exercise, although these relations are correlational and not causal. Happy people do appear to be engaged in the pursuit of meaningful activity rather than the pursuit of happiness itself. Self-esteem does not predict happiness, achievement, or social skills or drug use, but is related to positive illusions such as the belief that one is more likeable than one really is. It may be that moderate amounts of self-esteem are more desirable than the extremes. Critics of positive psychology note that optimists may gloss over their mistakes rather than prepare themselves for the worst. Positive psychology, however, may be seen as promoting a positive way of viewing and coping with the negative in life rather than attempting to eliminate or ignore the negative.

Motivation refers to drives that propel us in specific directions. According to drive reduction theory, drives such as hunger and thirst motivate us to minimize aversive states. Motivation is to obtain homeostasis or equilibrium. One factor that affects the strength of our drives is arousal. The Yerkes-Dodson law proposes that optimal arousal is at moderate levels—neither too high nor too low. Kurt Lewin proposed how drives can conflict when the desire to approach and to avoid situations occur simultaneously. Some behaviors are not easily explained in terms of drives. Incentive theories propose how we are motivated by goals. These goals can reflect incentives that come from within us (e.g., interest) or incentives from outside of us (e.g., money).

Although we believe we feel hunger in our stomachs, hunger is actually quite complicated and also involves a variety of additional factors including the brain, blood, glucose levels, and hormones. Obesity seems to involve biological predispositions such as differences in sensitivity to the hormone leptin that signals to reduce appetite. Set point theory suggests people differ in "set point" by their number of fat cells and their metabolic rate. Overweight people have also been found to be more sensitive to environmental cues to eat. Bulimia is an eating disorder that involves periods of binge eating (often feeling as if one cannot stop) followed by efforts to minimize weight gain (often including purging by vomiting or abusing laxatives). The disorder affects 1–3% of women, but even higher percentages are found among college-aged women. Anorexia is a less common disorder involving a refusal to maintain normal weight. The disorder appears rooted in both biology and culture. With a 5–10% mortality rate, it is the most life threatening of the psychological conditions.

The hormone testosterone can enhance sexual interest but researchers are finding that neurotransmitters also play a role in levels of sexual desire. Masters and Johnson's pioneering work on human sexual responses reported that basic sexual arousal was the same for men and women and involved four phases: (1) desire, (2) excitement, (3) orgasm, and (4) resolution. Many married men and women continue to be sexually active over age 60.

Cultures differ in their approval of premarital sex. Non-Western cultures are more clearly disapproving compared with Western cultures. Same-sex romantic relations develop in all cultures, and have throughout history. A reported 2.8% of males and 1.4% of females identify themselves as gay or lesbian. Homosexuality is not a disease. Psychologists don't fully understand the biological-environment interactions influencing sexual orientation. As with most psychological processes, biology, cultural, and social factors play a role.

Three principles guide attraction and relationship formation: proximity, similarity, and reciprocity. We are more likely to be friends with people we see on a regular basis and with people we have things in common. For attraction to develop there must be give and take. Physical attractiveness does play a role in attraction for both men and women. In terms of romantic partners, women tend to be attracted to those with financial resources. Some psychologists suggest that these preferences have adaptive bases. Physical attractiveness may predict fertility; resources may enhance offspring survival. Other researchers suggest that these preferences are related to social roles.

Average faces tend to be seen as attractive perhaps because they are free of mutations or because they are familiar. Love takes many forms. Sternberg has proposed three dimensions—passion, intimacy, and commitment. These dimensions can combine in various ways. Together they reflect the deepest form of love. The opposite of love, hate, can be seen as the opposite of these three dimensions.

BEFORE YOU READ ... LEARNING OBJECTIVES

After reading Chapter 11 you should be able to:
11.1 Describe the major theories of emotion
11.2 Identify unconscious influences on emotion
11.3 Explain the importance of nonverbal expression of emotion
11.4 Describe the four levels of personal space
11.5 Identify major lie detection methods and their pitfalls
11.6 Describe the emerging discipline of popular psychology
11.7 Identify common myths and realities about happiness and self-esteem
11.8 Define motivation
11.9 Explain basic principles and theories of motivation
11.10 Describe the determinants of hunger, weight gain, and obesity
11.11 Identify the symptoms of bulimia and anorexia
11.12 Describe the human sexual response cycle and factors that influence sexual activity
11.13 Identify common misconceptions about sexual orientation
11.14 Describe potential influences on sexual orientation
11.15 Identify principles and factors that guide attraction and relationship formation
11.16 Describe the major types of love and the elements of love and hate

---

BEFORE YOU READ ... TERM IDENTIFICATION

affective forecasting (p. 466)
broaden and build theory (p. 463)
Cannon-Bard theory (p. 452)
cognitive theories of emotion (p. 450)
companionate love (p. 486)
defensive pessimism (p. 468)
desire phase (p. 477)
discrete emotions theory (p. 447)
display rules (p. 450)
drive reduction theory (p. 469)
durability bias (p. 466)
excitement phase (p. 477)
facial feedback hypothesis (p. 455)
glucostatic theory (p. 473)
guilty knowledge test (p. 461)
hedonic treadmill (p. 466)
hierarchy of needs (p. 472)
homeostasis (p. 471)
incentive theories (p. 471)
integrity tests (p. 462)
internal-external theory (p. 474)
James-Lange theory of emotion (p. 451)

leptin (p. 474)
mere exposure effect (p. 454)
motivation (p. 469)
motivation-structural rules (p. 450)
nonverbal leakage (p. 456)
orgasm (climax) phase (p. 477)
passionate love (p. 486)
Pinocchio response (p. 459)
positive illusions (p. 468)
positive psychology (p. 462)
positivity effect (p. 465)
primary emotions (p. 448)
proxemics 458)
proximity (p. 482)
reciprocity (p. 483)
resolution phase (p. 477)
somatic marker theory (p. 451)
set point (p. 474)
similarity (p. 483)
social identity support (p. 483)
two-factor theory (p. 452)
Yerkes-Dodson law (p. 471)

AS YOU READ ... PRACTICE ACTIVITIES

THEORIES OF EMOTION: WHAT CAUSES OUR FEELINGS?

1. According to discrete emotions theory, our feelings are linked to physical responses. Your text gives the example of disgust. Similarly, apply this example to what you think might go on physically when you experience happiness. (LO 11.1)

2. Compare primary and secondary emotions. List some additional examples of secondary emotions that are not listed in your text. (LO 11.1)

3. Paul Ekman, whose work is discussed in several sections of this chapter, has partnered with Disney's Pixar animation studios to help them with facial expressions for such animated feature films as *Toy Story, Cars,* and *Monsters, Inc*. You can read about some of his work at http://www.sfgate.com/cgi-bin/article.cgi?f=/c/a/2002/09/16/MN241376.DTL&type=science. (LO 11.1)

Discuss how you would draw a new character's facial expressions so that he or she could convey the following:

(a) Happiness

(b) Sadness

(c) Surprise

(d) Anger

(e) Fear

4. You have probably had some experiences in your life where you've observed different cultural display rules. Describe such an experience and the situation surrounding it. (LO 11.1)

5. Compare the James-Lange, somatic marker, facial feedback, Cannon-Bard, and Schachter-Singer two-factor theories of emotion. You should make a table to help you organize your comparisons. Which of these do you personally favor? Why? (LO 11.1)

NONVERBAL EXPRESSION OF EMOTION: THE EYES, BODIES, AND CULTURES HAVE IT

1. You will recall from Chapter 3 Biological Psychology, that most people are right-handed, and for most right-handed people their primary language centers are in the left hemisphere. However, the right hemisphere is very important for processing extralinguistic, nonverbal aspects of language. Now imagine that you are having a conversation with someone who has right hemisphere damage near the areas that normally correspond to speech areas in the left hemisphere. How do you think the conversation might be affected? What specific aspects of humor do you think might be disordered? (LO 11.3)

2. Think of a time when you had to stand in line, for example at the airport, waiting to check your luggage before a flight. You have probably experienced the feeling that the person in front of you was not "moving along"; or you may have felt that the person behind you was "crowding." Relate a personal experience for each of these situations. Estimate the distance that you think was annoying to you and what you think would have been a more appropriate distance. How do these distances match up with the guidelines on p. 458 of your text? (LO 11.4)

3. Explain why a polygraph is not truly a "lie detector" test. Include in your explanation how the polygraph is supposed to detect lies, the procedure and types of questions asked by the polygraph examiner, and the limitations and accuracy of these devices. (LO 11.5)

4. Your professor comes to class the day after an exam and announces that several students cheated on the exam and that he is going to give a lie-detector test to find out who the main culprit was. Would you take the test? Why or why not? (LO 11.5)

5. How does "truth serum" work to get people to tell the truth, and what are the potential problems with using this method of getting at the truth? (LO 11.5)

HAPPINESS AND SELF-ESTEEM: SCIENCE CONFRONTS POP PSYCHOLOGY

1. One could make the argument that happiness is really a pathological state—a psychological disorder. Look ahead to Chapter 15, Psychological Disorders (p. 622), where you will find several approaches that psychologists use to determine whether a particular behavior is "normal" or "abnormal." Then, make the case that happiness is really an abnormal state. (LO 11.6)

2. Bozena is really excited; she just won the lottery! How long do you think her happiness will last, and why? (LO 11.7)

3. Examine the five misconceptions that people have about happiness. Which of these did you know was a misconception? Why? Which of these did you most believe in? Are you now convinced that it is, in fact, a misconception? Why or why not? (LO 11.7)

4. Relate the concept of "hedonic treadmill" to the concept of "durability bias." How might the former predict the latter? (LO 11.7)

5. Which myth about self-esteem did you find most surprising? Does the research evidence the authors of your text provide convince you of the correct conception? If not, what else would you need to know to change your belief? (LO 11.7)

6. Happiness can predict many positive lifetime outcomes. Consider each of the variables discussed in the chapter that correlate with happiness and note how you can implement each one to enhance the quality of your life. Some of them may go against your basic values, on the surface, so think about how each can fit your life (e.g., "religion" can be defined in different ways). (LO 11.7)

MOTIVATION: OUR WANTS AND NEEDS

1. Apply the Yerkes-Dodson law to test anxiety. What would you tell a person with low test anxiety about drinking coffee just before an exam? What about a person with high test anxiety? Why? (LO 11.8)

2. Describe a situation in your life when you experienced an approach-avoidance conflict. How did you resolve the conflict? Did you have to completely give up on one option? (LO 11.8)

3. Compare intrinsic and extrinsic motivation. Suggest some ways that we can increase children's internal motivation to read. (LO 11.9)

4. Discuss the evidence for each of the following theories of hunger. (LO 11.10)

   (a) Stomach contraction hypothesis

   (b) Separate "satiety" and "feeding" centers in the brain (including their locations)

   (c) Glucostatic theory

5. Discuss the role of each of the following factors in affecting eating behaviors.
   (LO 11.10)
   (a) Leptin

   (b) Set point

   (c) Genes

   (d) Internal-external theory

6. Compare anorexia and bulimia in terms of symptoms, frequency rates, underlying causes, gender differences, and effects on overall health. Making a table should help you to organize your comparison. (LO 11.11)

7. T or F: Men have a stronger sex drive than women. Explain your answer. (LO 11.12)

8. List the myths regarding homosexuality that are described in your text, and then note the correct conceptions. Include the misconceptions regarding changing sexual orientations. (LO 11.13)

As with many human characteristics, sexual orientation appears to be part nature and part nurture. Discuss the evidence for each contribution. In the end, do you believe the evidence is stronger for nature or for nurture? (LO 11.14)

ATTRACTION, LOVE, AND HATE: THE GREATEST MYSTERIES OF THEM ALL

1. Summarize the effects of proximity, similarity, and reciprocity in intimate relationships. (LO 11.15)

2. At http://www.soc.ucsb.edu/sexinfo/?article=cj2w you can read about romantic love and some of the factors that influence relationships (in contrast to popular belief, opposites do NOT attract, and, in fact, birds of a feather DO flock together). Given this information how might the mere exposure effect influence the relationships between similarity, proximity, familiarity, and love? (LO 11.2, LO 11.15)

3. List the personal and physical characteristics that American men prefer in women, and that American women prefer in men. (LO 11.15)

4. Compare social role theory to evolutionary models of attraction. (LO 11.15)

5. What is the evidence that an average face is actually most often labeled as "attractive"? (LO 11.15)

6. Summarize Sternberg's six varieties of love, and relate them to other types of love, such as "Hollywood" love, or friendship. (LO 11.16)

AS YOU READ ... CONCEPT MAP ACTIVITIES

ACTIVITY 1: Complete this concept map for the theories of emotion.

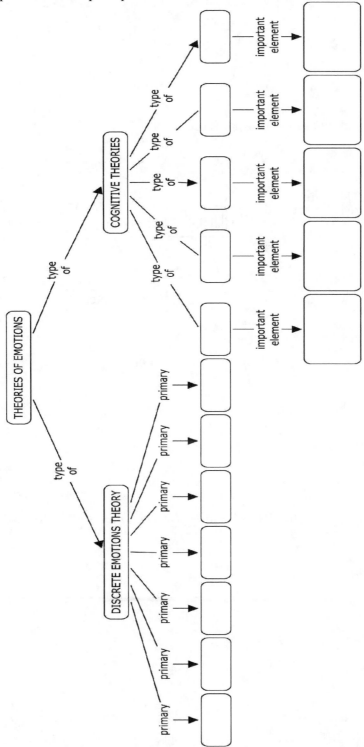

Author activity content supported by *IHMC Cmap Tools* Copyright ©1998-2007 Institute for Human & Machine Cognition

ACTIVITY 2: Complete this concept map for the variables associated with hunger.

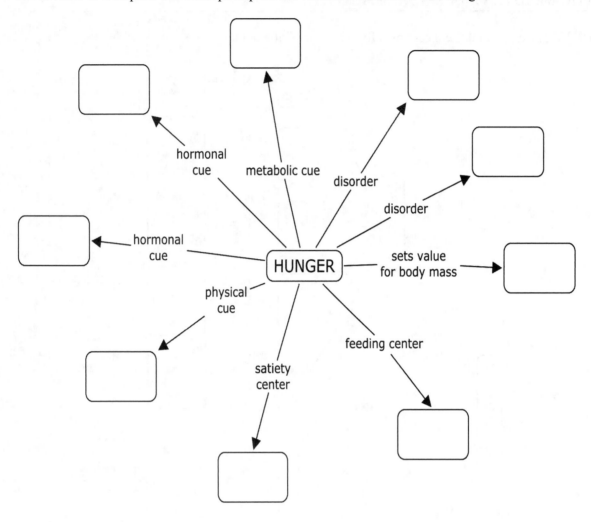

Author activity content supported by *IHMC Cmap Tools* Copyright ©1998-2007 Institute for Human & Machine Cognition

ACTIVITY 3: For this concept map, make your own, using the following terms:

ATTRACTION, social influences, proximity, similarity, reciprocity, models, evolutionary, social roles; LOVE, Hollywood love, passionate love, companionate love, friendship, intimacy, passion, consummate love, romantic love, liking, intimacy, commitment, empty love, fatuous love, hate.

AS YOU READ ... MYTH OR REALITY?

Myth: Women talk more than men.
Reality: Men and women use the same amount of words in a fixed time frame.

1. Your text notes in a "Fictoid" box the myth that men and women have distinctly different styles of emotional communication. In reality, research studies fail to find any such differences. Indeed, as your text notes, there is great similarity in the communication styles of men and women.

    To bolster this finding, recent independent studies have provided clear evidence that men and women also talk about the same amount. You can find the results of two studies, each conducted independently of the other and using a different methodology at:
    http://www.sciencedaily.com/releases/2007/11/071108171518.htm
    http://www.npr.org/templates/story/story.php?storyId=11762186

2. Have you heard any everyday wisdom about differences in men's and women's communication styles? In what aspects of language have you heard that men and women differ? Do you believe that the similarity of language usage is a good measure of whether men and women experience emotions similarly? Why or why not?

Myth: Fat people are fat because they are lazy and lack willpower.
Reality: Obesity is a complicated disorder that is an aggregate of many variables.

1. Your text notes many of the factors that contribute to obesity. You can also read much more about obesity at:
    http://www.obesityinamerica.org/causes.html
    http://www.weight.com/causes.asp

    Synthesize all your readings into an argument that would speak against fat people being lazy or lacking willpower, and instead make an argument for other factors that contribute to obesity.

AS YOU READ … PUT YOUR CRITICAL THINKING SKILLS TO THE TEST

1. Because current lie detection technology is flawed, a new technology is now being developed for lie detection: the use of functional MRIs.
   a. Read about this new technology at these websites:
      http://www.usatoday.com/tech/science/2006-06-26-mri-lie_x.htm
      http://www.sciam.com/article.cfm?id=lie-brain-fmri-polygraph&page=1
   b. Read about the potential ethical problems with this type of technology at
      http://ethicsinthenews.typepad.com/practicalethics/2007/11/lie-detection-u.html
   c. After reading the information at these websites what do you think about the usage of functional MRIs versus current technology? Would you want to rely on either one if a critical life decision had to depend on it? If you had to pick one technique and were given a choice, which one would you pick? Why?

2. Maslow's hierarchy of needs has often been criticized.
   a. Read about some of these criticisms by scrolling through these two websites:
      http://www.abraham-maslow.com/m_motivation/Hierarchy_of_Needs.asp
      http://webspace.ship.edu/cgboer/maslow.html.
   b. Maslow based his model on cases of individuals he considered to have achieved self-actualization; can you think of cases that contradict this model?
   c. How could you reformulate the model to better explain a wider range of human achievements?

AS YOU READ... MYPSYCHLAB CONNECTION

Theories of Emotion: What Causes Our Feelings?
When reviewing different theories of emotions, **explore** *Physiological, Evolutionary, and Cognitive Theories of Emotion* and learn about the universality of emotions and how cognitive appraisal influences emotional states.   Why does familiarity breed liking? Complete the *Mere Exposure* **simulation** to find out. To further illustrate the universal nature of emotional expression, complete the **simulation** *Recognizing Facial Expressions of Emotions*. In this simulation, you will have a chance to identify the emotion being expressed.

Nonverbal Expressions of Expressions: The Eyes, Bodies, and Cultures Have It
Watch *Lie Spy* to see new techniques in lie detection - a heat-sensitive camera.

Happiness and Self-Esteem: Science Confronts Pop Psychology
Complete the **simulation** *Survey on Happiness*. By taking this survey, you may learn what factors truly make you happy.

Motivation: Our Wants and Needs
To master the theories of motivation **explore** *Maslow's Hierarchy of Needs* and *Theories of Motivation and Job Performance*. To learn about how the brain plays a role in eating **watch** *The Effects of the Hypothalamus on Eating Behavior* and *Your Brain on Food*. Learn about various eating disorders by **watching** *Eating Disorders* and *Anorexia Nervosa: Kim.*

Attraction, Love and Hate: The Greatest Mystery of All?
Complete the **explore** *Passionate Love Scale* when reviewing different types of love.

AFTER YOU READ ... PRACTICE TEST #1

Before beginning this practice test, estimate the percent you expect to get correct.
Anticipated percent correct: _____

1. Science fiction characters are sometimes portrayed as being emotionless and rational, with expert decision-making skills. This depiction
   a. underscores how emotions are opposite of clear, rational thinking.
   b. is consistent with scientific evidence from brain-damaged individuals.
   c. is in contrast to real case studies where brain damage leaves people emotionless but also less rational.
   d. fails to show that despite the rational thinking of brain-damaged individuals, their relationships with others are often unsuccessful.

2. Worldwide, the easiest emotion to recognize is
   a. anger.
   b. surprise.
   c. contempt.
   d. happiness.

3. Ekman conducted many studies of facial expressions associated with emotions and concluded that
   a. across cultures people disagree on how to name the different emotions.
   b. almost everyone agrees on seven fundamental emotions.
   c. only happiness and sadness have common expressions across cultures.
   d. expression of the same emotion varies from culture to culture.

4. Fear has been shown to be associated with several physical markers, including
   a. digestive system activation.
   b. slowing of heart rate.
   c. brain activation of the amygdala.
   d. a curling up of both corners of the mouth.

5. Markeesah reads an article that informs her that "if you see a bear, you are frightened because your heart is pounding." She immediately recognizes this statement as describing the
   a. James-Lange theory.
   b. somatic marker theory.
   c. Schachter-Singer theory.
   d. motivation-structure theory.

6. According to the Cannon-Bard theory of emotion,
   a. different types of arousal exist, and they are each named to correspond to an emotion.
   b. the amygdala is most important in experiencing the correct emotion, given a particular situation.
   c. the thalamus simultaneously triggers both an emotion and bodily reactions.
   d. the experience of emotion depends on cognitive interpretation of arousal.

7. Crystal's mother buys store-brand sodas that come in red cans. When offered Coke (which comes in a red can) or Pepsi (which comes in a blue can), Crystal always picks Coke. Crystal's behavior might best be explained as the result of
   a. somatic markers.
   b. autonomic arousal.
   c. affective forecasting.
   d. the mere exposure effect.

8. Which of the following statements regarding lie detectors is TRUE?
   a. Polygraph examiners make correct decisions 99% of the time.
   b. Evidence from lie detectors is admissible in most courts of law.
   c. Lie detectors assume a Pinocchio response: a perfect physiological indication of lying.
   d. Examiners are more likely to produce false negatives (i.e., to identify liars as truthful people).

9. It is most accurate to describe a polygraph as
   a. a confidence detector.
   b. an arousal detector.
   c. a truth detector.
   d. a lie detector.

10. Unlike a polygraph test, the integrity test
    a. is a pencil and paper test.
    b. yields few false positives.
    c. is a valid "honesty" detector.
    d. corrects for the shortcomings of the polygraph test.

11. Hector just won the Pennsylvania State Lotto! He is extremely excited and looks forward to a happy rest of his life, as well as that of his children.
    a. Hector should move to California to ensure his happiness.
    b. Hector should get divorced and stay single if he wants to stay happy.
    c. Hector should stop going to church because religious people are less happy.
    d. Unfortunately, according to research evidence, Hector is unlikely to be happy for very long.

12. You've received a mailing announcing the local engagement of a world-renowned motivational speaker. Should you shell out the shekels to attend?
    a. No, motivational speakers are charlatans, experts in cold-reading and Barnum effects.
    b. No, the research evidence shows only a small and temporary positive motivational effect.
    c. Yes, research evidence shows these speakers jump-start long-term changes in people's lives.
    d. Yes, the fact that the speaker sells out each time means he must be good at motivating others.

13. You've just written a new book and titled it *Homeostasis*. What would be a good subtitle for your book?
    a. *Maintaining of an Optimal Level of Equilibrium*
    b. *The Maximum Amount of Arousal Needed for Best Performance*
    c. *Engaging in an Act for Its Own Sake, Without Any External Reward*
    d. *A Positive Illusion in Which We Perceive Ourselves More Positively Than Others Do.*

14. An inverted-U function describes the relationship between
    a. drives and motives.
    b. approach and avoidance.
    c. arousal and performance.
    d. incentives and intrinsic motives.

15. Helga likes to paint for the fun of it; she has a(n) _____. Hans paints because he sells his paintings at high prices; he has a(n) _____.
    a. incentive; drive
    b. aesthetic reward; financial reward
    c. extrinsic motivation; intrinsic motivation
    d. intrinsic motivation; extrinsic motivation

16. Dr. Brown implanted an electrode in the hypothalamus of a rat. Then Dr. Brown electrically stimulated this area of the hypothalamus and the rat stopped eating. The electrode was probably implanted in the
    a. lateral hypothalamus.
    b. ventromedial hypothalamus.
    c. anterior hypothalamus.
    d. posterior hypothalamus.

17. An important source of energy for all parts of the body is
    a. insulin.
    b. sodium.
    c. glucose.
    d. serotonin.

18. Miranda will sometimes eat like there is no tomorrow and then feel guilty over her lack of control. She then forces herself to vomit and takes laxatives to avoid gaining weight. Miranda is probably suffering from what is called
    a. bulimia nervosa.
    b. anorexia nervosa.
    c. poor impulse control.
    d. irritable bowel syndrome.

19. A man who has a homosexual orientation is most likely to have a brother who is also homosexual if that brother is
    a. unfamiliar.
    b. an identical twin.
    c. a fraternal twin.
    d. adopted.

20. The variable that best predicts whether a relationship will develop between two individuals is
    a. proximity.
    b. reciprocity.
    c. serendipity.
    d. attractiveness.

After completing the test, calculate your percent correct
(/ 20 =   ) x 100 = _____.

How accurate were your expectations? Does your performance suggest the need for additional study?
For the items you missed, go back and identify why the "correct" answer is the best answer.

AFTER YOU READ ... PRACTICE TEST #2

Before beginning this practice test, estimate the percent you expect to get correct.
Anticipated percent correct: _____

1. Which of the following is NOT generally considered to be one of the primary emotions?
   a. Envy
   b. Anger
   c. Disgust
   d. Contempt

2. Evidence that emotions may be innate in all people includes which of the following?
   a. Newborn infants smile while in REM sleep.
   b. Babies smile back at anyone who smiles at them.
   c. Babies smile when they have intestinal gas bubbles.
   d. Blind children smile when their caretakers are happy.

3. Cross-cultural guidelines for how and when to express emotion are called
   a. motivational-structural rules.
   b. Duchenne guidelines.
   c. somatic markers.
   d. display rules.

4. According to the James-Lange theory, experiencing emotion starts with
   a. using "gut reactions" to determine our response to a specific situation.
   b. our interpretation of our own body's reaction to external stimuli.
   c. our interpretation of pure autonomic failure.
   d. exhibiting the proper display rules.

5. Schachter's two-factor theory of emotion suggests that we distinguish between different emotions on the basis of
   a. different levels of arousal.
   b. whether we decide on fight or flight.
   c. our interpretation of an internal state or an external situation.
   d. whether the emotion was experienced in the presence or absence of arousal.

6. The idea that blood vessels in the face send information to the brain and that this affects the emotion we feel is known as
   a. the James-Lange theory.
   b. Ekman's Pan-Am theory.
   c. Schachter's cognitive theory.
   d. the facial feedback hypothesis.

7. People sometimes misinterpret each others' statements in e-mail discussions because e-mail lacks
   a. proper use of grammar.
   b. adequate personal space.
   c. an emotional social intelligence prosthesis.
   d. nonverbal cues present in spoken language.

8. When a polygraph operator asks a subject, "Have you ever lied to your parents?" he or she is using _____, which are designed to make almost anyone anxious.
   a. critical questions
   b. control questions
   c. irrelevant questions
   d. minor deception questions

9. The main objection to the polygraph test is that
   a. it is biased against the innocent.
   b. it is difficult and time consuming to administer.
   c. it is too invasive and costly to administer on a regular basis.
   d. it is no more accurate than the average person is at identifying dishonesty.

10. In an effort to get at the truth of Ernest's past criminal history, investigators injected him with "truth serum." According to careful research studies,
   a. this might result in Ernest owning up to crimes he didn't commit.
   b. this can force Ernest to own up to some of his crimes, but still omit others.
   c. this is unlikely to produce any new, accurate information about Ernest's crimes.
   d. this will lower Ernest's inhibitions, allowing him to provide the information in his past history.

11. Carolina is an elementary school teacher who wants her students to excel in their classwork. To this end, she spends a large part of each day working on self-esteem–boosting exercises with her students.
   a. You applaud her efforts because the research evidence suggests that people with high self-esteem are always less aggressive than those with low self-esteem.
   b. You caution her that the research evidence suggests that she should spend her class time on classwork, because high self-esteem does not automatically translate into better school performance.
   c. You point out to Carolina that this strategy is good because higher self-esteem alone is likely to boost her students' test scores significantly.
   d. You tell Carolina about the research evidence that this will also prevent her students from becoming self-centered, which will also benefit them in life.

12. An internal state of tension that motivates an organism to engage in activities that should reduce this tension defines
   a. incentive.
   b. emotion.
   c. drive.
   d. motive.

13. Sue works on a factory line. Her tasks are simple, but because she wants a promotion, she needs to be productive and make few errors. The Yerkes-Dodson law would advise Sue to be
   a. unemotional in making decisions at work.
   b. moderately aroused for peak performance.
   c. in a very high state of arousal.
   d. in a low state of arousal.

14. Fernando loves to play baseball. Now that he is on a travel team his dad has told Fernando he will pay him $1 for every hit he gets, and $5 for every home run. This new plan is likely to
   a. increase Fernando's internal motivation to play baseball.
   b. decrease Fernando's external motivation to play baseball.
   c. decrease Fernando's internal motivation to play baseball.
   d. undermine Fernando's external motivation to play baseball.

15. The start-eating center is located in the _____, and the stop eating center is located in the _____.
   a. amygdala; stomach
   b. lateral hypothalamus; ventromedial hypothalamus
   c. melanocortin receptor-4; leptin center
   d. homeostatic center, pleasure circuits

16. People tend to maintain a nearly constant body weight over the course of months, unless something unusual happens. That constant weight is referred to as
    a. a set point.
    b. homeostasis.
    c. healthy weight.
    d. the ideal weight.

17. The typical personality trait of people with bulimia nervosa is described as
    a. extroverted.
    b. unmotivated.
    c. perfectionist.
    d. introverted.

18. The typical order of human sexual response is
    a. excitement, desire, plateau, orgasm.
    b. pleasure, plateau, orgasm, relaxation.
    c. desire, excitement, orgasm, resolution.
    d. excitement, euphoria, climax, relaxation.

19. Which of the following sayings best describes what research evidence tells us is true of long-term relationships?
    a. Opposites attract.
    b. Birds of a feather flock together.
    c. The enemy of my enemy is my friend.
    d. Absence makes the heart grow fonder.

20. Evolutionary models of attraction suggest that women place more emphasis than men on the _____ of a potential mate.
    a. height
    b. finances
    c. youthfulness
    d. attractiveness

After completing the test, calculate your percent correct
(/ 20 =   ) x 100 = _____.

How accurate were your expectations? Does your performance suggest the need for additional study?
For the items you missed, go back and identify why the "correct" answer is the best answer.

AFTER YOU READ ... PRACTICE TEST ANSWER KEYS

Practice Test 1.

1. c (p. 446)
2. d (p. 448)
3. b (p. 448)
4. c (p. 449)
5. a (p. 451)
6. c (p. 452)
7. d (pp. 454–455)
8. c (p. 459)
9. b (p. 460)
10. a (p. 462)
11. d (pp. 465–466)
12. b (p. 469)
13. a (p. 470)
14. c (p. 470)
15. d (p. 471)
16. b (p. 473)
17. c (p. 473)
18. a (p. 475)
19. b (p. 480)
20. a (p. 482)

Practice Test 2.

1. a (p. 448)
2. a (p. 448)
3. d (p. 450)
4. b (p. 451)
5. c (pp. 452–453)
6. d (p. 455)
7. d (p. 456)
8. b (p. 460)
9. a (p. 460)
10. c (p. 461)
11. b (pp. 467–468)
12. c (p. 469)
13. b (p. 470)
14. c (p. 471)
15. b (p. 473)
16. a (p. 474)
17. c (p. 476)
18. c (p. 477)
19. b (p. 483)
20. b (p. 484)

AFTER YOU READ ... CONCEPT MAPPING ACTIVITY ANSWERS

ACTIVITY 1: Complete this concept map for the theories of emotion.

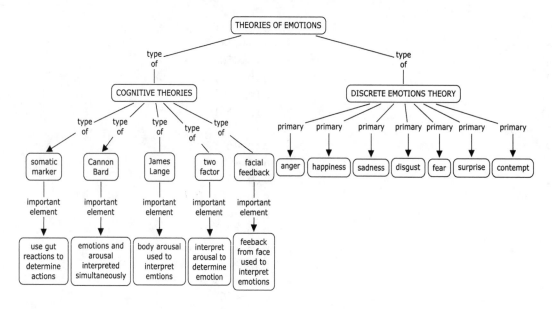

ACTIVITY 2: Complete this concept map for the variables associated with hunger.

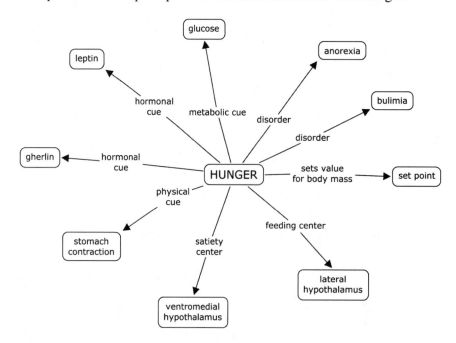

CHAPTER 12
STRESS, COPING, AND HEALTH
THE MIND-BODY INTERCONNECTION

BEFORE YOU READ ... CHAPTER PREVIEW

The terrorist attacks on September 11, 2001, provide us insights into stress and coping. This chapter examines what happens after we experience a traumatic event and how we cope. Most people (60%–90%) have experienced at least one traumatic event in their lifetimes, and surprisingly, most people successfully cope with these traumatic events.

Stress, trauma and anxiety are all distinct concepts. Stress consists of the tension, discomfort, or physical symptoms that arise when a situation strains our ability to cope effectively. Trauma has the potential to create stress, and anxiety is but one response to trauma and stress. Researchers perceive stress from one of three perspectives: as a stimulus, as a transaction, and as a response. Stress has been studied in terms of major life events and in terms of everyday hassles.

Research studies of stress indicate both common and distinctly individual responses to stress. For example, Hans Selye proposed a general adaptation syndrome with three stages that are common across individuals: alarm, resistance, and exhaustion. During the alarm stage the autonomic nervous system is activated, adrenaline is released, the midbrain is excited, and people show a fight-or-flight response. During the resistance stage people find ways to cope with the stress, which can vary across individuals. At the exhaustion stage resistance breaks down and with prolonged stress damage can occur to various organ systems, or people may become depressed. Although this model has been accepted for a long time, other researchers are finding differences, especially among genders. Women tend to take a "tend and befriend" response to stress, turning to others for support. In addition, women secrete an additional hormone, oxytocin. With prolonged stress some people develop posttraumatic stress disorder (PTSD), in which they continue to re-experience an extremely stressful event over a prolonged period of time. Finally, generalized anxiety and depression may result from prolonged stress. However, other people seem to cope well, and are more resilient. In fact, the majority of people, as mentioned before, are resilient.

Psychological stress has been shown to produce physical responses. Our immune system, which protects us from pathogens by producing antigens, suffers under stress. Normally we have specialized white blood cells called phagocytes, including neutrophils, and lymphocytes, as well as macrophages protecting us from bacteria and viruses. But when the immune system becomes overly active we can develop autoimmune disorders in which the immune system mistakes healthy body tissues for unhealthy invaders, such as bacteria and viruses, and attacks healthy tissues. A new field of psychology, psychoneuroimmunology has developed to study these complex relationships between stress, the mind, and the body. This field has found clear research evidence that immunity is decreased during times of stress and that people are more prone, for example, to develop colds at such times. Other disorders are also being linked to psychophysiological and biopsychosocial factors. In particular, coronary heart disease is being linked, via cholesterol levels and atherosclerosis, to stress levels. Several independent lines of research have shown a clear relationship between stress and coronary heart disease, with a mediating factor being personality type, especially "Type A." Although many people might be labeled as Type A, which is generally seen as an ambitious, goal-driven personality, being high on the traits of anger and hostility best predicts coronary artery disease. Controlling anger and hostility leads to a lessening of heart disease, especially as shown by research into the "Type D" personality type, characterized by social inhibition and negative feelings. In terms of illness, some researchers find that illness can be the cause, rather than the result of stress. For example, people with asthma experience stress because of their illness. Another good example of the interplay between stress and illness comes from studies of ulcers. Several hypotheses have been proposed for what causes ulcers, including a specific emotion hypothesis and a belief that spicy foods are to blame, but both have been discredited. A specific bacterium seems to be the real culprit; it takes hold particularly during stressful times.

Coping with stress shows wide individual differences. Factors that research have verified as being important for successful coping include social support and a perception of control over the stressful situation, including behavioral, cognitive, decisional, informational, and emotional control. Although many people believe that catharsis is a good way to handle stress, research shows this is not the case. Furthermore, although crisis debriefing can help a few people, it may not only be ineffective, depending on the type of trauma and the individual, but might even increase PTSD. So what helps? Wide individual differences characterize successful coping. For some people it's a matter of expressing their emotions and accepting that some things cannot be controlled. Attitudes, personality, and socialization interact to produce what researchers call hardiness: the ability to resist the negative effects of stress. Hardy individuals see stressors as a challenge rather than as a threat. Other individual difference variables that affect coping include being optimistic, having a strong sense of self-worth, being spiritual and religiously involved, and spending less time mulling over negative events.

Psychologists and other health practitioners look to promote good health and reduce stress, because these factors go hand in hand. The fields of behavioral medicine and health psychology have been rapidly growing over the past decade, focusing on preventing both illness and stress. Here are five tips for promoting good health: stop smoking, reduce alcohol consumption, lose weight, exercise, and follow medical advice. Of course, the problem with many of these tips is that they are difficult to put into effect. Prevention programs offer one approach to reducing bad health behaviors, but lessons learned from the failure of DARE programs need to be accounted for. Another approach for many people when it comes to poor health is to seek help from alternative and complementary medicine. Americans spend $22 billion each year on unsupported vitamins, herbs, and food supplements. Other unsupported approaches include chiropractic medicine, acupuncture, and homeopathy.

BEFORE YOU READ ... LEARNING OBJECTIVES

After reading Chapter 12 you should be able to:

12.1   Explain how stress is defined and approached in different ways
12.2   Identify different approaches to measuring stress
12.3   Describe Selye's general adaptation syndrome
12.4   Explain the tend and befriend response to stress
12.5   Describe the diversity of stress responses, including PTSD, anxiety, and depression
12.6   Describe how the immune system functions
12.7   Understand the field of psychoneuroimmunology
12.8   Appreciate the contributions of the biopsychosocial model to understanding psychophysiological disorders
12.9   Describe the role of personality in everyday experience, and socioeconomic factors in coronary heart disease, and stress in asthma and ulcers
12.10   Describe the role of social support and different types of control in coping with stress
12.11   Explain how spirituality, hardiness, self-enhancement, and rumination may influence responses to stress
12.12   Identify the goals and practices of behavioral medicine and health psychology
12.13   Distinguish alternative medicine from complementary medicine
12.14   Describe different alternative medical approaches and compare their effectiveness with placebo

BEFORE YOU READ ... TERM IDENTIFICATION

acquired immune deficiency syndrome
 (AIDS) (p. 504)
acupuncture (p. 525)
alternative medicine (p. 523)
asthma (p. 509)
biopsychosocial perspective (p. 506)
coping (p. 496)
complementary medicine (p. 523)
coronary heart disease (CHD) (p. 507)
corticosteroids (p. 496)
emotion-focused coping (p. 496)
fight-or-flight response (p. 500)
general adaptation syndrome (GAS) (p. 499)
hardiness (p. 514)
hassles (p. 498)
health psychology (p. 516)

homeopathic medicine (p. 526)
immune system (p. 504)
peptic ulcer (p. 510)
primary appraisal (p. 496)
proactive coping (p. 512)
problem-focused coping (p. 496)
psychoneuroimmunology (p. 505)
psychophysiological (p. 506)
secondary appraisal (p. 496)
social support (p. 511)
spirituality (p. 514)
stress (p. 495)
tend and befriend (p. 501)
Type A personality (p. 507)
Type D personality (p. 508)

AS YOU READ ... PRACTICE ACTIVITIES

WHAT IS STRESS?

1. Differentiate between stress, anxiety, and trauma. (LO 12.1)

2. Stress can be perceived in three ways: as a stimulus, as a transaction, or as a response. Summarize these three perspectives here. (LO 12.1)

3. Compare problem-focused and emotion-focused coping. Provide an original example of how each of these coping approaches might be implemented. (LO 12.1)

4. Score yourself on the Social Readjustment Rating Scale (p. 497). How did you score? What insights does this assessment provide into your own stress levels? What changes can you make in your life to reduce some of the major stressors that might later affect your health? (LO 12.2)

5. Go to http://www.drstephanie.org/dailyhassles.htm where you will find a "Hassles and Uplifts Scale." One of the things to note is that some things can be both a hassle *and* an uplift. Go over the list of events and note which ones are more often hassles for you, which are more often uplifts, and which are about half and half. What changes could you make in your life to maximize the uplifts and minimize the hassles? (LO 12.2)

HOW WE ADAPT TO STRESS: CHANGE AND CHALLENGE

1. Summarize, in your own words, the three stages of Selye's general adaptation syndrome (GAS). (LO 12.3)

2. Imagine yourself taking an extremely important exam (maybe the SATs, AP exam, or an important final exam) and you find yourself unable to answer item after item after item. Note the progression of activation through the hypothalamus-pituitary-adrenal (HPA) axis over the course of taking this exam. (LO 12.3)

3. Compare the fight-or-flight response with the tend-and-befriend reaction to stress. (LO 12.3, LO 12.4)

4. Bonanno and colleagues examined the effects of severe stress on individuals. Describe their studies. (LO 12.5)

        Study:

        Results:

        Lesson learned:

5. We've seen that even positive events can be stressful. Another paradox is that stress can be a good thing. Provide an example from your own life, or the life of someone close to you, of an instance in which a stressful event (positive or negative) led to a more positive outcome. (LO 12.5)

THE BRAIN-BODY REACTION TO STRESS

1. Ikema and Nakagawa (1962) elicited a poison-ivy type of rash. Describe their study here. (LO 12.8)

        Study:

        Results:

Lesson learned:

2.   Know the key terms related to the immune system, including *antigen, pathogen, phagocyte, lymphocyte, neutrophil, macrophage,* and *antibodies.* (LO 12.6)

3.   Discuss the work of Cohen and colleagues who examined the relationship between stress and colds. (LO 12.7)

Study:

Results:

Lesson learned:

4.   Several independent sources of correlational evidence link stress and coronary heart disease. Go over the evidence and determine whether the evidence is sufficient to convince you of a causal relationship. Are you convinced? Why or why not? (LO 12.8)

5.   Take the Type D Personality test at the following websites: (LO 12.9)
http://www.msnbc.msn.com/id/9087408/site/newsweek
http://www.wsbt.com/news/health/1971792.html

How did you do? What changes can you make to your life right now and for the rest of your life to protect you from coronary heart disease, on the basis of this test?

6.   Recent studies investigating bacterial infections as a basis for stomach ulcers show that the relationship is complex and bidirectional, with stress and bacterial ulcers both implicated. Describe the evidence for this complex interrelationship. (LO 12.9)

COPING WITH STRESS

1.   Describe the evidence that supports the following statement: "Social support is probably the single most important factor affecting successful coping with stress." (LO 12.10)

2.   Think of a stressful situation in your life and develop a coping plan based on each of the five areas in which you can gain control: behavioral, cognitive, decision, informational, and emotional. (LO 12.10)

3.   **T or F**: Catharsis is a good thing. What evidence supports your conclusion? (LO 12.10)

4.   **T or F**: Crisis debriefing is always a good thing. What evidence supports your conclusion? (LO 12.10)

5.   What are some of the characteristics of a "hardy" individual when it comes to coping with stress? Which of these characteristics do you possess? What personal characteristics should you try to develop to increase your hardiness? (LO 12.11)

PROMOTING GOOD HEALTH—AND LESS STRESS!

1.   Compare the fields of behavioral medicine and health psychology. (LO 12.12)

2.   Working under the assumption that everyone could improve personal health habits to some extent, pick one of the five health tips elaborated in your text and set up a plan for yourself to enhance your adherence to that health tip. Work out that plan here. (LO 12.12)

3.   Relate the concepts of "portion distortion" and "unit bias" as potential explanations of obesity. (LO 12.12)

4.   Why do you think it is so difficult to make lifestyle changes, even if we know it is the best thing to do for ourselves? In addition to coming up with some ideas of your own, discuss some of the reasons suggested by the text. (LO 12.12)

5.   Each year the government earmarks more than $6 million for DARE.
        T or F: DARE is an effective program. Evaluate the evidence based on carefully controlled research studies. (LO 12.12)

6.   What is the difference between alternative medicine and complementary medicine? (LO 12.13)

7.   **T or F**: The fact that many herbal supplements are "natural" makes them safe. Why? (LO 12.13)

8.   Discuss why "sham" (fake) acupuncture treatments may still provide pain relief to patients. (LO 12.13)

AS YOU READ ... CONCEPT MAP ACTIVITIES

ACTIVITY 1: Complete this concept map for general concepts related to stress.

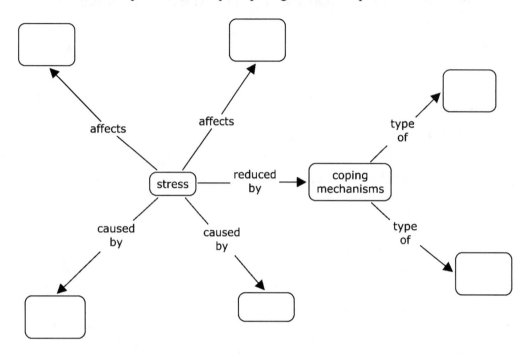

Author activity content supported by *IHMC Cmap Tools* Copyright ©1998-2007 Institute for Human & Machine Cognition

ACTIVITY 2: Complete this concept map for alternative medicine.

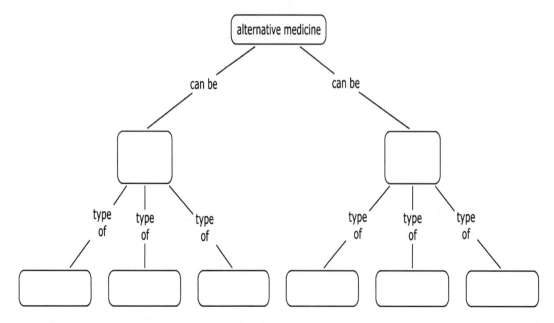

Author activity content supported by *IHMC Cmap Tools* Copyright ©1998-2007 Institute for Human & Machine Cognition

AS YOU READ... MYTH OR REALITY?

Myth: Only negative events produce stress in our lives.
Reality: Even good things can cause stress in our lives.

1.   Provide two examples of events that have occurred in your own life that were positive events, but that created "stress" for you.

2.   Do you believe that this type of stress can be as damaging to your overall health as the stress created by negative life events? Why or why not?

Myth: By applying the principles of *The Secret* your life can be stress and illness-free.
Reality: There is no "quick fix" to stress and illness in our lives.

1.   The secret is based on the "Law of Attraction" in which people's feelings and thoughts attract real events in the world into their lives. Thus, if you think good, positive thoughts, good and positive things will happen to you, and if you think bad, negative thoughts, bad and negative things will happen to you. Review the official website at http://www.thesecret.tv and provide a critique of the content.

AS YOU READ … PUT YOUR CRITICAL THINKING SKILLS TO THE TEST

---

1. Cohen and Cohen (1984) described what they called "the clinician's illusion." This illusion results from a bias that develops from a single clinician (psychological or medical) who comes to see a certain illness through the representation of the small sample of patients that clinician has seen, rather than in the big picture of all patients with the same diagnosis. (LO 12.1)
a. Consider how this might occur not only in clinical practice but in everyday life.
b. Also consider how this might lead anyone, including you, to make some errors in decision making.

2. The Social Readjustment Rating Scale has been criticized as not being applicable to large segments of the population, such as younger adults, older adults, and many minority groups. (LO 12.2)
a. Go through the items and evaluate the items individually to decide which items might not apply to all people across the board.
b. Can you think of major life events that are more likely to involve these different subgroups of people? What are they?

3. Two of the problems with correlational evidence include the two-way nature of the relationship and the potential of a third variable responsible for both of the related variables. (LO 12.7)
a. Point out the evidence that stress causes illness and then point out the evidence that illness causes stress. Which seems more convincing to you?
b. Alternatively, consider some potential third variables that might be responsible for causing both stress and illness.

AS YOU READ… MYPSYCHLAB CONNECTION

What is Stress?

Review how stress is measured with the **simulation** *How Stressed Are You?* **Explore** *The Effect of Cognitive Appraisal on Responses to Stressors* to see how people appraise stress. To see examples of the effects of life stressors and traumatic events on stress, **watch** *9/11 and Post Traumatic Stress Disorder.* **Explore** *Selye's General Adaptation Syndrome* and **listen** to the corresponding podcast to review Selye's theory on the General Adaptation Syndrome (G.A.S.).

How We Adapt to Stress: Change and Challenge

Go to the **simulation** *Stress and the Fight-or Flight Response* for more on how we adapt to stress and the effect of stress on health. Gender differences and stress are discussed in **watch** *Gender Differences in Stress Vulnerability.*

The Brain-Body Reaction to Stress

Watch *Stress and Sleep* to see how specific stressors affect the body.

Coping with Stress

E**xplore** *Coping Strategies and Their Effects* for an interesting activity illustrating how various coping strategies can affect how individuals can approach daily stressors. **Watch** *Coping with Stress*, *Socializing and Stress* and *Optimism and Resilience* for more on understanding how individuals cope with stress. **Watch** *Emotion Regulation: James Coan* to see how social support affects our reactions to stress.

Promoting Good Health –Less Stress

How does your lifestyle affect your health? To find out take the **simulation** *How Healthy Are You?*

AFTER YOU READ... PRACTICE TEST #1

Before beginning this practice test, estimate the percent you expect to get correct.
Anticipated percent correct: _____

1. Research shows that, on average, approximately _____% of people experience a major traumatic event in their lifetime.
   a. 10–30
   b. 40–50
   c. 60–90
   d. 90–95

2. When asked about stress in his life, Josh sees it as coming from specific events. Josh sees stress
   a. as a transaction.
   b. as an appraisal.
   c. as a response.
   d. as a stimulus.

3. When we compare hassles to major life events,
   a. only hassles can predict subsequent psychological health.
   b. hassles are a better predictor of subsequent psychological health.
   c. only major life events can predict subsequent psychological health.
   d. major life events are a better predictor of subsequent psychological health.

4. Dat feels a sudden shaking throughout his house. At first he is alarmed, but then calmly gets under a sturdy table and waits to see whether it is a serious earthquake or just a little shaker. Dat is now in the _____ stage of the general adaptation syndrome.
   a. fight
   b. befriend
   c. resistance
   d. exhaustion

5. Men's and women's stress responses tend to differ because women are more likely to produce the hormone _____ during stress.
   a. oxytocin
   b. adrenaline
   c. cholesterol
   d. epinephrine

6. Soldiers who fought in wars such as Vietnam or Iraq may sometimes experience nightmares and anxiety, as well as fear and anger long after their military service is over. Such an experience reflects
   a. rumination.
   b. homeopathy.
   c. posttraumatic stress disorder.
   d. the exhaustion phase in Selye's general adaptation syndrome.

7. Rochelle is convinced that her pessimistic style of thinking has led to her development of cancer. You reassure her that
   a. no research evidence supports the idea that a pessimistic attitude "causes" cancer.
   b. research shows that she can protect herself from cancer with a positive attitude.
   c. research evidence supports the link between negative thinking and serious illness, so she had better get some therapy.
   d. although negative thinking can cause colds, it has been found to protect individuals from serious illnesses, such as cancer.

8. Psychoneuroimmunology examines the relationship between
a. antigens and pathogens.
b. nocebo effects and placebo effects.
c. social support and the benefits of catharsis.
d. the immune system and the central nervous system.

9. Jamal studies hard because he really wants to get good grades in his classes. He wants to get into a good medical school and go far in his career. However, Jamal is cheerful and happy despite feeling "driven" to succeed. Jamal probably has a _____ personality.
a. Type A
b. Type B
c. Type C
d. Type D

10. The personality trait that best predicts coronary heart disease is
a. perfectionism.
b. irritability.
c. ambition.
d. hostility.

11. One of the most important factors for coping with stress is
a. strong social support.
b. the immediacy of crisis counseling.
c. having a positive attitude.
d. whether one responds with anxiety or with depression.

12. Behavioral control can be _____, whereas cognitive control can be _____.
a. exercise-based; informational
b. restructuring; avoidance-oriented
c. problem-focused; emotion-focused
d. proactive coping; retroactive coping

13. At Janet's school a student recently died in a horrific car accident. The next day crisis counselors were present in all of Janet's classrooms, asking students to talk through their grief. Janet did not know this student personally, and felt a bit sad for her family at first. However, after the counseling sessions she was particularly upset and felt guilty that her sadness was not deeper.
a. This is surprising because crisis counseling reduces the effects of trauma.
b. This is not surprising in that crisis counseling is not necessary for everyone.
c. This is surprising in that Janet was allowed to disclose her emotions in a public forum.
d. This is not surprising because Janet might have been withholding her emotions prior to the counseling session.

14. Viewing change as a challenge rather than a threat is called
a. optimism.
b. hardiness.
c. rumination.
d. self-enhancement.

15. Jerry is very religious. He is
a. less likely to be overweight and obese.
b. more likely to have good health habits.
c. more likely to be pessimistic about life events.
d. less likely to suffer from stress-related health problems.

16. The specialty area of psychology that studies how to prevent illness and promote good health is called
a. stress psychology.
b. health psychology.
c. behavioral psychology.
d. psychoneuroimmunology.

17. The most serious consequences of binge drinking include
a. a hangover the next day.
b. a weakened immune system.
c. an increase in certain types of cancer and even fatal liver problems.
d. an inability to cope with stress, leading to increased autoimmune disorders.

18. All of the following are reasons for generalized weight gain in society EXCEPT
a. a lack of sufficient sleep.
b. Darwinian natural selection.
c. having good indoor climate control.
d. mothers giving birth at a younger age.

19. Although acupuncture has been practiced for at least 2,000 years, doubt is cast on its validity because
a. the realignment of qi (chi) as the source of relief has recently been falsified.
b. studies show the needles can be placed incorrectly and still relieve migraines.
c. the needles would need to be placed much deeper to produce the supposed effect.
d. research studies have shown only symptom relief, but underlying causes of the illness remain.

20. Homeopathic treatments probably work so well because
a. like-goes-with-like, the same as why vaccines work to prevent illness.
b. symptom relief may simply occur because the illness, such as a cold, has run its course naturally.
c. memory of the substance is just as effective as the substance itself, thereby eliminating all side-effects.
d. the small dosages have fewer side effects than comparable medical prescription drugs that are usually given in higher dosage levels.

After completing the test, calculate your percent correct
(/ 20 =   ) x 100 = _____.

How accurate were your expectations? Does your performance suggest the need for additional study?
For the items you missed, go back and identify why the "correct" answer is the best answer.

AFTER YOU READ ... PRACTICE TEST #2

Before beginning this practice test, estimate the percent you expect to get correct.
Anticipated percent correct: _____

1. Following severely traumatic events, _____ turn out to be psychologically resilient.
   a. most people
   b. a few people
   c. about half of all people
   d. about 10% of all people

2. JoBeth finds the loss of her home following a hurricane is a major loss to her; but she can rebuild, and is grateful to be alive to do so. JoBeth has engaged in looking at stress
   a. as a stimulus.
   b. as a response.
   c. as an appraisal.
   d. as a transaction.

3. People with higher scores on the Social Readjustment Rating Scale
   a. cope better with stress.
   b. can manage more hassles.
   c. are more vulnerable to illness.
   d. react more negatively to stress.

4. Being late for an appointment because you couldn't find a parking space is an example of _____, but getting fired from your job is an example of _____.
   a. a stressor; a trauma
   b. a frustration; an irritation
   c. a hassle; a major life event
   d. a inconvenience; a pressure

5. The three stages of the general adaptation syndrome (GAS) include
   a. alarm, resistance, and exhaustion.
   b. fight, flight, and tend-and-befriend.
   c. stimulus, response, and transactions.
   d. major life events, major daily pressures, and hassles.

6. The greatest health risk for coronary heart disease comes from
   a. smoking.
   b. a hostile attitude.
   c. being overweight.
   d. having high cholesterol.

7. Aisha has occasional severe asthma attacks. At such times it is quite possible that when Aisha becomes frightened her response can
   a. lessen the attack if she also becomes depressed.
   b. aggravate the attack if she forgets to laugh it off.
   c. aggravate the attack if she also becomes anxious.
   d. lessen the attack if she has to restrict her everyday activities.

8. Ulcers provide a nice example of
   a. how stress and personality type interact to cause a physical illness.
   b. how gender differences in stress and resilience act to produce illness.
   c. which alternative treatments are most effective in treating stress-related illnesses.
   d. the interaction of a physical cause (bacterium) interacting with a psychological cause (stress) to result in illness.

9. We can gain control of stressors in our lives several ways, including
a. through faith, religion, and spirituality.
b. with crisis counseling, catharsis, and rumination.
c. increasing behavioral, cognitive, and emotional control.
d. using alternative, complementary, and homeopathic medicines.

10. When Suzanne realized that her dream wedding was on the verge of being a disorganized disaster, she hired a wedding planner to arrange all of the contracts she needed with other people. This example illustrates
a. proactive coping.
b. decisional coping.
c. emotion-focused coping.
d. problem-focused coping.

11. Proactive coping helps people to cope with stress because they can
a. anticipate problems and be prepared for them.
b. forget earlier stressful events by focusing on later, happier events.
c. automatically take part in crisis debriefing, which is always helpful.
d. build up their immune system to better protect against any ill effects on body systems.

12. Jessica has always heard that it's best to get stress "out of her system," so whenever she feels stressed she throws things. Jessica's coping behavior is a _____ idea, because research evidence shows that _____.
a. good; indeed, this is a surefire way to reduce overall internal stress
b. bad; "getting things off one's chest" helps in the long run but not in the short run
c. bad; "getting it [anger] out of your system" can actually increase anger and stress
d. good ; catharsis is successful in psychoanalytic and humanistic therapy in reducing stress

13. People who "see the glass as half empty"
a. are more optimistic.
b. have a more difficult time handling frustration.
c. show less commitment to their lives and work.
d. relive the negative events in their lives, over and over again.

14. Clemente sees each of life's hassles as a challenge that he can master and overcome. Clemente is likely to have a strong sense of
a. rumination.
b. hardiness.
c. religiosity.
d. helplessness.

15. Which of the following statements is true regarding smoking?
a. Each time people try to stop smoking they smoke even more.
b. Each time people try to stop smoking their chances of succeeding improve.
c. Approximately 50% of American men smoke.
d. Smoking in both men and women is on the decline.

16. Binge drinking is, unfortunately, not rare among college students. According to your text, it is defined as

a. drinking to the point of a blackout each time you drink.

b. drinking to the point of intoxication, but only very infrequently.

c. five or more drinks for men, four or more drinks for women, on a single occasion.

d. drinking almost to the point of intoxication, waiting to sober up, and repeating this process in a single session of drinking.

17. Lupe wants to lose weight. She shows you the advertising slogans of several weight loss programs, all of which cost the same. Which would you advise her to pursue as potentially the best, based on its slogan?

a. "We May Be Slow, But We Are Steady."

b. "Lose All the Weight You Want in Less Than a Month."

c. "Miracle Sleep: Take Our Sleeping Aid, and the More You Sleep, the More Comes Off."

d. "No Special Foods, No Special Appliances, Just Pure, Clean Water from Our Private Glacier Flushes Away That Fat."

18. Studies suggest that genetics play a role in weight control. In reality,

a. prior beliefs have the most powerful effect on weight.

b. about 50% of the predisposition to obesity appears to be genetic.

c. environmental factors appear to play a larger role in weight control.

d. most of the people who take off weight in a medically managed program keep it off.

19. Chiropractic manipulation is most likely effective due to

a. the realignment of spinal subluxations.

b. the medications that the chiropractors prescribe.

c. the nutritional advice the chiropractor provides.

d. the attention, support, and advice the patient receives from the chiropractor.

20. The bottom line on alternative treatments is

a. none of them have been shown to be effective as of this time.

b. some work, some don't; it's best to consult an authority and the scientific literature.

c. small doses may not help at all, but they won't harm you, and they might actually help.

d. many work; large pharmaceutical companies tell people they don't work for financial gain reasons.

After completing the test, calculate your percent correct
(/ 20 =   ) x 100 = _____ .

How accurate were your expectations? Does your performance suggest the need for additional study? For the items you missed, go back and identify why the "correct" answer is the best answer.

AFTER YOU READ... PRACTICE TEST ANSWER KEYS

Practice Test 1.

1. c (p. 494)
2. d (p. 496)
3. b (p. 498)
4. c (p. 500)
5. a (p. 501)
6. c (p. 502)
7. a (p. 505)
8. d (p. 505)
9. a (p. 507)
10. d (p. 508)
11. a (p. 511)
12. c (p. 512)
13. b (p. 513)
14. b (p. 514)
15. d (p. 515)
16. b (p. 516)
17. c (p. 517)
18. d (p. 519)
19. b (p. 525)
20. b (p. 526)

Practice Test 2.

1. a (p. 495)
2. d (p. 496)
3. c (p. 498)
4. c (p. 498)
5. a (pp. 500–501)
6. b (p. 508)
7. c (p. 509)
8. d (p. 510)
9. c (p. 512)
10. a (p. 512)
11. a (p. 512)
12. c (pp. 512–513)
13. b (p. 514)
14. b (p. 514)
15. b (p. 517)
16. c (p. 517)
17. a (p. 520)
18. b (p. 520)
19. d (p. 525)
20. b (p. 527)

AFTER YOU READ ... CONCEPT MAPPING ACTIVITY ANSWERS

ACTIVITY 1: Complete this concept map for general concepts related to stress.

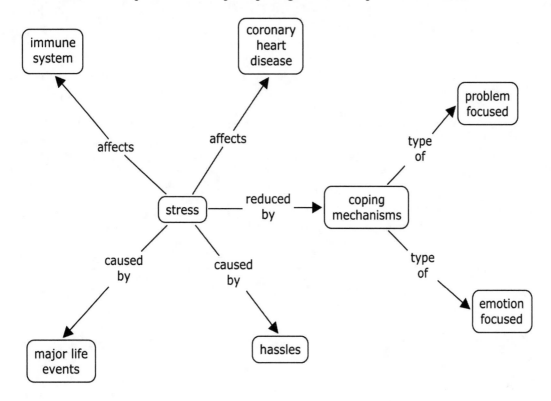

ACTIVITY 2: Here is a list of terms in alphabetical order that you might have included in this concept map.

acupuncture
biologically based
body-based
chiropractic
herbal
homeopathy
supplement
vitamins

CHAPTER 13
SOCIAL PSYCHOLOGY
HOW OTHERS AFFECT US

BEFORE YOU READ...CHAPTER PREVIEW

Social psychology studies social influences on people's thoughts, feelings, and behaviors. Social influences are powerful, but they are often qualified by individual characteristics and situational contexts. Biological needs for interpersonal connectedness (acceptance), cognitive mechanisms (attributions, perceptions), personality traits, and external factors (number and characteristics of others, culture) all play a role. Despite these multiple influences, we often assume that internal dispositions play the major role in causing other people's behavior and fail to see the power of situational influences on behavior. This perceptual tendency is called *the Fundamental Attribution Error*. In contrast to making dispositional attributions for others' behavior, we tend to make situational attributions for our own behavior.

Social comparison reflects the process of looking to others to help us interpret the meaning of a situation and how to behave in the situation. *Conformity* is the tendency for people to change their behavior as a result of group influence. Conformity is affected by dispositions (self-esteem) and characteristics of the group (unanimity, size). Groupthink occurs when a tightly knit group conforms to group pressure and avoids dissent. As with conformity, the presence of a deviant voice can be critical in avoiding groupthink. In obedience, pressure comes from a person in authority. In Milgram's study, over half of his participants followed orders to deliver what they believed were severe shocks to another person. The study is considered a classic because it resulted in surprising findings and because it created an ethical controversy surrounding the degree of stress experienced by the participants. Replication studies show that obedience may be influenced by the prestige of the authority, proximity to the authority or victim, and the presence of another who disobeys.

Research on bystander nonintervention suggests that people are less likely to help when others are present. This lack of intervention may be due to pluralistic ignorance (an ambiguous situation is interpreted by social comparison – others are not intervening) and diffusion of responsibility ("There are many other people. Am I the best person to intervene?"). *Social loafing* describes the phenomenon where people slack off in groups. Research on aggression suggests that males tend to be more physically aggressive and females tend to be more relationally aggressive. Although individual factors influence aggressive behavior (arousal), social factors (the culture of honor) do, as well.

Attitudes are beliefs that include an emotional component. Attitudes do not always predict behavior. Cognitive dissonance theory proposes that inconsistencies in our cognitions produce a feeling of uneasiness that we are motivated to reduce. When we behave in a manner that is discrepant from our attitudes, one way to reduce dissonance is to change our attitude. The dual process model suggests that persuasion can occur along a central route, in which we evaluate merits of an argument, or a peripheral route, in which we make quick judgments. Pseudoscientific marketers often use techniques that persuade us through peripheral routes such as the foot-in-the door, the door-in-the face, and the low-ball techniques.

Stereotypes are mental shortcuts that stem from adaptive cognitive processes. Stereotypes, however, can mislead us when we cling to them too rigidly. Prejudice can result when selected information is used to heighten our perception that others are different from us — the out group.

Discrimination is the behavior of treating members of the out group differently. We can combat prejudice by having groups work together.

BEFORE YOU READ... LEARNING OBJECTIVES

After reading Chapter 13 you should be able to:

13.1 Identify the ways in which social situations influence the behavior of individuals
13.2 Discover how and why our attributions about the causes of others' behaviors are accurate in some cases but biased in others
13.3 Explain the power our observations of others have in influencing our thoughts, beliefs, and decisions
13.4 Determine the factors that influence when we conform to the behaviors and beliefs of others
13.5 Recognize the dangers of group decision-making and identify ways to avoid mistakes common in group decisions
13.6 Identify the contexts that maximize or minimize obedience to authority
13.7 Recognize why individuals may not help others in distress when in a group context
13.8 Distinguish those aspects of a situation that increase or decrease the likelihood of helping
13.9 Describe the social and individual difference variables that contribute to human aggression
13.10 Describe how attitudes relate to behaviors
13.11 Evaluate theoretical accounts of how and when we alter our attitudes
13.12 Identify common and effective persuasion techniques and how they're exploited by pseudoscientists
13.13 Distinguish prejudice and stereotypes as beliefs from discrimination as a behavior
13.14 Identify theoretical explanations of the causes of prejudice
13.15 Identify ways to combat prejudice

BEFORE YOU READ...TERM IDENTIFICATION

adaptive conservatism (p. 565)

aggression (p. 556)

altruism (p. 555)

attitude (p. 558)

attribution (p. 536)

belief (p. 558)

cognitive dissonance (p. 561)

conformity (p. 539)

cults (p. 545)

deindividuation (p. 542)

diffusion of responsibility (p. 553)

discrimination (p. 565)

door-in-the-face technique (p. 563)

enlightenment effect (p. 555)

foot-in-the door technique (p. 563)

Fundamental Attribution Error (p. 537)

group polarization (p. 545)

groupthink (p. 544)

implicit and explicit stereotypes (p. 567)

impression management theory (p. 563)

in-group bias (p. 565)

inoculation effect (p. 546)

jigsaw classrooms (p. 570)

just-world hypothesis (p. 569)

low-ball technique (p. 563)

mass hysteria (p. 538)

obedience (p. 546)

out-group homogeneity (p. 565)

parametric studies (p. 540)

pluralistic ignorance (p. 552)

prejudice (p. 565)

relational aggression (p. 557)

scapegoat hypothesis (p. 569)

self-monitoring (p. 559)

self-perception theory (p. 563)

social comparison theory (p. 538)

social facilitation (p. 536)

social loafing (p. 553)

social psychology (p. 534)

stereotype (p. 566)

ultimate attribution error (p. 569)

As You Read…Practice Activities

WHAT IS SOCIAL PSYCHOLOGY?

1. **T or F:** *Social influence processes are adaptive under most circumstances.*
   Explain your answer.   (LO 13.1)

2. Demonstrating the phenomenon of social facilitation, Zajonc found that cockroaches run faster when
   _____. (LO 13.1)

3. Our explanations for the causes of our own or another person's behavior are called _____.
   (LO 13.2)

4. Describe the Fundamental Attribution Error and give an example from your own experience.
   (LO 13.2)

5. How do our attributions tend to differ when it comes to explaining our own behavior? (LO 13.2)

6. Social comparison theory suggests we look to _____ for guidance on how to interpret a
   situation, what to believe, and how to behave. (LO 13.3)

7. How can social comparison theory be used to explain collective delusions? (LO 13.3)

SOCIAL INFLUENCE: CONFORMITY AND OBEDIENCE

1. Describe Asch's study of conformity. (LO 13.4)

    Study:

    Results:

    Lesson learned:

2. John does not smoke but is offered a cigarette by a friend. He is with five other friends; all of these friends take a cigarette. Research suggests John's conformity to group pressure would be very likely because the group is unanimous in its behavior. If one of John's five friends *does not* take a cigarette, would John's own conformity be more or less likely? Why? (LO 13.4)

3. Describe the Stanford Prison Study. (LO 13.4)

    Study:

    Results:

    Lesson learned:

4. How can the lessons of this study help explain the behavior of prison guards at Abu Ghraib? (LO 13.4)

5. Differentiate between "groupthink" and "group polarization". (LO 13.5)

Groupthink _____

_____

Group polarization _____

_____

6. You are a member of a group charged with an important decision. What could you do to decrease the group's chances of falling prey to groupthink? (LO 13.5)

7. Explain how extreme forms of groupthink can lead to cults. How can one best resist cult influence? (LO 13.5)

8. Describe Milgram's study: (LO 13.6)

    Study:

    Results:

    Lesson learned:

9. The results of Milgram's study were "shocking" because... (LO 13.6)

It created an ethical controversy because...

HELPING AND HARMING OTHERS: PROSOCIAL BEHAVIOR AND AGGRESSION

1. Everyone knows that there is safety in numbers. Or is there? What does the empirical evidence suggest about this common knowledge? (LO 13.7)

2. Draw lines linking each major influence on nonintervention with the appropriate question and example. (LO 13.7)

                                                          "Am I the right person to provide help?"

Pluralistic ignorance   "Is this situation an emergency?"

Diffusion of responsibility   A person is lying on the sidewalk.

                                                            A person is having a heart attack in a crowd.

3. List the factors that are likely to increase the probability of helping. (LO 13.8)
    Situational factors

    Dispositional factors

4. Social loafing: (LO 13.8)
    Is defined as...

    Is influenced by...

Can be demonstrated using the example of…

Can be remedied by…

5. For each of the situational influences on aggression below, provide a brief explanation and example. (LO 13.9)

Interpersonal provocation

Frustration

Media

Aggressive Cues

Arousal

Drug/Alcohol

Temperature

6. Boys tend to be higher in physical aggression; girls tend to be higher in relational aggression. (LO 13.9)

What is relational aggression?

Have you ever been a victim of relational aggression?

ATTITUDES AND PERSUASION: CHANGING MINDS

1. T or F *Attitudes predict behaviors with a high level of certainty.*
    Explain. (LO 13.10)

2. How can the recognition heuristic be used to help explain the acquisition of Urban Legends?
    (LO 13.10)

3. Cognitive dissonance theory suggests that when we behave in ways that are discrepant from our
    cognitions we feel _____ and are motivated to _____ (LO 13.10)

4. What are three ways we can reduce dissonance? Give an example of each. (LO 13.10)

    1) _____

    Example: _____

    2) _____

    Example: _____

    3) _____

    Example: _____

5. Briefly describe the Festinger & Carlsmith study. (LO 13.10)

    Study:

    Results:

    Lesson learned:

6. In the Dual Process model, Petty & Cacippo (1986) propose two routes to attitude persuasion, the Central and Peripheral routes. The _____ route involves critical thinking. Promoters of Pseudoscience are likely to rely on the _____ route. (LO 13.12)

7. Match the following persuasion techniques with the appropriate example. (LO 13.12)

    a. Door-in-the face.   _____ "Thank you for agreeing to stay at my
                                             house to take care of my cats while I'm
                                             gone. By the way, there are 7 of them."

    b. Low ball   _____ "Well if you can't help with our Beach
                                             Clean-up this weekend could you donate $10 to help
                                             others get there?"

    c. Foot-in-the door   _____ "Thank you for wearing our 'Save the
                                             trees' button. Could you help the trees
                                             by joining our organization at the $35 level?"

8. How does the foot-in-the door technique rely on the process of cognitive dissonance? (LO 13.12)

9. Match each of the following techniques used to market pseudoscience with the applicable principle of persuasion. (LO 13.12)

    a. Phantom goal   _____ "University researchers endorse
                                              the use of our subliminal tapes."

    b. Manufacture source credibility _____ "Ours are the best selling
                                              subliminal tapes on the market."

    c. Scarcity heuristic   _____ "These subliminal tapes will
                                              only be offered for a limited time."

    d. Consensus heuristic   _____ "Our subliminal tapes can help
                                              you master psychology while
                                              you sleep!"

PREJUDICE AND DISCRIMINATION

1. Explain the two major biases that contribute to our tendency to ally with others. (LO 13.14)

   In-group bias

   Out-group homogeneity

2. T or F *Jane Elliot's study with brown-eyed and blue-eyed children found that it is hard to get children to discriminate against one another.* Explain your answer. (LO 13.14)

3. Match the following contributors to the development of prejudice with its example. (LO 13.14)

   a. Scapegoating   _____New frat members are likely to express
                                      dislike of rival frat members.

   b. Just-world   _____The belief that times are bad because
                                      illegal aliens have taken away jobs.

   c. Social conformity   _____Rev. Jerry Falwell's statement after 9/11
                                      that America brought this harsh
                                      punishment on itself because God
                                      was displeased with the country's
                                      godlessness.

4. Describe the Robber's Cave study. (LO 13.15)

   Study:

   Results:

   Lesson learned:

5. How did Aronson's Jigsaw Classroom incorporate lessons from the Robber's Cave study? (LO 13.15)

As You Read… Concept Map Activities

ACTIVITY 1:

As examples of social influence, conformity and obedience are similar concepts, yet they are also different. Complete the following concept map indicating some basic differences. (LO 13.6)

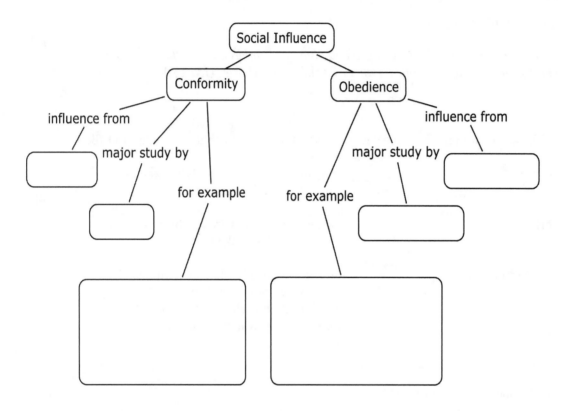

Author activity content supported by *IHMC Cmap Tools* Copyright ©1998-2007 Institute for Human & Machine Cognition

ACTIVITY 2:

The presence of others can have positive or negative effects, depending on the situation. Complete the Concept map below, outlining these differences. (LO 13.1)

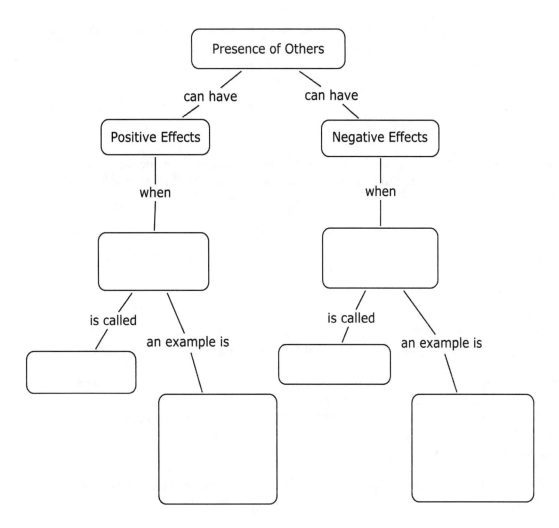

AS YOU READ... MYTH OR REALITY?

Myth: There's no adequate scientific explanation for UFO reports.
Reality: The overwhelming majority of UFO reports can be accounted for, with only 2% remaining truly unidentified.

1. Extraordinary claims require extraordinary evidence. What are some of the ordinary explanations for UFO sightings?

2. A hypothesis is scientific if it is falsifiable – evidence could be found to show the theory false. Why do the UFO believers' claims often fail to meet this criterion of falsifiability? Can you think of examples?

Myth: Women are yackers, men are slackers.
Reality: There is greater variability among members of the same gender than between genders.

Claims that there are gender differences in chatter are countered by research suggesting that differences between men and women are not statistically significant.
    http://www.npr.org/templates/story/story.php?storyId=11762186&ft=1&f=1024
In addition, who talks more depends on the situation
    www.pbs.org/speak/speech/prejudice/women

1. How might the concepts discussed in this chapter on social influence help explain why we hold gender stereotypes?

2. Why might we hold on to our stereotypes despite disconfirming evidence?

AS YOU READ... PUT YOUR CRITICAL THINKING SKILLS TO THE TEST

1. An important characteristic of critical thinking is being able to see that the answer to many questions is, "It all depends." For example, although the chapter suggests brainstorming may not be all it's cracked up to be, there are situations where bringing groups of people together to work on a common task is effective. When is group work likely to be problematic? When can it be useful?

2. This website http://www.thesecret.tv (and many others) describes a book and DVD called *The Secret*. Using Table 13.3 as a guide, identify as many persuasion techniques as you can. Check out this article for some discussion of these techniques:
   http://www.msnbc.msn.com/id/17314883/site/newsweek

3. *Thinking critically about your own behavior...* According to a Pew Research Center survey, the number of things Americans say they can't live without has multiplied in the past decade:
   http://pewresearch.org/pubs/323/luxury-or-necessity
   To what extent do you think these perceptions reflect the processes of social comparison and conformity? Do you think these processes have affected your own perceptions of necessities?

4. How many of the urban legends in Figure 13.3 have you heard? Have you ever asked yourself why you believe these claims? What are some of the social influences that may have contributed to your belief?

AS YOU READ... MYPSYCHLAB CONNECTION

What is Social Psychology?
Explore *Fundamental Attribution Error* and engage in the **simulation** *Social Facilitation*. Read more about urban legends and how they can use critical thinking skills to question such stories that circulate by choosing **explore** *Urban Legends*. **Explore** *Internal & External Attributions* to learn more about causal attributions and how they differ cross-culturally.

Social Influence: Conformity and Obedience
To learn more about the Stanford Prison Experiment, **watch** *The Stanford Prison Experiment*. **Watch** the shocking re-creation of the *Milgram Obedience Study Today*.

Helping: When We Intervene and When We Don't
For more about how the presence of others affects our likelihood of providing assistance, **explore** *Bystander Intervention*. Participate in the **simulation** *Helping a Stranger* to gain a better understanding of why we don't always provide help.

Attitudes and Persuasion
To learn more about how we modify our attitudes, **explore** *Cognitive Dissonance & Attitude Change*. To experience how your own attitudes may not always be consistent with your actual behaviors, participate in a replication of a cognitive dissonance study with the **simulation** *Cognitive Dissonance*. **Watch** the video *Attitudes and Attitude Change*, which illustrates how attitudes change.

Prejudice and Discrimination
For a way to better understand that all individuals engage in implicit stereotyping, participate in the **simulation** *Unconscious Stereotyping*.

AFTER YOU READ... PRACTICE TEST #1

Before beginning this practice test estimate the percent you expect to get correct
Estimated percent correct: _____

1. Demonstrating the phenomenon of _____, Zajonc found that cockroaches will run faster when _____.
   a. conformity; running together.
   b. learning; reinforced
   c. social facilitation; other cockroaches are present
   d. social loafing; they are alone.

2. Which of the following statements appears to be true on the basis of social psychological findings?
   a. There is safety in numbers.
   b. Social influences can be adaptive.
   c. Groups are superior to individuals at decision-making.
   d. Drinking can calm us down, lowering our risk for aggression.

3. The effect of an audience on performance can be positive or negative depending on the situation. Social facilitation tends to occur when tasks are _____; social disruption tends to occur when tasks are _____.
   a. unmastered; well-learned
   b. meaningful; meaningless
   c. meaningless; meaningful
   d. well-learned; unmastered

4. When we try to figure out why others (or ourselves) are engaging in a behavior, we are trying to form _____ for the causes of the behavior.
   a. stereotypes
   b. cognitive categories
   c. attitudes
   d. attributions

5. Prejudice is to discrimination as
   a. attitude is to behavior.
   b. cognition is to thought.
   c. action is to behavior.
   d. obedience is to conformity.

6. Julian, Taiwo, and Zora each think Dr. Strange can be a little rude to students at times. After discussing why each of them believes this to be so, they all conclude that Dr. Strange is a terrible teacher and start telling others. This episode provides an example of
   a. social facilitation.
   b. deindividuation.
   c. group polarization.
   d. the inoculation effect.

7. Which of the following characteristics tends to result in higher levels of conformity?
   a. being part of a collectivist culture.
   b. high self-esteem
   c. observing non-conformists
   d. someone who self-identifies as an individualist.

8. "Sam and I had a big fight. He had been home all day but when I came home from work, the place was a disaster. I told him he was a lazy slob, and he had the nerve to tell me I was one, too! He said that I leave the bathroom a mess every morning. He's too stupid to see that I have to or I'd be late for work." In explaining the causes of the man's behavior, the woman in this example is demonstrating the social psychological principle of
   a. diffusion of responsibility.
   b. the Fundamental Attribution Error.
   c. impression management.
   d. the scapegoat hypothesis.

9. _____ refers to the tendency for people to alter their behavior as a result of group pressure.
   a. In-group biasing
   b. Conformity
   c. The Fundamental Attribution Error
   d. Obedience

10. We come to believe strange things for no other reason than we've heard them from a lot of people. This phenomenon
   a. contributes to our belief in Urban Legends.
   b. reflects the recognition heuristic.
   c. reflects pluralistic ignorance.
   d. both a and b.

11. Cults seem to result when
   a. a group of mentally unstable individuals come together.
   b. a group of individuals share unquestioning loyalty to a leader.
   c. people are brainwashed.
   d. both a and b.

12. Keoki believes that global warming is a real threat. During a social gathering, however, most of the people discussing the issue appear to agree that the threat is greatly exaggerated. Keoki is most likely to express his opinion if
   a. all others in the group agree that the threat is exaggerated.
   b. the beliefs of the group are clearly wrong.
   c. there are five people in the group.
   d. one other person is expressing his belief that global warming is a real threat.

13. When a situation is unclear, we often look to others for guidance about what to do and how to behave. This phenomenon is known as
   a. social comparison.
   b. cognitive dissonance.
   c. social loafing.
   d. groupthink.

14. Based on replications of Milgram's original study of obedience, which of the following soldiers would have the most difficulty following orders to injure another person?
   a. a soldier armed with a machine gun in a fortified bunker
   b. a soldier launching a missile
   c. a soldier armed only with a knife
   d. a bombardier releasing a load of bombs

15. Results of the Milgram study are "shocking" because
   a. even people surveyed before the study did not suspect the high level of obedience Milgram observed.
   b. Milgram gave electric shocks to human beings.
   c. Milgram showed that people have a need to harm others.
   d. both a and b.

16. Which of the following statements is most likely to contribute to groupthink?
    a. "Let's hear some differing opinions."
    b. "What do you think?"
    c. "I'm sure we all agree on this."
    d. "We need to look at all of the evidence."

17. "If you can't come to our $100-a-plate *Save the Trees* dinner, could you donate $5.00 to our campaign?" This statement reflects which of the following persuasive techniques?
    a. door-in-the face
    b. foot-in-the door
    c. low-ball
    d. the natural is commonplace

18. We often assume that _____ play a major role in causing other people's behavior while we fail to see the power of _____.
    a. internal dispositions; situational influences
    b. pressures to conform; biological factors
    c. biological factors; internal dispositions
    d. situational influences; internal dispositions

19. Which of the following is an example of discrimination?
    a. using judges who are blind to musician sex to evaluate musical performance
    b. believing that all teens are bad drivers
    c. denying housing to individuals because of their race
    d. thinking Asians are good students

20. The need to blame others for our own misfortune is
    a. the Fundamental Attribution Error.
    b. the Ultimate Attribution Error.
    c. an example of the scapegoating hypothesis.
    d. an example of relational aggression.

After completing the test, calculate your percent correct
(/ 20 =   ) x 100 = _____.

How accurate were your expectations? Does your performance suggest the need for additional study?
For the items you missed, go back and identify why the "correct" answer is the best answer.

AFTER YOU READ... PRACTICE TEST #2

Before beginning this practice test, estimate the percent you expect to get correct.
Estimated percent correct _____.

1. Which of the following is a TRUE statement about aggression?
    a. Humans are the only species that wages all-out war against its own members.
    b. The presence of a gun can increase the chances one will act violently in response to provocation.
    c. The calming effects of alcohol reduce aggressive tendencies.
    d. There is little evidence that warmer temperatures are associated with higher rates of violence.

2. Bystander non-intervention appears to result from
    a. bystander apathy and pluralistic ignorance.
    b. pluralistic ignorance and diffusion of responsibility.
    c. social debilitation and bystander apathy.
    d. conformity and obedience.

3. According to the research, which of the following is true?
    a. Compared with females, males tend to be more physically and relationally aggressive.
    b. Men tend to be more physically aggressive; females tend to be more relationally aggressive.
    c. Studies across the animal kingdom suggest there is no real difference between male and female aggression.
    d. Differences in aggression are biological, not cultural.

4. In high school, you wore your pants baggy, loose, and low—like the rest of the guys. When you got to college you notice a dramatic difference in pant wearing style. You are MOST likely to CHANGE your pant style if
    a. no one on campus wears their pants loose and low.
    b. your group of friends wears their pants low.
    c. others you know wear crazy clothes.
    d. your advisor tells you to buy some new pants.

5. During the Vietnam War, Lt. William Calley ordered his men to shoot women and children in what came to be known as the My Lai massacre. This incident most closely which of the following studies?
    a. Zajonc's study of social facilitation
    b. Solomon Asch's study of conformity
    c. Stanley Milgram's study of obedience
    d. Festinger & Carlsmith's study of cognitive dissonance

6. Mike sees a man lying on a park bench. The man doesn't look well, but Mike notices that there are a lot of people passing by so he doesn't feel the need to stop. This is an example of
    a. pluralistic ignorance.   c. deindividuation.
    b. groupthink.   d. social loafing.

7. Which of the following people would be most likely to come to the aid of another?
    a. someone who read about bystander intervention research.
    b. a member of a crowd.
    c. someone in a hurry.
    d. someone concerned about social approval.

8. During Orson Welles' *War of the Worlds* radio broadcast, tens of thousands of people came to believe that aliens had actually landed at Grover's Mill. Which of the following contributed to this phenomenon?
    a. People openly discussed alternative explanations.
    b. Social comparison processes drove people to look to others for what to think.
    c. Orson Wells did not tell people the radio show was fictitious.
    d. Other stations also covered the event.

9. The belief that times are bad because illegal aliens have taken away jobs is an example of
    a. the just-world hypothesis.
    b. social conformity.
    c. scapegoating.
    d. discrimination.

10. John smokes cigarettes despite warnings that smoking causes cancer. He justifies his smoking by saying he also exercises so smoking isn't that dangerous for him. His justification is an example of
    a. insufficient justification.
    b. cognitive dissonance.
    c. diffusion of responsibility.
    d. conformity.

11. An ad for a new book claims it is an *Oprah* Book Club pick. This marketing technique relies on
    a. the consensus heuristic.
    b. the scarcity heuristic.
    c. manufactured source credibility.
    d. the goddess within.

12. Which of the following claims reflects the findings of social psychological research?
    a. Act as if you like someone and you soon will.
    b. Brainstorming is an effective way to come up with ideas.
    c. Brainwashing is a unique means of permanently changing behavior.
    d. The primary reason for bystander nonintervention is the apathy of the onlookers.

13. In Festinger & Carlsmith's study of cognitive dissonance, the participants who received _____ experienced the most attitude change.
    a. $1.00
    b. $20.00

14. Which of the following would be most effective in combating prejudice?
    a. allowing people to speak with a minority group member in a café setting
    b. providing information to groups about cultural differences
    c. creating a task in which the groups have to cooperate in order to succeed
    d. having groups compete against one another at a sporting event

15. During wartime, countries often emphasize the differences between their own culture and that of the enemy, pointing out differences such as race, language, religion, dietary habits, and fashion. This focus contributes to prejudice
    a. by emphasizing out-group homogeneity and in-group similarity.
    b. through implicit stereotyping.
    c. through social disruption.
    d. by increasing cultural knowledge.

16. You have been assigned a psychology project in which six of you must write and present a group paper on an urban legend for only one group grade. Which of the following is likely to be true?
    a. The group paper will be better than any individual paper.
    b. Individuals are likely to work less hard than if they were working on individual papers.
    c. Students will feel personally responsible for group products.
    d. By brainstorming, the group will come up with twice as many creative ideas as you would have on your own.

17. The just-world-hypothesis
    a. explains altruism.
    b. reflects the need to see the word just as it is.
    c. underlies why some believe cancer victims are responsible for their plight.
    d. avoids "blaming the victim."

18. Which of the following describes a difference between the central and peripheral routes to persuasion?
    a. The central route involves reasoning; the peripheral route promotes snap judgments.
    b. The central route relies on techniques such as low-ball and door-in-the face.
    c. The central route is often relied upon by promoters of pseudoscience.
    d. The central route relies more heavily on the appearance and likeability of the communicator.

19. Which of the following accurately describes Milgram's study of obedience?
    a. The learners were given electric shocks.
    b. The "teachers" were stressed.
    c. Most participants refused to obey the authority figure.
    d. both a and b

20. Zimbardo's prison study and the Abu Ghraib situation are similar because both reflect
    a. the process of deindividuation.
    b. the influence of social roles.
    c. the strong link between attitudes and behavior.
    d. both a and b.

After completing the test, calculate your percent correct
(/ 20 =   ) x 100 = _____.

How accurate were your expectations? Does your performance suggest the need for additional study? For the items you missed, go back and identify why the "correct" answer is the best answer.

AFTER YOU READ... PRACTICE TEST ANSWER KEYS

Practice Test 1.
1. c (p. 536)
2. b (p. 534 – 536)
3. d (p. 536)
4. d (p. 536)
5. a (p. 565)
6. c (p. 545)
7. a (p. 541)
8. b (p. 537)
9. b (p. 539)
10. d (p.539, 559)
11. b (p. 545 – 546)
12. d (p. 540)
13. a (p. 538)
14. c (p. 549)
15. a (p. 548 - 550)
16. c (p. 545)
17. a (p. 563)
18. a (p. 537)
19. c (p. 565 - 566)
20. c (p. 569)

Practice Test 2.
1. b (p. 556, 547)
2. b (p. 552 - 553)
3. b (p. 557)
4. a (p. 539)
5. c (p. 546)
6. a (p. 552)
7. a (p. 555)
8. b (p. 534)
9. c (p. 569)
10. b (p. 561)
11. c (p. 564)
12. a (p. 562)
13. a (p. 562)
14. c (p. 570)
15. a (p. 565)
16. b (p. 553)
17. c (p. 569)
18. a (p. 563)
19. b (p. 548 - 549)
20. d (p. 543)

AFTER YOU READ... SAMPLE CONCEPT MAPS

ACTIVITY 1:

ACTIVITY 2:

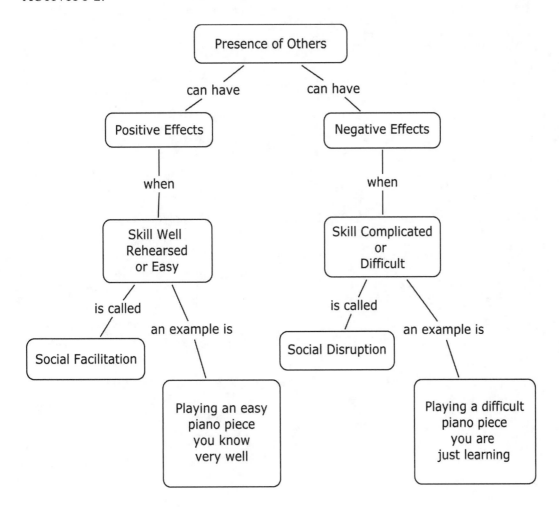

CHAPTER 14
PERSONALITY WHO WE ARE

BEFORE YOU READ ... CHAPTER PREVIEW

Personality is composed of traits, which reflect the stable ways in which people respond to a wide range of situations. The study of personality follows three broad influences on behavior: genetic factors, shared environmental factors, and nonshared environmental factors. Research studies show that the genetic component for many personality traits is strong in identical twins, even when reared apart. Furthermore, adopted children share more personality traits with their biological parents than with their adoptive parents. Nevertheless, the evidence for genetic factors is not perfect, demonstrating the influence of nonshared environmental factors. Shared environmental factors seem to play only a small role, especially among identical twins reared apart.

Most psychologists approach the study of personality through several major frameworks, including the psychoanalytic, trait, behavioral, and humanistic approaches. The psychoanalytic approach, developed by Sigmund Freud, suggests the mind and the body have distinct influences on behavior, called psychogenic and somatogenic effects, respectively. Freud suggested three core assumptions for psychoanalytic theory: psychic determinism, symbolic meaning, and unconscious motivation. These three assumptions can then be seen within the interactions of the three parts of human personality: the id, the ego, and the superego. These three components are often in conflict. One of the coping mechanisms people use to reduce the anxiety caused by this conflict is the use of defense mechanisms. According to Freud's approach to personality, early psychosexual development is critical, proceeding through a series of stages, including, in order, an oral stage, an anal stage, a phallic stage, a latency stage, and a genital stage. Although Freud's work has had a powerful impact on society, several major criticisms of his approach include an inability to falsify major features of this approach, a failure of predictions, a lack of evidence for defense mechanisms, a questionable conception of the unconscious, a reliance on a limited and unrepresentative sample, and flawed assumptions of shared environmental influence. Freud's students and followers tended to tone down the emphasis on sexuality and Freud's pessimistic view of our ability to change while retaining his focus on the unconscious and the importance of early life experiences in shaping personality. However, many of the approaches developed by Freud's followers suffer from the same criticisms as did Freud's approach, particularly an inability to falsify many of the central premises of their approaches.

Another approach to personality grew from the behaviorist's influence on psychology. This group of theorists rejected the influence of early childhood experiences in shaping personality and believed that external contingencies cause our behaviors. The two major assumptions underlying the behavioral view of personality include a focus on genetics and on reinforcers and punishers in the environment. A more moderate approach was proposed by social learning theorists who emphasized our perceptions and cognitions as the cause of personality. Social learning approaches proposed observational learning as important to development. In addition, people's attributions were accounted for by internal or external locus of control. Behavioral and social learning approaches are favored for their empirical attitude. However, strict behaviorist explanations of personality are criticized for excluding a causal role for thinking in shaping personality. Finally, the predictions of observational learning have not panned out.

Humanistic approaches to personality provide a third view. Humanistic approaches emphasize free will and self-actualization, a desire to be the best that we can be, at the core of personality development. In contrast to a Freudian view of a pleasure-seeking id driving our behavior, the humanistic view sees human nature as constructive. Humanists see personality as made up of three components: the organism, the self, and conditions of worth. Incongruence between these various components leads to psychological disorders. Humanistic approaches have been criticized for being difficult to falsify and suffering from confirmation bias.

A final approach is concerned with understanding personality as a cluster of individual traits. Research evidence strongly suggests that traits are stable within individuals. Many models have been proposed, but the most scientifically supported model is called the Big Five. According to this approach all people fall along a continuum in five dimensions of extraversion, neuroticism, conscientiousness, agreeableness and openness to experience. This approach strongly relies on the language skills of individuals and is prone to a circular reasoning fallacy. A criticism of this approach is the finding of inconsistency of behaviors across situations. This criticism, however, has been countered by other research that shows that traits are good at predicting behavior on average, rather than in specific situations, therefore predicting behavioral trends, if not specific behaviors. Culture has recently gained importance for its influence on how personality traits are expressed. For example, some of the Big Five traits are not found in all cultures, but different important traits emerge. Individualism (a focus on individual goals) versus collectivism (behavior tempered by its effect on society) may explain some cross-cultural differences. Furthermore, individuals may have the same trait but express it quite differently. Thus, traits are useful in predicting long-term average behavior of individuals, and they describe individuals very well, but trait approaches are descriptive and do not explain *why* people behave the way they do.

No discussion of personality is complete without an exploration of different approaches to personality assessment. Phrenology, one of the earliest attempts to assess personality based on the pattern of bumps on the skull, failed to withstand empirical testing. These days, assessments are evaluated for their reliability (consistency) and validity (the truthfulness of the measure). Personality tests fall into two broad categories. Structured personality tests are paper-and-pencil tests with fixed responses. The most widely used of these is the MMPI-2. Validity and reliability of the MMPI-2 are high, and the test is widely used for this reason. Although many structured tests have fair validity and reliability, others, such as the Myers-Briggs Type Indicator (MBTI) have doubtful validity and reliability based on research studies. In contrast to structured tests, projective tests require a person to interpret an ambiguous stimulus, such as the Rorschach Inkblot Test or the Thematic Apperception Test. Such tests are favored by the psychoanalytic approach because their underlying premise is that the interpretation of a vague, ambiguous stimulus allows for unconscious motives to be revealed. Unfortunately, reliability and validity are both very poor. Furthermore, because it requires a subjective interpretation by the test-giver, the final interpretation may reflect biases of the test-giver, rather than characteristics of the test-taker. A final caution regarding all types of personality assessments involves the Barnum effect: an interpretation that is sufficiently vague and general and could fit almost anybody.

BEFORE YOU READ ... LEARNING OBJECTIVES

After reading Chapter 14 you should be able to:

14.1   Distinguish between the two major approaches to studying personality
14.2   Describe how twin and adoption studies shed light on genetic and environmental influences on personality
14.3   Describe the core assumptions of psychoanalytic theory
14.4   Distinguish among the three Freudian agencies of the psyche and understand their interactions
14.5   Identify the five psychosexual stages of psychoanalytic theory
14.6   Describe key criticisms of psychoanalytic theory
14.7   Identify the central features of neo-Freudian theories

14.8   Identify the core assumptions of behavioral views of personality
14.9   Identify the core assumptions of social learning theories of personality and their differences from traditional behavioral views
14.10   Describe key criticisms of behavioral and social learning approaches
14.11   Explain the concept of self-actualization and its role in humanistic models
14.12   Identify Maslow's characteristics of self-actualized individuals
14.13   Describe key criticisms of humanistic approaches
14.14   Describe key challenges to trait models of personality
14.15   Explain what personality traits can and cannot predict
14.16   Identify models of personality structure and their implications and limitations
14.17   Identify cultural influences on personality
14.18   Identify key criticisms of trait models
14.19   Describe structured personality tests, particularly the MMPI-2, and their methods of construction
14.20   Describe projective tests, particularly the Rorschach, and their strengths and weaknesses
14.21   Identify common pitfalls in personality assessment

BEFORE YOU READ ... TERM IDENTIFICATION

anal stage (p. 590)
archetypes (p. 595)
Big Five (p. 604)
catharsis (p. 585)
collective unconscious (p. 595)
conditions of worth (p. 601)
defense mechanisms (p. 588)
denial (p. 589)
displacement (p. 589)
ego (p. 587)
Electra complex (p. 591)
empirical method of test construction (p. 609)
erogenous zone (p. 590)
face validity (p. 609)
factor analysis (p. 603)
genital stage (p. 592)
graphology (p. 614)
id (p. 587)
identification with the aggressor (p. 590)
idiographic approach (p. 579)
incongruence (p. 601)
incremental validity (p. 613)
inferiority complex (p. 594)
intellectualization (p. 590)
latency stage (p. 592)
lexical approach (p. 604)
locus of control (p. 598)
Minnesota Multiphasic Personality Inventory (MMPI) (p. 609)
molecular genetic studies (p. 582)
neo-Freudian theories (p. 594)

nomothetic approach (p. 579)
object relations theorists (p. 596)
Oedipus complex (p. 591)
oral stage (p. 590)
P. T. Barnum effect (p. 615)
peak experiences (p. 601)
penis envy (p. 591)
phallic stage (p. 591)
pleasure principle (p. 587)
projection (p. 589)
projective hypothesis (p. 612)
projective tests (p. 612)
psychic determinism (p. 585)
psychogenic (p. 584)
rational/theoretical method of test construction (p. 611)
rationalization (p. 589)
reaction-formation (p. 589)
reality principle (p. 587)
regression (p. 589)
repression (p. 589)
Rorschach Inkblot Test (p. 612)
self-actualization (p. 600)
social learning theorists (p. 598)
somatogenic (p. 584)
structured personality tests (p. 609)
style of life (p. 594)
sublimation (p. 590)
superego (p. 587)
Thematic Apperception Test (TAT) (p. 613)
traits (p. 579)

AS YOU READ ... PRACTICE ACTIVITIES

PERSONALITY: WHAT IS IT AND HOW CAN WE STUDY IT?

1. Your text does not provide a definitive definition of "personality." Formulate a definition that takes into account your text's description of the factors that determine those behaviors we can call a person's "personality." (LO 14.1)

2. Review the logic of the evidence underlying the statement that shared environmental influences appear to have little effect on personality development. Write out at least two sources of converging evidence to support this conclusion. (LO 14.2)

3. Scarr, Webber, Weinberg, and Wittig (1981) provide information on adoption studies in terms of personality development. Provide the following information: (LO 14.2)

    Study:

    Results:

    Lesson learned:

PSYCHOANALYTIC THEORY: THE CONTROVERSIAL LEGACY OF SIGMUND FREUD AND HIS FOLLOWERS

1. Differentiate between somatogenic and psychogenic causes of a disorder. (LO 14.3)

2. Keep track of your "slips of the tongue" for the next several days. Then, look at the core assumptions of the psychoanalytic approach to personality (psychic determinism, symbolic meaning, and unconscious motivation). Do you believe that your "slips of the tongue" have provided an insight into your unconscious? If not, what do they tell you about your behavior? (LO 14.3)

3. Although the analogy between consciousness and an iceberg is intuitively appealing, and captures the static essence of the three components of personality, it fails to capture the dynamic interplay between the id, ego, and superego. Keeping in mind that the ego is constantly mediating between the desires of the id and the morality of the superego, suggest another analogy that would capture the essence of this active part of personality. (LO 14.4)

4. Match the defense mechanism to the example: (LO 14.4)

    a. Jamal, a professional golfer, missed an easy putt. Afterward, he banged his putter so hard into the ground that he bent the shaft.   _____ displacement

    b. During her first semester away at college, Tanya called home every day to ask her mom how to do things around her dorm room.   _____ regression

    c. Maria can't understand why her neighbors gossip so much.   _____ projection

    d. Although Mike claims he was fired from his sales job because the boss's nephew was brought into the company, in reality his sales figures were very low.   _____ rationalization

    e. Sharona never really liked to be around children, but after having two of her own, she spends her days volunteering as room mother at her children's school.   _____ reaction-formation

    f. Bill is a successful basketball player, but as a child his parents had many phone calls from teachers about his aggressive nature on the playground.   _____ sublimation

5. Go back to Chapter 10 on Human Development. Complete this table mapping out the stages of psychosexual development in comparison to Piaget's stages of cognitive development based on age. Note the similarities and contrasts between these two descriptive approaches to development. (LO 14.5)

	birth -				
Piaget's Cognitive Development					
Freud's Psychosexual Development					

6. Your text provides six criticisms of Freud's psychoanalytic approach to personality. Go back to Chapter 1 and reread the section on ruling out rival hypotheses. Then suggest specific examples of ruling out rival hypotheses in Freud's approach. (LO 14.6)

7. Discuss the elements that neo-Freudians retained from the classic psychoanalytic approach, and those elements that they modified, and note what each neo-Freudian did individually to advance studies of personality. (LO 14.7)

BEHAVIORAL AND SOCIAL LEARNING THEORIES OF PERSONALITY

1. Some aspects of behavioral and social learning approaches to personality are perhaps surprisingly similar to psychoanalytic approaches. Compare the two approaches. Note which aspects you found most surprising, and why. (LO 14.8)

2. How do you think that observational learning relates to the finding that social learning approaches were among the first to rely on "thinking" as important to personality development? (LO 14.9)

3. Go to http://www.similarminds.com/locus.html and take this test to determine whether you have an internal or external locus of control. Do you think the test results accurately reflect how you think about yourself when you think about locus of control? Did the items on this test reflect the tone of sample items in your text? (LO 14.9)

4. Commercials are notorious for taking advantage of observational learning and social learning principles. Pick a commercial from TV that has borrowed from these principles and develop your reasoning for picking this commercial. (LO 14.9)

5. Go back to the first part of this chapter and reread the section on shared and unshared environments and then develop the argument that observational learning and the findings on shared environments are in opposition to one another. (LO 14.10)

HUMANISTIC MODELS OF PERSONALITY: THE THIRD FORCE

1. Rogers's humanistic approach is often described in terms of conditional versus unconditional positive regard. In conditional positive regard, love and respect are only given when a person behaves in accordance with a significant other's wishes. However, in unconditional positive regard a person is always valued, even if the person's actions are not. To quote another famous Mr. Rogers, "Sometimes, good people do bad things." Relate the notion of unconditional positive regard to the personality component, "conditions of worth." (LO 14.11)

2. How would a "whistle-blower" (a person who publicly discloses some negative aspect of a company's operations that the company prefers be kept secret) fit into Maslow's definition of a self-actualized person? (LO 14.12)

3. Some writers have provided evidence that Mother Theresa was no saint (c.f. see the review of Hitchins' scathingly negative view of Mother Theresa at http://www.population-security.org/swom-96-09.htm and http://www.rtis.com/reg/bcs/pol/touchstone/April96/hand.htm).Given her need to seek funds for causes that most governments and organizations gave low priority to, and her strict religious beliefs, her attitudes should not be surprising. With this new insight do you still consider Mother Theresa to be a fully actualized person? Why or why not? Can your conclusion be falsified? How or why not? (LO 14.13)

TRAIT MODELS OF PERSONALITY: CONSISTENCIES IN OUR BEHAVIOR

1. Rank order where you might fall along the dimensions of the Big Five personality traits.
    Agreeableness _____ Openness _____ Neuroticism _____
    Conscientiousness _____ Extraversion _____

    Now go to http://www2.wmin.ac.uk/~buchant/wwwffi/ and complete the Big Five test.

    How did your predictions compare to the test results? If your predictions were "off," what accounted for the differences? Is this type of test helpful in understanding your personality dynamics? Discuss the validity of your test results.

    Now try this version: http://webspace.ship.edu/cgboer/bigfiveminitest.html.
    Did you have trouble discriminating between some of the terms? Does this help you to better understand the criticism of the lexical approach? Why or why not?

    You took two different tests that measured your five traits. Were your results consistent and reliable across both tests? What can you conclude about the reliability of Big Five testing? (LO 14.14)

2. The argument against trait approaches—that behaviors are inconsistent across situations—is tempered by the finding that traits do predict behavior averaged across many situations. Consider two traits of your own and note situations in which you behaved *in*consistently. Would you agree that on average, across a wide-range of situations your behavior is consistent? Why or why not? (LO 14.15)

3. Match the trait to its definition: (LO 14.16)

    a. Tendency to be lively and sociable   _____   conscientiousness

    b. Tendency to be tense and moody   _____   agreeableness

    c. Tendency to be careful and responsible   _____   neuroticism

    d. Tendency to be easy to get along with   _____   openness (to new experiences)

    e. Tendency to be curious and unconventional   _____   extraversion

4. Cosmetic psychopharmacology for one's personality is an interesting but controversial proposal, much like cosmetic surgery for the body. Do you believe it would be good for individuals and for society as a whole if we could take a pill to make our personalities more "attractive"? Why or why not? (LO 14.17)

5. Consider the effects of caffeine on arousal. How might caffeine differentially affect introverts and extraverts? What about having a cup of coffee just before a crucial exam? Yes or no for introverts, extraverts, neither, or both? (LO 14.18)

6. Complete the following table to help you summarize the key points of the four different approaches to personality (LO 14.1–LO 14.18)

	Psychoanalytic	Behavioristic	Humanistic	Trait
Importance of unconscious				
Behavior determined or free will?				
Personality structures				
Concept of conscience				
Principal motives				
View of human nature				

PERSONALITY ASSESSMENT: MEASURING AND MISMEASURING THE PSYCHE

1. Look in your text at Sheldon's body types in Figure 14.5. Based on the information provided in the text, which type are you? Do you believe the traits associated with this body type match you? Why or why not? Which ones match and which ones don't? (LO 14.19)

2. Imagine that you are ordered by a judge to have a psychological assessment. The court-appointed psychologist plans to base his entire assessment on the Rorschach Inkblot Test. What would you tell your attorney to convince him to ask the judge for a different psychologist? (LO 14.20)

As You Read ... Concept Map Activities

ACTIVITY 1: Of the four approaches to personality, the psychoanalytic is the most complicated. Complete this concept map to simplify this approach.

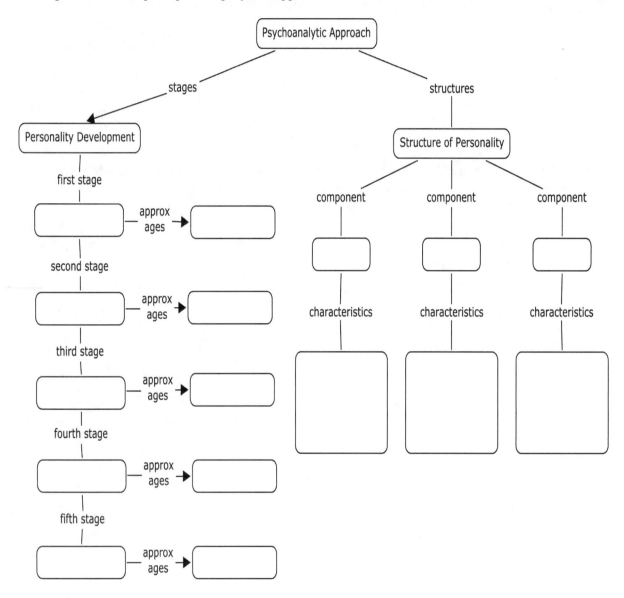

ACTIVITY 2: Complete this concept map for personality assessment:

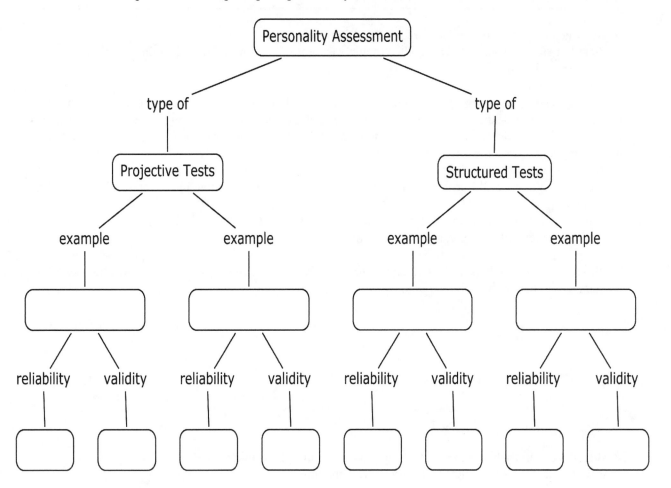

AS YOU READ... MYTH OR REALITY?

Myth: Personality tests are good predictors of job performance.
Reality: Personality tests only work when they measure traits important to performing specific job tasks.

Personality testing in the workplace is becoming increasingly pervasive. Many employers are being sold by personality test salespeople's clever marketing that claims personality testing as the best way to assure the best employees. Some even go so far as to suggest that the resume or interview adds nothing that a quick computerized personality test can't detect.

1. Read about some of the critical reviews of personality testing in general and in the workplace at these websites.
   http://www.simonsays.com/content/book.cfm?tab=6&pid=503846&agid=2
   http://www.enotalone.com/article/5584.html

2. Based on your readings of the text and these book excerpts, develop a rationale against the use of personality testing by potential employers.

Myth: It is generally better to express anger openly than to hold it in.
Reality: Catharsis leads to increased aggressive behaviors.

1. Do you believe that holding in anger only makes you angrier? Freud advocated catharsis as a way of relieving pent up anxiety, thereby leading to a feeling of relief.

2. See what the following websites have to say about catharsis.
   http://home.hiwaay.net/~garson/venting.html
   http://www.apa.org/releases/catharsis.html
   http://whyfiles.org/118anger/3.html

3. After examining these three websites what do you think? Do you see any remaining flaws in what you have read about?

AS YOU READ ... PUT YOUR CRITICAL THINKING SKILLS TO THE TEST

1. At http://www.myersbriggs.org/my%2Dmbti%2Dpersonality%2Dtype/mbti%2Dbasics/ you can read promotional information on the Myers-Briggs Type Indicator (MBTI). Then go to http://skepdic.com/myersb.html to read a critique of the MBTI. Take what you read there and in your text about the Jungian approach to personality, as well as reading about personality assessment later in the chapter, and develop an argument and come to a conclusion, with evidence for whether you believe the MBTI is a good measure of personality.

2. Go to http://www.wizardrealm.com/tests/personality.html and pick any of the tests. Take the test and read about your results. What elements of personality did this test measure? Was this a projective or structured test? How appropriate do you think that the test is for measuring the personality characteristics that were in your report? What do you think would be its validity and reliability? Compare the test items in that test with the kinds of items that *should* be included in tests of personality that would correspond to the aspects of personality described in your textbook.

AS YOU READ... MYPSYCHLAB CONNECTION

Personality: What Is It and How Can We Study It?
To see the roles nature and nurture played in the development of their personalities **watch** *Twins Separated at Birth, Reunited.*

Psychoanalytic Theory: The Controversial Legacy of Sigmund Freud and His Followers
For a good review of Freud's theories on personality development, go to the following **explore** modules: *Id, Ego, Superego, Freud's Five Psychosexual Stages of Personality Development*, and *Defense Mechanisms.*

Behavioral and Social Learning Theories of Personality
Compare behavioral and social learning theories of personality in **explore** *Behavioral Versus Social Learning Theories of Personality.*

Humanistic Models of Personality: The Third Force
To compare Humanistic Theories against other personality theories go to **explore** *Psychodynamic, Behavioral, Trait & Type, Humanistic and Cognitive Approaches to Personality.*

Trait Models of Personality: Consistencies in Our Behavior
For review of Trait Models of personality, **explore** *The Five Factor Model* and *Mischel's Theory of Personality.*

Personality Assessment: Measuring and Mis-measuring the Psyche
For more on how researchers and clinicians attempt to measure personality and diagnose personality disorders, **explore** *Personality Assessment.*

AFTER YOU READ... PRACTICE TEST #1

Before beginning this practice test, estimate the percent you expect to get correct.
Anticipated percent correct: _____

1. Jane is listening to a radio talk show host and decides she is going to follow the advice given out to someone else. You tell Jane she needs to follow this radio host's advice
   a. confidently, this personality's training has prepared her to synthesize complicated constructs into simpler ones.
   b. confidently, because this personality takes primarily a nomothetic approach to understanding the caller's problem.
   c. cautiously, because this personality often takes a complicated, multifaceted construct, and speaks about it unidimensionally.
   d. confidently, this personality tries to interpret problems based on wide-ranging influences such as genetic, familial, and social forces.

2. Personality is generally a function of three broad influences that include
   a. culture, family life, and school experiences.
   b. nomothetic factors, idiographic factors, and genetic factors.
   c. traits, early childhood experiences, and reward contingencies.
   d. genetics, shared environmental factors, and nonshared environmental factors.

3. A strong conclusion about personality development, based on various studies of identical twins raised both together and apart, is that
   a. genetic factors have, at best, only a small effect on adult personality.
   b. genetics and shared environmental factors together determine adult personality.
   c. shared environmental factors have, at best, only a small effect on adult personality.
   d. shared and nonshared environmental factors contribute equally to personality development.

4. Jermaine argues that psychic determinism, symbolic meaning, and unconscious motivations influence our personality. Jermaine believes in the _____ approach to personality.
   a. trait   c. behaviorist
   b. humanistic   d. psychoanalytic

5. In purely Freudian psychoanalytic terms, the core assumptions of determinism and unconscious psychic motivation suggest
   a. people have little free will.
   b. free will is limited by the id's desires.
   c. we can choose our own actions, as long as the superego permits them.
   d. we have the power to control forces outside of our conscious awareness.

6. The pleasure principle drives the _____, whereas the reality principle drives the _____.
   a. ego; id   c. id; superego
   b. id; ego   d. ego; superego

7. In order, from birth onward, the stages of psychosexual development are
   a. oral, anal, penile, phallic, genital.
   b. oral, penile, anal, latency, phallic.
   c. oral, anal, phallic, latency, genital.
   d. oral, anal, genital, latency, phallic.

8. Compared to strict Freudian approaches, the neo-Freudians shared Freud's idea of _____, but differ in _____.
   a. cross-cultural archetypes; am emphasis on unconscious forces
   b. psychosexual development; an emphasis on a personal unconscious
   c. unconscious influences on behavior; placing less emphasis on the central role of sexuality
   d. optimism for personality change in adulthood; the importance of early experiences in shaping behavior

9. Because radical behaviorist views of personality focus on contingencies in the environment, they rely heavily on the principles of
   a. psychoanalysis.
   b. operant conditioning.
   c. classical conditioning.
   d. information-processing.

10. Justin always wears a helmet when riding a motorcycle. He knows that he can actively do something to keep himself safe. Justin must have a(n) _____ locus of control.
    a. primary
    b. internal
    c. external
    d. secondary

11. Which of the following individuals shows the greatest self-actualization?
    a. John. During the baseball season, he likes to take in a ballgame after work.
    b. Carmen. She was recently voted "most popular" by her many friends in her sorority.
    c. Mike. He regularly runs errands for his grandmother because he has no job and has the time to help her out.
    d. Tasha. After retiring from her teaching job, she spends six months out of each year working in a refugee camp in Darfur.

12. Which of the following is true of the Big Five traits?
    a. Tenacity is a sixth trait found among chimpanzees.
    b. The traits are found universally.
    c. Scores on the Big Five are correlated with intelligence.
    d. These traits show up most consistently in factor analyses.

13. Mamoru is taking the Big Five personality test, but he's stuck. One of the problems with trait approaches is reliance on a lexical approach in which it's important that people know themselves in terms of fine differences between the meanings of words. Mamoru is having a difficult time discriminating between the two traits of
    a. kind and rude.
    b. bashful and shy.
    c. jealous and creative.
    d. careless and thoughtful.

14. When a particular test is consistent in assessing some characteristic, this is known as
    a. validity.
    b. reliability.
    c. standardization.
    d. truthfulness of the measure.

15. Personality tests can be divided into two broad categories. These include
    a. implicit and explicit.
    b. intrinsic and extrinsic.
    c. structured and projective.
    d. conscious and subconscious.

16. Andrzej has been asked by a potential new employer to complete the MBTI as part of his job application process. Andrzej should
    a. complete the test because knowing his "type" will provide useful information both for his new employer and for himself.
    b. walk out the door, any potential employer who uses such a poor test is not worth working for, no matter the quality of the position.
    c. refuse to complete the test because he knows it will reveal his weaknesses, which may lead the new employer to not hire him.
    d. complete the test, then tactfully provide references to scientific sources to the personnel director, noting that the validity and reliability of this measure are questionable.

17. The Rorschach and the TAT are considered
    a. honest tests.
    b. projective techniques.
    c. unstructured interviews.
    d. personality questionnaires.

18. Janet is taking the TAT. She is looking at a series of
    a. inkblots.
    b. genetic tests.
    c. observations of others.
    d. ambiguous-situation drawings.

19. Graphology, the psychological interpretation of handwriting,
    a. has the lowest validity and reliability of all projective measures.
    b. has successfully helped people change their personalities, by changing their handwriting.
    c. shows high reliabilities when the content of what is written is neutral, so that the handwriting sample is pure.
    d. should be used by employers who hire people to handle money, because of how well it predicts dishonest behavior.

20. You are writing a review article that evaluates a new personality inventory. Based on a potential problem with all personality tests, you title your paper
    a. "Beware of the Dog."
    b. "Beware the Ides of March."
    c. "Beware of Cheap Imitations."
    d. "Beware the P. T. Barnum Effect."

After completing the test, calculate your percent correct
(/ 20 =   ) x 100 = _____ .

How accurate were your expectations? Does your performance suggest the need for additional study? For the items you missed, go back and identify why the "correct" answer is the best answer.

AFTER YOU READ ... PRACTICE TEST #2

Before beginning this practice test, estimate the percent you expect to get correct.
Anticipated percent correct: _____

1. The idiographic approach to personality examines a person's _____, whereas a nomothetic approach to personality examines a person's _____.
   a. early history; sexual orientation
   b. common aspects; unique aspects
   c. global traits; individualistic traits
   d. idiosyncrasies; degree of being average

2. In terms of identical twins,
   a. a correlation of sharing a given trait that is lower than for fraternal twins indicates the influence of genetics on personality development.
   b. a correlation of sharing a given trait that is higher than for fraternal twins indicates the influence of unshared environmental factors on personality development.
   c. a strong correlation for both twins possessing the same trait, even if they are raised apart, provides evidence for the influence of genetics on personality development.
   d. studies show high correlations for some traits, which points to the importance of shared environmental factors in personality development.

3. Overall, molecular genetic studies find
   a. little consistency between specific genes and personality traits.
   b. great consistency between specific genes and personality traits.
   c. consistent results and so no further studies are currently underway.
   d. little consistency for half of all personality traits, and good consistency for the other half.

4. Your friend, Thasnim, is getting divorced for the third time, just like her mother did. She laughs about inheriting the "divorce gene." You respond by saying,
   a. "Yes, you must be right, especially if your dad and siblings also have high divorce rates."
   b. "No, you only had a 25% chance of inheriting that gene, unless your dad also had many divorces."
   c. "Well, I suppose it's possible for a single gene to control such complex behavior, but it would probably be numbered, and not named."
   d. "There is no such thing as a 'divorce gene,' although you might have inherited other genes that predispose you to make poor decisions in picking partners."

5. Your "id" is talking to you. It is telling you it wants to
   a. apply moral values in satisfying wishes.
   b. pursue pleasure and satisfy biological drives.
   c. satisfy wishes through socially acceptable methods.
   d. push unacceptable biological drives into the unconscious.

6. According to Freud, any serious threat to the ego results in a state of
   a. anxiety.   c. misalignment.
   b. depression.   d. defensiveness.

7. Tanikwa is a 21-year-old who smokes two packs of cigarettes a day. According to psychodynamic approaches to personality, she
   a. has an external locus of control.
   b. may be fixated in the oral stage.
   c. may be sublimating an Electra complex.
   d. is exhibiting signals from her collective unconscious.

8. Perhaps the greatest difference between psychoanalytic and strict behaviorist conceptions of personality is that behaviorists, relative to Freudians, minimize
   a. their views of determinism.
   b. the importance of early childhood experience.
   c. our unconscious awareness underlying our own behaviors.
   d. explanations of behavior as a result of processing certain personality traits.

9. When a parent tells a child, "Do as I say, and not as I do," the parent is ignoring the principles of
   a. unconscious forces.
   b. observational learning.
   c. an external locus of control.
   d. our free will to depart from behavioral contingencies.

10. Behaviorists focus on external contingencies, whereas humanists focus on
    a. ego strength.
    b. trait analysis.
    c. personal growth.
    d. observational learning.

11. The lifelong process of striving to realize one's potential is known as
    a. self-promotion.
    b. self-actualization.
    c. ego enhancement.
    d. psychological narcissism.

12. Three important components of Rogers's humanistic approach to personality development are
    a. id, ego, and superego.
    b. the organism, traits, and collective unconscious.
    c. external contingencies, rewards, and punishments.
    d. genetic makeup, sense of self, and sense of worth.

13. One of the main arguments Walter Mischel levied against trait approaches to personality is that
    a. specific situations appear to be subject to behavioral inconsistencies.
    b. the roots of trait development in early childhood are overemphasized.
    c. the effects of culture are greater than traits could ever be.
    d. unconscious forces affect trait expression in ways that cannot be scientifically determined.

14. Carlos is friendly, sociable, lively, and easy to get along with. Based only on this description, Carlos is probably high on the Big Five traits of
    a. openness and neuroticism.
    b. openness and agreeableness.
    c. agreeableness and extraversion.
    d. extraversion and conscientiousness.

15. After completing the Big Five personality test, which of these people's behavior will be most difficult to predict based on an interaction of culture and test results?
    a. Akina, who lives in a collectivistic culture. Her behavior will be modified by social norms.
    b. Indira, who lives in a collectivistic culture. Her behavior will reflect her personal goals.
    c. Amy, who lives in an individualistic culture. Her behavior will be modified by social norms.
    d. Chantal, who lives in an individualistic culture. Her behavior will reflect her personal goals.

16. Phuong is taking a personality test with good reliability and validity. She must complete nearly 600 true-false items as they best describe her. She is probably taking the
    a. MBTI.
    b. MMPI-2.
    c. Rorschach Test.
    d. Thematic Apperception Test.

17. Projective tests
    a. are favored by trait psychologists because people with certain traits consistently interpret the images in similar ways.
    b. are favored by psychoanalytic psychologists because they assume test-takers project their personalities onto the stimuli.
    c. are favored by humanistic psychologists because the interpretation of ambiguous stimuli allows a clear picture of the "true self" to emerge.
    d. are favored by behaviorists because the images provide a direct stimulus for eliciting a clear response related to environmental contingencies.

18. A critique of the Rorschach shows it
    a. has both high test-retest reliability and interrater reliability
    b. has little relationship between interpretations and actual disorders.
    c. contributes little additional information above and beyond more efficient measures.
    d. can detect faking by respondents, including particular disorders.

19. Juanita went to a fortune-teller at the county fair and was amazed at how accurate the fortune-teller was in describing her personality. It is likely that the fortune-teller's accuracy was due to
    a. ESP.
    b. inside information.
    c. the Barnum principle.
    d. projective techniques.

20. A tragic event in Sharon's life was the murder of her uncle. Because the police were making little progress in their investigation, Sharon's family wanted to hire a high-priced criminal profiler. You advise Sharon to
    a. save her money and watch all three *CSI* shows on TV—they use all of the same principles.
    b. go ahead with the plan; research evidence reliably confirms the success of trained profilers.
    c. save her money and call in the FBI. Their track record of solving crimes using profiles is excellent.
    d. save her family's money! Even chemistry majors with no training in criminology have been shown to provide more accurate profiles than professional profilers.

After completing the test, calculate your percent correct
(/ 20 =) x 100 = _____.

How accurate were your expectations? Does your performance suggest the need for additional study? For the items you missed, go back and identify why the "correct" answer is the best answer.

AFTER YOU READ ... PRACTICE TEST ANSWER KEYS

Practice Test 1.

1. c (p. 578)
2. d (pp. 579–580)
3. c (p. 582)
4. d (pp. 585–586)
5. a (pp. 585–586)
6. b (p. 586)
7. c (p. 590)
8. c (p. 594)
9. b (p. 597)
10. b (p. 598)
11. d (p. 600)
12. d (p. 604)
13. b (p. 605)
14. b (p. 608)
15. c (pp. 609, 612)
16. d (p. 611)
17. b (pp. 612–613)
18. d (p. 613)
19. a (p. 614)
20. d (p. 615)

Practice Test 2.

1. d (p. 579)
2. c (pp. 580–581)
3. a (p. 582–583)
4. d (p. 583)
5. b (p. 587)
6. a (p. 588)
7. b (p. 590)
8. b (pp. 594, 597)
9. b (p. 598)
10. c (p. 600)
11. b (p. 600)
12. d (p. 601)
13. a (pp. 603–604)
14. c (p. 604)
15. a (pp. 605–606)
16. b (p. 609)
17. b (p. 612)
18. b (p. 613)
19. c (p. 615)
20. d (p. 616)

AFTER YOU READ ... CONCEPT MAPPING ACTIVITY ANSWERS

ACTIVITY 1:
Of the four approaches to personality, the psychoanalytic is the most complicated. Complete this concept map to simplify this approach.

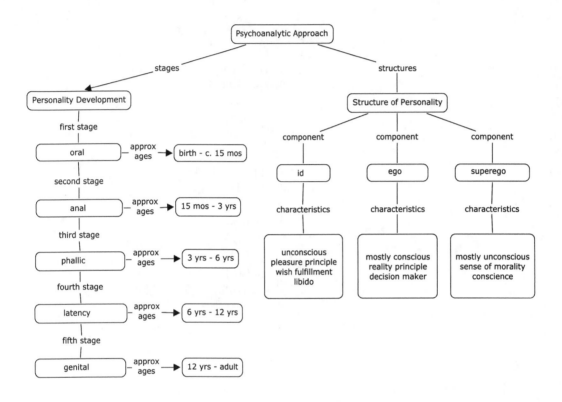

ACTIVITY 2:
Complete this concept map for personality assessment:

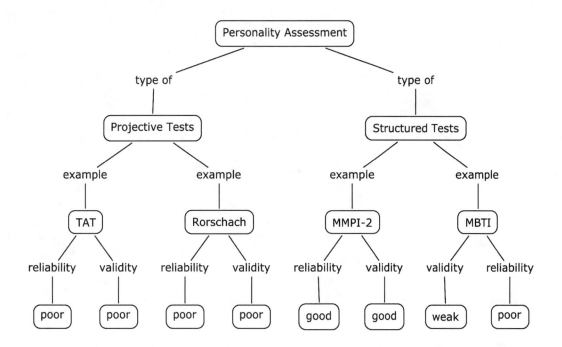

CHAPTER 15
PSYCHOLOGICAL DISORDERS
WHEN ADAPTATION BREAKS DOWN

BEFORE YOU READ ... CHAPTER PREVIEW

The most important issue in examining mental disorders is determining what distinguishes abnormality from normality. Psychopathology, or mental illness, covers a broad range of disorders. Five criteria are used to define a mental disorder, including statistical rarity, subjective distress, impairment, societal disapproval, and biological dysfunction. Mental disorders don't all have one thing in common but rather share a cluster of features. Throughout history people have suffered with "demons," and the earliest models were based on demonic possession. After the Middle Ages, a medical model dominated in which the mentally ill were seen as in need of medical treatment. At that time the treatments included placement in asylums, bloodletting, or being tossed into a snake pit. In the 1800s, an approach called moral treatment led to improved care of the mentally ill. In the modern era of psychiatric treatment one focus has been on treatment with drugs. With the rise in medication-based treatment, many mentally ill patients are doing better and have been deinstitutionalized. This has been a double-edged sword; although patients are allowed to lead normal lives, many are unable to sustain a truly normal life because of their illness. In addition to changes in treatment over time, diagnostic criteria have also changed. Conditions that were present in the 1800s are no longer present and new ones have taken their place, some of which are controversial. It is becoming more important to be certain that people are given diagnoses and not just labels. An additional complication is that some diagnoses are culture-bound, appearing in some cultures and not in others, whereas most diagnoses are made worldwide, including schizophrenia, alcoholism, and psychopathic personality disorder. The general public operates under many misconceptions about psychiatric diagnosis, including that it just sorts people into categories, is unreliable, is invalid, and stigmatizes people. In reality, it helps pinpoint problems and makes it easier for professionals to communicate with one another. Diagnoses follow an official system based on the *Diagnostic and Statistical Manual of Mental Disorders*, in which the number of symptoms, their frequency, and duration are all considered. Other misconceptions affect the relationships between mental illness and the law. For example, it is not true that the mentally ill are more violent; many people don't understand that "insanity" is a legal definition and not a psychiatric definition that the use of the insanity defense is rare across all legal cases, and even when used, is rarely successful. Nevertheless, some people do need to be committed against their will, a controversial practice.

Many categories of disorders need to be considered. The most commonly occurring disorders include the anxiety-based disorders. Some of these manifest themselves physically and others are clearly mental disorders. Generalized anxiety disorders are characterized by an almost constant sense of worry, in contrast to panic disorders, where extreme anxiety comes on suddenly and for no apparent reason. Many different types of phobias, including agoraphobia, specific phobias, and social phobia, are experienced by many people. In posttraumatic stress disorders, some precipitating event results in persistent anxiety. In obsessive-compulsive disorder, a person has repetitive thoughts (obsessions) that result in repetitive and unnecessary behaviors (compulsions). The explanations for anxiety disorders vary, including classical and operant conditioning models, individual differences in anxiety sensitivity, and genetic and biological influences.

The second most common category of disorders consists of the mood disorders, which more than 20% of Americans experience across their lifetime. Mood disorders affect twice as many women, although some cultures show no gender difference. Explanations for depression are complicated by combined biological, psychological, and social factors. Stressful life events can bring on depression. According to Beck's cognitive model of depression, negative beliefs and expectations are responsible for bringing on and maintaining a depressed state. Seligman proposed that a prior inability to control events in one's life leads to a subsequent learned helplessness, accompanied by depressive symptoms. Studies of twins provide evidence for a genetic component, and other evidence points to problems with various neurotransmitters. Sometimes periods of depression alternate with periods of extreme elation and mania, in which case a diagnosis of bipolar disorder is appropriate. Of all the mental disorders the evidence for the heritability of bipolar disorder is the strongest. One of the most serious consequences of depression is suicide. Although 30,000 people commit suicide annually in the United States, it is estimated that for each completed suicide, approximately 8–25 attempts are made. Known risk factors for suicide can be used to intervene and prevent suicide with some individuals.

Another category of mental disorders includes the dissociative disorders, which are controversial. In depersonalization disorder, a person feels detached from the self. Dissociative amnesia, in which a person forgets important autobiographical details, is more severe, but not as severe as dissociative fugue in which a person not only forgets important details of his or her life, but often ends up lost in a strange city or country. Finally, the most controversial disorder is dissociative identity disorder (DID), characterized by the presence of two or more distinct identities within a single person. Some people attribute this compartmentalization of different personalities to severe early trauma, but other evidence fails to support this explanation. Many cases of DID may be incorrectly diagnosed cases of other disorders, and some evidence suggests that poor psychotherapy techniques might induce a belief in alternate personalities. The number of documented cases of DID has grown since a much publicized case in the 1970s, which might have been a misdiagnosed case of schizophrenia. Thus alters may be created by therapists, rather than discovered.

The most serious disorder of all is schizophrenia, which is often confused with DID. The term literally means "split mind" and many people confuse it with having multiple personalities within a single person. More accurately it refers to a disordered single personality. Most schizophrenics cannot function on their own without both social support and medication. However, many of them can become functional with such support. Schizophrenia is characterized by delusions, which are strongly held beliefs that have no basis in reality. Auditory hallucinations are common, and speech can become highly disorganized with thoughts rapidly jumping in the person's mind so that others just hear a jumbled word salad. In more severe cases people might become catatonic, alternating between extreme bodily rigidity to constant, aimless movement. Researchers have examined the causes of schizophrenia and rejected parents and family members as "causing" this disorder. Instead, researchers have found that the brains of schizophrenics show distinct differences, including a disorder of the function of the neurotransmitter dopamine. Finally, a strong heritability factor is also evidenced by research. Currently, the dominant model is the diathesis-stress model, which focuses on the interaction between a genetic predisposition that is triggered by environmental factors. Only a fraction of the people with the genetic predisposition develop the disorder, although some develop a schizotypal personality disorder, in which symptoms are much reduced and everyday functioning is intact.

Personality disorders often appear as a "quirk" in personality. DSM-IV groups these disorders into clusters of eccentric, dramatic, and anxious. A dramatic personality disorder is borderline personality disorder, which is marked by unstable mood, identity, and impulse control. In psychopathic personality disorder (antisocial personality disorder), a person lacks a sense of guilt or remorse and shows a strong sense of self-interest. Explanations for psychopathic personality disorder show an inability to develop classical conditioning to painful stimuli and a general underarousal of the nervous system. Substance abuse disorders are characterized by abuse and dependence on drugs, with signs of tolerance and withdrawal. Substance abuse often begins when drugs become available, and the consequences for using them don't seem serious. Cultural differences in rates of alcoholism are based on acceptance of drinking in various cultures, but this finding might also be confounded with genetic predispositions.

BEFORE YOU READ ... LEARNING OBJECTIVES

After reading Chapter 15 you should be able to:

15.1   Identify criteria for defining mental disorders
15.2   Describe conceptions of diagnoses across history and cultures
15.3   Identify common misconceptions about psychiatric diagnoses, and the strengths and limitations of the current diagnostic system
15.4   Identify popular misconceptions about the law and mental illness
15.5. Describe the many ways people experience anxiety
15.6   Identify explanations of anxiety disorders that center on the environment, catastrophic thinking, and biological causes
15.7   Identify the characteristics of different mood disorders
15.8   Identify risk factors for suicide
15.9   Describe the interplay of personal, genetic, and interpersonal factors in producing the symptoms of depression
15.10 Describe depersonalization, dissociative amnesia, and fugue
15.11 Explain the controversies that surround dissociative disorders, especially dissociative identity disorder
15.12 Recognize the characteristic symptoms of schizophrenia
15.13 Explain how psychosocial, brain, biochemical, and genetic determinants can create the vulnerability to schizophrenia
15.14 Identify differences between normal variations in personality and personality disorders
15.15 Identify the characteristics of borderline and psychopathic personality disorders
15.16 Identify differences between substance abuse and dependence
15.17 Identify sociocultural, learning, and genetic explanations for drug abuse

Before You Read ... Term Identification

agoraphobia (p. 640)

anorexia nervosa (p. 630)

antisocial personality disorder (p. 662)

anxiety sensitivity (p. 643)

asylums (p. 626)

axes (p. 635)

bipolar disorder (p. 649)

borderline personality disorder (p. 661)

bulimia nervosa (p. 629)

catatonic symptoms (p. 657)

categorical model (p. 635)

cognitive model of depression (p. 647)

comorbidity (p. 635)

compulsions (p. 642)

deinstitutionalization (p. 627)

delusions (p. 655)

demonic model (p. 626)

depersonalization disorder (p. 652)

Diagnostic and Statistical Manual of Mental Disorders (p. 632)

diathesis-stress models (p. 659)

dimensional model (p. 635)

dissociative amnesia (p. 652)

dissociative disorders (p. 652)

dissociative fugue (p. 652)

dissociative identity disorder (DID) (p. 653)

generalized anxiety disorder (p. 640)

hallucinations (p. 656)

hypocondriasis (p. 639)

incompetence to stand trial (p. 638)

insanity defense (p. 636)

involuntary commitment (p. 638)

labeling theorists (p. 633)

major depressive episode (p. 644)

manic episode (p. 649)

medical model (p. 626)

moral treatment (p. 627)

obsessions (p. 642)

obsessive-compulsive disorder (OCD) (p. 642)

panic attacks (p. 639)

panic disorder (p. 640)

personality disorder (p. 660)

phobia (p. 640)

posttraumatic stress disorder (PTSD) (p. 641)

prevalence (p. 634)

psychopathic personality (p. 662)

psychotic symptoms (p. 655)

schizophrenia (p. 654)

social phobia (p. 641)

somatoform disorders (p. 639)

specific phobias (p. 641)

AS YOU READ ... PRACTICE ACTIVITIES

CONCEPTIONS OF MENTAL ILLNESS: YESTERDAY AND TODAY

1. Your text provides five guidelines for determining whether a behavior should be considered to be "abnormal." Briefly describe each of the five guidelines here, in your own words. Which one do you think is the most important? Why? (LO 15.1)

2. Consider a disorder such as anorexia, with which most people are at least somewhat familiar. Which of the five criteria for a mental disorder best describes anorexia? Do you believe that more than one criterion should be used? Which ones should be used? (LO 15.1)

3. Deinstitutionalization has led to both positive and negative effects. Outline several of each of the positive and negative effects. (LO 15.2)

4. **T or F:** Psychiatric diagnoses can truly be culture-bound. Explain your answer and provide examples as appropriate. (LO 15.2)

5. Psychiatric diagnosis is frequently made by assessing symptoms as well as their frequency and duration. How might this approach lead to the creation of diagnostic labels for behaviors that together describe problem behaviors? Be sure to consider how "labels" differ from "diagnoses." (LO 15.2)

6. Write out the four misconceptions about psychiatric diagnosis, leaving some space between them. Next, in the space you left, go back and briefly state the correct information about each misconception. (LO 15.2)

7. How might confirmation bias lead a person to not only believe that vaccinations "cause" autism, but to actually strengthen that belief over time? (LO 15.3)

ANXIETY DISORDERS: THE MANY FACES OF WORRY AND FEAR

1. Match the symptom complex to the diagnosis for that disorder. (LO 15.5–LO 15.15)

a. Agoraphobia

b. Attention deficit hyperactivity disorder

c. Bipolar disorder

d. Generalized anxiety disorder

e. Hypochondriasis

f. Major depression

g. Obsessive-compulsive disorder

h. Panic disorder

i. Posttraumatic stress disorder

j. Psychopathic personality disorder

k. Schizophrenia

1. Constant, underlying, worry and anxiety

2. Inattention, impulsivity, and overactivity

3. Fear of being in open places and spaces

4. Increased sensitivity to anxiety-provoking symptoms following a severe trauma

5. Unpredictable, sudden terror with racing heart rate and light-headedness

6. Repeated thoughts to perform unnecessary actions on a repetitive basis

7. A longtime lingering depressed mood that prevents normal everyday functioning

8. Having periods of deep depression followed by periods of manic hyperactivity

9. Having disordered thought patterns, hallucinations, and delusions

10. Continuous preoccupation of suffering from a physical disorder

11. Showing no sense of remorse or guilt for harmful behaviors

2. Have you ever experienced an "earworm"? If you have, then you must certainly remember what it was. What was it? Were there particular times you seemed to experience it? Can you remember what you had to do to get it out of your mind? (LO 15.5)

3. Learning models of anxiety and explanations based on genetic and biological influences suggest an interplay between nature and nurture in anxiety. Based on the readings in the chapter, discuss how these two influences (learning and genetics) might interact to produce an anxiety disorder in an individual. (LO 15.6)

4. People who have been in therapy for anxiety and have seen a successful decrease in their symptoms often see them recur. How might anxiety sensitivity act to increase this vulnerability to relapse? (LO 15.6)

5. As you consider all of the major anxiety disorders, how could you tell whether a new college roommate might suffer from a specific anxiety disorder? (LO 15.4–15.6)

MOOD DISORDERS AND SUICIDE

1. Depression appears to beget depression: Most people do not really like to interact with depressed individuals. How might this lead to a vicious cycle that maintains depression? (LO 15.7)

2. A frequent analogy is made between depression as the mental health equivalent of the common cold. The authors of your text, however, argue that this analogy is not a particularly good one. Compare the two conditions: depression and the common cold. In the end, do you agree or disagree with your text's authors? Why? (LO 15.7)

3. If the interplay between nature and nurture is complicated for the anxiety disorders, it seems even more so for the mood disorders. Describe some of the complicated interactions of the contributions of nature and nurture to depression. (15.9)

4. Describe Seligman's (1975) study of leaned helplessness. (LO 15.9)

    Design:

    Results:

    Lesson learned:

5. How does bipolar disorder differ from major depression? What are some of the objective biological findings that discriminate between these two disorders? (LO 15.7)

6. Your new roommate seems sad, isn't eating, and cries much of the time. Describe specific behaviors and risk factors that would lead you to believe that she might consider attempting suicide, and might need intervention. You can see more risk factors for younger adults at http://www.yellowribbon.org/WarningSigns.html. (LO 15.8)

DISSOCIATIVE DISORDERS: THE DIVIDED SELF

1. If extraordinary claims require extraordinary evidence, just what would it take to convince you that a person has more than 100 distinct personalities? Would you need to meet each one on a one-to-one basis and at which point would you be convinced that each one is truly unique and distinct? (LO 15.10)

2. Because many people have experienced either derealization or depersonalization, it shouldn't be too hard for you to find someone among your friends who has. Describe one of their experiences and why you think it would fit the definition of either experience, based on your text's description. (LO 15.10)

3. Differentiate between a dissociative fugue and dissociative amnesia. (LO 15.10)

4. Compare the posttraumatic model to the sociocognitive model for explaining DID. (LO 15.11)

5. A quick web search shows that comedienne Roseanne Barr claims to have been diagnosed with DID, bipolar disorder, and obsessive-compulsive disorder. Some people are truly in distress but cannot settle on, or "fit" a particular disorder or diagnosis. Why might it not be surprising that such a person is eventually diagnosed with DID?

THE ENIGMA OF SCHIZOPHRENIA

1. Although schizophrenia is the least diagnosed mental disorder, with less than 1% of the population suffering from schizophrenia, people with this diagnosis account for the largest percentage of patients hospitalized with any mental disorder. Why might this be? (LO 15.12)

2. Rather than think of schizophrenia as a single disorder, it might be better to think of it as a family or range of disorders. Which aspects of this disorder, as described in your text, would lead to this conclusion? (LO 15.12)

3. Your text describes schizophrenics as having a "flat affect." What does this mean? You may have to go to the web to find a satisfactory definition. (LO 15.12)

4. Differentiate between the various subtypes of schizophrenia. (LO 15.12)

5. Show how the diathesis-stress model of vulnerability to schizophrenia is a good example of the interaction of nature and nurture. (LO 15.13)

PERSONALITY DISORDERS AND SUBSTANCE ABUSE

1. In everyday life we talk about people with a "bad" personality. Compare this everyday way of talking about personality to the way that psychologists talk about personality disorders. (LO 15.15)

2. **T or F**: Personality disorders are every bit as debilitating as schizophrenia or major depressive disorders. Provide evidence to support your answer. (LO 15.15)

3. A person is arrested for theft. He says he is sorry and will never steal again. How can you tell whether he is sincere or has a sociopathic personality disorder? (LO 15.15)

4. Your sister tells you that she thinks her best friend has an antisocial personality disorder because her friend is very shy. Explain to your sister why she is wrong. Discuss the true characteristics of someone with antisocial personality disorder. (LO 15.15)

5. Go back to Chapter 5 on Consciousness and review the critical terms related to substance abuse, including *tolerance*, *withdrawal*, and *addiction*. Do you believe that people can "use," without "abusing" drugs? Explain your answer. (LO 15.16)

AS YOU READ ... CONCEPT MAP ACTIVITIES

ACTIVITY 1: Complete this concept map for personality disorders, then read the assignment for Activity 2 and follow this model.

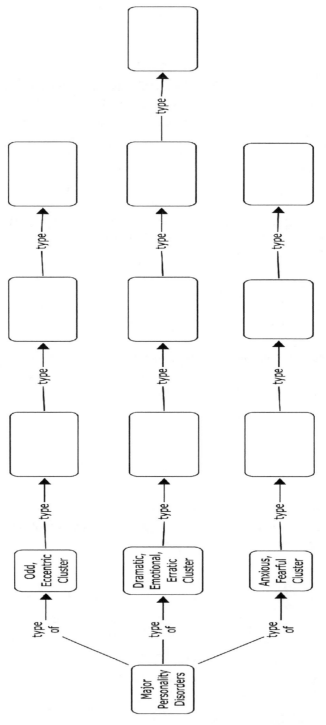

ACTIVITY 2: Make your own concept map for disorders. Be sure to include the major categories of disorders, such as anxiety disorders, mood disorders, substance abuse disorders, and schizophrenia and dissociative identity disorder. Then include subtypes of each. You could connect these to nodes containing symptoms that distinguish each disorder. You can also connect them to related explanations via connections from multiple disorders to particular explanations, such as shared genetic components.

AS YOU READ ... MYTH OR REALITY?

Myth: Homeless people are too lazy to get a job.

Reality: Many homeless people are not able to maintain an independent lifestyle. In the past they might have been institutionalized, but following deinstitutionalization, many of these people who are unable to take care of themselves find themselves homeless.

1. Read about deinstitutionalization and its effects on increasing the population of homeless people at: http://www.pbs.org/wgbh/pages/frontline/shows/asylums/special/excerpt.html http://www.psychservices.psychiatryonline.org/cgi/content/full/55/10/1112

2. Has this information changed your perception of homeless people? How could you tell whether someone is "lazy" or is truly unable to maintain an independent lifestyle? Make a list of all the tasks it would take to live independently. Do you take for granted your ability to do these things on a daily basis?

3. What can you, as an individual in society, do to help the homelessness problem?

Myth: Many people define schizophrenia as a split personality.

Reality: Schizophrenia is really the fracturing of a single personality. The more commonly accepted terminology of a "split personality" refers to the type of multiple personality disorder seen in dissociative identity disorder (DID).

1. You should be clear about the distinction between schizophrenia and DID. They are distinct disorders, one of which has been around perhaps as long as recorded history, and the other a newcomer to mental disorder diagnoses.

2. Review the two disorders and map out the differences between them, making note of the more prominent and less prominent symptoms that would lead to a diagnosis.

Myth: Most suicides are committed by 15- to 24-year-olds.

Reality: Most suicides are committed by males over the age of 65.

1. You can download all of the suicide facts for the most recent year for which they are available at the following website: http://www.suicidology.org/associations/1045/files/2004datapgv1.pdf

2. Examine Table 15.10 in your text, which lists major suicide risk factors. Additional risk factors are available at http://www.cdc.gov/ncipc/dvp/Suicide/Suicide-risk-p-factors.htm. Evaluate how each of these might differentially impact the 15- to 24-year-old age group and the over-65 age group. In addition, it is the case that older white males in particular are more vulnerable to suicide. Why do you think this might be?

AS YOU READ… PUT YOUR CRITICAL THINKING SKILLS TO THE TEST

---

1. One of the biggest critics of the entire concept of mental disorders is Thomas Szasz. To quote Szasz from his book, *The Second Sin* (1973): "If you talk to God, you are praying; if God talks to you, you have schizophrenia. While people behave and think in ways that are very disturbing, this does not mean they have a disease." To Szasz, mental illness is simply another way of talking about behaviors we do not approve of, such as talking to one's self, going on spending binges, or taking another person's life.

   a. Consider the implications of this idea, that psychopathology is a myth, an epiphenomenon—a consequence of some other event, but not a real part of that event. Do you agree or disagree? Why?

2. Some people consider schizophrenia to be the ultimate attention deficit disorder. At times people with schizophrenia cannot focus on any one relevant stimulus, at other times they cannot disengage their attention from an irrelevant stimulus.

   a. For example, you can read abstracts of some of the work by Michael Posner and his collaborators at http://stinet.dtic.mil/oai/oai?verb=getRecord&metadataPrefix=html&identifier=ADA184483 http://www.blackwell-synergy.com/doi/abs/10.1046/j.1440-1819.2003.01150.x?journalCode=pcn

   b. In reading through your text, find examples of typical indicators or symptoms of schizophrenia that fit this idea of a disorder of the attentional system.

AS YOU READ... MYPSYCHLAB CONNECTION

Conceptions of Mental Illness: Yesterday and Today

For more on mental illness, complete the **simulations** *Psychological Disorders*, *Overview of Clinical Assessment Methods,* and *Overview of Clinical Assessment Tools.* When reviewing the DSM-IV, **explore** *The Axes of the DSM.*

Anxiety Disorders: The Many Faces of Worry

When reviewing anxiety disorders use **simulate** *Obsessive Compulsive Test* and **watch** *Anxiety Disorders* and *When Does a Fear Become a Phobia: Sue Mineka.*

Mood Disorders and Suicide

Explore *Bipolar Disorder* for information on the seriousness of this disorder with regards to suicidal ideation. **Watch** *Nathan: Bipolar Disorder* and *Helen: Major Depression* to learn more about mood disorders and how it affects patients. For more on emotion and cognition **watch** *Interaction of Cognition and Emotion: Jutta Joormann.*

Dissociative Disorders: The Divided Self

Explore *Dissociative Identity Disorder* to learn more about the clinical presentation of an individual with DID.

The Enigma of Schizophrenia

To review the different subtypes of Schizophrenia use the **simulation** *Schizophrenia.* **Watch** *Rodney: Schizophrenia* and *Genetic Schizophrenia* to learn more about the etiology, symptoms, and clinical presentation of the disorder.

Personality Disorders and Substance Use

Watch *Janna: Borderline Personality Disorder* to view a real case study of an individual with this disorder.

AFTER YOU READ ... PRACTICE TEST #1

Before beginning this practice test, estimate the percent you expect to get correct.
Anticipated percent correct: _____

1. Lorena likes to put Tabasco sauce on her ice cream. Her favorite dessert is vanilla ice cream with strawberries, smothered in hot sauce. Most people might consider Lorena's taste in desserts "abnormal" based on which criterion of abnormality?
   a. Impairment
   b. Statistical rarity
   c. Subjective distress
   d. Biological dysfunction

2. Which of the following was NOT an early medical treatment for mental illness?
   a. Blood-letting
   b. Use of chlorpromazine
   c. Use of the tranquilizing chair
   d. Placement in a pit with snakes

3. In the 1800s, slaves in the United States who repeatedly tried to escape their master were considered to be
   a. lazy.
   b. homeless.
   c. mentally ill.
   d. codependent.

4. In the United States, one is more likely to experience _____, whereas in Japan one would be more likely to experience _____.
   a. bulimia; koro
   b. koro; anorexia
   c. amok; windigo
   d. anorexia; amok

5. The criteria for validity of psychiatric diagnoses suggest that the diagnosis
   a. is more descriptive than predictive.
   b. can fully explain the person's behavior.
   c. provides the proper label for the individual.
   d. predicts a person's performance on various assessments.

6. DSM-IV
   a. refers to a book that lists the drugs that are used in psychiatry and their side effects.
   b. is a system of classifying psychological disorders.
   c. specifies ethical standards for the treatment of patients with psychological disorders.
   d. lists the diagnostic schizophrenic methods.

7. Comorbidity means that
   a. obese people tend to have more problems than thin ones.
   b. some problems are more life-threatening than are others.
   c. individuals with one diagnosis often shows signs of another, as well.
   d. some disorders fit better along a continuum, rather than being considered all-or-none.

8. Insanity
   a. can easily be faked.
   b. is a legal definition of responsibility for a crime.
   c. refers to a severe psychopathology, such as schizophrenia.
   d. is a good defense in criminal trials, as seen in the cases of Andrea Yates and Jeffry Dahmer.

9. _____ disorders are more prevalent than _____ disorders, which are more prevalent than _____ disorders.
   a. Phobia; mood; alcoholism
   b. Substance abuse; anxiety; mood
   c. Mood; anxiety; substance abuse
   d. Anxiety; mood; substance abuse

10. Abdallah will often be sitting in class, when suddenly he starts to sweat, his heart races, he feels he is going to pass out and has to get out of the room, but he cannot move. Abdallah is showing the symptoms of
    a. panic disorder.
    b. a manic episode.
    c. schizophrenia.
    d. social phobia.

11. Studies of biological influences on anxiety show that people with obsessive-compulsive disorder seem to have a particular problem with the neurotransmitter
    a. serotonin.
    b. dopamine.
    c. adrenaline.
    d. acetylcholine.

12. Approximately _____ % of people are likely to develop a mood disorder in their lifetime.
    a. 20
    b. 40
    c. 60
    d. 80

13. Jamal is depressed. To make it worse, he has isolated himself from his friends because he doesn't find any rewards in interacting with them. This isolation actually prolongs his depression. Jamal's situation illustrates the _____ model of depression.
    a. cognitive
    b. biological
    c. behavioral
    d. interpersonal

14. According to learned helplessness as described by Seligman, after several uncontrollable events in their life, people
    a. expend excessive effort to control their lives, resulting in exhaustion.
    b. attribute negative events to external factors and positive events to internal factors.
    c. just stop trying to effect changes and later fail to change controllable circumstances for the better.
    d. spend more time trying to escape from all circumstances in their lives, even the ones they can control.

15. Sophie has fluctuated between episodes of feeling sad and depressed, and at other times feeling energized and as if she can do anything. Sophie probably suffers from
    a. histrionic personality disorder .
    b. bipolar disorder.
    c. major depression.
    d. dysthymia.

16. Pam has been severely depressed for several weeks, to the point of not getting out of bed for several days at a time. With psychotherapy and medications her depression is lifting. This could be a warning sign that
    a. her risk of suicide is actually rising.
    b. she is leaving a prolonged period of susceptibility to suicide.
    c. you should avoid talking to her about suicide because it will reverse her progress.
    d. she might relapse as she considers the time she wasted by being depressed, creating a vicious cycle.

17. As long as Ernie lines his underwear with aluminum foil so that "rays" cannot penetrate to his skin, he is able to function fairly normally on a day-to-day basis. He does, however, need to wear long sleeves and pants and keep everything lined. His fear of "rays" reflects a
    a. shadow.
    b. delusion.
    c. diathesis.
    d. hallucination.

18. Lottie has completely stopped bathing or taking care of herself. She was diagnosed with schizophrenia after a prolonged period of immobility. Although her doctor could freely move her limbs, she could not respond to his commands to move her limbs by herself. Lottie probably has the _____ type of schizophrenia.
    a. residual
    b. catatonic
    c. disorganized
    d. undifferentiated

19. In the movie *Girl, Interrupted*, the main character's behaviors showed an instability in mood, impulsivity, sexual promiscuity, and difficulty in controlling her emotions. She was (probably correctly) diagnosed with _____ personality disorder.
    a. avoidant
    b. borderline
    c. schizotypal
    d. psychopathic

20. Jadzia tells you that her life is difficult because she is constantly tempted by food, alcohol, and gambling. She tells you she has an addictive personality. You tell her that
    a. she is probably correct, and ample evidence indicates the existence of such a personality trait.
    b. she is probably correct, but new-age therapy can best help her with her addictive personality disorder.
    c. she is incorrect; research shows that she most likely has traits of agreeableness and sociability that promote her behavior.
    d. she is incorrect; the research evidence for the existence of a specific addictive personality just cannot be demonstrated.

After completing the test, calculate your percent correct
(/ 20 =   ) x 100 = _____.

How accurate were your expectations? Does your performance suggest the need for additional study? For the items you missed, go back and identify why the "correct" answer is the best answer.

AFTER YOU READ ... PRACTICE TEST #2

Before beginning this practice test, estimate the percent you expect to get correct.
Anticipated percent correct: _____

1. The oldest notions about mental illness reflected a belief that people
   a. had a physical disorder.
   b. were possessed by the devil.
   c. could best be cured with blood-letting.
   d. could best be cured with placebo drugs.

2. Chlorpromazine was developed to particularly treat
   a. bedlam.
   b. bulimia.
   c. drapetomania.
   d. schizophrenia.

3. People who suffer from bulimia show a pattern of behavior that consists of
   a. intensive sadness followed by a period of uncontrollable behavior.
   b. eating too much (binging) and then vomiting the food back up (purging).
   c. a panicky belief that their sexual organs (testes in men, breasts in women) are shriveling up.
   d. excessive weight loss due to not eating because the person has a false belief of being overweight.

4. Evidence for the reliability of psychiatric disorders comes from
   a. studies that show that they are valid.
   b. high agreement between different diagnosticians.
   c. different expert witnesses coming to different conclusions.
   d. predictions of how well people with a particular diagnosis respond to treatment.

5. The number of children diagnosed with autism is on the rise, which can most likely be attributed to
   a. the increase in the number of children getting vaccinated.
   b. the increase in the number of vaccinations each child is required to get.
   c. looser diagnostic criteria, so more children meet the minimum definition.
   d. the increased use of thimerosol as a preservative in children's vaccinations.

6. DSM-IV
   a. lists more than 350 classes of disorders.
   b. provides labels everyone can easily understand.
   c. helps therapists diagnose their clients' disorders.
   d. includes diagnostic criteria for medically related problems, such as hypothyroidism.

7. Calvin has always been happy and healthy. Recently, while reading the chapter on psychopathology for his psychology class he started to notice how often his heart races for no reason, and then he started feeling light-headed and broke out into a sweat. Most likely Calvin is now suffering from
   a. medical students' syndrome.
   b. generalized anxiety disorder.
   c. anxious personality disorder.
   d. panic attack syndrome.

8. Across your lifetime you have an almost _____% chance of developing a mental disorder.
   a. 25
   b. 50
   c. 75
   d. 90

9. Natsumi is afraid to leave her home. She worries she will do something embarrassing and shame herself and her family. She is completing her college degree online, calls Safeway for home delivery of groceries to her home, and buys everything else at Costco.com. Natsumi has all the symptoms of
   a. PTSD.
   b. agoraphobia.
   c. claustrophobia.
   d. social inhibition.

10. Howie is concerned about catching an illness. He avoids touching things in public and doesn't allow other people to shake his hand or hug him in greeting. Howie probably suffers from
    a. bipolar disorder.
    b. hypochondriasis.
    c. histrionic personality disorder.
    d. obsessive-compulsive disorder.

11. Studies of gender show that in terms of mood disorders
    a. no differences are evident between men and women.
    b. generally more men than women develop mood disorders.
    c. generally more women than men develop mood disorders.
    d. across cultures sometimes many more men and sometimes many more women are affected.

12. In which of these ways is depression MOST like the common cold?
    a. Both tend to occur more often in women.
    b. Major depression, like a cold, produces severe impairment.
    c. The symptoms can develop gradually over days and weeks.
    d. People will typically experience several episodes over their lifetimes.

13. Jasmine is depressed, and her conversations with friends often revolve around her sad feelings. Pretty soon Jasmine's friends start to avoid her because their conversations are draining for them. Jasmine's situation illustrates the _____ model of depression.
    a. cognitive
    b. biological
    c. behavioral
    d. interpersonal

14. According to Beck's cognitive model,
    a. depressed individuals have negative schemas and cognitive distortions.
    b. genetic factors dominate all other factors that might contribute to depression.
    c. early life events set the stage for later responses to stressful situations with depression.
    d. a low rate of response-contingent positive reinforcement is instrumental in the development of depression.

15. The mental disorder with the highest rate of heritability is
    a. bipolar disorder.
    b. major depression.
    c. panic attack syndrome.
    d. obsessive-compulsive disorder.

16. Hilda remembers going to summer camp when she was 10 years old. She remembers the beach, camp fires, and hikes, but she cannot remember any of the children or leaders. It is likely that
    a. she is repressing a traumatic experience from camp.
    b. a good hypnotherapist can help Hilda recover her memories of the other people.
    c. this is a perfectly normal example of forgetting something she hasn't thought about in a while.
    d. she has a dissociative identity disorder, and only one of her alters remembers the other people.

17. As a child Yumi's parents sent her for figure skating lessons. She is 18 now and never really developed into a very good skater. Yumi believes that she is the Olympic gold medalist, Kristi Yamaguchi, who is hiding from people who would steal her gold medals. She spends all her time at the skating rink and does not work or go to school. She just skates around the rink telling everyone she is Kristi Yamaguchi. Yumi probably suffers from
    a. a temporary manic episode associated with bipolar disorder.
    b. a delusion associated with schizophrenia.
    c. a narcissistic personality disorder.
    d. a histrionic personality disorder.

18. Which of the following is NOT a brain abnormality found among schizophrenia patients?
    a. The sulci are larger, resulting in less brain tissue in surrounding areas.
    b. The ventricles are enlarged, resulting in shrinkage of other brain areas.
    c. The frontal lobes are less active, possibly resulting in reduced ability to concentrate.
    d. The corpus callosum is smaller, resulting in slower transmission across hemispheres.

19. Studies of identical twins raised apart show
    a. a strong genetic component to schizophrenia.
    b. no evidence for a genetic component to schizophrenia.
    c. that the environment plays a role only if a history of schizophrenia is present in the adoptive family.
    d. a powerful effect of the environment, especially mothers, on the development of schizophrenia.

20. Sam tells you that although he uses drugs recreationally, he is not abusing them. You tell him that
    a. his pattern of having problems, such as missing school at least 2 or 3 days per month and being fired from his job, suggests that he is having a problem with abuse.
    b. even though he seems to be drinking more and more each week, and is now occasionally using other street drugs as well, he is probably just young and going through a phase.
    c. he is probably right because his problems are also found among people who don't use drugs.
    d. he should be careful because he probably has an addictive personality.

After completing the test, calculate your percent correct
(/ 20 =   ) x 100 = _____.

How accurate were your expectations? Does your performance suggest the need for additional study? For the items you missed, go back and identify why the "correct" answer is the best answer.

AFTER YOU READ ... PRACTICE TEST ANSWER KEYS

Practice Test 1.

1. b (p. 625)
2. b (p. 626)
3. c (p. 627)
4. a (pp. 628–629)
5. d (p. 631)
6. b (p. 634)
7. c (p. 635)
8. b (p. 636)
9. d (p. 639)
10. a (p. 640)
11. a (p. 643)
12. a (p. 644)
13. c (p. 646)
14. c (p. 648)
15. b (p. 649)
16. a (p. 650)
17. b (p. 655)
18. b (p. 657)
19. b (p. 661)
20. d (pp. 664–665)

Practice Test 2.

1. b (p. 626)
2. d (p. 627)
3. b (p. 629)
4. b (pp. 630–631)
5. c (pp. 632–633)
6. c (p. 634)
7. a (p. 636)
8. b (p. 639)
9. b (p. 640)
10. d (p. 642)
11. c (p. 644)
12. d (p. 645)
13. d (p. 646)
14. a (p. 647)
15. a (p. 649)
16. c (p. 652)
17. b (p. 655)
18. d (p. 658)
19. a (p. 659)
20. a (p. 664)

AFTER YOU READ ... CONCEPT MAPPING ACTIVITY ANSWERS

ACTIVITY 1: Complete this concept map for personality disorders, then read the assignment for Activity 2 and follow this model:

Alphabetically, the answers you should have properly placed in the diagram are:

Odd, eccentric: paranoid personality disorder, schizotypal personality disorder, and schizoid personality disorder

Dramatic, emotional, erratic: antisocial personality disorder, borderline personality disorder, histrionic personality disorder, and narcissistic personality disorder

Anxious, fearful: avoidant personality disorder, dependent personality disorder, and obsessive-compulsive personality disorder

ACTIVITY 2: There is no "right" answer to this one; a reasonable diagram of the interrelationships between concepts should be most helpful to you.

CHAPTER 16
PSYCHOLOGICAL AND BIOLOGICAL TREATMENTS
HELPING PEOPLE CHANGE

BEFORE YOU READ ... CHAPTER PREVIEW

The picture of therapy painted in this chapter differs from the common image of couches and mustached men. Therapies include the classic, the effective, the not evaluated, and the harmful. An estimated 20% of Americans of all ages and backgrounds will receive some form of therapy. People go into therapy for a range of problems, from those that are severe and longstanding to those that are minor and temporary. Patients who are better adjusted to begin with benefit the most. Therapy can be provided by a variety of individual with a variety of backgrounds. For example, those with professional degrees include clinical psychologists (PhD/PsyD), psychiatrists (MD), and social workers (MSW/LCSW). Paraprofessionals working in the field may have little formal training. Although consulting with professionals provides certain advantages, paraprofessionals may be able to provide needed hope, support, and advice.

The image of the couch originates with the first of the psychotherapies, Freud's psychoanalysis. According to psychoanalytic theory, behavior is based on unconscious conflicts. Therapy can help the individual uncover the unconscious motives underlying behavior by exploring childhood memories, dreams, and behaviors that occur during therapy, such as resistance and transference. Psychoanalytic therapists believe *insight* into the meaning of behaviors will provide a basis for reducing guilt and distress, but they also believe that change is difficult and conflict will be ongoing. Neo-Freudian therapists are more optimistic about change and consider a broader range of influences on personality including culture. Interpersonal psychotherapy attempts to discover unrealistic attitudes and to work on developing social skills. Many psychodynamic therapies can be criticized for their lack of scientific rigor. Psychoanalytic theory is based on anecdotal evidence from biased samples, it makes unfalsifiable claims, and the claims that can be tested tend not to be supported. For example, although insight is believed crucial in psychodynamic therapy, research suggests that insight is not required in the relief of distress.

Humanistic and existential therapies share the belief that human nature is basically positive. The goal of therapy is to help people overcome their sense of alienation and actualize their potential. Person-centered therapies provide a warm, nonjudgmental setting in which the client can accept him- or herself and think more realistically about his or her situation.

Behavior therapies focus on change rather than insight. These therapies are based on the principles of learning outlined in Chapter 6. Exposure therapy, for example, confronts individuals with the fear-producing stimulus with the goal of reducing the fear through extinction. Systematic desensitization teaches the client to relax while exposing the individual to the fear producing stimuli in gradual steps. Other behavior therapies use techniques such as role playing and modeling to teach skills such as assertiveness and communication. Token economies modify behavior through operant conditioning principles. Behavior therapies are effective for a variety of disorders. Therapists are cautioned not to overinflate claims and to continue conducting research to dismantle the therapy's ineffective components.

Cognitive therapies emphasize that irrational thoughts underlie psychological disorders. The goal of such therapy is to identify and replace the irrational thoughts with more rational cognitions. Therapists play an active role, encouraging clients to rethink their assumptions. Stress inoculation therapies help patients prepare for stress by developing cognitive skills to minimize its harm. The trend in therapy today is for therapists to be eclectic—tailoring their therapeutic approach to individual clients and problems.

Group therapies are an efficient way of providing many of the forms of therapy. Group therapies recognize that problems of living are shared. They offer the advantage of the group setting for individuals to practice developing skills. The best known of the group therapies is Alcoholics Anonymous. Because only some people choose to participate in AA and a large percentage drop out, research is needed to clarify which alcoholics are best served by AA. Another form of group therapy, family therapy, views psychological problems as rooted in the family. Its goal is to improve communication and relationships in the family.

Although most therapies are more effective than no therapy and all are about equal in effectiveness, some exceptions exist. Cognitive therapy is more effective than other forms of therapy for depression; behavioral therapy is more effective than other forms of therapy for phobias. Some forms of psychotherapy can actually make clients worse. Examples include some treatments that have been discussed throughout this text including facilitated communication, recovered memories, critical incident debriefing, and coercion restraint. Effective therapies share common features including empathic listening, hope that things will improve, and a new way of thinking. Some therapies challenge thoughts and teach skills—techniques that also appear to influence outcomes. Advocates of empirically supported therapies (ESTs) point out that clarifying which therapies have demonstrated effectiveness with specific disorders is an important guide for therapists looking for techniques that are most likely to help their clients. Self-help books can help when the book is based on research and used by individuals who are motivated to read the book and whose problems are relatively minor.

Unfortunately, some therapies practiced today lack empirical support. These therapies can appear effective for reasons other than actual effectiveness. For example, individuals may feel better because of the effect of spontaneous remission—individuals improve with the passage of time. Individuals may also improve because of the placebo effect—their improvement may be due to their belief that they were given an effective treatment. Individuals may also report improvement because of the self-serving bias—they overestimate success as a way of justifying their investment in the treatment or retrospective rewriting. In expecting to change, they rewrite the past to fit expectations. Finally, improvement may be due to the phenomenon of regression to the mean.

Biological treatments are those that alter brain chemistry or physiology. Although many psychological disorders do appear to be associated with chemical imbalances, biological treatments have been criticized for a variety of reasons. Beginning with Thorazine in the 1950s, the number of medical treatments for psychological disorders continues to proliferate; we don't know how many of these medications work and all of these medications have side effects—including many serious side effects. Although in most states only psychiatrists (MDs) can prescribe medications, a movement is growing that would allow psychologists, who lack specific medical training, to have prescription privileges. Other controversies include the overprescribing of medications to populations for whom the medication's effectiveness is not demonstrated. Critics of medication also point out that some therapies, like CBT for depression, have been shown to be as effective as medication with less likelihood of relapse. Most admit that medication should be at least combined with other forms of therapy.

Electroconvulsive therapy, another controversial treatment, involves brief electrical pulses to the brain to produce a seizure. It may be used as a last resort to treat certain disorders, such a severe depression. It is a misconception that it results in drastic personality change or brain damage. Psychosurgery, at least as performed during the mid-1900s, did produce dramatic personality change. Today it is used only as a last resort in only a few cases.

BEFORE YOU READ ... LEARNING OBJECTIVES

After reading Chapter 16 you should be able to:

16.1   Describe who seeks treatment, who benefits from psychotherapy, and who practices psychotherapy
16.2   Identify the training and effectiveness differences between professionals and paraprofessionals
16.3   Describe what it takes to be an effective therapist
16.4   Describe the core beliefs of psychodynamic therapists
16.5   Determine how neo-Freudians, including Jung and Sullivan, departed from traditional psychoanalysis
16.6   Identify criticisms of psychodynamic therapies
16.7   Identify important aspects of humanistic-existential therapies
16.8   Evaluate the effectiveness of Rogers's person-centered therapy
16.9   Describe the characteristics of behavior therapy
16.10   Identify different behavior approaches
16.11   Describe the features of cognitive-behavioral therapies
16.12   List the advantages of group methods
16.13   Describe the research evidence concerning the effectiveness of AA
16.14   Identify different approaches to treating the dysfunctional family system
16.15   Evaluate the claim that all psychotherapies are equally effective
16.16   Identify common factors in psychotherapy
16.17   Explain why ineffective therapies can appear to be effective
16.18   Recognize different types of drugs and cautions associated with drug treatment
16.19   Outline key considerations in drug treatment
16.20   Identify misconceptions about biological treatments

BEFORE YOU READ ... TERM IDENTIFICATION

abstinence violation effect (p. 692)
Alcoholics Anonymous (p. 691)
aversion therapy (p. 687)
behavior therapists (p. 683)
cognitive-behavior therapy (p. 687)
dismantling (p. 684)
electroconvulsive therapy (p. 703)
empirically supported therapies (ESTs) (p. 695)
experiential therapy (p. 681)
exposure therapy (p. 683)
free association (p. 676)
Gestalt therapy (p. 680)
group therapy (p. 690)
humanistic-existential psychotherapy (p. 680)
insight therapies (p. 676)
interpersonal therapy (p. 678)

logotherapy (p. 681)
paraprofessional (p. 673)
participant modeling (p. 686)
person-centered therapy (p. 680)
pharmacotherapy (p. 699)
phenomenological approach (p. 680)
psychosurgery (p. 704)
psychotherapy (p. 672)
resistance (p. 677)
response prevention (p. 685)
strategic family intervention (p. 692)
structural family therapy (p. 693)
systematic desensitization (p. 683)
token economy (p. 687)
transference (p. 677)
work through (p. 677)

AS YOU READ ... PRACTICE ACTIVITIES

PSYCHOTHERAPY: PATIENTS AND PRACTITIONERS

1. How does the common image of psychotherapy differ from the reality? (LO 16.1)

2. Those that benefit most from therapy are those who need it least. Discuss the reasons this statement is true. (LO 16.1)

3. Therapists don't necessarily need to be professionally trained to be effective. Based on the discussion of the characteristics of effective therapists and therapies, explain why this is true. (LO 16.2, LO 16.3)

4. Review the characteristics to look for in a therapist in Table 16.2. How does characteristic #6 "My therapist uses scientifically based approaches and discusses the pros and cons of alternative approaches," reflect the characteristics of critical thinking discussed in this text? (LO 16.3)

5. **T or F:** There is no difference between psychologists and psychiatrists. (LO 16.2)

6. Summarize the *Consumer Reports* study (discussed on p. 674). (LO 16.3)

Design:

Results:

Lessons learned:

Why should we be cautious in drawing conclusions from this study?

INSIGHT THERAPIES: ACQUIRING UNDERSTANDING

1. Compare the discussion of dreams and dream analysis conducted by psychoanalytic therapists with the research on dreams discussed in Chapter 5. (LO 16.4)

2. The Skeptic's Dictionary notes that New Age therapies share an emphasis on past trauma, a determination to uncover the cause of the disorder, and a lack of interest in objective evidence. How does this description parallel the first therapy, psychoanalysis? (LO 16.6)

3. The Skeptic's Dictionary also describes psychoanalytic therapy as a search for what probably does not exist (repressed childhood memories), on an assumption that is probably false (childhood experiences cause problems), and therapeutic theory with little probability of being correct (bringing repressed memories to consciousness is essential to cure). Describe the research evidence that supports the idea that psychoanalysis is based on illusion. (LO 16.6)

4. Although both humanistic therapies and psychoanalytic therapies are interested in their clients' gaining insight into their disorders, they differ in a number of ways. Complete this table differentiating these therapies along the following dimensions. (LO 16.4)

	Psychoanalytic	Humanistic
View of human nature		
Potential for change		
Therapeutic techniques		
Who interprets information		
Focus on past		

5. Which of the insight therapies is based on a philosophical perspective? What is this perspective and how does it influence the goals of therapy? (LO 16.4)

BEHAVIORAL APPROACHES: CHANGING MALADAPTIVE ACTIONS

1. Review the principles of conditioning discussed in Chapter 6. Show how the behavior therapies listed here are based on learning principles. (LO 16.8, LO 16.9)

Exposure

Systematic desensitization

Participant modeling

Token economies

Aversion therapies

2. Sophia is a college freshman. She is so terrified of speaking in public it makes her sick to her stomach just to think about it. She just found out that one of her classes will require a presentation to the class for the final project. She cannot sleep or concentrate and has come to you, a counselor, for help. How would you help Sophia as a behavioral therapist? How would you help if you were a cognitive therapist? (LO 16.8–LO 16.10)

3. Cognitive therapy attempts to replace irrational with rational thoughts. Complete this table. (LO 16-10)

Event	Irrational Thought	Rational Alternative
Getting an "F" on a test		
A relationship breaking up		
Being let go from a job		

4. Cognitive-behavioral therapies will often help individuals identify irrational thought by recommending they keep a journal. Once thoughts are identified, the therapist might give the client homework assignments designed to test out their beliefs. We all think irrationally, at least occasionally. Such thoughts can lead to stress. Keep a journal for a week. Note the thoughts you have following events. At the end of the week, review the thoughts. How "rational" are your thoughts? How can you think differently about the events you experienced? (LO 16.10)

5. Compare the chapter's coverage on Thought Field Therapy (TFT) with the information provided at www.tftrx.com. What do you conclude about the effectiveness of TFT? Why do you think so many therapists (and patients) believe in it? (LO 16.10)

Chapter 16 Psychological and Biological Treatments

GROUP AND FAMILY SYSTEMS THERAPIES: THE MORE, THE MERRIER

1. AA studies are affected by self-selection and dropout. What characteristics would a study need to provide clear evidence for the effectiveness of AA? (LO 16.13)

2. What are the advantages of group therapy? Of family therapy? (LO 16.11, LO 16.13)

3. The different therapeutic approaches are based on different views of what underlies psychological disorders. Complete the following table outlining these differences (LO 16.4, LO 16.8, LO 16.10)

	Basis of Psychological Disorder	Basis of Therapy
Psychoanalytic		
Humanistic		
Behavioral		
Cognitive		

4. If therapies are based on views of what underlies psychological disorders, what beliefs would contribute to a therapist being eclectic? (LO 16.14)

5. Which type of therapist would say the following: (LO 16.4, LO 16.8, LO 16.10)

"So tell me about your dream." _____

"It sounds like you may be feeling angry about that test grade." _____

"So we are going to start with a picture of the spider." _____

"You're saying you will never be happy without this person. Let's think about that." _____

IS PSYCHOTHERAPY EFFECTIVE?

1. Look carefully at the graph in Figure 16.3 (p. 694). Describe the effectiveness of therapy in your own words. (LO 16.15)

2. How can most therapies be generally effective, but some therapies be more effective than others? Look at the keys to effective therapeutic outcomes. How does each of the forms of therapy provide hope and a new way of thinking? (LO 16.14)

3. Which therapies are clearly helpful for which disorders? Why should therapists be aware of these relations? (LO 16.15)

4. How can therapies with no demonstrated effectiveness appear effective? (LO 16.15)

Describe each of the following:

Spontaneous remission

Placebo effect

Self-serving bias

Regression to the mean

Rewriting the past

5. Self-help books can be beneficial in certain situations. What are the characteristics of such books? Have you ever read a self-help book? Do you think its success (or failure) was influenced by its meeting the criteria listed? (LO 16.17)

BIOLOGICAL TREATMENTS: DRUGS, PHYSICAL STIMULATION, AND SURGERY

1. What are the pros and cons of drug therapy? (LO 16.18)

2. What are the criticisms of the current emphasis on medication for psychological disorders? (LO 16.19)

3. Compete this table. (LO 16.18)

Type of Drug	Example	Disorder for Which It Might Be Prescribed
Anitianxiety		
Antidepressants	Prozac	
Mood stablizers	Lithium	
Antipsychotics		

4. **Just for fun** … check out this flash parody http://www.astonishedhead.com/images/OVOID_123.swf.

5. What are the myths and realities concerning electroconvulsive therapy? (LO 16.20)

6. Review the discussion of neurotransmission in Chapter 3. Describe how researchers think Prozac works. (LO 16.18)

As You Read … Cognitive Map Activities

ACTIVITY 1: The chapter suggests that many forms of therapy are available. Many of these therapies are based on theories of personality or learning described in the text. Creating a map of the various forms of therapy (e.g., psychodynamic, behavior), their theoretical basis (e.g., unconscious conflict), and features of therapy will help you organize and remember the relations.

ACTIVITY 2: This alternative to Practice Activity 1 under Behavioral Approaches should provide you with a representation of the links between learning principles and therapeutic techniques.

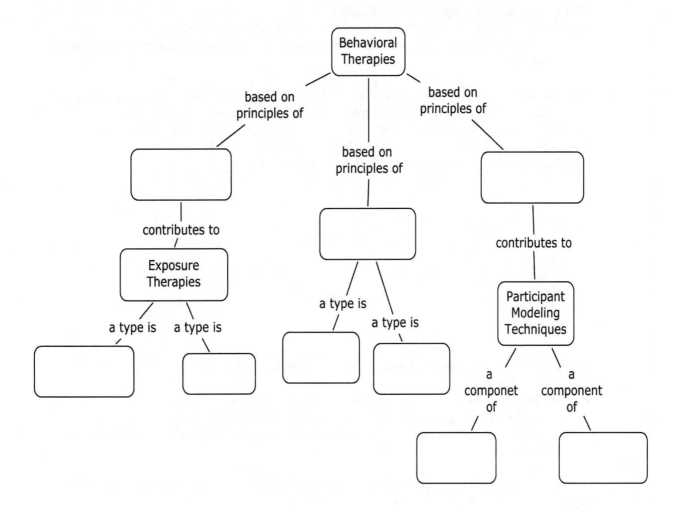

AS YOU READ... MYTH OR REALITY?

Myth: Psychologists psychoanalyze people.

Reality: Traditional psychoanalysis is rarely used today. Most therapists are eclectic in their practice, selecting from cognitive-behavioral and interpersonal forms of therapy.

1. Why do you think most people think of Freud and psychoanalysis as representing psychology?
2. Do you think telling them that psychology is more than Freud would convince them?
3. Look at some of these articles for a discussion of how difficult it is to change misconceptions.
   http://www.encyclopedia.com/doc/1G1-126582634.html
   http://teachpsych.org/resources/e-books/eit2004/eit04-03.rtf

Myth: Insight into the cause of one's disorder will result in dramatic improvement.

Reality: Insight is not required for success in therapy. Some individuals who improve do not gain "insight"; some who gain insight do not improve. In addition, it is not possible to know whether what is perceived to be "insight" reflects reality.

1. How is this insight myth perpetuated by film? Describe a film you have seen that perpetuates this myth.

AS YOU READ … PUT YOUR CRITICAL THINKING SKILLS TO THE TEST

1. Despite some evidence that type of training makes little difference, some characteristics of therapists do make a difference. One of these is whether the individual responds to scientific literature. Read Tavris's discussion of the mind games. Why is scientific literacy a concern?
    http://chronicle.com/free/v49/i25/25b00701.htm

2. Searching for a therapy? Among the hundreds of "therapies" being practiced today, many New Age therapies are mixes of metaphysics and pseudoscience. Angel therapy, for example, works with your guardian angel to heal and harmonize every aspect of your life.
    http://www.angeltherapy.com/about_at.php

    The Skeptic's Dictionary suggests the popularity of New Age therapies reflect a rise in irrationality as well as a demand created by talk shows and book circuits. Take a look at angel therapy or search for other therapies on the web. On what claims are the therapies based? For example, some New Age therapies believe children demonstrating symptoms labeled ADHD are really examples of a newly evolved human species, the Indigo children (www.indigochild.com or http://skepdic.com/indigo.html). How do the underlying assumptions for these therapies and the support for these therapies differ from the EST discussed in the text?

3. Based on "A Nation of Wimps" at
    http://psychologytoday.com/articles/pto-20041112-000010.html, answer the following question: Why do young people today seem "psychologically fragile" (i.e., prone to anxiety and depression)?

4. In medical studies of antidepressants, "active placebos" (i.e., drugs that are not antidepressants but do have noticeable subjective or physiological effects) can produce substantial changes on measures of depression. http://www.biopsychiatry.com/placebo.htm
    Why might individuals respond more to "active placebos" compared with placebos without noticeable effects?

AS YOU READ ... MYPSYCHLAB CONNECTION

Therapy: Patients and Practitioners

Explore *Psychotherapy Practitioners and Their Activities* to learn about the different career fields and professional training requirements.

Insight Therapies: Acquiring Understanding

For review on insights therapies, **explore** *Key Components in Psychoanalytic, Humanistic, Behavior, and Cognitive Therapies* where you can summarize and compare psychotherapeutic approaches.

Behavioral Approaches: Changing Maladaptive Actions

For more on evidence-based therapeutic approaches **watch** *Cognitive-Behavioral Therapy*.

Group and Family Systems Therapies: The More, the Merrier

Watch the *Family Therapist* interview as she discusses the challenges and rewards of being a family crisis counselor.

Is Psychotherapy Effective?

Watch *The Secret* to learn more about this self-help book and how students should apply their critical thinking skills to the claims.

Biological Treatment: Drugs, Stimulation, and Surgery?

Explore *Drugs Commonly Used to Treat Psychiatric Disorders* to learn about the different psychotropic medications that are used to treat psychiatric disorders.

AFTER YOU READ ... PRACTICE TEST #1

Before beginning this practice test, estimate the percent you expect to get correct.
Anticipated percent correct: _____

1. Which of the following best represents the perceived cause of psychological disorders according to cognitive therapists?
   a. Problems are rooted in unconscious conflicts left over from childhood.
   b. Problems are rooted in negative thoughts and errors in thinking.
   c. Problems are rooted in biochemical malfunctions.
   d. Problems are rooted in conditioned behaviors.

2. Which of the following best describes the principle assumption of behavior therapy?
   a. All types of therapy are based on classical conditioning.
   b. Unconscious conflicts can be uncovered and eliminated.
   c. Problems in behavior are learned and can be changed.
   d. Symptoms cannot be alleviated until the causes are diagnosed.

3. Which statement about psychotherapy is FALSE?
   a. Therapy's major benefit is that it provides comfort, support, and a way to make positive changes.
   b. Therapy usually brings about a dramatic end to a person's suffering.
   c. Effective therapies provide hope and new perspectives.
   d. Spontaneous remission refers to improvement in symptoms with the passage of time.

4. Ron has a great fear of final exams. Using systematic desensitization, his therapist begins by asking Ron to make a list of his exam-related fears from lowest to highest. The next step in Ron's therapy will be
   a. to think about taking a major final exam.
   b. to learn how to relax.
   c. to complete a homework assignment (e.g., take an exam and report back to the therapist).
   d. to question how rational his fears really are.

5. The most convincing evidence for the effectiveness of psychotherapy comes from
   a. studies of client satisfaction with treatment received.
   b. reports from therapists concerning their perceptions of client improvement.
   c. analyses of multiple psychotherapeutic outcome studies.
   d. reactions of friends and family to those who have undergone therapy.

6. Which of the following statements about drug therapy is TRUE?
   a. Most medications, while improving behavior, have many negative side effects.
   b. The use of Thorazine in the 1950s resulted in scores of "dehumanized zombies."
   c. Medication without additional support and psychotherapy is likely to result in relapse.
   d. Both a and c.

7. Psychotherapy outcome studies suggest that
   a. therapy is no more effective than a good friend and a bottle of Scotch.
   b. it is not possible to measure therapeutic effectiveness.
   c. evidence supports the effectiveness of therapy.
   d. therapy harms as many people as it helps.

8. Which of the following statements regarding psychoanalytic theory is TRUE?
   a. Freud is the founding father of modern psychological science.
   b. Freud's theory of catharsis, releasing aggressive energy relieves aggressive urges, has been supported by empirical research.
   c. By ignoring the falsifiabilty criterion, psychoanalytic theorizing contributes to an illusion of understanding.
   d. Psychoanalysis is the dominant form of therapy practiced today.

9. Mike is a 19-year-old with a fear of bees. Whenever he sees a bee, even at a distance, he gets so anxious and afraid that he runs the other way. A therapist who sees Mike's problem as the result of learning
   a. is likely to investigate his childhood experiences.
   b. is a psychoanalytic therapist.
   c. is a behavior therapist.
   d. is likely to promote a biomedical treatment.

10. Research studies dismantling the components of EMDR suggest its effectiveness is likely due to
    a. exposure therapy.
    b. highly trained therapists.
    c. the brain alignment.
    d. eye movement.

11. In a survey conducted by *Consumer Reports*, 90% of respondents believed they were helped by psychotherapy. Why are such client testimonials not the best source of evidence for the effectiveness of therapy?
    a. Therapists, not clients, know when there's been improvement.
    b. Because the study was not an experimental design, alternative explanations have not been ruled out.
    c. Individuals' improvement could have been due to the placebo effect.
    d. Both b and c.

12. Alicia was having problems in relationships so she bought the self-help book, *Change Your Life!* The book claimed its techniques would change your life and encouraged readers to attend the seminar offered by the authors. Alicia has now attended several seminars and bought every book and DVD available from the authors. Now despite the fact that Alicia is still having relationship problems, she is convinced that the Change Your Life program is effective. What might explain Alicia's thinking?
    a. Her investment in time and money has resulted in her convincing herself it has worked.
    b. Self-help books and seminars are effective in most cases.
    c. When we expect to change, we may adjust our memories of the past.
    d. Both a and c.

13. Lenita is afraid of flying. In therapy she is asked to create a hierarchy of stimuli related to flying that produce anxiety for her. She then learns relaxation techniques. The form of therapy Lenita is in is probably
    a. existential therapy.
    b. person-centered therapy.
    c. systematic desensitization.
    d. aversive conditioning.

14. Of the following individuals, who would be most likely to benefit from Prozac?
    a. Sharena feels she has little control over the bad things in her life, feels helpless, and worthless.
    b. Billie hears voices that he believes come from outer space.
    c. John experiences episodes of such incredible energy he doesn't sleep for days.
    d. Rhonda is feeling sad that her best friend just moved away.

15. Which of the following is NOT one of the key ingredients of effective psychotherapy?
    a. Insight into the cause of one's problems
    b. A new perspective
    c. A supportive relationship
    d. A sense of hope

16. Which of the following statements about group therapy is TRUE?
    a. The self-help group, AA, has been proven more effective for alcoholics than other forms of therapy.
    b. In family therapy, usually one targeted family member is treated in therapy.
    c. Group therapy is more costly and time consuming than individual therapy.
    d. Groups provide opportunities for individuals to practice new skills.

17. Which of the following statements regarding electroconvulsive therapy is TRUE?
    a. ECT is painful.
    b. ECT invariably produces memory loss.
    c. ECT invariably produces personality changes.
    d. ECT is used in cases of very severe depression.

18. Which of the following psychotherapies emphasizes the individual's inherent potential for self-actualization?
    a. Behavior therapy
    b. Humanistic therapy
    c. Psychoanalytic therapy
    d. Cognitive-behavioral

19. An eclectic therapist
    a. bases treatment on the existential search for meaning in life.
    b. may use any of a variety of techniques, depending on the client and the problem.
    c. emphasizes achieving insight into the root causes of the problem.
    d. views maladaptive behaviors as expressions of unfulfilled wishes.

20. Antipsychotic drugs appear to have their effect by blocking receptor sites for the neurotransmitter
    a. dopamine.
    b. GABA.
    c. norepinephrine.
    d. acetylcholine.

After completing the test, calculate your percent correct
(/ 20 =   ) x 100 = _____.

How accurate were your expectations? Does your performance suggest the need for additional study? For the items you missed, go back and identify why the "correct" answer is the best answer.

AFTER YOU READ... PRACTICE TEST #2

Before beginning this practice test, estimate the percent you expect to get correct.
Anticipated percent correct: _____

1. Selective serotonin reuptake inhibitors (SSRI) are prescribed
   a. to help lessen the manic episodes in bipolar disorder.
   b. to eliminate hallucinations in schizophrenic individuals.
   c. to lessen symptoms of depression.
   d. to increase focus and attention in individuals with ADHD.

2. Manny has been diagnosed as experiencing severe attention-deficit-hyperactivity disorder. He attends a school in which his teacher gives him poker chips following specific desired behaviors such as raising his hand to speak. It's likely this school is trying to modify Manny's behavior by using
   a. systematic desensitization.
   b. a token economy.
   c. exposure.
   d. aversive conditioning.

3. The meta-analysis described in your text evaluated 475 studies of the effectiveness of psychotherapy. What were the conclusions of this meta-analysis?
   a. Professionals are much more effective than paraprofessionals in providing therapy.
   b. Paraprofessionals are more effective than professionals in providing therapy.
   c. Overall, paraprofessionals and professionals are about equal in effectiveness in providing therapy.
   d. Therapy is ineffective in 80% of the cases.

4. Elgin suffers from auditory hallucinations and believes that the people on TV can see him. Elgin's symptoms may be relieved by
   a. antipsychotic drugs.
   b. psychoanalytic psychotherapy.
   c. counterconditioning.
   d. both a and c.

5. The "Dodo bird verdict" refers to the finding that
   a. many therapies should become extinct.
   b. most therapies are equivalent in terms of their therapeutic outcomes.
   c. most therapies are for the birds.
   d. therapies that appear odd are often the most effective therapies.

6. Which of the following claims is TRUE?
   a. Current difficulties stem from the repression of traumatic events.
   b. Insight into the origin of one's problem is always a crucial ingredient in therapeutic change.
   c. Dreams are important in expressing unconscious content or foretelling the future.
   d. Psychodynamic and humanistic therapies all share a goal of expanding awareness and insight.

7. Tabitha had been feeling quite anxious, but since seeing her alien abduction therapist she now reports feeling much better. What might explain Tabitha's improvement?
   a. Spontaneous remission
   b. The placebo effect
   c. Insight
   d. Both a and b

8. Which of the following statements is TRUE?
   a. Only biological treatments can produce chemical changes in the brain.
   b. Psychological treatments affect our biology.
   c. Biological treatments affect out psychology.
   d. Both b and c are true.

9. Humanistic and psychoanalytic therapies differ in all of the following ways EXCEPT
   a. humanistic therapies are more optimistic for change.
   b. humanistic therapies are more positive about human nature.
   c. humanistic therapies focus more on the importance of insight.
   d. humanistic therapies focus more on present relationships.

10. Your roommate is having problems with her boyfriend and has decided to go to the bookstore and check out the books about relationships. You recommend she look for a book
    a. based on published research that supports its claims.
    b. based on many years of observations of improvement in therapy.
    c. that promises positive results will be achieved for everyone, not just a few people.
    d. that simplifies concepts so they are easy to understand, like *Men are from Mars*.

11. Yolanda went to a therapist hoping he'd tell her what was "wrong" with her and how to fix it. Instead she found that the therapist was expecting her to discover ways of dealing with her problems. It is likely that Yolanda's therapist is
    a. a humanistic therapist.   c. a psychoanalytic therapist.
    b. a behavioral therapist.   d. a family therapist.

12. Jeremy's therapist has asked him to recount his dreams and has interpreted the dream's content. It is likely the therapist has a _____ orientation toward therapy.
    a. humanistic   c. psychoanalytic
    b. cognitive   d. behavioral

13. _____ therapy has been criticized for offering interpretations that cannot be verified.
    a. Psychoanalytic   c. Cognitive
    b. Behavioral   d. Biomedical

14. In which of the following ways are clinical psychologists and psychiatrists similar?
    a. They are similar in education and training.
    b. They are likely to work in similar settings such as hospitals and in private practice.
    c. They are both authorized to prescribe medication.
    d. They are both trained in providing psychotherapy.

15. Which type of therapist would say "It sounds like you're feeling really angry right now"?
    a. A cognitive therapist   c. A psychoanalytic therapist
    b. A person-centered therapist   d. A behavioral therapist

16. Which of the following has been shown to be a potentially harmful therapy?
    a. Facilitated communication   c. EMDR
    b. Recovered memory techniques   d. Both a and b

17. Which of the following statements regarding drug therapy is TRUE?
    a. Medications today have few side effects.
    b. Changes in brain chemistry can only be produced with medications.
    c. Drugs are being prescribed for individuals whose behavior could be treated with other methods.
    d. The effectiveness of a drug in curing a disorder proves the cause of the disorder is biological.

18. Which of the following is TRUE?
    a. Extensive professional training is necessary to produce good therapeutic outcomes.
    b. Behavioral therapies place a great deal of importance on insight.
    c. AA is more effective than other alcohol abuse treatments.
    d. Common factors may help explain why many different therapies are equally effective.

19. _____ is an empirically supported therapy for _____.
    a. Dolphin therapy; autism
    b. Laughter therapy; depression
    c. Cognitive-behavioral therapy; bulimia
    d. Both b and c

20. Which of the following therapists would you want to avoid?
    a. Dr. Who is quite friendly and likes to chat about his family and personal life.
    b. Ms. Duno listens carefully to what is said and provides useful feedback.
    c. Dr. Sure is confident in his techniques because he has seen them help many people.
    d. Both a and c.

After completing the test, calculate your percent correct
(/ 20 =   ) x 100 = _____.

How accurate were your expectations? Does your performance suggest the need for additional study?
For the items you missed, go back and identify why the "correct" answer is the best answer.

AFTER YOU READ ... PRACTICE TEST ANSWER KEYS

Practice Test 1.

1. b (p. 687)
2. c (p. 683)
3. b (p. 6 95)
4. b (pp. 683–684)
5. c (pp.674, 693–696)
6. d (pp. 702–703)
7. c (p. 694)
8. c (pp. 678–679)
9. c (p. 684)
10. a (pp. 684–686)
11. d (p. 674)
12. d (pp. 697–698)
13. c (p. 684)
14. a (pp. 699–700)
15. a (pp. 679, 695)
16. d (p. 690)
17. d (pp. 703–704)
18. b (p. 680)
19. b (pp. 689–690)
20. a (p. 700)

Practice Test 2.

1. c (pp. 699–700)
2. b (p. 687)
3. c (pp. 693–694)
4. a (p. 703)
5. b (p. 693)
6. d (pp. 680–681)
7. d (p. 698)
8. d (pp.701–702)
9. c (p. 680)
10. a (p. 697)
11. a (p. 680)
12. c (p. 676)
13. a (p. 679)
14. b (p. 674)
15. b (p. 680)
16. d (p. 694)
17. c (p. 699)
18. d (p. 695)
19. c (p. 696)
20. d (p. 675)

AFTER YOU READ ... COGNITIVE MAP ACTIVITIES ANSWERS

ACTIVITY 1:
The chapter suggests that many forms of therapy are available. A map of the various forms of therapy, their theoretical basis, and features of therapy is likely to be complicated and could take different forms. However, your map should at least include the following:

> psychoanalytic therapy, humanistic therapy, behavioral therapy, cognitive therapy, unconscious conflict, alienation, maladaptive learning, irrational thoughts, free association, unconditional regard, operant and classical conditioning, challenging thoughts

ACTIVITY 2: This alternative to Practice Activity 1 under Behavioral Approaches should provide you with a representation of the links between learning principles and therapeutic techniques.

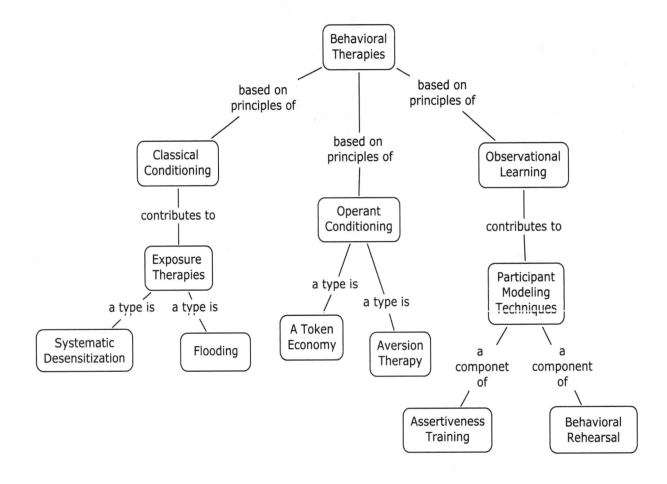

NOTES

NOTES

NOTES

NOTES

NOTES

NOTES

NOTES

NOTES

NOTES

NOTES

NOTES

NOTES

NOTES

NOTES

NOTES

NOTES

NOTES

NOTES

NOTES